Critical Thinking

Fifth Edition

Richard L. Epstein

with the collaboration of

Michael Rooney

and illustrations by

Alex Raffi

Advanced Reasoning Forum

No cats were harmed in the making of this book.

For more information contact:
Advanced Reasoning Forum
P. O. Box 635
Socorro, NM 87801 USA
rle@advancedreasoningforum.org

Or visit us at:
www.AdvancedReasoningForum.org

ISBN 978-1-938421-32-7 paperback

ISBN 978-1-938421-33-4 e-book

THE SLEEP OF REASON BEGETS MONSTERS

Critical Thinking

Fifth Edition

THE FUNDAMENTALS

THE STRUCTURE OF ARGUMENTS

7 Compound Claims

8 General Claims

AVOIDING BAD ARGUMENTS

9 Concealed Claims

14 Generalizing

15 Cause and Effect

Truth-Tables
Aristotelian Logic
} available as free downloads at www.AdvancedReasoningForum.org/CT/supplements

Formal Logic—see the companion volume *An Introduction to Formal Logic* by Richard L. Epstein, also published by ARF.

Cast of Characters

To the Student

Critical thinking will teach you how to see the consequences of what you and others say and do, to write well, and to make decisions. In your studies, in your work, you will go far if you can think clearly and write clearly.

It's all here in the text. There are plenty of examples and lots of exercises to illustrate the ideas and skills you're supposed to master. In the discussion and exchanges in class, your understanding will crystallize. You'll get the most out of those discussions if you've worked through the material first. Read the chapter through once. Get an overview. Mark the passages that are unclear. You need to understand what is said—not all the deep implications of the ideas, not all the subtleties, but the basic definitions.

Once the words make sense and you see the general picture, you need to go back through the chapter paragraph by paragraph, making sure that you understand each part or marking it so you can ask questions in class. Then you're ready to try the exercises.

Many of them will be easy applications of the material you've read. Others will require more thought. And some won't make sense until you talk about them with your classmates and instructor. When you get stuck, look in the back where there are answers to many of them.

By the time you get to class, you should be on the verge of mastering the material. Some discussion, some more examples, a few exercises explained, and you've got it.

Have fun!

To the Instructor

- Rigorous.
  - Fun.
    - One story, from start to finish.
      - Practical.
        - Easy to teach.
          - Great for classroom discussions.

Rigorous Clear and correct definitions and concepts are set out, based on the deep analysis of critical thinking developed by the author in *The Fundamentals of Argument Analysis* and the other volumes in *Essays on Logic as the Art of Reasoning Well*. You won't get lost in a maze of confusion. You won't have to keep correcting the text. This is a text you can rely on.

Fun The ideas and methods are illustrated with cartoons drawn especially for this text. They're memorable and amusing, and the text as a whole is infused with a biting humor that makes students think. Your students, and you, won't get bored.

One whole story There is a vision of how to understand, how to reason, how to teach that unifies the presentation and keeps students moving forward. The chapters build on one another to the end.

Practical More than 400 worked examples and more than 1,000 exercises teach students how to use critical thinking in their studies, in their work, and in their lives.

Easy to teach The Instructor's Manual has all you need to find an easy path to teaching and grading: teaching suggestions for each chapter; answers to all the exercises; handouts for correcting the writing lessons; analyses of the cartoon writing lessons; sample exams; and hundreds more examples that you can use for classroom or exams. You are not alone.

Great for classroom discussions The text is designed to be the basis of classroom discussion so lectures won't be necessary, minimizing the jargon while retaining the ideas. The material is more challenging than in other texts, yet more accessible.

Overview of the material

The Fundamentals (Chapters 1–6) is all one piece. It's the heart of the course. Here and throughout, learning the definitions is emphasized. It's best to go through this in a direct line.

The Structure of Arguments (Chapters 7 and 8) is important. Chapter 7 on compound claims—an informal version of propositional logic—is probably the hardest for most students. There's a temptation to skip it and leave that material for a formal logic course. But some skills in reasoning with conditionals are essential. If you skip this chapter, you'll end up having to explain the valid and invalid forms piecemeal when you deal with longer arguments. It's the same for Chapter 8 on general claims—an informal introduction to quantifiers in reasoning—except that the material is easier for students.

Avoiding Bad Arguments (Chapters 9–11) is fun. Slanters and fallacies give the students motive to look around and find examples from their own lives and from what they read and hear. For that reason, many instructors like to put this material earlier. But if you do, you can only teach a hodgepodge of fallacies that won't connect and won't be retained. Fallacies are placed alongside the good reasoning they mock—for example, mistaking the person for the claim with a discussion of when it's appropriate to accept an unsupported claim. Chapter 11 is a summary and overview. Covering this material here helps students unify the earlier material and gives them some breathing room after the hard work in Chapters 7 and 8.

It's only at the end of this section by working through *Short Arguments for Analysis* that students will begin to feel comfortable with the ideas from the earliest chapters. You can conclude a course for the quarter system here.

Reasoning About Our Experience (Chapters 12–16) covers specific kinds of reasoning: analogies, generalizations, cause and effect, and explanations. Chapter 13 on numerical claims could follow directly after Chapter 4.

Making Decisions places this material most directly in the lives of your students. Chapter 17 on evaluating risk requires students to use all the skills they've developed in the course. Chapter 18 on making decisions is an exhortation and a chance for students to see the importance of this course.

Reasoning in the Sciences is new to this edition. The first two chapters get students used to seeing scientific talk in reasoning. Chapter 3S explains what experiments are, what it means to say an experiment is reproducible, and how to evaluate experiments. Chapter 4S shows what can go wrong in an experiment, from lying and self-deception to placebos and positive publication bias. Chapter 5S draws on all they've learned to explain what models and theories are and how we evaluate them. Chapter 6S discusses the role of explanations in science, and Chapter 7S compares science, magic, and religion. Together, these chapters constitute a basic scientific literacy course, one that is needed by all of us as we encounter scientific or pseudoscientific claims and which is crucial background for students beginning the study of any science. No background in any science is assumed.

Exercises in each chapter, in each section, build from routine ones—mostly recalling definitions—to fairly hard ones. There are always easy exercises to help students build their confidence. This method helps them learn how to read, how to pick out their confusions, how to work on their own—in short, it teaches them how to learn. On our website we have the exercise sets formatted in both PDF and RTF as free downloads so your students can answer them on those pages and bring them to class or send them to you online.

Writing Lessons are an integral part of this text. There are enough for courses that require a substantial writing component. The *Essay Writing Lessons* require the student to write an argument for or against a given claim, where the method of argument is tied to the material that's just been presented. In the Instructor's Manual there are suggestions for making the grading of those easy. About midway through the course your students can read the section "Composing Good Arguments" that summarizes the lessons they should learn.

Cartoon Writing Lessons present a situation or a series of actions in a cartoon and require the student to write the best argument for a claim based on what they see. These do more to teach students reasoning than any other work. Students have to distinguish between observation and inference; they have to judge whether a good argument is possible; they have to judge whether the claim is objective or subjective; they have to judge whether a strong argument or a valid argument is called for. These are great for class discussion.

Formal logic is quite a separate subject, important but not clearly applicable to reasoning in daily life beyond what's presented in Chapters 7 and 8. If you want to include more than that in your course, ARF publishes *An Introduction to Formal Logic* that uses the same teaching techniques and is based on the author's extensive research in *Propositional Logics*, *Predicate Logic*, and most recently *The Internal Structure of Predicates and Names*.

New to this edition

- Many new examples and exercises are included in Chapters 1–15.
- Material on explanations has been added. The basics are in Chapter 16 and the use of explanations in science is covered in Chapter 6S.
- There is a new section of seven chapters on reasoning in the sciences.
- There is now enough material in the text for a two-semester course. Suggested course outlines are given at the beginning of the Instructor's Manual.

I've tried to steer between the Scylla of saying nonsense
and the Charybdis of teaching only trivialities. I hope
you find the journey memorable. The water is deep.

Acknowledgments

I am grateful to many people who have been willing to give their time and ideas to help make this text. Many of them I have thanked in previous editions. For this edition I am especially indebted to:

- Michael Rooney, whose collaboration on this work has been essential; a great colleague and a great teacher.
- Peter Adams, whose editorial advice has directed so much of what I have done in this volume and over the years.
- Juan Francisco Rizzo, whose suggestions and encouragement have greatly improved the text.
- Andrew Higgins for many useful suggestions for the reasoning in the sciences chapters.
- Sandy Nelson for her excellent work copyediting, even though I stubbornly didn't follow some of her suggestions.
- My many students at the Socorro County Detention Center who provided me with examples, whose quizzical looks made me rewrite, and whose interest motivated me to finish this book.

I am grateful to them all. Much of what is good in this text comes from them. What is bad is mine, all mine.

The FUNDAMENTALS

1 Critical Thinking?

A. Are You Convinced?

Everyone's trying to convince you of something: You should go to bed early. You should drop out of college. You should buy a Ram truck. You should study critical thinking . . . . And you spend a lot of time trying to decide what you should be doing, that is, trying to convince yourself: Should I take out a student loan? Is chocolate bad for my complexion? Should I really date someone who owns a cat?

Are you tired of being conned? Of falling for every pitch? Of making bad decisions? Of fooling yourself? Or of just being confused?

Thinking critically is a defense against a world of too much information and too many people trying to convince us. But it is more. Reasoning is what distinguishes us from beasts. Many of them can see better, can hear better, and are stronger. But they cannot plan, they cannot think through, they cannot discuss in the hopes of understanding better.

An older student was in the spring term of his senior year when he took this course. He was majoring in anthropology and planned to do graduate work in the fall. Late in the term he brought me a fifteen-page paper he'd written for an anthropology class. He said he'd completed it, then he went over it again, analyzing it as we would in class, after each paragraph asking "So?" He found that he couldn't justify his conclusion, so he changed it and cut the paper down to eleven pages. He showed me the professor's comments, which were roughly "Beautifully reasoned, clear. A+." He said it was the first A+ he'd ever gotten. I can't promise that you'll get an A on all your term papers after taking this course. But you'll be able to comprehend better what you're reading and write more clearly and convincingly.

Once in a while I'll tune in to a sports talk show on the radio. All kinds of people call in. Some of them talk nonsense, but more often the comments are clear and well reasoned. The callers know the details, the facts, and make serious projections about what might be the best strategy based on past experience. They comment on what caused a team to win or lose. They reason with great skill and reject bad arguments. I expect that you can too, at least on subjects you consider important. What we hope to do in this course is hone that skill, sharpen your judgment, and show you that the methods of evaluating reasoning apply to much in your life.

In trying to understand how to reason well, we'll also study bad ways to convince, ways we wish to avoid, ways that misuse emotions or rely on deception. You could use that knowledge to become a bad trial lawyer or advertising writer, but I hope you will learn a love of reasoning well, for it is not just ethical to reason well; it is, as we shall see, more effective in the long run. Critical thinking is part of the study of philosophy: the love of wisdom. We might not reach the truth, but we can be searchers, lovers of wisdom, and treat others as if they are too.

B. Claims

We'll be studying the process of convincing. An attempt to convince depends on someone trying to do the convincing and someone who is supposed to be convinced.

- Someone tries to convince you.
- You try to convince someone else.
- You try to convince yourself.

Let's call an attempt to convince an "argument."

But, you say, an argument means someone yelling at someone else. When my mom yells at me and I yell back, that's an argument. Yes, perhaps it is. But so, by our definition, is you and your friend sitting down to talk about your college finances to decide whether you need to get a job. We need a term that will cover our attempts to convince. The word "argument" has become pretty standard.

Still, that isn't right. Suppose the school bully comes up to Flo and says, "Hand over your candy bar." Flo won't. She hits Flo on the head with a stick. Flo gives up her candy bar. Flo's been convinced. But that's no argument.

The kind of attempts to convince we'll be studying here are ones that are or can be put into language. That is, they are a bunch of sentences that we can think about. But what kind of sentences?

When we say an argument is an attempt to convince, what exactly is it we're supposed to be convinced of? To do something? If we are to try to reason using arguments, the point is that something is true. And what is that something? A sentence, for it's sentences that are true or false. And only certain kinds of sentences: not threats, not commands, not questions, not prayers. An attempt to convince, in order to be classified as an argument, should be couched in plain language that is true or false: declarative sentences.

You should already know what a declarative sentence is. For example:

This course is a delight.
The author of this book sure writes well.
Intelligent beings once lived on Mars.
Everyone should brush their teeth at least once every day.
Nobody knows the troubles I've seen.

The following are not declarative sentences:

Shut that door!
How often do I have to tell you to wipe your feet before you come into the house?
Dear God, let me be a millionaire instead of a starving student.

Still, not every declarative sentence is true or false: "Green dreams ride donkeys" is a declarative sentence, but it's nonsense. Let's give a name to those sentences that are true or false, that is, that have a ***truth value***.

Claim A *claim* is a declarative sentence used in such a way that it is true or false, but not both.

We don't have to make a judgment about whether a sentence is true or whether it's false in order to classify it as a claim. We need only judge that it is one or the other. A claim need not be an *assertion*: a sentence put forward as true by someone.

One of the most important steps in trying to understand new ideas or new ways of talking is to look at lots of examples.

Examples Are the following claims?

Example 1 Your instructor for this course is male.

Analysis This is a claim. It's either true or false.

Example 2 Your instructor is short.

Analysis Is this a claim? What does "short" mean? We'll consider problems with vagueness in Chapter 2.

Example 3 Cats are nasty.

Analysis If when you read this you disagreed, then you've accepted it as a claim. You can't disagree unless you think it has a truth value.

Example 4 2 + 2 = 4

Analysis This is a claim, though no one is going to disagree with you about it.

Example 5 I wish I could get a job.

Analysis How is this being used? If Maria, who's been trying to get a job for three weeks, says it to herself late at night, then it's not a claim. It's more like a prayer or an extended sigh.

But if Dick's parents are berating him for not getting a job, he might say, "It's not that I'm not trying. I wish I could get a job." That might be true, but it also might be false, so "I wish I could get a job" would be a claim.

Example 6 How can anyone be so dumb as to believe that cats can think?

Analysis This is not a claim; it's a question. But in some contexts we might rewrite it as "Someone must be dumb to think that cats can think" or perhaps "Cats can't think." The process of rewriting and reinterpreting is something we'll consider throughout this course.

Example 7 Never use gasoline to clean a hot stove.

Analysis Instructions and commands are not claims because they're not true or false.

Example 8 Every mollusk can contract myxomatosis.

Analysis If you don't know what these words mean, you shouldn't try to reason with this as a claim. But that doesn't mean you should just dismiss any attempt to convince that uses language you don't understand. A dictionary is an important tool of a good reasoner.

Example 9 Something is rotten in the state of Denmark.

Analysis This is from *Hamlet*. That's fiction and isn't intended to be true or false. This isn't a claim.

C. Arguments

We're trying to define "argument." We said it was an attempt using language to convince someone that a claim is true. The only language we should allow in an argument, then, should be sentences that are true or false.

> ***Arguments*** An *argument* is an attempt to convince someone (possibly yourself) that a particular claim is true by giving one or more other claims as reasons.

The point of an argument is to convince someone that a claim—the ***conclusion*** —is true. The conclusion is sometimes called the ***issue*** that's being debated. The reasons offered for why the conclusion is true are called the ***premises***.

Critical thinking is evaluating whether we should be convinced that some claim is true or some argument is good, as well as formulating good arguments.

Examples Are the following arguments?

Example 10

Analysis The nurse is making an argument. She's trying to convince the doctor that "Your patient in Room 47 is dying" is true. She offers the premise "He's in cardiac arrest." Sounds pretty convincing.

Example 11

Analysis Dick is making an argument, trying to convince the police officer that the following claim is true: "The accident was not my fault" (reworded a bit). He uses two premises: "She hit me from the rear" and "Anytime you get rear-ended it's not your fault."

Example 12 The sky is blue. That's because sunlight is refracted through the air in such a way that other wavelengths of light are diminished.

Analysis This is not an attempt to convince you that the sky is blue—that's obvious. This is an explanation, and *an explanation is not an argument.* We'll study explanations in Chapter 16.

Example 13 Out? Out? I was safe by a mile. Are you blind? He didn't even touch me with his glove!

Analysis This was spoken at a baseball game by a runner who'd just been called out. He was trying to convince the umpire to believe "I was safe." He used only one premise: "He didn't even touch me with his glove." The rest is just noise.

Example 14 Give me that *$!#&* wrench.

Analysis I can remember who said this to me. He was trying to convince me. But it was no argument, just a series of commands and threats. And what he was trying to convince me of wasn't that some claim was true.

Example 15 (From a label on a medication) Follow the directions provided by your doctor for using this medicine. This medicine may be taken on an empty stomach or with food. Store this medicine at room temperature, away from heat and light.

Analysis This is not an argument. Instructions and descriptions, though they may use declarative sentences, aren't arguments. They're not intended to convince you that some claim is true.

Example 16

HOW COME YOU DON'T CALL ME? WHAT'S WRONG? YOU DON'T LOVE YOUR MOTHER? WHERE DID I GO WRONG?...

Analysis Zoe's mother is attempting to convince her, but not of the truth of a claim. So there's no argument. Perhaps we could interpret what's being said as having an unstated conclusion "You should feel guilty for not calling your mother," and premises (disguised as questions) "Anyone who doesn't call her mother doesn't love her mother" and "If you don't love your mother, then your mother did something wrong." But it would be the interpretation that is an argument, not the original. And we would have to consider whether the interpretation is faithful to what Zoe's mother intended. We'll consider re-interpreting what's said in Chapter 5.

Example 16 You see a chimpanzee trying to get some termites out of a hole. She can't manage it because the hole is too small for her finger. So she gets a stick and tries to pull the termites out. No success. She licks the end of the stick and puts it in the hole and pulls it out with a termite stuck to it. She eats the termite and repeats the process. Is she convincing herself by means of an argument?

Analysis There's no argument here. Whatever the chimpanzee is doing, she's not using claims to convince herself that a particular claim is true.

But isn't she reasoning? That's a hard question you can study in psychology and philosophy courses.

Summary We said that this course will be about attempts to convince. But that's too much for one course. We narrowed the topic to attempts to convince that use language. That was still too broad. An argument, we decided, should mean an attempt to convince someone that a sentence is true. We defined a claim as a declarative sentence used in such a way that it is true or false. Arguments, then, are attempts to convince that use only claims.

Now we'll begin to look at methods and make distinctions. Because your reasoning can be sharpened, you can understand more, you can avoid being duped. And, we can hope, you will reason well with those you love and work with and need to convince, and you will make better decisions. But whether you will do so depends not just on method, not just on the tools of reasoning, but on your goals, your ends. And that depends on virtue.

Key Words	truth value	conclusion
	true	premise
	false	issue
	claim	critical thinking
	argument	virtue

Exercises for Chapter 1

These exercises are meant to help you become familiar with the ideas we've seen in this chapter. They should raise enough worries about the nature of claims and arguments that you'll be glad to see how we clarify those in the next few chapters.

To make it easier to answer these exercises, use the formatted versions of them which you can find at www.AdvancedReasoningForum.org/CT5/exercises.

1. What is this course about?
2. How did I try to convince you that this course is important? Pick out at least two places where I tried to convince you and decide whether they are arguments.
3. Explain how to divide up all attempts to convince in terms of who is trying to convince whom.

4. Which of the following are claims?
   a. Justin Bieber is a woman.
   b. College is really expensive now.
   c. Pass the salt, please.
   d. Bill Gates founded Apple.
   e. Your instructor believes that Bill Gates founded Apple.
   f. A friend in need is a friend indeed.
   g. Puff is a cat.
   h. Puff is a cat?
   i. Distance makes the heart grow fonder.
   j. No se puede vivir sin amar.
   k. Whenever Spot barks, Zoe gets mad.
   l. The Dodgers aren't going to win a World Series for at least another ten years.
   m. If you don't pay your taxes on time, you'll have to pay more to the government.
   n. $2 + 2 = 5$
   o. I feel cold today.
   p. There are an odd number of stars in the universe.
5. Write down five sentences, four of which are claims and one of which is not. Exchange with a classmate and see if he or she can spot which are the claims.
6. What is an argument?
7. What is the point of making an argument?
8. What is a premise? What is a conclusion?
9. Why isn't every attempt to convince an argument? Give an example.
10. Bring to class an example of an argument you heard or read in the last two days.
11. Bring in a short article from a news website or a newspaper. Are all the sentences used in it claims? Is it an argument?
12. Your friend goes outside, looks up at the sky, and sees it's cloudy. She goes back inside and gets her raincoat and umbrella. Is she making an argument? Explain.
13. Bring an advertisement to class that uses an argument. State the premises and the conclusion.

Here are two exercises done by Tom, along with Dr. E's comments.

Tom Wyzyczy
Critical Thinking, Section 4

Sheep are the dumbest animals. If the one in front walks off a cliff, all the rest will follow it. And if they get rolled over on their backs, they can't right themselves.

Argument? (yes/no) Yes.
Conclusion: Sheep are the dumbest animals.
Premises: If a sheep walks off a cliff, all the rest will follow it.
If a sheep gets rolled over on its back, it can't right itself.

This is good work, Tom.

How can you go to the movies with Sarah and not me? Don't you remember I helped you fix your car last week?

Argument? (yes/no) Yes.
Conclusion: You should go to the movies with me.
Premises: I helped you fix your car last week.

Is what you are given an argument? No. There are just two questions, and questions aren't claims. So it can't be an argument. And if there's no argument, there are no premises and no conclusion. Sure, it seems that we ought to interpret what's said as an argument—as you have done. But before we go putting words in someone's mouth, we ought to have rules and a better understanding of when that's justified.

For each of Exercises 14–28 answer the following:

Argument? (yes or no)
Premises:
Conclusion:

Remember: Answer the last two only if it's an argument.

14. You shouldn't eat at Zee-Zee Frap's restaurant. I heard they did really badly on their health inspection last week.

15. You liked that movie? Boy, are you dumb. I guess you just can't distinguish bad acting from good. And the photography was lousy. What a stupid ending, too.

16. If it's O.K. to buy white mice to feed a pet boa constrictor, why isn't it O.K. to buy white mice for your cat to play with?

17. We shouldn't fix the car now. The oil leak is slow, and it would cost a lot of money.

18. Flo: She pulled my hair and stepped on my hand and wrecked my toy. I hate her.

19. (Advertisement) The bigger the burgers, the better the burgers, the burgers are bigger at Burger King.

20. I would not live forever, because we should not live forever, because if we were supposed to live forever, then we would live forever, but we cannot live forever, which is why I would not live forever.
(A contestant's response to the question "If you could live forever, would you and why?" in the 1994 Miss USA contest.)

21. Flo has always wanted a dog, but she's never been very responsible. She had a fish once, but it died after a week. She forgot to water her mother's plants, and they died. She stepped on a neighbor's turtle and killed it.

22. Maria: Ah-choo.
    Lee: Bless you.
    Maria: I'm just miserable. Stuffy head and trouble breathing.
    Lee: Sounds like the allergies I get.
    Maria: No, it's the flu. I'm running a fever.

23. Look Dick! Look Zoe! See Spot. See Spot run.

24. If you don't take a course on critical thinking, you'll always end up being conned, a dupe for any fast-talker, an easy mark for politicians. So you should take a course on critical thinking. You'd be especially wise to take one from the instructor you've got now—she [he] is a great teacher.

25. Whatever you do, you should drop the critical thinking course from the instructor you've got now. She [he] is a really tough grader, much more demanding than the other professors who teach that course. You could end up getting a bad grade.

26. [A review on Netflix of *Fifty Shades of Grey*—1 star out of 5] This movie plodded along like getting a root canal . . . painfully slow. Perhaps more insight into Christian Grey's psychological workings would have made the movie more interesting and engaging. I didn't read any of the books but I am wondering why all the fascination with an abusive physical relationship? It seemed to border on domestic violence and the papers are full of it with real people. Say "no" to this movie and do something better with your time . . . like bake cookies or shovel snow.

27. Dick: The gas pump stopped pumping by itself.
    Zoe: I can't get it to pump any more gas.
    Dick: So the gas tank must be full.

28. Dick: You shouldn't dock your dog's tail because it will hurt her, it'll make her insecure, and she won't be able to express her feelings.

29. In order to choose good courses of action in our lives, we need not only knowledge of the world and the ability to reason well, but what else?

Further Study There's much more to learn about the nature of claims and truth and the relation of language to our experience. We'll touch on some of those in the next chapter. An introductory philosophy course goes much deeper.

Attempts to convince that use language but aren't arguments, such as fables and examples, are studied in courses in rhetoric. Courses in marketing, advertising, and psychology study both verbal and nonverbal ways to convince that aren't arguments. Convincing that uses body language is at the heart of acting classes.

A good place to begin reading about whether animals can reason is *The Animal Mind* by James and Carol Gould, Scientific American Library.

Writing Lesson 1

Write an argument either for or against the following:

> *Student athletes should be given special leniency when the instructor assigns course marks.*

Your argument should be at most one page long.

2 What Are We Arguing About?

We want to arrive at truths from our reasoning. So we need to be able to recognize whether a sentence is true or false—or whether it's just nonsense.

A. Vague Sentences

1. Too vague?

Zoe heard a radio advertisement that said, "Snappy detergent gets clothes whiter." So when she went to the supermarket she bought a box. She's not very happy.

Some sentences look like claims, or people try to pass them off as claims, but they're worthless for reasoning. If we can't figure out what someone's saying, we can't investigate whether it's true or false.

> ***Vague sentence*** A sentence is too vague to be a claim if there are different ways to understand it and we can't settle on one of those without the speaker making it clearer.

We hear vague sentences all the time:

You can win a lot playing blackjack.
Public education is not very good in this state.
Freedom is worth fighting for.

They sound plausible, yet how can anyone tell whether they're true?

But isn't everything we say somewhat vague? After all, no two people have identical perceptions; and, since the way we understand words depends on our experience, we all understand words a little differently. There has to be some wiggle room in the meaning of words and sentences for us to be able to communicate. You say, "My math professor showed up late for class on Tuesday." Which Tuesday? Who's your math professor? What do you mean by late? 5 minutes? 30 seconds? How do you determine when she showed up? When she walked through the door? At exactly what point? When her nose crossed the threshold?

That's silly. We all know "what you meant," and the sentence isn't too vague for us to agree that it's true or false. The issue isn't whether a sentence is vague but whether it's *too vague* given the context for us to be justified in saying that it is true or false.

Examples Are the following too vague to be taken as claims?

Example 1 Men are stronger than women.
Analysis Don't bother to argue about this one until you clarify it, even though it may seem plausible. What's meant by "stronger"? Stronger for their body weight? Stronger in that the "average man" (whoever that is) can lift more than the "average woman"? Stronger emotionally?

Example 2 On the whole, people are much more conservative than they were 30 years ago.
Analysis We get into disagreements about sentences like this and make decisions based on them. But the example is too vague to be true or false. What does "people" mean? All adults? What does "conservative" mean? That's really vague. Is the head of Fox News conservative? Your uncle? Your senator?

Example 3 Aquarius: What you thought would be a quick dance is turning out to be a long slog. What makes this so cumbersome is all of the baggage you have to carry.

Horoscopes by Holiday, February 2, 2012

Analysis Ever notice how vague horoscopes are? How could you tell if this one was false? There's no claim here.

Example 4 Susan Shank, J.D., has joined Zia Trust Inc. as Senior Trust Officer. Shank has 20 years' experience in the financial services industry including 13 years' experience as a trust officer and seven years' experience as a wealth strategist.

Albuquerque Journal, April 29, 2010, and the Zia Trust website

Analysis "Wealth strategist" looks impressive. But when I called Ms. Shank and asked her what it meant, she said, "It can have many meanings, whatever the person wants it to mean." This is vagueness used to try to convince you she's doing something important.

Example 5 If a suspect who is totally uncooperative is hit once by a policeman, that's not unnecessary force. Nor twice, if he's resisting. Possibly three times. If he's still resisting, shouldn't the policeman have the right to hit him again? It would be dangerous not to allow that. So, you can't say exactly how many times a policeman has to hit a suspect before it's unnecessary force. So the policeman did not use unnecessary force.

Analysis This argument convinced a jury to acquit the policemen who beat up Rodney King in Los Angeles in the 1990s. But it's an example of the drawing the line fallacy.

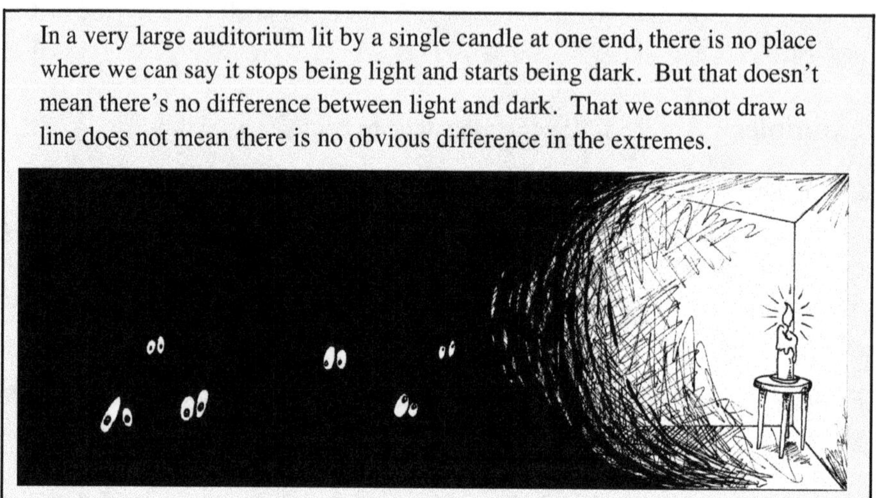

In a very large auditorium lit by a single candle at one end, there is no place where we can say it stops being light and starts being dark. But that doesn't mean there's no difference between light and dark. That we cannot draw a line does not mean there is no obvious difference in the extremes.

Throughout this text we'll often point out a common mistake in reasoning and label it a *fallacy*.

> ***Drawing the line fallacy*** It's bad reasoning to argue that if you can't make the difference precise, then there's no difference.

Example 6 Tom: That guard on the 76ers is better than LeBron James.

Analysis Manuel shouldn't start arguing about this until Tom makes it clear what he means by one basketball player being better than another (Scoring? Defense? Passing? All of those somehow combined?). Suppose you were a coach and you asked your assistant, "Who should I put in the game?" and she answered, "The best player, coach." You'd want to get a new assistant.

Example 7 Dad: Whoa, little guy. Be careful with that gallon of milk. Let me help you.

Little Boy: No, no, Daddy. I can do it. I'm strong.

Analysis If someone came up to you on the street and asked, "Are you strong?" how could you answer that? It's too vague. But here the dad understands his son means that he's strong enough to lift the milk without dropping it. Either his son can do it or he can't, so it's a claim. *Whether a sentence is too vague to be a claim can depend on context.*

2. Ambiguous sentences

An ***ambiguous*** sentence is one that can be understood in two or a very few obviously different ways. An ambiguous sentence is definitely not a claim.

Example 8 There is a reason I haven't talked to Robert [my ex-lover] in seventeen years (beyond the fact that I've been married to a very sexy man whom I've loved for two-thirds of that time).

Laura Berman, *Ladies' Home Journal,* June 1996

Analysis The rest of the time she just put up with him?

Example 9 Tom: Saying that having a gun in the home is an accident waiting to happen is like saying that people who buy life insurance are waiting to die. We should be allowed to protect ourselves.

Analysis Tom, perhaps without even realizing it, is trading on two ways to understand "protect": physically protect vs. emotionally or financially protect.

Example 10 Dr. E's dogs eat over 10 pounds of meat every week.

Analysis Is this true or false? It depends on whether it means "Each of Dr. E's dogs eats over 10 pounds of meat every week" (big dogs!), or "Dr. E's dogs together eat over 10 pounds of meat every week." *It's ambiguous whether the individual or the group is meant.*

Example 11 Homosexuality can't be hereditary. Homosexual couples can't reproduce, so genes for homosexuality would have died out long ago.

Analysis The argument appears good but only because "Homosexual couples can't reproduce" is ambiguous. It's true if understood as "Homosexuals can't reproduce *as a couple*," but it's false in the sense needed to make the argument good: "Homosexuals, who happen to be in couples, each can't reproduce." Again there's ambiguity between the individual and the group. It's easy to get confused when an ambiguous sentence is used as a premise. We can tolerate some vagueness, but we should never tolerate ambiguity in reasoning.

Exercises for Section A

To make it easier to answer these exercises, use the formatted versions of them, which you can find at www.AdvancedReasoningForum.org/CT5/exercises.

1. Give an example of a vague sentence that someone tried to pass off to you as a claim.
2. Which of the following are too vague to be considered claims?
   (You may have to suggest a context in which the sentence is spoken.)
   a. Manuel: Maria is a better cook than Lee.
   b. Lee: Manuel looks like he has a cold today.
   c. Public animal shelters should be allowed to sell unclaimed animals to laboratories for experimentation.
   d. Tuition at state universities does not cover the entire cost to the university of a student's education.
   e. All unnatural sex acts should be prohibited by law.
   f. All citizens should have equal rights.
   g. People with disabilities are just as good as people who are not disabled.
   h. Boy, are you lucky to get a date with Jane—on a scale of 1 to 10, she's at least a 9.
   i. Zoe has beautiful eyes.
   j. Dog food is cheaper at Albertson's grocery store than at Smith's grocery.
   k. Alpo in cans is cheaper at Albertson's grocery store than at Smith's grocery.
   l. Spot is a big dog.
   m. Cholesterol is bad for you.
   n. Parents should be held responsible for crimes their children commit.
   o. "Pasadena City College: a global community college for the 21st century" (radio ad)
   p. We offer no-hassle loans.
   q. "Each one of us has an important contribution to make in terms of shaping our collective vision and helping us create a welcoming and positive environment that truly serves the needs of our students and community."
      (memo to faculty from Kathleen F. Burke, Ed.D., Pierce College president, 2016)
   r. "Coaching people to unleash their aspirations, move beyond what they already think and know, and maximize their results fulfills one of our highest aspirations of what it is to be a human being."
      Robert Hargrove, *The Masterful Coaching Fieldbook*, 2007

3. Find an advertisement that treats a vague sentence as if it were a claim.

4. What's wrong with the following attempt to convince?

   Look, officer, if I were going 36 in this 35 m.p.h. zone, you wouldn't have given me a ticket, right? What about 37? But at 45 you would? Well, isn't that saying that the posted speed limit is just a suggestion? Or do you write the law on what's speeding?

5. a. Can a claim be ambiguous?
   b. Can a claim be vague?

6. How much ambiguity can we tolerate in an argument?

7. Decide whether each of the following sentences is a claim. If it is ambiguous, give at least two sentences corresponding to the ways it could be understood.
   a. Zoe saw the waiter with the glasses.
   b. Americans bicycle thousands of miles every year.
   c. If someone is under 18 years old, then he cannot vote in this country.
   d. I am over 6 feet tall.
   e. Zoe is cold.
   f. The players on the basketball team had a B average in their courses.
   g. All men are created equal.
   h. It is better to be rich than famous.
   i. "VA Reaches Out To Blind Vets"
      Albuquerque Journal, headline, August 18, 2009
   j. Cats are a species of reptile.
   k. "I remember meeting a mother of a child who was abducted by the North Koreans right here in the Oval Office." George W. Bush, June 26, 2008
   l. Public education in California is on the decline.
   m. He gave her cat food.

8. Give an example of an ambiguous sentence you've heard recently.

9. The following argument depends on ambiguity to sound convincing. Rewrite at least one of the sentences to eliminate the ambiguity.

   Dick to Zoe: Anything that's valuable should be protected. Good abdominal muscles are valuable—you can tell because everyone is trying to get them. A layer of fat will protect my abs. So I should continue to be 11 pounds overweight.

10. A special kind of ambiguity occurs when we're talking about what we say. Suppose I say:

    The Taj Mahal has eleven letters.

    I don't mean that the building has eleven letters but that the name of it does. In speech we use a different tone of voice or make quotation marks in the air with our fingers. In writing we use quotation marks around a word or phrase to show that we're talking about that word or phrase. In writing I can indicate that with:

    "The Taj Mahal" has eleven letters.

We also use quotation marks as an equivalent of a wink or a nod in conversation, a nudge in the ribs indicating that we're not to be taken literally or that we don't really subscribe to what we're saying. We call these "scare quotes," and when used this way they allow us to get away with "murder."

For each of the following, indicate if any quotation marks should be inserted.

a. Suzy can't understand what argument means.

b. Suzy can't understand the argument Dr. E gave in class.

c. The judge let the defendant get away with murder.

d. O'Brien says that there are seven legal ways to never pay taxes.

B. Subjective and Objective Claims

Sometimes the problem with a sentence that seems vague is that we're not clear what standards are being used. Suppose Dick hears Harry say,

> "New cars today are really expensive."

Harry might have some clear standards for what "expensive" means, perhaps that the average price of a new car today is more than 50% of what the average person earns in a year.

Or Harry might just mean that new cars cost too much for him to be comfortable buying one. That is, Harry has standards, but they're personal, not necessarily shared by anyone else. They're how he thinks or believes or feels.

Or Harry might have no standards at all. He's never thought hard about what it means for a car to be expensive.

It's convenient to have terms for these different possibilities.

> ***Subjective and objective claims*** A claim is *subjective* if whether it is true or false depends on what someone (or some thing or some group) thinks, believes, or feels. A claim is *objective* if it's not subjective.

So Harry might have objective standards for what it means for a car to be expensive, or he might have subjective standards, or he might have no standards at all. Until we know what he meant, we shouldn't accept what he said as a claim.

An example of an objective claim is "Every car made by Volkswagen has a gasoline engine." It's false, and that doesn't depend on what anyone thinks or believes. But when Dick says, "Steak tastes better than spaghetti," that's subjective. Whether it's true depends on whether Dick believes or thinks that steak tastes better than spaghetti.

If Tom says, "It's cold outside," is that objective or subjective? If it's meant as shorthand for "I feel cold when outdoors," then it's subjective, and it's a claim. But if it's meant as objective, that is, Tom means to assert that it's cold independently of me or anyone, then it's too vague for us to consider it to have a truth value.

A sentence that's too vague to be an objective claim might be perfectly all right as a subjective one if that's what the speaker intended. After all, we don't have very precise ways to describe our feelings.

But what if it's so cold that everyone agrees that it's cold outside? Is "It's cold outside" still subjective? Yes. Whether it's true or false depends on what a lot of people think—no standard independent of people has been put forward. But we can note that agreement.

> ***Intersubjective claims*** A subjective claim is *intersubjective* if (nearly) everyone agrees that it's true or (nearly) everyone agrees that it's false.

Examples Are the following objective or subjective claims, or not claims at all?

Example 12 All ravens are black.
Analysis This is an objective claim.

Example 13 Wanda weighs 195 pounds.
Analysis This is an objective claim. Whether it's true or false doesn't depend on what anyone thinks or believes. Registering a number on a scale is an objective criterion.

Example 14 Wanda is overweight.
Analysis If Wanda's doctor says this, he's probably thinking of some standard for being overweight, and he intends it as an objective claim. If you or I say it, it's probably subjective, just as if we were to say someone is ugly or handsome.

Example 15 Wanda is fat.
Analysis "Fat" isn't a technical term used by a doctor. It's a term we use to classify people as unattractive or attractive, like "beautiful." The claim is subjective. But what if Wanda is so obese that almost everyone would say she is fat? In that case the claim is intersubjective.

Example 16 Lee: I felt sick yesterday, and that's why I didn't hand in my work.
Analysis Lee didn't feel sick yesterday—he left his critical thinking writing assignment to the last minute and couldn't finish it before class. This is a false subjective claim.

Example 17 Dick: Spot eats canned dog food right away, but when we give him dry dog food, he doesn't finish it until half the day is over.

Zoe: So Spot likes canned dog food better than dry.

Analysis Dick makes two objective claims about how Spot acts. Zoe concludes from them a subjective claim about what Spot thinks or feels.

Example 18 Compare:

There are no oil reserves worth exploiting in Iowa.

I think that there are no oil reserves worth exploiting in Iowa.

Analysis There's a big difference between these two. The first is objective. The second is subjective.

Example 19

Analysis Sure, "too loud" is vague. It's subjective, too. But it serves its purpose here. We understand what the guy means.

Example 20 There are more rabbits alive now than there were 50 years ago.

Analysis You might think it's easier to know whether objective claims are true compared to subjective ones. But this example is objective and no one has any idea how to go about finding out whether it's true.

Example 21 Spot is outdoors. He's wet. It's well below freezing. Spot is whining and shivering. Dick says, "Spot feels cold."

Analysis This is subjective, and we all know it's true.

Example 22 There's enough oil available for extraction by current means to fulfill the world's needs for the next 47 years at the current rate of use.

Analysis This is objective. People disagree about it because there's not enough evidence one way or the other.

Example 23 Zoe (to Dick): Tom loves Suzy.

Dick: I don't think so.

Analysis Dick and Zoe disagree about whether this subjective claim is true, but it's not for lack of evidence. There's plenty; the problem is how to interpret it.

Whether a claim is subjective or objective does not depend on:

- How many people believe it.
- Whether it's true or false.
- Whether anyone can know whether it's true or false.

Subjectivist fallacy It's a mistake to argue that because there is a lot of disagreement about whether a claim is true, it's therefore subjective.

The subjectivist fallacy is just one way of ***confusing objective with subjective***.

Example 24 Lee: I deserve a higher mark in this course.
Dr. E: No, you don't. Here's the record of your exams and papers. You earned a C.
Lee: That's just your opinion.

Analysis Lee is treating the claim "I deserve a higher mark in this course" as if it were subjective. But if it really were subjective, there'd be no point in arguing about it with Dr. E any more than arguing about whether Dr. E feels cold.

Example 25

Analysis What are Dick and Zoe arguing about? He likes the tie; she doesn't. Treating a subjective claim as objective is also a mistake.

Often it's reasonable to question whether a claim is really objective. But sometimes it's just a confusion. All too often people insist that a claim is subjective ("That's just your opinion") when they're unwilling to examine their beliefs or engage in dialogue.

Exercises for Section B

1. a. What is a subjective claim?
   b. What is an objective claim?
   c. Are there any claims that are neither objective nor subjective?
2. a. Give an example of a true objective claim.
   b. Give an example of a false objective claim.
   c. Give an example of a true subjective claim.
   d. Give an example of a false subjective claim.

3. Explain why a sentence that is too vague to be taken as an objective claim might be acceptable as a subjective claim.

4. Make up a list of five claims for your classmates to classify as objective or subjective.

5. State whether each of the following is objective, or subjective, or not a claim at all. In some cases you'll have to imagine who's saying it and the context. Where possible, explain your answer in terms of the standards being used.

   a. Wool insulates better than rayon.
   b. Silk feels better on your skin than rayon.
   c. Pablo Picasso painted more oil paintings than Norman Rockwell.
   d. Bald men are more handsome.
   e. You intend to do your very best work in this course.
   f. He's sick! How could someone say something like that?
   g. He's sick; he's got the flu.
   h. Cats enjoy killing birds.
   i. Murder is wrong.
   j. Your answer to Exercise 3 in Chapter 1 of this book is wrong.
   k. Demons caused me to kill my brother.
   l. (In a court of law, said by the defense attorney) The defendant is insane.
   m. Zoe is more intelligent than Dick.
   n. Zoe gets better grades in all her courses than Dick.
   o. Suzy believes that the moon does not rise and set.
   p. Dick's dog Spot ran to his bowl and drooled when Dick got his dog food.
   q. Dick's dog Spot is hungry.
   r. Fifty-four percent of women responding to a recent Gallup Poll said they think that women do not have equal employment opportunities with men.
   s. Fifty-four percent of women think that women do not have equal employment opportunities with men.
   t. Zeke failed the lie-detector test.
   u. Zeke is lying.
   v. God exists.

6. Bring to class two advertisements, one that uses only subjective claims and another that uses only objective claims.

7. a. Give an example of someone treating a subjective claim as if it were objective.
   b. Give an example of someone treating an objective claim as if it were subjective.

8. What, if anything, is wrong with these?

   a. Tom: It is more likely for a teenage girl to get into an automobile accident than a boy.
      Zoe: That's a sexist remark!

   b. Zoe: I'm so tired.
      Dick: C'mon. You can't be tired, you just got 12 hours of sleep.

c. Dick: You're going for a run now? That's crazy. It's way too hot for a run.
Tom: No it isn't. It's just right.

9. 
IF YOU DON'T SLOW DOWN WE'RE GOING TO GET IN AN ACCIDENT! YOU NEARLY WENT OUT OF CONTROL GOING AROUND THAT LAST CORNER!
THAT'S JUST WHAT YOU THINK.
25

Is Zoe right? How should Dick respond?

10. Go back to some of the essays you've written for other courses and find where you used a phrase like "I think" or "It seems to me that." Did you really mean your words to be taken as just your personal opinion?

11. Give an example of a claim that you thought was intersubjective but later you found out that you were wrong.

12. Bring to class a movie criticism (Netflix is a good place to look) and decide whether the writer is trying to convince you that claims he or she is making are not just his or her opinion. Explain how the writer does it.

C. Prescriptive Claims and Value Judgments

"Dick should take Spot for a walk this afternoon." "Suzy should study more." "People shouldn't litter." Sometimes we don't describe how the world is but rather how we think it should be.

> ***Descriptive and prescriptive claims*** A claim is *descriptive* if it's meant to describe what is. A claim is *prescriptive* if it's meant to describe what should be.

Every claim is either descriptive or prescriptive.

Examples Are the following prescriptive or descriptive claims?

Example 26 Drunk drivers kill more people than sober drivers do.
Analysis This is a descriptive claim.

Example 27 There should be a law against driving drunk.
Analysis This is a prescriptive claim.

Example 28 Selling cocaine is against the law.
Analysis This is a descriptive claim.

Example 29 Zeke shouldn't sell cocaine.
Analysis This is a prescriptive claim.

Example 30 Dick: I'm hot.
Zoe: You should take your sweater off.
Analysis Dick has made a descriptive claim. Zoe responds with a prescriptive one.

Example 31 The government must not legalize marijuana.
Analysis This is a prescriptive claim where "must" is meant as a stronger idea of "should."

Often when someone says that something is "good," "better," "best," "bad," "worse," "worst," or makes some other ***value judgment***, it's meant as prescriptive in the sense that we shouldn't do what is bad/wrong/worse and that we should do or choose what is good/better/best.

Example 32 Texting while driving is bad.
Analysis This is prescriptive. It's meant that no one should text while driving.

Example 33 Dr. E: It's just plain wrong to cheat on an exam.
Analysis This is prescriptive, for by "wrong" Dr. E means that his students shouldn't do it.

Example 34 Physician to Professor Zzzyzzx: You should see some improvement in your chest pains by the end of the week.
Analysis Sometimes people use "should" to mean that they think it's probable. There's no prescription here.

Example 35 Dick: Cats are really disagreeable animals.
Analysis Dick is making a value judgment, but there's no "should" in it or implied by it. Not every value judgment is prescriptive.

Example 36 Tom: Abortion is wrong.
Analysis What standard is Tom invoking? In disagreement with the commands of the Bible? In disagreement with what a priest said? In disagreement with the Koran? In disagreement with moral principles that are not codified but are well-known? Until he and Zoe are clear about the standard, there's nothing to debate.

On the other hand, Zoe might say, "Maybe abortion is wrong to you, but it's O.K. to me." No further standard is needed then, for she views "Abortion is wrong" as a subjective claim—the standard is personal. But if so, there's nothing to debate.

Prescriptive claims and standards A prescriptive claim either asserts a standard—this is what should be, and there's nothing more fundamental to say than that—or else it assumes another prescriptive claim as standard.

Example 37 Ahmad: Eating dogs is bad.

Analysis This is intended as a prescriptive claim, since it carries with it the idea that we should not eat dogs.

Zoe agreed with Ahmad when he said this to her, but did she really know what standard Ahmad had in mind? Perhaps he's a vegetarian and believes:

> You should treat all animals humanely, and butchering animals is not humane.

Or Ahmad might believe just:

> Dogs taste bad, and you shouldn't eat anything that tastes bad.

Or perhaps Ahmad believes:

> We should not eat anything forbidden by the standard interpretation of the Koran, and it is forbidden to eat carnivores.

Or Ahmad might just believe what almost all Americans believe:

> Dogs should be treated as companions to people and not as food.

Until Zoe knows what Ahmad means by "bad," she has no reason to view what he's said as a claim.

Example 38 Harry: The Federal Reserve Board ought to lower interest rates.

Analysis This is a prescriptive claim. Zoe's mother disagrees with Harry, since she wants to see her savings earn more interest. Harry says the standard he's assuming is "The Federal Reserve Board should help the economy grow," which is what he and Zoe's mom should debate.

Example 39 Zoe: That's enough ice cream for you, Dick.
Dick: What do you mean? There's no such thing as too much ice cream.

Analysis Zoe is making a prescriptive claim. When she says "That's enough," she means that Dick should stop eating. Dick challenges her unstated standard.

Example 40 It's wrong to kill people.

Analysis This is a prescriptive claim. It's usually taken as a standard rather than assuming any other standard.

People who believe that all prescriptive claims are subjective are called ***relativists***. They think that all standards—for beauty, morality, and every other value—are relative to what some person or group of people believe. Most people, though, believe that at least some prescriptive claims are objective, such as "You shouldn't torture dogs."

Often when you challenge people to make their standard explicit, they'll say, "I just mean it's wrong (right) to me." Yet when you press them, it turns out they're not so happy that you disagree. What they really mean is "I have a right to believe that." Of course they do. But do they have a *good reason* to believe the claim? It's rare that people intend their moral views to be taken as subjective.

I've got a right to believe this. ≠ *I have a good reason to believe this.*

Example 41 [The author cites various conflicting standards on which to base economic policy.] The problem with all these criteria is that the choice among them seems entirely arbitrary. . . . I suspect though that the choice of a normative [prescriptive] criterion is ultimately a matter of taste. Stephen Landsburg, *The Armchair Economist*

Analysis This author seems to be a relativist. But he might just be committing the subjectivist fallacy, mistaking lack of agreement for subjectivity.

Example 42 Almost all economists believe that rent control adversely affects the availability and quality of housing and is a very costly way of helping the most needy members of society. Nonetheless, many city governments choose to ignore the advice of economists and place ceilings on the rents that landlords may charge their tenants. Gregory Mankiw, *Principles of Economics*

Analysis That "nonetheless" slips in a value judgment that city governments shouldn't adopt a policy that adversely affects availability and quality of housing and is a costly way of helping the most needy members of society. You may agree, but you need to be aware that in doing so you're accepting a prescriptive standard.

Exercises for Section C

1. What is a prescriptive claim? A descriptive claim?

For each of the exercises below, explain why you understand the sentence as prescriptive or descriptive, and if necessary provide a standard to make it clear enough to be a claim. That is, for each answer the following:

Prescriptive or descriptive?
Standard needed?

2. Dissecting monkeys without anesthetic is cruel and immoral.
3. Dissecting monkeys without anesthetic is prohibited by the National Science Foundation funding guidelines.
4. Larry shouldn't marry his sister.
5. Employees must wash their hands before returning to work.
6. Downloading a pirated copy of this textbook is wrong.
7. It's better to conserve energy than to heat a room above 68°.
8. It's about time that the government stop bailing out the bankers.
9. Dick and Zoe have a dog named "Spot."
10. The government should raise the tax rate for the upper 1% of all taxpayers.
11. This school should require students to take critical thinking their first year so that they can improve their comprehension in all their other courses.
12. Dogs are good and cats are bad.

D. Definitions

We've seen that we can get into problems, waste our time, and generally irritate each other through misunderstandings. It's always reasonable and usually wise to ask people we are reasoning with to be clear enough that we can agree on what it is we are discussing.

There are two general methods of making clear what we say.

- Replace the entire sentence by another that is not vague or ambiguous.
- Use a definition to make a specific word or phrase precise.

> ***Definition*** A *definition* explains or stipulates how to use a word or phrase.

"Dog" means "domestic canine."

Puce is the color of a flea, purple-brown or brownish-purple.

"Puerile" means boyish or childish, immature, trivial.

There are several ways we can make a definition. One, as with the definition of "dog," is to give a *synonym*, a word or phrase that means the same and that could be substituted for "dog" wherever that's used.

Another way is to describe: A lorgnette is a kind of eyeglass that is held in the hand, usually with a long handle.

Or we can explain, as when we say a loophole is a means of escaping or evading something unpleasant.

Or we can point:

Though pointing isn't part of language, it serves to make our language clear.

> *A definition is not a claim.* A definition is not true or false but good or bad, apt or wrong. Definitions tell us what we're talking about.

People often use what sounds like a definition to hide a claim that should be debated. For example, if someone defines "abortion" as "the murder of an unborn child," she's made it impossible to have a reasoned discussion about whether abortion is murder and whether a fetus is a person. A ***persuasive definition*** is a claim that should be argued for but which is made to sound like a definition.

> If you call a tail a leg, how many legs has a dog? Five?
> No, calling a tail a leg don't *make* it a leg.
>
> attributed to Abraham Lincoln

Examples Which of the following are definitions? Persuasive definitions?

Example 43 A dog is a mammal.
Analysis This is not a definition. We can't use "mammal" in place of "dog" in our reasoning. It doesn't tell us how to use the word "dog"; it tells us something about dogs. Not every sentence with "is" in it is a definition.

Example 44 "Exogenous" means "developing from without."
Analysis This is a definition, not a claim. It's an explanation of how to use the word "exogenous."

Example 45 Fasting and very low calorie diets (diets below 500 calories) cause a loss of nitrogen and potassium in the body, a loss which is believed to trigger a mechanism in the body that causes us to hold on to our fat stores and to turn to muscle protein for energy instead. *Jane Fonda's New Workout and Weight Loss Program*
Analysis Definitions aren't always labeled but are often made in passing, as with this definition of "very low calorie diet."

Example 46 Meyer Friedman and Ray Rosenman . . . identified a cluster of behavioral characteristics—constant hurriedness, free-floating hostility, and intense competitiveness—that seemed to be present in most of their patients with coronary disease. They coined the term *Type A* to describe this behavior pattern; *Type B* describes people who do not display these qualities. Daniel Goleman and Joel Gurin, *Mind Body Medicine*
Analysis Here the definitions are embedded in a text, too. But these are not good unless some standards are given for what is meant by "constant hurriedness," "free-floating hostility," and "intense competitiveness" (none were given in the text). How could you determine whether someone you know is Type A or Type B from this definition? A good definition must use words that are clearer and better understood than the word being defined.

Example 47 —Maria's so rich, she can afford to pay for your dinner.
—What do you mean by "rich"?
—She's got a Mercedes.

Analysis This is not a definition since by "rich" we don't mean "has a Mercedes." Many people who are rich don't have a Mercedes, and some people who own a Mercedes aren't rich. This is an argument: "Maria has a Mercedes" is given as evidence that Maria is rich; "means" is used in the sense of "because."

I just tried to convince you that "has a Mercedes" is not a good definition of "rich." How? I pointed out that someone could own a Mercedes and not be rich, or be rich and not own a Mercedes.

Example 48 Microscope: an instrument consisting essentially of a lens or combination of lenses, for making very small objects, as microorganisms, look larger so that they can be seen and studied. *Webster's New World Dictionary*

Analysis This is from a dictionary, so it's got to be a good definition. But if you're trying to convince someone that what she sees through a microscope is actually there —that it's not in the lens or inside the microscope like a kaleidoscope—then this definition won't do. "See, there really are little living things there. After all, it's part of the definition of a microscope that it's just enlarging what's there." What counts as a persuasive definition can depend on the context.

Example 49 Pluto is not a planet.

Analysis There was a lot of heated debate about this in 2006 when astronomers re-classified Pluto using a new and what they considered better definition of "planet." But really the only issue was whether that was a better or worse definition.

Example 50 According to the U.S. Supreme Court, to be obscene, material must meet a three-prong test:

> (1) an average person, applying contemporary community standards, must find that the material, as a whole, appeals to the prurient interest (i.e., material having a tendency to excite lustful thoughts); (2) the material must depict or describe, in a patently offensive way, sexual conduct specifically defined by applicable law; and (3) the material, taken as a whole, must lack serious literary, artistic, political, or scientific value. From the FCC.gov website

Analysis This is the definition the Federal Communications Commission uses to determine whether speech broadcast on public airwaves is obscene—in which case it is not protected by the First Amendment and may be punishable by multimillion dollar fines. However, saying some expression is not serious, is patently offensive, and is prurient to a hypothetical "average person" is not any clearer than saying it's obscene.

Example 51 Intuition is perception via the unconscious. Carl G. Jung

Analysis This is a definition, but a bad one. The words doing the defining are no clearer than what's being defined.

Example 52 Dogs are domesticated canines that obey humans.

Analysis This is a bad definition because it's ***too narrow***: it doesn't cover cases it should, like feral dogs.

Example 53 A car is a vehicle with a motor that can carry people.

Analysis This is a bad definition because it's ***too broad***: it covers cases that it shouldn't, like a golf cart. So we can't use the words doing the defining in place of the word being defined.

> ***Good definition*** For a definition to be good:
> - The words doing the defining are clear and better understood than the word or phrase being defined.
> - The words being defined and the defining phrase can be used interchangeably. That is, it's correct to use the one exactly when it's correct to use the other.

The key to making a good definition is to look for examples where the definition does or does not apply in order to make sure that it is not too broad or too narrow. For example, suppose we want to define "school cafeteria." That's something a lawmaker might need in order to write a law to disburse funds for a food program. As a first go, we might try "A place in a school where students eat." But that's too broad, since that would include just a room where students can take their meals. So we might try "A place in a school where students can buy a meal." But that's too broad, too, since that would include a room where you could buy a sandwich from a vending machine. How about "A room in a school where students can buy a hot meal that is served on a tray"? But if there's a fast-food restaurant like Burger King at the school, that would qualify. So it looks like we need "A room in a school where students can buy a hot meal that is served on a tray, and the school is responsible for the preparation and selling of the food." This looks better, though if adopted as a definition in a law, it might keep schools that want money from the legislature from contracting out the preparation of their food. Whether that's too narrow will depend on how the lawmakers intend the money to be spent.

> ***Steps in making a good definition***
> - Show the need for a definition.
> - State the definition.
> - Make sure the words make sense.
> - Give examples where the definition applies.
> - Give examples where the definition does not apply.
> - If necessary, contrast it with other likely definitions.
> - Possibly revise your definition.

Exercises for Section D

1. What is required of a good definition?
2. Why should we avoid persuasive definitions?

3. Classify each of the following as a definition, a persuasive definition, or neither. If it is a definition, state why you think it is good or bad.
   a. "Dog" means "a canine creature that brings love and warmth to a human family."
   b. Domestic violence is any violent act by a spouse or lover directed against his or her partner within the confines of the home of both.
   c. A feminist is someone who thinks that women are better than men.
   d. A conservative, in politics, is one who believes that we should conserve the political structure and laws as they are as much as possible, avoiding change.
   e. A liberal is someone who wants to use your taxes to pay for what he thinks will do others the most good.
   f. Love is blind.
   g. Sexual intercourse is when a man and a woman couple sexually with the intent of producing offspring.
   h. *Less-developed countries* (LDCs) The economies of Asia, Africa, and Latin America. (From an economics textbook)
   i. A killer whale has a sleek, streamlined, fusiform (tapered at both ends) body shape.
   j. A real fan has season tickets.
   k. Critical thinking is a habit of mind characterized by the comprehensive exploration of issues, ideas, artifacts, and events before accepting or formulating an opinion or conclusion. Association of American Colleges and Universities

4. For each of the following, give both a definition and a persuasive definition:
   a. Homeless person.
   b. Spouse.
   c. School bus.

5. For each of the following, replace "believes in" with other words that mean the same:
   a. Zoe believes in free love.
   b. Dick believes in God.
   c. Zoe believes in the Constitution.
   d. Zoe believes in herself.

6. Bring in an example of a definition used in one of your other courses. Is it good?

7. Sometimes we can make an apparently subjective claim objective by making a definition. For example, "Harry is intelligent" can be objective if we define "intelligent" to mean "has a B average or better in university courses." Give definitions that make the following subjective claims objective.
   a. It's hot outside.
   b. Eating a lot of fat every day is unhealthy.

8. Go to one of your other textbooks and find a definition that is made in passing, not explicitly stated as a definition.

9. Verify whether the presentation of the definition of "claim" in Chapter 1 follows the steps in making a good definition.

Summary We need to be able to distinguish different kinds of claims and be aware of sentences that look like claims but aren't.

A sentence is vague if it's unclear what the speaker intended. We can learn to recognize when a sentence is too vague to use in our reasoning. But it's bad reasoning to say that just because we can't draw a precise line, there's not any clear meaning to a word. An ambiguous sentence is vague in a bad way, for it has two or more clear interpretations. Ambiguous sentences should never be taken as claims.

Often the problem with a vague sentence is to determine what standards are being assumed. They could be objective—independent of what anyone or anything thinks/believes/feels, or they could be subjective, or there might not be any standard at all. A sentence that's too vague to be an objective claim might be all right as a subjective claim.

Considering whether a claim is objective or subjective can save us a lot of heartache because we won't debate someone else's feelings. Confusing subjective and objective claims leads to bad arguments.

Often we make prescriptive claims about what should be, not just what is. Moral claims usually are meant as prescriptive and objective, though often people retreat to saying they're subjective when they can't defend their views.

We need to eliminate ambiguity and excessive vagueness if we are to reason together. We can do so by rewriting our arguments or speaking more precisely. Or we can define the words that are causing the problem. A definition isn't a claim, though; it's something added to an argument to make the words in it clearer. A definition shouldn't prejudge the issue by being persuasive.

Key Words

- vague sentence
- drawing the line fallacy
- ambiguous sentence
- objective claim
- subjective claim
- intersubjective claim
- subjectivist fallacy
- confusing objective with subjective
- prescriptive claim
- descriptive claim
- value judgment
- relativist
- definition
- synonym
- persuasive definition
- good definition

Exercises for Chapter 2

Here are a few of Tom's attempts to do exercises using all the ideas we've learned in this chapter, along with Dr. E's comments. Tom's supposed to underline the terms that apply.

Dogs bark.

<u>claim</u>	subjective	ambiguous or too vague	
not claim	objective	definition	persuasive definition

Yes, it's a claim. But if it's a claim, then it has to be either objective or subjective.

Cats are nasty.

<u>claim</u> <u>subjective</u> <u>ambiguous or too vague</u>
not claim objective definition persuasive definition

No–if it's ambiguous or too vague, then it's not a claim. This is an example of a subjective claim.

Rabbits are the principal source of protein for dogs in the wild.

<u>claim</u> subjective ambiguous or too vague
not claim <u>objective</u> <u>definition</u> persuasive definition

No–if it's a definition, it's not a claim. And this is not a definition—what word is it defining? Certainly not "rabbit."

Dogs are canines that bring warmth and love to a family.

claim subjective ambiguous or too vague
<u>not claim</u> objective definition <u>persuasive definition</u>

No. If it's a persuasive definition, then it's a claim—masquerading as a definition.

1. State which of the following can together apply to a single sentence.

   claim subjective ambiguous or too vague
   not claim objective definition persuasive definition

For each of the following, indicate which of the terms from Exercise 1 apply. If you think your instructor might disagree, provide an explanation.

2. Donkeys can breed with other equines.
3. The manifest content of a dream is what a dream appears to be about to the dreamer.
4. A grade of A in this course means you know how to parrot what the professor said.
5. Public Health Is the Greatest Good for the Most Numbers
   (on the logo of the New Mexico Department of Health)
6. Too much TV is bad for children.
7. China has the largest land mass of any single country.
8. I've already seen the new *Star Wars* movie.
9. There are five countries in North America.
10. I'm going to throw up.
11. "We [the United States] are the leader of the free world."
    Senator J. Rockefeller on "Day to Day," National Public Radio, July 23, 2004
12. Science, when well digested, is nothing but good sense and reason.
13. Remember loved ones lost through Christmas concert.
    Headline, *The Spectrum*, December 4, 1998
14. If America shows uncertainty and weakness in this decade, the world will drift toward tragedy.

15. Buying low-cost property and renting it out is a great way to create wealth and constant cash flow. (from an extension course description)

16. Suzy: I can't take any more of these exercises!

17. That test was easy. (Tom to Suzy after Dr. E's last critical thinking exam)

Further Study Much of philosophy is concerned with attempts to give criteria that will turn apparently subjective claims into objective ones. A course on ethics will discuss whether claims about what's wrong or right can be made objective. A course on aesthetics will analyze whether all claims about what is beautiful are subjective. And a course on the philosophy of law or criminal justice will introduce the methods the law uses to give objective criteria for determining what is right or wrong.

Philosophy courses debate whether a claim being objective just means that it is believed by enough people—that is, whether objectivity is just intersubjectivity.

Courses in nursing discuss how to deal with subjective claims by patients and vague instructions by doctors.

For a fuller discussion of prescriptive claims and how to reason with them, see *Prescriptive Reasoning*, also published by the Advanced Reasoning Forum.

Some courses in English composition or rhetoric deal with the correct forms and uses of definitions. Courses on the philosophy of language and linguistics study the nature of definitions, ways in which definitions can be made, and misuses of definitions. Ambiguity and vagueness are also covered in English composition and rhetoric courses.

Writing Lesson 2

We know that before we begin deliberating we should make the issue precise enough that someone can agree or disagree.

Make the following sentence sufficiently precise that you could debate it:

Student athletes should be given special leniency when the instructor assigns course marks.

Your definition(s) or explanation should be at most one page long.
(At most one page, not at least or exactly one page.)

To give you a better idea of what you're expected to do, here are Tom's and Mary Ellen's homework on another topic, along with Dr. E's comments.

Tom Wyzyczy
Critical Thinking
Section 4
Writing Lesson 2

"All unnatural sex acts should be prohibited by law."

Before we can debate this we have to say what it means. I think that "unnatural sex act" should mean any kind of sexual activity that most people think is unnatural. And "prohibited by law" should mean there's a law against it.

You've got the idea, but your answer is really no improvement. You can delete the first sentence. And you can delete "I think." We can guess that, because you wrote the paper.

Your proposed definition of "unnatural sex act" is too vague. It's reminiscent of the standard the U.S. Supreme Court uses to define obscenity: prevailing community standards. In particular, what do you mean by "sexual activity"? Does staring at a woman's breasts count? And who are "people"? The people in your church? Your neighborhood? Your city? Your state? Your country? The world?

Of course, "prohibited by law" means there's a law against it. But what kind of law? A fine? A prison sentence? A penalty depending on the severity of the offense? How do you determine the severity?

Mary Ellen Zzzyzzx
Critical Thinking
Section 4
Writing Lesson 2

"All unnatural sex acts should be prohibited by law."

By "unnatural sex act" I shall mean any sexual activity involving genitals, consensual or not, *except* between a man and a woman who are both over 16 and in a way that could lead to procreation if they wanted it to and which is unobserved by others.

By "prohibited by law" I shall mean it would be a misdemeanor comparable to getting a traffic ticket.

I don't really think that everything else is unnatural, but I couldn't figure out any other way to make it precise. Is that what we're supposed to do?
Mary Ellen

You did just fine. Really, the burden to make it precise would be on the person suggesting that the sentence be taken as a claim. Most attempts are going to seem like a persuasive definition. But at least you now have a claim you could debate. If the other person thinks it's the wrong definition, that would be a good place to begin your discussions.

3 What Is a Good Argument?

A. Good Reason to Believe

Dr. E is a professor.
Dr. E wears a tie to class.
Dr. E teaches critical thinking.
So Dr. E is a vegetarian.

This is an awful argument. What's being a professor, wearing a tie, and teaching critical thinking got to do with Dr. E being a vegetarian?

But what about this one?

All dogs bark.
Ralph barks.
So Ralph is a dog.

It sounds good. Should we be convinced that Ralph is a dog?

It isn't a matter of whether we're convinced. Bad advertisements convince, but they're not good arguments. You can give a great argument to your friend but it won't convince him if he's weeping because his dog died. What's important is whether we *should* be convinced.

> ***Good arguments*** A good argument is one in which the premises give good reason to believe that the conclusion is true.

Our intuition was enough for us to know that the first argument is bad. But without some criteria for what counts as good reason, we're lost with the second one.

B. The Conclusion Follows from the Premises

We said that the first argument above is bad because the premises don't have anything to do with the conclusion. But that easy phrase is no guide for evaluating the second argument.

The problem with the first argument is that though all the premises are true, the conclusion could be false: Dr. E could be gluten intolerant; Dr. E could enjoy eating meat; Dr. E could wants a woman he's dating to think he's a real man who eats steak and barbecued ribs. There's nothing in the premises that rules out those possibilities, which for all we know are likely.

The second argument sounds better. But with that one, too, the premises don't rule out a likely possibility for how the premises could be true and the conclusion false: Ralph could be a seal or a fox.

> ***Weak arguments*** An argument is *weak* if there is some way, some possibility, for its premises to be true and conclusion false (at the same time) that doesn't seem unlikely.

If an argument is weak, the premises don't rule out likely possibilities for the conclusion to be false. So even if they're true, we wouldn't have good reason to believe the conclusion. Any weak argument is bad.

Example 1 Maria is at Dick and Zoe's place when she says,

"Spot is scratching at the door. So he must have to go outside to poop."

Analysis Or maybe he saw a cat through the window and wants to chase it. Or he wants to go for a walk. Or he's hungry and wants Dick to go outside to fill his bowl. These are ways the premise could be true and conclusion false which don't seem unlikely.

For an argument to be weak, it isn't just that there's *some* possible way for the premises to be true and conclusion false. There has to be a *likely* possibility.

Example 2 Dick heard this morning that there are parakeets for sale down at the mall. He knows that his neighbor has a birdcage in her garage and he wonders if it will be big enough for one of those parakeets. He reasons:

> All parakeets anyone I know has ever seen, or heard of, or read about are under 2 feet tall. So the parakeets on sale at the mall are under 2 feet tall.

Analysis Surveying all the ways the premise could be true, Dick thinks that, yes, a new supergrow bird food could have been formulated and the parakeets at the local mall are really 3 feet tall, he just hasn't heard about it. Or a rare giant parakeet from the Amazon forest could have been discovered and brought here. Or a UFO might have abducted a parakeet by mistake, hit it with growing rays, and made it gigantic.

All of these ways that the premise could be true and the conclusion false are so unlikely that Dick has good reason to believe the conclusion, even though it's possible that the conclusion is false.

> ***Strong arguments*** An argument is *strong* if there is some way, some possibility, for its premises to be true and conclusion false (at the same time), but every such possibility seems unlikely.

Sometimes we can make an argument where there's no way at all that the premises could be true and conclusion false.

Example 3 Every student at this school has paid tuition. Suzy is a student at this school. So Suzy has paid tuition.
Analysis Any way the premises could be true, the conclusion would be true, too.

> ***Valid arguments*** An argument is *valid* if there is no way, no possibility, for the premises to be true and conclusion false (at the same time). An argument that is not valid is *invalid*.

An argument is either valid or it isn't. There are no degrees to it, no judgment involved. But evaluating the strength of an argument does involve judgment, for it depends on how likely certain possibilities seem. The strength of an argument is a matter of degree, and *we classify invalid arguments on a scale from strong to weak.*

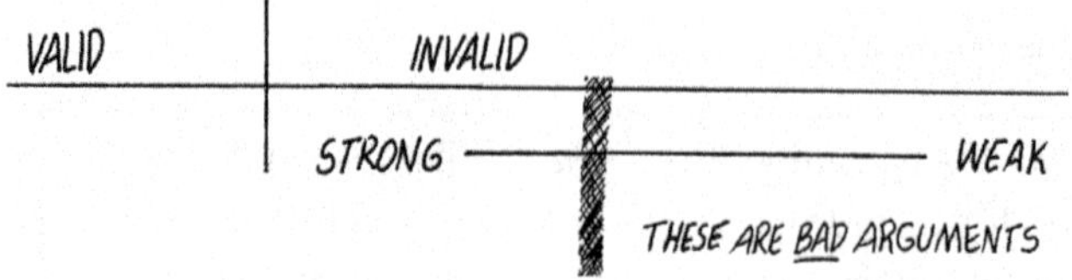

To evaluate an argument, you have to imagine ways the premises could be true. You have to be creative. *Imagine the possibilities.*

Weak arguments are bad. It's only with strong or valid arguments that the conclusion follows from the premises.

> In an argument, ***the conclusion follows from the premises*** means that the argument is strong or valid.

C. The Premises Are Plausible

If we don't have good reason to believe the premises, then the premises won't give us good reason to believe the conclusion. From a false claim you can prove any claim. For example:

All textbooks are written by women.
So the author of this textbook is a woman.
False premise, false conclusion.

All textbooks are written by women.
All women are human beings
So the author of this textbook is a human being.
False premise, true conclusion.

Here it's obvious that these have a false premise. But often it's not so obvious. We have to use our judgment whether we have reason to believe the premises.

> ***Plausible claims*** A claim is *plausible* if we have good reason to believe it is true. It is less plausible the less reason we have to believe it is true. It is ***implausible*** or ***dubious*** if we have no good reason to believe it.

A good argument has to be strong or valid and have plausible premises. But that's not enough.

Example 4 Suzy: Dr. E is mean.
Wanda: Why do you say that?
Suzy: Because he's not nice.

Analysis "He's not nice" is no more plausible than "Dr. E is mean." So Suzy hasn't given Wanda good reason to believe that Dr. E is mean.

Example 5 Dogs have souls. So you should treat dogs humanely.

Analysis Even if you agree that the premise is plausible, it's less plausible than the conclusion. So it doesn't give us more reason to believe the conclusion than we had before we heard the argument.

> ***Begging the question*** An argument begs the question if one of its premises is no more plausible than the conclusion.

Now we have the conditions for an argument to be good.

D. Tests for an Argument to Be Good

> ***Tests for an argument to be good***
> - The premises are plausible.
> - The premises are more plausible than the conclusion.
> - The argument is valid or strong.

Each of these tests is independent of the others: each can fail while the other two hold, as we saw in the examples above. So in evaluating whether an argument is good, we can start with whichever of them is easiest to determine.

But why should we be interested in whether the argument is strong or valid if we don't know whether the premises are true? Compare that to applying for a home loan. A couple goes in and fills out all the forms. The loan officer looks at their answers. She might tell them right then that they don't qualify. That is, even though she doesn't know if the claims they made about their income and assets are true, she can see that even if they are true, they won't qualify for a loan. So why bother to investigate whether what they said is true? On the other hand, she could tell them that they'll qualify if those claims are true. Then she goes out and makes phone calls, checks credit references, and so on, and finds out if they were telling the truth.

With an argument that is strong or valid you can say: grant me these premises and the conclusion follows. Good reasoning is concerned with what follows from what, as well as with what is true.

We've seen that a good argument gives us good reason to believe its conclusion. ***A bad argument tells us nothing about whether the conclusion is true or false***. If we encounter a bad argument, we have no more reason to believe or disbelieve the conclusion than we had before we heard it. *A bad argument does* not *show that the conclusion is false or even doubtful.*

Evaluating whether an argument passes the three tests to be good requires skills, ones you'll learn as you go along in this course. But evaluating whether an argument is good also depends on your knowledge, because as you know more you become better at evaluating whether premises are plausible and whether possibilities are likely.

Exercises for Sections A–D

1. What is an argument?
2. What does it mean to say an argument is valid?
3. What does it mean to say an argument is strong?
4. Can an argument be both valid and strong?
5. If an argument is valid or strong, does that mean it's a good argument? Explain.
6. If an argument is valid and its premises are true, is its conclusion true, too? Explain.
7. If an argument is strong and its premises are true, is its conclusion true, too? Explain.
8. Does whether an argument is good depend on whether it convinced anyone?
9. If an argument is good, what does that show about its conclusion?
10. If an argument is bad, what does that show about its conclusion?
11. To be classified as good, an argument must pass three tests. What are they?
12. Can we show that an argument is not valid by showing that its conclusion is false? Give an example or explanation.
13. Make up three arguments, two of which are bad and one good. Exchange them with a classmate to evaluate.

For Exercises 14–19, select the claim that makes the argument valid. *You're not supposed to judge whether the claim is plausible, just whether it makes the argument valid.* These examples may seem artificial, but we need simple practice on recognizing possibilities.

14. The dogs are drinking a lot of water today. It must be hot.
    a. Dogs always drink when they are hot.
    b. Every dog will drink when the weather is hot.
    c. Hot weather means dogs will drink.
    d. Only on hot days do dogs drink a lot of water.
    e. None of the above.
15. Every Yangakuchi monitor I've had either was defective and had to be returned or else burned out in less than a year. So you'd be foolish to buy a Yangakuchi monitor.
    a. You should do what I tell you to do.
    b. Every Yangakuchi monitor will be defective or go bad.

c. All monitors that are reliable are not Yangakuchi.
d. None of the above.

16. Puff is a cat. So Puff meows.
    a. Anything that meows is a cat.
    b. Dogs don't meow.
    c. All cats meow.
    d. Most cats meow.
    e. None of the above.

17. Suzy is a cheerleader. So Suzy goes to all the football games.
    a. Cheerleaders get in free to the football games.
    b. Cheerleaders are expected to attend all football games.
    c. Suzy is dating Tom, who is the football captain.
    d. All cheerleaders attend all football games.
    e. None of the above.

18. If Spot gets into the garbage, Dick will hit him with a newspaper. So Dick will hit Spot.
    a. The garbage is a bad thing for Spot to get into.
    b. Whenever Spot gets into the garbage, Dick hits him.
    c. Whenever Dick hits Spot, Spot was in the garbage.
    d. Spot got into the garbage.
    e. None of the above.

19. The President is on every channel on television. So he must be making an important speech.
    a. Only Presidents make important speeches on television.
    b. When the President makes an important speech on television, he's on every channel.
    c. When the President is on every channel on TV, he's making an important speech.
    d. Presidents only make important speeches.
    e. None of the above.

E. Indicator Words

Sometimes it's hard to know whether what you hear is an argument. But certain words let us see that someone intends to introduce a premise or a conclusion.

> ***Indicator word*** An indicator word is a word or phrase added to a claim to tell us the role of the claim in an argument or what the speaker thinks of the claim.

Indicator words are flags put on claims—they are not part of a claim. They are good to use in our own arguments in order to structure our writing and to help others understand us, though most arguments we encounter won't have such clear signposts. Here are some common ones.

conclusion indicators	*premise indicators*
so	since
therefore	because
hence	for
thus	in as much as
consequently	given that
we can then derive	suppose that
it follows that	it follows from

Now compare:

Manuel says he visited Mexico.
He speaks Spanish and he described the towns he visited.
So Manuel really visited Mexico.

Manuel says he visited Mexico.
He speaks Spanish and he described the towns he visited.
So maybe Manuel visited Mexico.

These are the *same argument*: they have the same premises, and the conclusion of both is "Manuel visited Mexico." The words "maybe" and "really" just tell us the speaker's attitude toward the argument. "So really" instead of "so maybe" lets us know that the speaker thinks the argument is valid or strong, but that doesn't make the argument valid or strong. You can't make an argument valid by calling it valid any more than Zoe can make Dick a pig by calling him a pig. These words are a comment on a claim, not part of the claim.

F. Evaluating Some Examples

Example 6 Every elected official in the United States is under thirty-four years old. So the president of the United States is under thirty-four years old.

Analysis This argument is valid: there's no way the premise could be true and conclusion false at the same time. Were the premise true—say if tomorrow the laws were changed and enforced to prohibit people older than thirty-four from holding elective office—then it would be impossible for the president to be older than thirty-four. But the argument is bad. It has a false conclusion, and that's because the premise is false. *Valid ≠ Good*

Example 7 Lee: Every garbage can that I've seen or anyone else I know has seen that's issued by the city is blue. So all city-issued garbage cans in this city are blue.

Analysis This is a strong argument, and it's good. Compare it to the valid argument:

This city issues only blue garbage cans.
Therefore, all city-issued garbage cans in this city are blue.

This one begs the question. Valid arguments aren't always best. *A strong argument can be better than a valid one with the same conclusion.*

Example 8 All dogs bark. Ralph is a dog. So Ralph barks.
Analysis This is a valid argument. But it's not good. The first premise is false: some dogs have had their vocal cords cut to keep them quiet, and there's a breed of dog from Africa called "Basenji" that can't bark at all (they just sort of whimper).

Those possibilities don't seem likely. Nonetheless we shouldn't rely on this argument because it has a premise that we know is false.

Example 9 Maria (to her supervisor): I was told that I would earn a bonus if I put in 100 hours of overtime and have a perfect attendance record for two months. I have since put in 110 hours of overtime and have a perfect attendance record for the last ten weeks. So I'm entitled to a bonus.
Analysis This is a valid argument. It's not possible for the premises to be true and the conclusion false. But we don't know if the argument is good because we don't know if the premises are true.

Example 10 Student athletes should not be given special leniency in assigning their course marks because that wouldn't be treating all students equally.
Analysis This is how Maria wrote her first writing lesson. But what does "treating all students equally" mean? It means "treat everyone the same way." So her argument is: You shouldn't treat athletes differently because you should treat everyone the same way. The premise may be true, but it's just a restatement of the conclusion. The argument begs the question, so it's bad.

Example 11 Good teachers give fair exams, and Dr. E gives fair exams. So Dr. E is a good teacher.
Analysis The premises of the argument are true. And the conclusion is true, too. But is it a good argument? Is there a way in which the premises could be true and the conclusion false? Yes: Dr. E might bore his students to tears and just copy fair exams from the instructor's manual for the textbook. After all, the premise doesn't say that *only* good teachers give fair exams. The argument is weak and hence bad.

> How do we show an argument is weak? *We describe at least one likely way in which the premises could be true and the conclusion false.*

Example 12 Maria's hair is naturally black. Today Maria's hair is red. So Maria dyed her hair.
Analysis Could the premises be true and the conclusion false? Perhaps: Maria is taking a new medication that has a strong effect or she might have gotten too close to the machinery when they were painting her car. These are possibilities, but not likely ones, and it doesn't seem that there's any other one that's likely. So the

argument is strong, not valid. Since we know that Maria's hair is naturally black, it's a good argument.

Example 13 Harry: Every time I can remember eating eggs the last couple of weeks, I've broken out in a rash. It couldn't be the butter or oil they're fried in, 'cause I remember it happening when I had hard-boiled eggs, too. I must have developed an allergy to eggs.

Analysis This is a strong argument, and we can trust that Harry isn't lying. So it's a good argument. But it's not valid. There could be a strange new virus that Harry caught whose only symptom is that it makes him sick when he eats eggs. In a week or two he might be fine.

Example 14 Prosecuting attorney: The defendant intended to kill Louise. He bought a gun three days before he shot her. He practiced shooting at a target that had her name written across it. He staked out her home for two nights. He shot her twice.

Analysis The argument is strong. If there's good reason to believe the premises, then the argument is good and establishes beyond a reasonable doubt "The defendant intended to kill Louise." But the argument isn't valid: we don't know the defendant's thoughts, and the conclusion might be false.

Example 15 Tom: You didn't have eggs in the house this morning, did you?
Dick: No. Why?
Tom: Well, you've got some in the refrigerator now.
Dick: Zoe must have bought eggs, since she knew we were out.

Analysis This isn't strong. Zoe's friend could have brought over the eggs; when they were out, the landlord might have brought them over; a guest who was staying with them might have bought them; . . . . These possibilities don't seem so unlikely, so the argument is weak.

Example 16 (continuing Example 15)
Tom: But what about your neighbor or your landlord?
Dick: No one else has a key to the house. And Zoe didn't plan to have any guests over today.

Analysis Dick has made his argument stronger by ruling out some of the possible ways the premises could be true and the conclusion false.

Example 17 (continuing Example 16)

Tom: But didn't your neighbor Mrs. Zzzyzzx say she had some eggs from her cousin's farm?

Dick: Yes, but Zoe said we should only bring food into the house we'd bought ourselves at the health-food store. And she always keeps her word.

Analysis Dick's argument is now a lot stronger because so many of the ways in which the premises could be true and conclusion false have been ruled out. Still, it's not valid: the landlord could have gotten a locksmith to open the door, and then before he went out put eggs in the refrigerator; or a burglar could have broken in and left some eggs behind; or Zoe could have bought a chicken and left it in the refrigerator and it laid eggs there; or . . . . These are possible ways that the premises could be true and the conclusion false, but they're all so unlikely that the argument is strong. And since we can trust Dick's word, it's a good argument. So Tom and Dick have good reason to believe that Zoe bought the eggs.

Though we can't say exactly where Example 16 lies on the scale from strong to weak, we can say that Example 15 is weak and Example 17 is strong. But if we can't say exactly how strong an argument is, isn't the whole business of classifying arguments worthless? That would be a drawing the line fallacy. There may be some fuzziness in the middle, but we can distinguish strong arguments from weak ones.

Example 18 Tom: All CEOs of computer software companies are rich. Bill Gates is a CEO of a computer software company. So Bill Gates is rich.

Lee: That's valid, just like Dr. E said. And Bill Gates is sure rich. So all CEOs of computer software companies must be rich.

Analysis Lee is *arguing backwards*. There are lots of CEOs of small software companies who are working hard just to make a living. An argument is supposed to convince someone that its conclusion is true, not that its premises are true.

When can we go from the conclusion to the premises? When the conclusion is false and the argument is valid, we know that one of the premises is *false*.

Now you're ready to begin evaluating arguments yourself. Before you do, review these points to make sure you understand them and can use them.

- Every good argument is strong or valid.
- Every weak argument is bad.
- Not every valid or strong argument is good
  (a premise could be implausible or it could beg the question).
- Only invalid arguments are classified from strong to weak.

Summary We said that a good argument is one that gives good reason to believe the conclusion. So we needed a standard for "good reason."

First, the conclusion should follow from the premises. We saw that means that the argument is valid or strong: either there's no way for the premises to be true and the conclusion false, or only unlikely ones. Also, we should have good reason to believe the premises of the argument. And those should be more plausible than the conclusion. These are the three tests an argument must pass to be good.

In evaluating whether what we hear is an argument, we saw that there are words that key us to finding the conclusion and the premises, and we learned to ignore words like "maybe" that are tagged onto a claim to show what the speaker thinks about it.

Key Words

good argument
weak argument
strong argument
valid argument
plausible claim
dubious (implausible) claim
begging the question
tests for an argument to be good
indicator word

Exercises for Chapter 3

1. a. How can you show that an argument is not valid?
   b. How can you show that an argument is weak?

2. a. What is an indicator word?
   b. List at least five words or phrases not in the chart that indicate a conclusion.
   c. List at least five words or phrases not in the chart that indicate premises.
   d. List five more words or phrases that show an attitude toward a claim or argument.
   e. Bring in an argument from some source that uses indicator words.

3. Mark which of the blanks below would normally be filled with a premise (P) and which with a conclusion (C).

   a. (i)_____, (ii)_____, (iii)_____, therefore (iv)_____.

   b. (i)_____, since (ii)_____, (iii)_____, and (iv) _____.

c. Because (i)_____, it follows that (ii)_____ and (iii)_____.
d. Since (i)_____ and (ii)_____, it follows that (iii)_____, because (iv)_____.
e. (i)_____ and (ii)_____, and that's why (iii)_____.
f. Due to (i)_____ and (ii)_____, we have (iii)_____.
g. In view of (i)_____, (ii)_____, and (iii)_____ we get (iv)_____.
h. From (i)_____ and (ii)_____, we can derive (iii)_____.
i. If (i)_____, then it follows that (ii)_____, for (iii)_____ and (iv)_____.

4. If an argument is bad, what does that tell us about the conclusion?
5. If we want to give a good argument with a subjective claim as its conclusion, would it be better for it to be valid or strong? Explain.
6. To prove an objective claim, should we always give an argument that is valid? Explain or give an example.
7. Which subjects in your school would employ only valid arguments? Which would employ primarily strong arguments? Which would rely on a mix of the two?

Here are some of Tom's answers to exercises that require all the ideas we've learned in this chapter. He's supposed to fill in the italicized parts. Dr. E has corrected his work.

Puff is a cat. So Puff has a tail.
Argument? (yes or no) Yes.
Conclusion: Puff has a tail.
Premises: Puff is a cat.
Classify: valid strong ———— weak
If not valid, show why:
Good argument? (Choose one)

- It's good (passes the three tests). ✓
- It's bad because a premise is false.
- It's bad because it's weak.
- It's bad because it begs the question.
- It's valid or strong, but you don't know if the premises are true, so you can't say if it's good or bad.

No! This isn't valid. Puff could be one of those cats that don't have tails. Or Puff could have had his tail cut off. But it's strong, so it is a good argument, since we know that Puff is a cat.

Whenever Spot barks, there's a cat outside. Since he's barking now, there must be a cat outside.
Argument? (yes or no) Yes.
Conclusion: Whenever Spot barks, there's a cat outside.
Premises: Spot's barking now. There must be a cat outside.
Classify: valid strong ————**X**– weak

If not valid, show why: Maybe he's barking at the garbageman outside.
Good argument? (Choose one)

- It's good (passes the three tests).
- It's bad because a premise is false.
- It's bad because it's weak. ✓
- It's bad because it begs the question.
- It's valid or strong, but you don't know if the premises are true, so you can't say if it's good or bad.

No. The conclusion is "There is a cat outside." Ask yourself where you could put "therefore" in the argument. Which claims are evidence for which others? The argument is valid but bad: The premise "Whenever Spot barks, there's a cat outside" is implausible. As you point out, what about the garbageman? So it's not good.

Alison is Kim's sister, right? So Alison and Kim have the same mother and father.
Argument? (yes or no) Yes.
Conclusion: Alison and Kim have the same mother and father.
Premises: Alison is Kim's sister.
Classify: valid strong ——————X– weak
If not valid, show why: They might be half sisters, or stepsisters, or adopted. It depends on what the speaker means by "sister."
Good argument? (Choose one)

- It's good (passes the three tests).
- It's bad because a premise is false. *Good work!*
- It's bad because it's weak. ✓
- It's bad because it begs the question.
- It's valid or strong, but you don't know if the premises are true, so you can't say if it's good or bad.

Bob has worked as a car mechanic for twenty years. Anyone who works that long at a job must enjoy it. So Bob enjoys being a car mechanic.
Argument? (yes or no) Yes.
Conclusion: Bob enjoys being a car mechanic.
Premises: Bob has worked as a car mechanic for twenty years. Anyone who works that long at a job enjoys it.
Classify: valid strong ——————X– weak
If not valid, show why: Bob might not be able to get any other job.
Good argument? (Choose one)

- It's good (passes the three tests).
- It's bad because a premise is false.
- It's bad because it's weak. ✓
- It's bad because it begs the question.
- It's valid or strong, but you don't know if the premises are true, so you can't say if it's good or bad.

Wrong! The argument is valid. What you showed is that the second premise is false or at least very dubious. So the argument is bad, but not for the reason you gave.

For the exercises below answer the following:

Argument? (yes or no)
Conclusion:
Premises:
Classify: valid strong ———— weak
If not valid, show why:
Good argument? (choose one)

- It's good (passes the three tests).
- It's bad because a premise is false.
- It's bad because it's weak.
- It's bad because it begs the question.
- It's valid or strong, but you don't know if the premises are true, so you can't say if it's good or bad.

To make it easier to answer these exercises, use the formatted versions of them, which you can find at www.AdvancedReasoningForum.org/CT5/exercises.

8. Flo's hair was long. Now it's short. So Flo must have gotten a haircut.
9. Intelligent students study hard. Zoe studies hard. So Zoe is intelligent.
10. Dr. E is a bachelor. So Dr. E is not married.
11. All cats meow. Puff is a cat. So Puff meows.
12. All licensed drivers in California have taken a driver's test. Lemuel has taken a driver's test in California. So Lemuel is a licensed driver in California.
13. No dog meows. Puff meows. So Puff is not a dog.
14. Flo's mother to Flo: We have to go because we are leaving. End of conversation!
15. Lee: I can't get wifi reception in the house. There must be something wrong with the router.
16. This book teaches how to reason. So this book costs less than $70.
17. Lee: My friend Judy manages a local bookstore. She drives a new Jaguar. So bookstore managers must make good money.
18. No cat barks. Spot is not a cat. So Spot barks.
19. What do you want to eat for dinner? Well, we had fish yesterday and pasta the day before. We haven't eaten chicken for a while. How about some chicken with potatoes?
20. Maria: Almost all the professors I've met at this school are liberals.
    Manuel: So to get a teaching job here, it must help to be a liberal.
21. Suzy: Every student who has ever taken a course from Professor Zzzyzzx has passed. So if I take his composition course, I'll pass, too.
22. Dick missed almost every basket he shot in the game. He couldn't run, he couldn't jump. He should give up basketball.

23. 

24. Some students don't have enough money for college. Anyone who wants an education but can't afford it should be given financial aid. So some students should receive financial aid.

25. Tom: If Louie bought a new car, then he must have had more money than I thought.
Harry: Well, look, there's the new hatchback he bought.
Tom: So Louie must have had more money than I thought.

26. Zoe: Spot got out of the yard somehow.
Dick: He must have got out under the fence.
Zoe: No way he got out under the fence. There's no sign of new digging.

27. Zoe: Spot got out of the yard somehow.
Dick: He must have got out under the fence.
Zoe: No way he got out under the fence. There's no sign of new digging. And we blocked all the old ways he used to get out under the fence.

28. Zoe: Spot got out of the yard somehow.
Dick: He must have got out under the fence.
Zoe: No way he got out under the fence. There's no sign of new digging. And we blocked all the old ways he used to get out under the fence.
Dick: But he pulled down that chicken wire last week.
Zoe: (*later*) I checked—all the wire and rocks we put up are still there, and there's no sign that the fence has been disturbed at the bottom.
Dick: I hope he hasn't learned how to jump over the fence.

29. Dick: Whenever the garbage gets picked up, the trash bins end up away from the curb.
Lee: The bins haven't been moved away from the curb. So the garbage hasn't been picked up.

30. 

31. All cats shed fur. There's fur on Suzy's couch. So a cat's been on Suzy's couch.
32. Suzy: Tom hasn't called in a week. So he doesn't want to see me anymore.
33. There are 30 seconds left in the football game. The 49ers have 35 points. The Dolphins have 7 points. So the 49ers will win.

Writing Lesson 3

We've been learning how to analyze arguments. Now it's time to try to write one.

You know what tests a good argument must pass. It must be composed of claims, and only claims. It shouldn't contain any ambiguous or excessively vague sentence. It must be valid or strong. And the premises should be plausible and more plausible than the conclusion.

Write an argument in OUTLINE FORM either for or against the following:

Everyone should use a bicycle as his or her main form of transportation.

- Just list the premises and the conclusion.
  You can include definitions, too. Nothing more.
- Your argument should be at most one page long.
- Check whether your instructor has chosen a different topic for this assignment.

It doesn't matter if you never thought about the subject or whether you think it's terribly important. This is an exercise, a chance for you to sharpen your skills in writing arguments. It's the process of writing an argument that should be your focus.

If you have trouble coming up with an argument, think how you would respond if you heard a friend say the claim. Make two lists: *pro* and *con*. Then write the strongest argument you can.

Don't get carried away. You're not expected to spin a one-page argument into three pages. You can't use any of the literary devices that you've been taught are good fillers. List the premises and conclusion—that's all. And remember, premises and conclusion don't have those words "therefore" or "I think" or "because" attached. Once you can write an argument in outline form, you can worry about making your arguments sound pretty. It's clarity we want first.

To give you a better idea of what you're expected to do, I've included Tom's argument on a different topic.

Tom Wyzyczy
Critical Thinking
Section 4
Writing Lesson 3

Issue: Students should be required to take a course on critical thinking.

Definition: I'll understand the issue as "College students should be required to take a course on critical thinking before graduating."

Premises:

1. A critical thinking course will help students to write better in their other courses.
2. A critical thinking course will help students to read assignments in all their other courses.
3. A critical thinking course will make students become better informed voters.
4. Most students who take a critical thinking course appreciate it.
5. Professors will be able to teach their subjects better if they can assume their students know how to reason.
6. Critical thinking is a basic skill and should be required, like Freshman Composition.

Conclusion: College students should be required to take a course on critical thinking before graduating.

Tom, it's good that you began by making the issue precise. Even better is that you realized the definition wasn't a premise. You've learned a lot from the last assignment.

Your argument is pretty good. You've used claims for your premises. Some of them are a bit vague. But only the fourth is so vague you should delete it or make it more precise. All of your premises support your conclusion. But the argument's not strong as stated. You're missing some glue, something to fill the gap. You're piling up evidence, but to what end? To your third premise, I'd just say "SO?" We really don't know what standard you have in mind for that "should." And you never used in your argument that you're talking about college students. Won't your argument work just as well for high school? Is that what you want?

We'll look at how to fill in what you've missed in Chapter 5.

Cartoon Writing Lesson A

Here is a chance to reason as in your everyday life, drawing conclusions from what you see.

Imagine encountering the scene depicted in the cartoon. Do you believe the claim that accompanies the cartoon? Why? Or why not? How would you convince someone to agree with you who hasn't witnessed the scene?

Here are the steps you can go through:

1. Write down what you see—nothing else.
   (Refer to the cast of characters at the front of the book.)
   We can assume that those claims are true.

2. Ask yourself whether it's possible for everything you've listed to be true yet the claim in question to be false.

3. If the answer is no, you've already got a valid argument for the claim in question. Since the premises are true, it's also good.

4. If the answer is yes and such a possibility isn't all that unlikely, you know that you can't get a good argument for the claim in question. So just describe one or more such possibilities, and say that no good argument can be made.

5. The last case is if each such possibility—where what you see is true but the claim in question is false—is very unlikely. Then look for a claim or claims that will rule out all or almost all such possibilities to get a valid or strong argument and add it. That's the *glue*. But don't make up a story; the claim(s) should be common knowledge, something we all know is true.

Steps (2)–(5) are exactly what's pictured on p. 41, except here you can add the glue.

So for each cartoon, write the best argument you can that has as its conclusion the claim that accompanies the cartoon. List only the premises and conclusion. If you believe there is no good argument, explain why by describing a likely way the conclusion could be false even if everything we see in the cartoon is true.

To give you a better idea of what to do, here is an example of what Tom did for his assignment.

Name Tom Wyzyczy Section 4

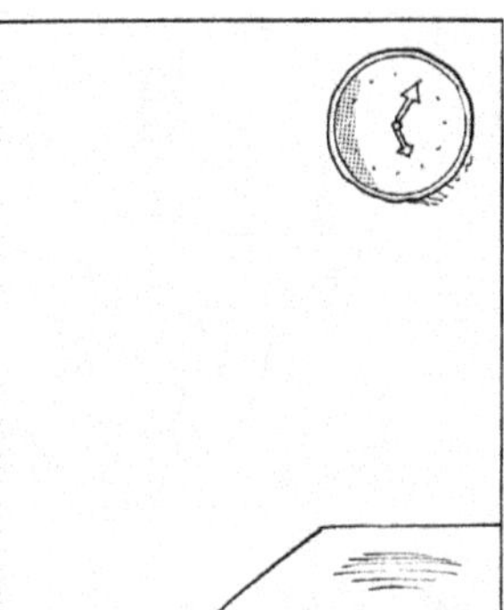

The fellow stole the purse.

The guy is in the room and he spots a purse on the table.
He looks around pretty shiftily and thinks that he can get away with taking the purse.
So he grabs it and goes.

This isn't a course in creative writing! How do you know he thinks that he can get away with it? That's just making up a story. How do you know he grabbed it? You didn't _see_ *that. And what makes you say he looks around shiftily? You need to distinguish what you see from what you deduce. If I didn't have the cartoon in front of me, I could never have imagined what you saw. You need to use the* _observation_ *that almost no time passed from the time he saw it to the time the purse was gone and that there was no one else around. Then you can conclude he took the purse.*

Also, be sure to put in the conclusion. "So he grabs it and goes" is only a step along the way. You need some glue to get from that to the conclusion "The fellow stole the purse," something like, "Almost anytime a guy looks around quickly and takes a purse, he's stealing it." But that's false. Maybe he just recognized that it belonged to his girlfriend or his mother, and when he didn't see her he decided to take it to her. It looks like there is no good argument you can make for the conclusion.

This was your first try, and I'm sure that next time you'll know better. Describe what you see, and try to get from that to the conclusion.

1.

Spot chased a cat.

2.

Professor Zzzyzzx is cold.

3.

Dick didn't wash his hands properly.

4.

Dick broke his leg skiing.

5.

Flo isn't really sick.

6.

Dick should not drink the coffee.

4 Is That True?

A. Evaluating Premises

For an argument to be good we should have good reason to believe its premises. But why simply believe a premise? Shouldn't every claim be backed up with an argument? We can't do that. If we want a justification for every claim, we'd have to go on forever. Sometimes when someone makes a claim we just have to decide whether to believe it.

Three choices for whether to believe a claim

- Accept the claim as true.
- Reject the claim as false.
- Suspend judgment.

We needn't pretend to be all wise nor force ourselves to make judgments. Sometimes it's best to suspend judgment. Rejecting a claim means to say that it's false.

not believe ≠ believe is false

lack of evidence ≠ evidence it is false

B. Criteria for Accepting or Rejecting Claims

There are no absolute rules for when to accept, when to reject, and when to suspend judgment about a claim. It's a skill, weighing up the criteria we'll see here in their order of importance.

1. Personal experience

• *Our most reliable source of information about the world is our own experience.*

What would you think of an adult who never trusted his own experience, who always deferred to authority? He goes to a priest and asks if it's daytime. He looks up in an atlas whether his hometown is in Nevada. He asks his wife whether the room they're standing in is painted white. You'd say he's crazy.

We need to trust our own experience because that's the best we have. Everything else is secondhand. Should you trust your buddy, your spouse, your priest, your professor, the president, the dictator, when what they say contradicts what you know from your own experience? That way lies demagoguery, religious intolerance, and worse. Too often leaders have manipulated the populace: All Muslims want to destroy the West? But what about my neighbor who's Muslim and a city councilor? You have to forget your own experience to believe the Big Lie. They repeat it over and over and over again until you begin to believe it, even when your own experience says it isn't so.

> Who you gonna believe, me or your own eyes?
> Chico Marx in *Duck Soup*

Oh, we get the idea. Don't trust the politicians. No. It's a lot closer to home than that. Every rumor, all the gossip you hear, compare it to what *you* know about the person or situation. Don't repeat it. Be rational, not part of the humming crowd.

Still, there are times we shouldn't trust our own experience. Sometimes our memory is not reliable. As Sgt. Carlson of the Las Vegas Police Department says, "Eyewitnesses are terrible. You get a gun stuck in your face and you can't remember anything." The police do lineups, putting a suspect to be identified by a witness among other people who look a bit similar. The police have to be very careful not to say anything that may influence the witness, because memory is malleable.

The state of the world around us can also affect our observations and make our personal experience unreliable. You could honestly say you were sure the other driver didn't put on a turn signal, when the rain and distractions made you not notice.

But even then, there are times we're right not to trust our own experience. You go to the circus and see a magician cut a lady in half. You saw it, so it has to be true. Yet you don't believe it. Why? Because it contradicts too much else you know about the world.

Or stranger still: Day after day we see the sun rise in the east and set in the west, yet we say the sun isn't moving, the earth is. We don't accept our own experience because there's a long story, a theory of how the earth turns on its axis and revolves around the sun. And that story explains neatly and clearly so many other phenomena, like the seasons and the movement of stars in the skies, that we accept it. A convincing argument has been given for us to reject our own experience, and that argument builds on other experiences of ours.

- We accept a claim if we know it is true from our own experience.
- We reject a claim if we know it is false from our own experience.

Exceptions

- We have reason to doubt our memory or our perception.
- The claim contradicts other experiences of ours, and there is a good argument (theory) against the claim.

Too often, though, we remember what we deduced from our experience, not what we actually experienced. Look at Tom's cartoon writing lesson on p. 57. He said he saw the guy grab the purse. But he didn't see that; he inferred it.

Example 1 Wanda: Chinese guys are all really smart. There are five of them in my algebra class, and they're all getting an A.

Analysis It's not Wanda's personal experience that all Chinese guys are really smart but a conclusion she's drawing from knowing five of them.

Exercises for Sections A and B.1

1. Why can't we require that every claim be backed up?
2. What three choices can we make about whether to believe a claim?
3. If the conclusion of a valid argument is false, why must one of the premises be false?
4. Give an example of a rumor or gossip you heard in your personal life recently that you believed. Did you have good reason to believe it? Why?
5. We can tell that a rumor or gossip is coming up when someone says, "Guess what I heard." Give five other phrases that alert us similarly.
6. Should you trust an encyclopedia over your own experience? Explain.
7. Give an example of a claim that someone made this week that you knew from your own experience was false.
8. Give an example of a time when you accepted or rejected a claim, but you should have suspended judgment.
9. Give an example of a claim that you believed was true from memory but really you were drawing a conclusion based on your experience.
10. When is it reasonable for us to accept a claim that disagrees with our own experience? Give an example (not from the text) of a claim that it is reasonable for you to accept even though it appears to contradict what you perceive.
11. Remember the last time this class met? Answer the following about your instructor.
    a. Male or Female?
    b. Hair color?
    c. Eye color?
    d. Approximate height?
    e. Approximate weight?
    f. Did he/she bring a backpack to class? Describe it.
    g. Did he/she use notes?
    h. Did he/she get to class early?
    i. Did he/she wear a jacket?
    j. Is he/she left-handed or right-handed?
12. Remember the last time this class met? Answer the following about the room.
    a. How many windows?
    b. How many doors?
    c. How many walls?
    d. Any pictures?
    e. Lectern?
    f. How high is the ceiling?
    g. How many light fixtures?
    h. How many chairs?
    i. How many students showed up?
    j. Wastebasket?
    k. What kind of floor (concrete, tile, linoleum, carpet)?
    l. Did you get out of class early?

13. Which of your answers to Exercises 11 and 12 were from actual memory and which were inferences?
14. List five ways that the physical conditions around us can affect our observations.
15. List five ways that your mental state could affect your observations.
16. Our personal observations are no better than ____________ .
17. What does a bad argument tell us about its conclusion?

2. Other sources

• *We can accept a claim made by someone we know and trust who is an expert on this kind of claim.*

Example 2 Zoe tells Harry to stay away from the area around South Third and Westermeyer Avenue. She's seen people doing drugs there and knows two people who were mugged at that corner.
Analysis Harry has good reason to believe Zoe's claims.

Example 3 Dick's mother tells him that he should major in business so he can get ahead in life.
Analysis Should Dick believe his mother? She can tell him about her friends' children. But what really are the chances of getting a good job with a degree in business? It would be better to check at the local colleges where they keep records on what jobs graduates get. Dick shouldn't reject her claim; he should suspend judgment until he gets more information.

• *We can accept a claim made by a reputable expert on this kind of claim who has no obvious motive to mislead.*

Example 4 Compare:

- The Surgeon General announces that smoking is bad for your health.
- The doctor hired by the tobacco company says there's no proof that smoking is addictive or causes lung cancer.
- The new Surgeon General says that marijuana should be legal.

Analysis The Surgeon General is a reputable physician with expertise in public health. She's in a position to survey the research on the subject. We have no reason to suspect her motives. So it's reasonable to believe her.

But is the doctor hired by the tobacco company an expert on smoking-related diseases, or an allergist, or a pediatrician? He has motive to mislead. There's no reason to accept his claim.

Nor is there any reason to accept what the Surgeon General says about what should be law. She's an expert on health, not an expert on law and society.

Example 5 Wanda tells Zoe that she shouldn't get vaccinated for the flu this year because the vaccine might give her the flu.

Analysis Zoe rejects Wanda's claim that you can catch the flu that way. She's read on the Centers for Disease Control website that flu vaccines contain inactive viruses or no viruses at all, so they can't give anyone the flu. The CDC has reliable experts. *We're justified in rejecting a claim that contradicts another claim or claims that we have good reason to believe*. That's the best after personal experience.

Example 6 The science says you've got to reduce emissions of greenhouse gases. The science says you've got to stabilize concentrations of greenhouse gases in the atmosphere. What may be subject to debate is who is to reduce how much.

Rajendra K. Pachauri, chairman, U.N. Intergovernmental Panel on Climate Change

Analysis The science says no such thing. Pachauri is an expert on the science of global warming but not on ethics or public policy.

When a scientist asks us to accept a prescriptive claim, he or she is no longer talking as a scientist but as someone qualified to make value judgments, playing the role of a politician, or philosopher, or priest. *No prescriptive claim follows from any scientific laws or data: some value judgment is required.* We have no reason to accept a prescriptive claim just because a scientist said it.

Which experts we trust and which we disregard change from era to era. It was the lying by Presidents Johnson and Nixon and Bush that led many of us to distrust pronouncements from the government. It was the Chicago police killing the Black Panthers in their beds and calling it self-defense that convinced many of us not to accept what big-city police say. Seeing videos of police shooting unarmed black men have convinced more people that official police denials are just as dubious today.

The moral is that some experts are more trustworthy than others, even in their own area of expertise. Some may have motive to mislead. The more you tell the truth, the more likely you are to be believed; but even one lie can ruin your reputation for reliability.

• *We can accept a claim in a reputable journal or reference source.*

Up to this point we've considered whether to believe people who claim to be knowledgeable. But sometimes we can rely on the quality and reputation of an organization or reference work. *The New England Journal of Medicine* is regularly quoted in newspapers, and for good reason. The articles in it are subjected to peer review; that is, experts in the subject are asked to evaluate whether the research was done to scientific standards. That journal is notable for having high scientific standards, and its official website is similarly reliable.

The *National Geographic* used to be reliable, though it paid for the research it printed. But now it's owned by NewsCorp and should be treated as a media outlet.

On the internet you're likely to come across sites with very impressive names. But anyone can start up an organization called the "American Institute for Economic Analysis" or any other title you like and get an address that ends with ".org". A name is not enough to go by. There's no reason to accept a claim made by an "institute" you don't know about. Don't be bluffed by appeals to unidentified "studies" or "research": every claim should be traceable to someone's experience. That's what any reliable source ultimately is: a person, not some abstract authority.

• *We can accept a claim in a media outlet that's usually reliable.*
Most remote from our experience and least reliable is what we hear and read from what's called "the media": print, radio, television, websites, mobile apps.

With these sources it's partly like trusting your friend and partly like trusting an expert. The more you read a particular news site and check it against other sources, for instance, the better you'll be able to judge whether there's an editorial bias. Remember, what you read or watch on the screen is not personal experience.

Here are three factors that are important in evaluating a news report.

— *The outlet has been reliable in the past.*
A local paper seems to get the information correct about local stories most of the time. It's probably trustworthy in its account of a car accident in town. The website TMZ pays its sources for celebrity gossip and has retracted several "scoops," so it may not be reliable about the love life of your favorite movie star.

— *The outlet doesn't have a bias on this topic.*
A television network consistently gives a bias against a particular presidential candidate. So when it says that the candidate contradicted himself twice yesterday, you should take that with a grain of salt. It may be true, but it may be a matter of interpretation. Or it may be plain false.

Bias often follows the money. Try to find out who owns the media outlet or who its principal advertisers are. If you hear NBC saying what a good job General Electric is doing in the "reconstruction" of Iraq, it's worth knowing that GE owns NBC.

— *The source being quoted is named.*
Do you know who wrote the articles you read on your local news site? "From our sources" or no byline at all often means that the article is simply a reprint of a publicity handout from a company. Remember those Department of Defense unnamed sources? Don't trust them. "Usually reliable sources" are not even as reliable as the person who is quoting them, and anyway, they've covered themselves by saying "usually." When someone is unwilling to admit being a source, it's a sign that he or she may have a motive to mislead. An unnamed source is no better than a rumor. *There's never good reason to accept a claim from an unnamed source.*

Criteria for judging unsupported claims

PERSONAL EXPERIENCE

Accept We know the claim is true from our own experience.

Reject We know the claim is false from our own experience.

Reject The claim contradicts another claim we know is true.

OTHER SOURCES

Accept The claim is made by someone we know and trust who is an expert on this kind of claim.

Accept The claim is made by a reputable expert on this kind of claim who has no motive to mislead.

Accept The claim is put forward in a reputable journal or reference.

Accept The claim is in a media source that's usually reliable and has no obvious motive to mislead, and the original source is named.

We don't have criteria for when to *suspend judgment* on a claim. That's the default choice when we don't have good reason to accept or reject a claim.

Remember that these criteria only apply when you're judging whether to accept a claim unsupported by other evidence. They're given in order of importance .

Example 7 A Nevada couple letting their SUV's navigation system guide them through the high desert of eastern Oregon got stuck in snow for three days when their GPS unit sent them down a remote forest road. *Albuquerque Journal*, December 29, 2009

Analysis How far down a remote snow-packed forest road do *you* have to go before you trust your own senses over your GPS unit?

Exercises for Section B

1. When should we suspend judgment on a claim?

2. a. Give five criteria for accepting an unsupported claim.
   b. Give two criteria for rejecting an unsupported claim.

3. a. Explain why we should apply the criteria for accepting or rejecting claims in the order in which they are listed.
   b. Do these criteria imply that you should believe your mom over your professor?

4. a. Describe two people you encounter regularly whose word you trust. Then say why you believe them.
   b. Give an example of a claim that one of them made that you shouldn't accept because he or she has doesn't really know about that subject.

5. List three *categories* of experts you feel you can trust. State for which kind of claims those kinds of people would be experts.

6. Give a recent example from some media outlet of an expert being quoted whose claims you accepted as true.

7. Give an example from some media outlet of an expert being quoted whose expertise does not bear on the claim being put forward, so you have no reason to accept the claim.

8. Give an example of an expert who made a claim recently that turned out to be false. Do you think it was a lie? Or did the person just not know it was false?

9. Find a story that the *New York Times* retracted. Does that show that we can't trust it any more than the website TMZ?

10. Give an example of a claim you've heard repeated so often you think it's true but which you really have no reason to believe.

11. See if you can determine who wrote each article on the home page of your favorite news website.

12. Which section of your local news website do you think is most reliable? Why?

13. Choose a website you often read, and tell the class what biases you expect from it. That is, for what kinds of claims in it should you suspend judgment rather than accept?

14. a. What part of a national newscast do you think is most likely to be true? Why?
    b. Which part do you think is least reliable? Why?

15. Give an example of a news story you heard or read that you knew was biased because it didn't give the whole story.

16. Find an article that has quotes from some "think tank" or "institute." Find out what bias that group might have.

17. Choose one of the large national news broadcasting outlets and find out who owns the company and what companies it owns or are owned by the same company.

18. Bring to class an article that praises some business or type of business that comes from a media source that has lots of advertising from that business or type of business.

19. 

    How should he respond?

20. Your friend who's an avid fan tells you that the basketball game on Saturday has been cancelled. Five minutes later you hear on the radio that tickets are on sale for the game on Saturday. Who do you believe? Why?

21. Your doctor tells you that the pain in your back can't be fixed without surgery. You go to the health-food store, and the clerk tells you they have a root extract that's made especially for back pain that'll fix your back. Whom do you believe? Why?

22. 

Comment on Tom's reasons for believing that steroids won't harm him.

Lee was asked to decide whether to accept, reject, or suspend judgment on some claims, with an explanation of what criteria he's using.

> **Suzy prefers to go out with athletes.**
> *accept*   *reject*   *suspend judgment*
> *criteria*: Personal experience. She told me so. *Good!*
>
> **Japanese are good at math.**
> *accept*   *reject*   *suspend judgment*
> *criteria*: I know everyone thinks this is so, but it's just a stereotype, isn't it? I know a couple who aren't real good at math, but maybe they mean "almost all"? It just seems so unlikely. *Good!*
>
> **Crocodiles are found only in Asia and Africa.**
> *accept*   *reject*   *suspend judgment*
> *criteria*: I think this is true. At least I seem to remember hearing it. Crocodiles are the ones in Africa and alligators in the U.S. But I'm not sure. So I guess I should suspend judgment. *Good!*
>
> **Donkeys only make that burbling noise flapping their lips when no one is around.**
> *accept*   *reject*   *suspend judgment*
> *criteria*: I don't know anything about donkeys, but how could anyone know if this is true? I mean, you have to be around to know whether they're burbling.
> *Great! You figured it out. Always ask: how could they know that?*

23. Evaluate the following claims by saying whether you *accept*, *reject*, or *suspend judgment*, citing the *criteria* you are using to make that decision.
    a. Toads give you warts. (said by your mother)
    b. Toads give you warts. (said by your doctor)
    c. The moon rises in the west.

d. The Pacers beat the Knicks 92–84 last night. (heard on your local news)

e. They're marketing a new liposuction machine you can attach to your vacuum cleaner. (told to you by your best friend)

f. You were speeding. (said by a police officer)

g. Boise-Cascade has plans to log all old-growth forests in California. (said by a Sierra Club representative)

h. The United States government was not involved in the recent coup attempt in Venezuela. (unnamed sources in the Defense Department, by the Associated Press)

i. Cats are the greatest threat to public health of any common pet. (said by the author of this book)

j. Cats are the greatest threat to public health of any common pet. (said by the Surgeon General)

k. Crocodiles weep after eating their victims, hence the term "crocodile tears." (in the travel section of your local newspaper)

l. Blood is blue without oxygen.

m. It is very unlikely that anyone could get infected with avian flu by eating thoroughly cooked chicken. (*New York Times*, Science and Health section, citing Professor William K. Hallman of Rutgers University)

n. Earlier this year, 56-year-old Spanish fisherman Luigi Marquez went through a nightmarish experience as he was swallowed whole by a whale, presumed dead by all who knew him. (SpiritScience website, September 2, 2016)

o. A DePauw University computer study sometime back turned up a remarkable finding. Coeds were asked to submit their grade point averages plus their bust, waist, and hip measurements. No significance was found in the upper-body measurements. But the larger the hips, the better the grades. *The Pantagraph*, Bloomington, IN, Dec. 9, 1981

p. The 54-study review of 3,000 asthma patients finds that no chemical or physical intervention to reduce exposure to house dust mites is effective.

"Dust Mites Outlast Heroic Efforts to Help Asthma Patients," *Science Daily*, April 16, 2008

C. Advertising and the Internet

1. Advertising

The truth-in-advertising laws weren't written because advertisers were always telling us the truth. Many advertisements are arguments with the (often unstated) conclusion that you should buy the product, or frequent the establishment, or use the service. Sometimes the claims are accurate, especially in print advertising for medicines. But sometimes they're not. There's nothing special about them, though. They should be judged by the criteria we've already considered. *If you think there should be more stringent criteria for evaluating ads, you're not judging other claims carefully enough.*

Example 8 Gold is the only asset that's not somebody else's liability.

Radio advertisement, spring 2010

Analysis That's false. When you've paid off your car it's not someone else's liability.

Example 9 We're Credit Card Relief . . . We've been helping people like you for more than a decade. We're an attorney-driven program. Radio advertisement, Spring 2010

Analysis This isn't true or false. "Attorney-driven program" is meaningless, though it sounds impressive.

Example 10 At the supermarket not long after the attack on 9-11 I saw small, soft magnetic strips for sale. On each was an American flag with "God Bless America" written below it. On the box was:

Show your support

CAR MAGNETS

A portion of the proceeds go to the

New York Firefighters and Victims

Key Bank Disaster Relief Fund

Nothing else was written on the box or magnets—no name nor address of the manufacturer. A search on the web for "Key Bank Disaster Relief Fund" turned up nothing.

2. The internet

Re-read the discussion about advertising. Now ask yourself what reason you have to believe something you read on the web. Next time you're ready, mouth agape, to swallow what's up there on the screen, imagine Zoe saying to you, "No, really, you believed *that*?" Don't check your brain at the door when you go online.

Example 11 Colonial records refer to small, nearly hairless dogs at the beginning of the 19th Century, one of which claims 16th-century Conquistadores found them plentiful in the region later known as Chihuahua.*

* Pedro Baptista Pino y Juan Lopez Cancelada, *Exposición sucinta y sencilla de la Provincia del Nuevo México y otros escritos*. Ed. Jesus Paniagua Perez. Valladolid: Junta de Castilla / León: Universidad de León, 2007, p. 244: "even in the desert the tiny dogs could be found, hunting rats, mice, and lizards." The footnote that follows alludes to starving Conquistadores reportedly hunting and stewing the dogs (Universidad Veracruzana, Arquivo Viejo, XXVI.2711).

Chihuahua dog, *Wikipedia*, February 2012

Analysis You believe what you read on Wikipedia, and quote it, too. Only this is pure fantasy written by Michael Rooney and me. There is such a book, but there's no such quote, and we made up the reference to Arquivo Viejo. Yet this has been on Wikipedia for four years and counting. What makes you think that any other entry in Wikipedia is more reliable?

Lots of ignorant people correcting one another does not result in a reliable source. At best, Wikipedia entries are useful to stimulate our imaginations and provide references that we can consult.

The July 31, 2006, piece on Wikipedia, "Know It All," by Stacy Schiff, contained an interview with a Wikipedia site administrator and contributor called Essjay, whose responsibilities included handling disagreements about the accuracy of the site's articles and taking action against users who violate site policy. He was described in the piece as "a tenured professor of religion at a private university" with "a Ph.D. in theology and a degree in canon law." Essjay was recommended to Ms. Schiff as a source by a member of Wikipedia's management team because of his respected position within the Wikipedia community. He was willing to describe his work as a Wikipedia administrator but would not identify himself other than by confirming the biographical details that appeared on his user page. At the time of publication, neither we nor Wikipedia knew Essjay's real name. Essjay's entire Wikipedia life was conducted with only a user name; anonymity is common for Wikipedia administrators and contributors, and he says that he feared personal retribution from those he had ruled against online. Essjay now says that his real name is Ryan Jordan, that he is twenty-four and holds no advanced degrees, and that he has never taught. He was recently hired by Wikia—a for-profit company affiliated with Wikipedia—as a "community manager"; he continues to hold his Wikipedia positions. He did not answer a message we sent to him; Jimmy Wales, the co-founder of Wikia and of Wikipedia, said of Essjay's invented persona, "I regard it as a pseudonym and I don't really have a problem with it."

New Yorker, <http://www.newyorker.com/archive/2006/07/31/060731fa_fact>

And speaking of lying, avoid those sites that sell you essays. "Plagiarism," after all, is just a fancy name for lying.

Exercises for Section C

1. What difference is there between how we evaluate an advertisement and how we evaluate any other apparent argument?

2. Find an advertisement and evaluate the claims in it.

3. Identify a website whose claims you believe, and explain why you consider it to be a reliable source. (Don't use a personal website of friends or family—or yourself.)

4. Print out a page of a website devoted to UFOs.
   a. Are any sentences too vague to be claims?
   b. Are the claims plausible?
   c. Do any claims contradict each other?
   d. Is there an argument?
   e. Is the argument good?

   Trade with a classmate to comment on each other's evaluation.

Evaluate the following in terms of the criteria in this chapter.

5. Maxell media—offers 100 years of archival life! Delivers quality you can trust!
   (MacMall catalogue, 2003)

6. Professor Rooney placed 11th out of 145 in the *Jeopardy!* Ultimate Tournament of Champions. ("Jeopardy! Ultimate Tournament of Champions", Wikipedia)

7. *Pet Healer* Pet Healer with psychic abilities to communicate with pets that have left this earthly plane. Contact 292–xxxx. Suggested donation: $25–$100.
   (*Crosswinds Weekly*, Albuquerque)

8. "I'm Katy Perry. I love being a free spirit onstage and off, but when you suffer with acne blemishes, you don't feel very free. I tried everything to get rid of my acne but nothing worked. So one day, I ordered Proactiv solution. Within a couple of weeks, my skin cleared up fast."
   (Proactiv commercial)

9. Evaluate the website of The BARK of DOG Foundation at <www.BARKofDOG.org>.

10. Evaluate the website of McWhortle Enterprises at <www.McWhortle.com>.

11. Dick: My uncle's doctor told him that he's got prostate trouble.
    Zoe: What does that mean? I don't even know what a prostate is.
    Dick: Beats me.

    Can you help Dick and Zoe? Search on the web for "prostate" and check out five of the sites on the first page of results. Which do you trust? Why? Do you now know what a prostate is and what kinds of problems there can be with them? Compare those sites to the printed version of the Encyclopedia Britannica in your school library.

D. Common Mistakes in Evaluating Claims

1. Confusing possibility with plausibility

The standard fare of conspiracy theorists is to think that if it's possible, it's true. Just because it could happen and you don't trust the folks who would benefit if you don't believe it, doesn't make it true. ***Possibility isn't plausibility***.

Example 13 Tom: Terrorists are attacking us by spreading disease with our money. Dollar bills are passed from hand to hand more than mail, more than menus, more than a few door handles in an office building. No one gives a second thought if you handle money with gloves in the winter. Do you ever think twice when Ahmad hands you your change at the convenience store? Now you know why the flu reached epidemic proportions this year.

Suzy: Yes, yes, that could be true. And it sure explains a lot. I'm going to be extra careful taking any money from Muslims now.

Analysis Tom's conspiracy theory is just feeding Suzy's prejudices and paranoia. What's possible isn't necessarily plausible.

An interesting story is just that—a story, which might be worth investigating. But we need evidence before we believe. Sometimes there really are conspiracies, like when the soldiers and Department of Defense tried to cover up the torture at Abu Ghraib. But with real conspiracies, we can be pretty sure evidence will eventually come out.

Three may keep a secret, if two of them are dead." —Benjamin Franklin

2. Bad appeals to authority

We've seen that we often have good reason to accept a claim because of who said it—that's an ***appeal to authority***. But folks often accept claims from people who aren't experts on the subject or who have a motive to mislead. That's a ***bad appeal to authority***.

Example 14 Zoe: What do you think of the president's new science funding plan?

Tom: It's awful. It'll cut back funding on military research. They said so on Fox News.

Analysis Not everything you hear on Fox News is true.

Example 15 Dick: This is terrible what's happening with global warming. We've got to cut back on driving.

Tom: Stop driving? Are you crazy? I heard an expert on Fox News say that the evidence isn't clear that global warming is caused by humans.

Dick: You believe everything you hear on Fox News?

Tom: No. But since it's controversial I figure it's best to suspend judgment.

Analysis Some folks think that suspending judgment is the best course, the most unbiased. But that's exactly what the big oil and coal companies want. If you suspend judgment on whether global warming is caused by humans using fossil fuels, then you won't have reason to cut back on driving or to oppose new coal-fired electricity-generating plants. There is overwhelming evidence, given by scientists who have no obvious motive to mislead, that burning fossil fuels has caused global warming and that global warming will get much worse and is very dangerous unless we stop using fossil fuels. That a very few scientists don't agree shouldn't count as equal to the weight of the most respected authorities and research, especially when so many of those doubting scientists are paid by big oil or big coal companies. It's a bad appeal to authority to suspend judgment in this case. Tom is being conned, just like a lot of people were in the 1950s and 1960s when the tobacco companies trotted out their "experts" to say that it wasn't certain that smoking causes cancer.

We often treat our friends as experts. We accept their claims because they sound like they know what they're talking about or because we'd be embarrassed not to. "How can you not believe Senator Hatch about the good intentions of the oil companies? All of us think he's right." Sometimes it's the conviction that if everyone else believes it or does it, it must be true or right.

Example 15 Lee: All my co-workers have iPhones, and they all make fun of Android phones. So once my contract is up, I'm going to get an iPhone.
Analysis Lee is making an appeal to common belief, which is just a bad appeal to authority.

> ***Appeal to common belief*** It's usually a mistake to accept a claim as true solely because a lot of other people believe it.

Example 16 Harry went to Japan and reasoned that since everyone there was driving on the left-hand side, he should, too.
Analysis Harry is appealing to common belief, or at least what he figures the people who are driving believe. And he's right to do so. An appeal to common belief isn't always bad.

3. Mistaking the person for the claim

Though it's OK to suspend judgment on a claim if you don't consider the person who's making it to be a reputable expert, it's never right to say a claim is false because of who said it.

> ***Mistaking the person (or group) for the claim*** It's a mistake to reject a claim solely because of who said it.

Example 17 Tom: The new global warming accord won't help the environment. That's just another lie our president said.
Analysis Tom's mistaking the person for the claim. Presidents don't always lie.

Example 18 There's no water shortage here in New Mexico. That's just one of those things environmentalists say.
Analysis This is mistaking the group for the claim.

4. Mistaking the person for the argument

Suppose Dr. E gives an argument in class that a critical thinking course should be required of every college freshman. His students are not convinced. So he makes the same argument tap-dancing on his desk while juggling beanbags, between each claim whistling "How much is that doggy in the window?" Is the argument any better? Suppose someone in class just found out that Dr. E lost his temper and threw Suzy's cat Puff over the hedge to his neighbor's yard. Is the argument any worse?

We have standards for whether an argument is good or bad. It may be more memorable if Dr. E stands on his head; you may be repulsed by him if you know he threw Puff over a hedge. But the argument is good or bad—independent of how Dr. E or anyone presents it and independent of their credentials. Just as a claim isn't false because of who said it, an argument isn't bad because of who said it.

> ***Mistaking the person (or group) for the argument*** It's a mistake to say an argument is bad solely because of who said it.

Example 19 Zoe: I went to Professor Zzzyzzx's talk about writing last night. He argued that the best way to start on a novel is to make an outline of the plot.

Suzy: Are you kidding? He could never get his published. And he doesn't even speak good English.

Analysis Suzy is mistaking the person for the argument. Professor Zzzyzzx's argument is good or bad independent of how good a writer he is.

Example 20 Dick: This proposed work corps program for the unemployed is a great idea. Look at the reasons they gave for it.

Tom: Are you kidding? Wasn't that on the Green Party platform?

Analysis Tom is mistaking the group for the argument.

Mistaking the group for the argument is a favorite ploy of demagogues. It's an important tool in establishing stereotypes and prejudice.

Example 21 Maria: The soldiers who stripped and beat prisoners in Abu Ghraib should go to jail, as well as the politicians who licensed it by changing the definition of torture. If you or I did anything like that, we'd be in prison for years. It's against the law.

Tom: You were never in the military, so you can't judge those soldiers. You don't know what war is like.

Analysis Sure, Maria has never been a soldier. She's never been a murderer, either, but that doesn't disqualify her from judging murderers. This is an example of a common way of rejecting arguments because of who said it: You've no authority to make an argument because you're not a soldier /a woman/a black person/ . . . .

To ***refute*** an argument is to show it is bad. Often we think we can refute an argument by showing that the person who made it doesn't believe one of the premises or even the conclusion itself.

Example 22 Harry: We should stop logging old-growth forests. There are very few of them left in the U.S. They are important watersheds and preserve wildlife. And once cut, we cannot recreate them.

Tom: You say we should stop logging old-growth forests? Who are you kidding? Didn't you just build a log cabin on the mountain?

Analysis Tom's rejection of Harry's argument is understandable: it seems Harry's actions betray the conclusion he's arguing for. But whether they do or not (perhaps the logs came from the land Harry's family cleared in a new-growth forest), Tom has not answered Harry's argument. Tom is not justified in ignoring an argument because of Harry's actions.

If Harry were to respond to Tom by saying that the logs for his home weren't cut from an old-growth forest, he's been suckered. Tom got him to change the subject, and they will be deliberating an entirely different claim than he intended. It's a phony refutation.

> ***Phony refutation*** It's not a real refutation of an argument to point out that the person who made the argument has done or said something that shows he or she doesn't believe one of the premises or the conclusion of the argument.

We have a desire for consistency in actions and words. We don't trust hypocrites. But when you spot a contradiction between actions and words, at most you can lay a charge of hypocrisy or irrationality. Sincerity of the speaker is not one of the criteria for an argument to be good, and insisting on it is just mistaking the person for the argument. Besides, the contradiction is often only apparent, not real.

Whether a claim is true or false is not determined by who said it.

Whether an argument is good or bad is not determined by who said it.

Always ask "Why?"

Always ask "So?"

Take as authority only those whose speech indicates knowledge and awareness and whose conduct indicates trustworthiness. Never rely solely on the position of an authority: many fools have been promoted to high place. Human desires, wills, fears can lead to fools prospering. But wisdom will out.

Don't believe because it's comfortable. A great desire for comfort, for no challenge, can lead to the enslavement of the truth and to the enslavement of us all.

If in doubt, suspend judgment. The seeker is wiser than the dogmatist.

> First, realize that it is necessary for an intelligent person to reflect on the words that are spoken, not the person who says them. If the words are true, he will accept them whether he who says them is known as a truth teller or a liar. One can extract gold from a clump of dirt, a beautiful narcissus comes from an ordinary bulb, medication from the venom of a snake.
>
> Abd-el-Kader, Algerian Muslim statesman, 1858

Exercises for Section D

1. a. What is an appeal to authority?
   b. Give an example of a bad appeal to authority you heard recently.
   c. Give an example of a good appeal to authority you heard recently.
2. When are we justified in rejecting a claim because of who said it?
3. Give an example of a bad appeal to common belief you heard recently.
4. Why should you never mistake the person for the argument?
5. What does it mean to say that a person has made a phony refutation?
6. Find a conspiracy theory presented on the web. Explain why you do or do not believe it.

Here are some more of Tom's exercises along with Dr. E's comments. He's trying to distinguish between good and bad reasons for accepting or rejecting claims.

Doctor Ball said that for me to lose weight I need to get more exercise, but he's so obese. So I'm not going to listen to him.

This person is mistaking the person for the claim. Looks like a phony refutation to me.

You're right—it's mistaking the person for the claim. But it's not a phony refutation because we don't know of any argument that Dr. Ball said.

Lucy said I shouldn't go see Doctor Williams because he's had problems with malpractice suits in the past. But Lucy also believes in herbs and natural healing, so she's not going to like any doctors.

Looks O.K. to me. The speaker is just questioning the authority of Lucy and deciding not to accept her claim.

Perhaps. But it might be a case of mistaking the person for the argument. It isn't clear whether the speaker is suspending judgment on a claim or is rejecting Lucy's argument.

Zoe: Everyone should exercise. It's good for you. It keeps you in shape, gives you more energy, and keeps away depression.

Dick: Are you kidding? I've never seen you exercise.

Phony refutation. *Right!*

For each of the exercises below answer the following:

What, if any, classifications of this section does this fit?

Is it a bad argument?

7. Suzy: I played doubles on my team for four years. It is definitely a more intense game than playing singles.
   Zoe: Yesterday on the news Maria Sharapova said that doubles in tennis is much easier because there are two people covering almost the same playing area.
   Suzy: I guess she must be right then.

8. Mom: You shouldn't stay out so late. It's dangerous, so I want you home early.
   Son: But none of my friends have curfews, and they stay out as long as they want.

9. Manuel: Barbara said divorce'll hurt her kids' emotions.
   Maria: But she goes out with her boyfriend every night leaving the kids and her husband at home. She won't divorce, but she's already hurt her kids. So it doesn't matter if she gets divorced or not.

10.

11. Zoe: You should be more sensitive to the comments you make around people.
    Dick: Of course you'd think that—you're a woman.

12. Zoe: The author of this book *Critical Thinking* said that bad people always make wrong decisions. You need to have virtue to make good use of critical thinking.
    Suzy: What does he know about virtue?

13. Zoe: That program to build a new homeless shelter is a great idea. We need to help get poor people off the streets so they can eventually fend for themselves.
    Suzy: How could you say that? You don't even give money to the homeless guy who was begging on the street corner there.

14. Zoe: That new law against panhandling is terrible. People have a right to ask for money so long as they aren't really bothering anyone.
    Tom: Sure. And I suppose you believe everything else the ACLU says.

15. Prof. Zzzyzzx: Mine doctor told me cigarettes I should be ceasing. He said bad lungs they will give me and mine skin wrinkle and mine blood pressure to increase. But I do not listen to his talk because he is always smoking like the chimney.

16. Zoe: You're going to explode our water bill the way you're watering the lawn!
    Dick: I'm going to increase the water bill? What about those 30-minute showers you take every day?

17. Tom: What do you think about requiring kids at school to wear uniforms?
    Lee: My mom said it was great, so I'm behind it.

18. Doctor: Well, your test results show you have very high cholesterol. You need to cut back on fatty foods and get more exercise, or else you're likely to develop heart disease.

    Prof. Zzzyzzx: Vat are you talking? I am very good feeling. Eating meat gives me strength!

19. Doctor: You are morbidly obese. If you don't lose some weight, you'll develop serious health problems.

    Wanda: You're just prejudiced against fat people.

20. Maria: What do you think about the new book on financial independence?

    Lee: It must be good; it's on the *New York Times* best seller list.

21. Suzy: Did you notice that only beautiful women advertise in the personal columns here?

    Zoe: How do you know?

    Suzy: Duh, they say so in their ads.

Summary We can't prove everything. We must take some claims as given or we'd never get started. But when should we accept a claim someone puts forward without proof? And when should we reject? And when is it best to suspend judgment?

We don't have hard and fast rules, but we can formulate some guidelines. Most important is experience: we can accept a claim that from experience we know is true; we can reject a claim that we know from experience is false. But we need to be sure that it is from our experience and not a faulty memory or an inference. And there are some times when we can reject what we seem to know from experience because it contradicts other claims that we know are true and which explain a lot.

We have reason to accept claims from people we trust who know what they're talking about. And we have reason to accept claims from respected experts, though we can give too much deference to an authority. But it's wrong to think a claim is false because of the source. We argue badly when we reject anything a particular person or group says. Worse is when we reject an argument because of who said it. Arguments are good or bad regardless of who made them.

Key Words

accept	bad appeal to common belief
reject	mistaking the person for the claim
suspend judgment	mistaking the person for the argument
personal experience	refuting an argument
bad appeal to authority	phony refutation

Further Study Courses in psychology deal with the reliability of witnesses and the nature of memory. Courses in journalism or communications discuss the reliability of various sources in the media and bias in the media. A short course on how to use the library is offered at most schools in order to help you find your way through reference sources.

You can see the Federal Trade Commission's guidelines against deceptive pricing in advertising at <http://www.ftc.gov/bcp/guides/decptprc.htm>.

The *Columbia Journalism Review* publishes "Who Owns What," a guide to the ownership of major media companies. It's available for free on their website, <www.cjr.org>.

In a philosophy or rhetoric course you might hear Latin names for some of the fallacies discussed here. All the ways of mistaking a person for a claim or an argument are referred to in Latin as *ad hominem* ("against the person"). Phony refutations are sometimes called by the Latin term *tu quoque* ("you, too").

Writing Lesson 4

Write an argument either for or against the following:

No unmanned spacecraft landed on Mars; the photos are faked.

- Just list the premises and the conclusion.
  You can include definitions, too. Nothing more.
- Your argument should be at most one page long.
- Check whether your instructor has chosen a different topic for this assignment.

You know whether you believe this claim. But why do you believe it or doubt it?

What if you're unsure? You write pro and con lists, yet you can't make up your mind. You're really in doubt. Then write the best argument you can for why someone should suspend judgment on the claim. That's not a cop-out; sometimes suspending judgment is the most mature, reasonable choice to take. But you should have good reasons for suspending judgment.

To give you an idea of what to do, here are arguments by Tom and Suzy on other topics.

Tom Wyzyczy
Critical Thinking
Section 4
Writing Lesson 4

Issue: Elvis is still alive.

Definition: By "Elvis" I understand Elvis Presley.

Premises:

Elvis Presley was reported to have died a number of years ago.

All the reputable press agencies reported his death.

Many people went to his funeral,[A] which was broadcast live.[B]

His doctor signed his death certificate, according to news reports.

There have been reports that Elvis is alive.

No such report has been in the mainstream media, only in tabloids.[C]

No physical evidence that he is alive has ever been produced.

No one would have anything to gain by faking his death.[D]

If Elvis were alive, he would have much to gain by making that known to the public.

Conclusion: Elvis is not alive.

Good. But it could be better. First, split the third premise into two (A and B). I don't know if it was broadcast live, yet I can accept part A.

Second, the sentence C is too vague—what's "mainstream media"? What counts as a "tabloid"? You should cite real sources if you want someone to accept your argument.

And premise D is dubious: any of his heirs had lots to gain.

Finally, you take for granted that the reader knows why some of your premises are important. But it isn't obvious. Why is A important? To explain, you need to add the glue, a premise or premises linking it to the conclusion. You're still leaving too much unstated. Don't rely so much on the other person making your argument for you.

Still, I think you have the idea and won't be suckered by the conspiracy theorists.

Suzy Queue
Critical Thinking
Section 2
Writing Lesson 4

Issue: The CIA started the cocaine epidemic in the ghettos in order to control and pacify African Americans.

Premises:

The CIA has lied to us a lot in the past.

Riots in the past in the ghettos have been a serious problem in the U.S.

The government wants to control African Americans, so they won't make any trouble.

African American people in the ghetto had too much to ~~loose~~ *lose* to start.

Many people in the ghettos believe that the CIA introduced cocaine to the U.S.

It was reported on national news that the CIA was involved with drug running from Latin America.

Conclusion: The CIA started the cocaine epidemic in the ghettos in order to control and pacify African Americans.

At best you've given reason to suspend judgment. You haven't given me any reason to believe the claim is true, only that it isn't obviously false.

Some of your premises are too vague ("national news," "serious problem"). And I can't see how they link to the conclusion. Are you suggesting that if the CIA lied to us in the past, that makes it highly probable that they introduced cocaine into the ghettos? That's weak. And big deal that a lot of people in the ghettos believe the CIA introduced cocaine there. A lot of people think the moon doesn't rise or that it rises in the west—that doesn't make it true. Are they experts?

Review the criteria in Chapter 4.

5 Repairing Arguments

A. We Need to Repair Arguments

Lee: Tom wants to get a dog.
Maria: What kind?
Lee: A dachshund. And that's really stupid, since he wants one that will catch a Frisbee.

Lee has made an argument, if we interpret what he said: Tom wants a dog that will catch a Frisbee, so Tom shouldn't get a dachshund. You might think this is a bad argument. There's no *glue*, no claim that gets us from the premise to the conclusion. We just ask "So?" But Maria knows very well, as do we, that a dachshund would be a lousy choice for someone who wants his dog to catch a Frisbee. Dachshunds are too low to the ground, they can't run fast, they can't jump, and the Frisbee is bigger than they are, so they couldn't bring it back. Any dog like that is a bad choice for a Frisbee partner. Lee just left out these obvious claims. But why should he bother to say them?

Folks normally leave out so much that if we look only at what's said, we'll be missing too much in trying to determine what we should believe. We can and must rewrite many arguments by adding an *unstated premise* or an *unstated conclusion*.

When are we justified in adding an unstated premise? How do we know whether we've rewritten an argument well or just added our own prejudices? And how can we recognize when an argument is beyond repair?

B. The Principle of Rational Discussion

What assumptions can we make about someone with whom we wish to reason?

> ***The Principle of Rational Discussion*** We assume that the other person who is discussing with us or whose argument we are reading:
>
> 1. Knows about the subject under discussion.
> 2. Is able and willing to reason well.
> 3. Is not lying.

What justification do we have for invoking this principle? After all, not everyone fits these conditions all the time.

Consider condition (1). Dr. E leaves his car at the repair shop because it's running badly, and he returns later in the afternoon. The mechanic tells him that he needs a new fuel injector. Dr. E asks, "Are you sure I need a new one?" That sounds like an invitation for the mechanic to give an argument. But she shouldn't. Dr. E doesn't have the slightest idea how his engine runs, and the mechanic might as well be speaking Greek. She should try to educate Dr. E, or she'll have to ask Dr. E to accept her claim because she's an expert.

Consider condition (2). Sometimes people intend not to reason well. Like the demagogic politician or talk-show host, they want to convince you by nonrational means and won't accept your arguments, no matter how good they may be. There's no point in deliberating with such a person.

Or you may encounter a person who is temporarily unable or unwilling to reason well, a person who is upset or in love. Again, it makes no sense at such a time to try to reason with that person. Calm him or her, address his or her emotions, and leave discussion for another time.

Then again, you might find yourself with someone who wants to reason well but just can't seem to follow an argument. Why try to reason? Give him a copy of this book.

What about condition (3)? If you find that the other person is lying—not just a little white lie, but serious lies—there's no point in reasoning with him or her, unless perhaps to catch and point out the lies.

The Principle of Rational Discussion does not instruct us to give other people the benefit of the doubt. It summarizes the necessary conditions for us to reason with someone. Compare it to playing chess with someone: what's the point if your opponent doesn't understand or won't play by the rules?

Still, you say, most people don't follow the Principle of Rational Discussion. They don't care if your argument is good. Why should you follow these rules and assume them of others? If you don't:

- You are denying the essentials of democracy.
- You are not going to know what to believe yourself.
- You are not as likely to convince others.

A representative democracy is built on the idea that the populace as a whole can choose good men and good women to write laws by which they can agree to live. If any appeal to the worst in people succeeds, then a democracy will degenerate into the rule of the mob. It is only by constantly striving to base our political discussions on good arguments that we have any hope of living in a just and efficient society.

And how can you know what to believe yourself if you've adopted methods of convincing that appeal to the worst in people? Abandoning the standards of good reasoning, you'll soon be basing your own life on illusions and false beliefs.

But most of all, you're wrong if you think that in the long run convincing with clever ads, sound bites, or appeals to prejudice work better than good arguments. They don't. I've seen the contrary in my city council meetings. I've seen it with my friends. I've seen it with my students. With a little education, most people, most of the time, prefer to have a sensible, good argument to think about.

> If you once forfeit the confidence of your fellow citizens, you can never regain their respect and esteem. It is true that you may fool all the people some of the time; you can even fool some of the people all the time; but you cannot fool all of the people all the time. — Abraham Lincoln

Still, there are times when an argument appears good but you think the conclusion is false. Then if you're a good reasoner, you should try to show the argument isn't good: the conclusion doesn't really follow from the premises, or one of the premises is false, or it begs the question.

Example 1 Dick: Cats are really dangerous pets. Look at all the evidence. See, it says so here in this medical journal, and it lists all the diseases you can catch from them, even schizophrenia. You know that lots of your friends get sick from cat allergies. And remember how Puff scratched Zoe last week? You can't deny it.

Suzy: O.K., O.K., I believe what you've said. So you can reason well like Dr. E. Still I don't believe that cats are dangerous pets.

Analysis Suzy recognizes that Dick has given a good argument for cats being dangerous pets, but she still doesn't believe it. She's not judiciously suspending judgment; she's just unwilling to reason about her beloved cat.

> ***The Mark of Irrationality*** If you recognize that an argument is good, it is irrational not to accept the conclusion.

What if you hear arguments for both sides, and you can't find a flaw in either? Then you should suspend judgment on whether the claim is true until you can investigate more.

Exercises for Sections A and B

1. Why add premises or a conclusion? Why not take arguments as they are?
2. State the Principle of Rational Discussion and explain why we are justified in adopting it when we reason with others.
3. What should you do if you find that the Principle of Rational Discussion does not apply in a discussion you're having?
4. You find that a close friend is an alcoholic. You want to help her. You want to convince her to stop drinking. Which is more appropriate: reason with her or take her to an Alcoholics Anonymous meeting? Explain.
5. Since often people don't satisfy the Principle of Rational Discussion, why not just use bad arguments to fit the circumstances?

C. The Guide to Repairing Arguments

With the Principle of Rational Discussion, we can formulate a guide to help us evaluate and interpret arguments. Since the person is supposed to be able to reason well, we can add a premise to his or her argument only if it makes the argument stronger or valid and doesn't beg the question. Since we assume that the person isn't lying and knows the subject under discussion, any premise we add should also be plausible and plausible to that person. We can delete a premise if it doesn't make the argument weaker.

> ***The Guide to Repairing Arguments*** Given an apparent argument that seems defective, we are justified in *adding* a premise or conclusion if all three of the following hold:
>
> 1. The argument becomes stronger or valid.
> 2. The premise is plausible and would seem plausible to the other person.
> 3. The premise is more plausible than the conclusion.
>
> If an argument is valid or strong, we may *delete* a premise if doing so does not make the argument weaker.

Example 2 Lee: I was wondering what kind of pet Dick has. It must be a dog.
Maria: How do you know?
Lee: Because I heard it barking last night.

Analysis Maria shouldn't dismiss Lee's reasoning just because the glue to get from the premises to the conclusion is missing. She should ask what claim(s) are needed to make it strong, since by the Principle of Rational Discussion we assume Lee intends to and is able to reason well. The obvious premise to add is "All pets that bark are dogs." But Maria knows that's false (seals, foxes, parrots can bark) and can assume that Lee does, too, since he's supposed to know about the subject. So she tries "Almost all pets that bark are dogs." That's plausible, and with it the argument is strong and good.

We first try to make the argument valid or strong because we don't need to know what the speaker was thinking in order to do so. Then we can ask whether that claim is plausible and whether it would be plausible to the other person. *By first trying to make the argument valid or strong, we can show the other person what he or she needs to assume to make the argument good.*

It's the same when you make your own arguments. You have premises and a conclusion, and you ask yourself: Is it possible for the premises to be true and the conclusion false? When you find a possible way for the premises to be true and the conclusion false, you try to eliminate it by adding a premise—of course a plausible one. As you eliminate ways in which the premises could be true and the conclusion false, you make the argument better.

But why go to all this bother when we hear a defective argument and can see how to make a better one for the same conclusion? Why not just use what we can from it and ignore the rest in order to come up with a good argument? After all, we're trying to learn what's true about the world. Fine, but first you should take seriously what the other person said. You can't learn if you don't listen. The Guide to Repairing Arguments is a method to hear and understand better by paying attention to what's actually said.

Examples

Are the following good arguments? Can they be repaired?

Example 3 Flo: No dog meows. So Spot doesn't meow.

Analysis "Spot is a dog" is the only premise that will make this a valid or strong argument. So we add that. Since that's true, the argument is good.

We don't add "Spot barks." That's true, too, and certain to seem obvious to Flo, but it doesn't make the argument valid or strong. So adding it violates requirement (1) of the guide. *We repair only as needed.*

Example 4 All professors teach. So Ms. Han is a professor.

Analysis The obvious claim to add is "Ms. Han teaches." But then the argument is still weak: Ms. Han could be an instructor, or a part-time lecturer, or a graduate student. *The argument can't be repaired because the obvious premise to add still leaves it weak.*

Example 5 Harry has a dog, Anubis. So Anubis barks.

Analysis We can't make this valid by adding "All dogs bark" because we know that's false. We could make it stronger by adding "Anubis is not a Basenji" and "Anubis didn't have her vocal cords cut." Those would rule out a lot of possibilities where Anubis is a dog but doesn't bark. And why not add "Anubis scares away the electric meter reader every month"? But this isn't a course in creative writing. We can't make up just anything to add to the argument to make it stronger or valid. We have no reason to believe those claims are true.

The only premise we can add here is a blanket one that rules out lots of possibilities without specifying any one of them: "Almost all dogs bark." That's the *glue* that links the premise to the conclusion. Then the argument is good.

Example 6 Dr. E is a good teacher because he gives fair exams.

Analysis The unstated premise needed to make this valid or strong is "Almost any teacher who gives fair exams is a good teacher." That gives a strong argument. But it's not plausible: a teacher could copy fair exams from the instructor's manual. (If you thought the claim that's needed is "Good teachers give fair exams" then reread Example 4.) *The argument can't be repaired because the obvious premise to add to make the argument strong or valid is false or dubious.*

But can't you make it strong by adding, say, "Dr. E gives great explanations," "Dr. E is amusing," "Dr. E never misses class," . . . ? Yes, all those are true and perhaps obvious to the person. But adding those doesn't repair this argument—it makes a whole new argument. *Don't put words in someone's mouth.*

Example 7 Dick: Dogs are loyal. Dogs are friendly. Dogs can protect you from intruders.

Maria: So?

Dick: So dogs make great pets.

Maria: Why does that follow?

Analysis Maria's right. Dick's argument is missing the "glue," the link between premises and conclusion that rules out other possibilities, in this case something like "Anything that is loyal, friendly, and can protect you from intruders is a great pet." But that's exactly what Maria thinks is false: dogs need room to run around, they need to be walked every day, it costs more to take care of a dog than a goldfish, ... *Just stating a lot of obvious truths doesn't by itself get you a conclusion.*

Example 8 Wanda to Suzy: Sure, you'll get a passing grade in English. After all, you paid tuition to take the course.

Analysis The argument is weak—and it *is* an argument: the last sentence is meant as a reason to believe the first. But there's no obvious repair: it's false that anyone who pays tuition for a course will pass it. *Wanda apparently can't reason*. Don't bother to repair this one.

Example 9 You're going to vote for the Green Party candidate for president? Don't you realize that means your vote will be wasted?

Analysis Where's the argument here? Aren't these just two questions?

If you heard this, you'd certainly think that the speaker is trying to convince you to believe "You shouldn't vote for the Green Party candidate for president." And the speaker is giving a reason to believe: "Your vote will be wasted." This is meant as an argument.

It sounds pretty good, though something is missing. A visitor from Denmark may not know "The Green Party candidate doesn't have a chance of winning." But even then she could ask, "So?" The argument is missing the glue that links the premises to the conclusion. We'd have to fill in the argument further: "If you vote for someone who doesn't have a chance of winning, then your vote will be wasted." And when we add that premise, we see the argument that used such "obvious" premises is really not very good. Why should we believe that if you vote for someone who doesn't stand a chance of winning then your vote is wasted? If that were true, then who wins is the only important result of an election, rather than, say, making a position understood by the electorate. At best we can say that when the unstated premises are added, we get an argument one of whose premises needs a substantial argument for us to accept that it's true. *Trying to repair an argument can reveal unstated assumptions that should be debated.*

Example 10 Cats are more likely than dogs to carry diseases harmful to humans. Cats kill songbirds and can kill people's pets. Cats disturb people at night with their screeching and clattering in garbage cans. Cats leave paw prints on cars and will sleep in unattended cars. Cats are not as pleasant as dogs and are owned only by people who have satanic affinities. So there should be a leash law for cats just as much as for dogs.

Analysis This letter to the editor is going pretty well until the next to last sentence. *That claim is a bit dubious, and the argument would be better without it. So we can delete it*. Then, by adding some obvious claims that glue the premises to the conclusion by ruling out other possibilities, we'll have a good argument.

Example 11 In a famous speech, Martin Luther King Jr. said:

> "I have a dream that one day this nation will rise up and live out the true meaning of its creed: 'We hold these truths to be self-evident—that all men are created equal.' . . . I have a dream that one day even the state of Mississippi, a desert state sweltering with the heat of injustice and oppression, will be

> transformed into an oasis of freedom and justice. I have a dream that my four little children will one day live in a nation where they will not be judged by the color of their skin but by the content of their character."
>
> . . . King is also presenting a logical argument . . . the argument might be stated as follows: "America was founded on the principle that all men are created equal. This implies that people should not be judged by skin color, which is an accident of birth, but rather by what they make of themselves ('the content of their character'). To be consistent with this principle, America should treat black people and white people alike."
>
> David Kelley, *The Art of Reasoning*

Analysis The rewriting of this passage is too much of a stretch—putting words in someone's mouth—to be justified. Where did David Kelley get "This implies . . ."? Stating my dreams and hoping others will share them is not an argument. Martin Luther King Jr. knew how to argue well and could do so when he wanted. We're not going to make his words more respectable by pretending they're an argument. *Not every good attempt to persuade is an argument.*

Example 12 Alcoholism is a disease, not a character flaw. People are genetically predisposed to be addicted to alcohol. An alcoholic should not be fired or imprisoned but should be given treatment.

Treatment centers should be established because it is too difficult to overcome the addiction to alcohol all by oneself. The encouragement and direction of others are what is needed to help people, for alcoholics can find the power within themselves to fight and triumph over their addiction.

Analysis On the face of it, "Alcoholism is a disease, not a character flaw" contradicts "Alcoholics can find the power within themselves to fight and triumph over their addiction." Both these claims are premises needed for the conclusion "Treatment centers should be established." *When premises contradict each other and can't be deleted, there's no way to repair the argument.*

Example 13 U.S. citizens are independent souls, and they tend to dislike being forced to do anything. The compulsory nature of Social Security therefore has been controversial since the program's beginnings. Many conservatives argue that Social Security should be made voluntary, rather than compulsory.

Brux and Cowen, *Economic Issues and Policy*

Analysis The first two sentences look like an argument. But the first sentence is too vague to be a claim. And even if it could be made precise, we'd have an explanation, not an attempt to convince. *Don't try to repair what isn't an argument.*

Example 14 It is only for the sake of profit that any man employs capital in the support of industry; and he will always, therefore, endeavour to employ it in the support of that industry of which the produce is likely to be of greatest value, or to exchange for the greatest quantity either of money or of other goods.

Adam Smith, *The Wealth of Nations*

Analysis The argument is valid, but *its single premise is false*. Lots of other considerations about where to invest money matter to many people: convenience, social responsibility, ... So there's no way to repair it, and it's bad.

Example 15 (a) Investors in 2016 invested more than twice as much money in no-load mutual funds as in other mutual funds. So, (b) investors in 2016 overwhelmingly preferred no-load mutual funds.

Analysis Typically, we invoke some evidence such as (a), which is objective, to conclude (b), which is subjective. But to have a good argument for (b) we also need a premise like "When people invest money in a fund, they prefer that fund to one that they do not invest in," which is plausible and makes this a good argument. That subjective claim is the link between the observed behavior and the inferred state of mind. *Often an unstated assumption linking behavior to thoughts is needed to make an argument good.*

Example 16 None of Dr. E's students are going to beg in the street. 'Cause only poor people beg. And Dr. E's students will be rich because they understand how to reason well.

Analysis This is a superb argument!

We've seen how to repair some arguments. Just as important, we've seen that some arguments can't be repaired.

Unrepairable Arguments We don't repair an attempt to convince if:

- There's no argument.
- The argument is so lacking in coherence there's nothing obvious to add.
- The obvious premise to add would still leave the argument weak.
- The obvious premise to add to make the argument valid or strong is false.
- A premise is false, dubious, or question-begging and cannot be deleted.
- Two of its premises are contradictory, and neither can be deleted.
- The conclusion is clearly false.

Example 17

Analysis Tom is making an argument (the second question is rhetorical):

> Environmentalists should not be allowed to tell us what to do.
> The federal government should not be allowed to tell us what to do.
> Therefore, we should go ahead and allow logging in old-growth forests.

When the argument is put this way, it seems obvious to us that Tom has confused whether we have the *right* to cut down the forests with whether we *should* allow them to be cut down.

Sometimes people say an argument like Tom's is bad because his premises are irrelevant to the conclusion. They say an argument is bad if in response to one or more premises your reaction is "What's that got to do with anything?" or "So?"

What would you do if someone told you a claim you made is irrelevant? You'd try to show it is relevant by adding more premises to link it to the conclusion. The trouble is that the premises needed to make the claim relevant are not obvious to the other person. When we say that a premise is irrelevant to the conclusion, all we're saying is that it doesn't make the argument any better and that we can't see how to add anything plausible that would link it to the conclusion. And when we say that all the premises are irrelevant, we're saying that we can't even imagine how to repair the argument. A premise is ***irrelevant*** if you can delete it and the argument isn't any worse.

Exercises for Section C

1. State the guide we have in judging when to add or delete a premise, and then what would count as a suitable unstated premise.
2. When can't we repair an argument?
3. When you show an argument is bad, what does that tell you about the conclusion?
4. If a strong argument has one false premise and thirteen true premises, what choice should we make about whether to believe its conclusion?
5. How should we understand the charge that a premise is irrelevant?

Here is some of Tom's homework on repairing arguments with Dr. E's comments.

Anyone who studies hard gets good grades. So it must be that Zoe studies hard.

Argument? (yes or no) Yes.

Conclusion (if unstated, add it): Zoe must study hard.

Premises: Anyone who studies hard gets good grades.

Additional premises needed to make it valid or strong (if none, say so):

Zoe gets good grades.

Classify (with the additional premises): <u>valid</u> strong ———— weak

Good argument? (Choose one and give an explanation.)

- It's good (passes the three tests). ✓ with the added premise.
- It's valid or strong, but you don't know if the premises are true, so you can't say if it's good or bad.
- It's bad because it's unrepairable (state which of the reasons apply).

No! First, "must" is an indicator word. The conclusion is "Zoe studies hard." Even then, Zoe could get good grades and not study hard if she's very bright. It's the obvious premise to add, all right, but it makes the argument weak. The argument is unrepairable. It's just like Example 4 on p. 90.

Celia must love the coat Rudolfo gave her. She wears it all the time.

Argument? (yes or no) Yes.

Conclusion (if unstated, add it): Celia loves the coat Rudolfo gave her.

Premises: She wears it all the time.

Additional premises needed to make it valid or strong (if none, say so):

Anyone who wears a coat all the time loves it.

Classify (with the additional premises): valid strong ——X———— weak

Good argument? (Choose one and give an explanation.)

- It's good (passes the three tests). ✓ with the added premise.
- It's valid or strong, but you don't know if the premises are true, so you can't say if it's good or bad.
- It's bad because it's unrepairable (state which of the reasons apply).

You've confused whether an argument is valid or strong with whether it's good. With your added premise, the argument is indeed valid. But the premise you added is clearly false. A premise to make the argument only strong won't do—the person making the argument intended it to be valid (that word "must" in the conclusion). So the argument is unrepairable because the obvious premise to add to make it valid is false.

I got sick after eating shrimp last month. Then this week again when I ate shrimp, I got a rash. So I shouldn't eat shellfish anymore.

Argument? (yes or no) Yes.

Conclusion (if unstated, add it): I shouldn't eat shellfish anymore.

Premises: I got sick after eating shrimp last month. This week again when I ate shrimp I got a rash.

Additional premises needed to make it valid or strong (if none, say so):
None.

Good argument? (Choose one and give an explanation.)

- It's good (passes the three tests).
- It's valid or strong, but you don't know if the premises are true, so you can't say if it's good or bad. ✓ Sounds very strong to me. I sure wouldn't risk eating shrimp again.
- It's bad because it's unrepairable (state which of the reasons apply).

First, a prescriptive claim is needed as premise. Then I agree that I wouldn't risk eating shrimp again. But that doesn't make the argument strong—there are lots of other possibilities for why the person got a rash. Risk may determine how strong an argument we're willing to accept, but it doesn't affect how strong the argument actually is.

Our congressman voted to give more money to people on welfare. So he doesn't care about working people.

Argument? (yes or no) Yes.

Conclusion (if unstated, add it): Our congressman doesn't care about working people.

Premises: Our congressman voted to give more money to people on welfare.

Additional premises needed to make it valid or strong (if none, say so):
I can't think of any that are plausible.

Classify (with the additional premises): valid strong ————X weak

Good argument? (Choose one and give an explanation.)

- It's good (passes the three tests).
- It's valid or strong, but you don't know if the premises are true, so you can't say if it's good or bad.
- It's bad because it's unrepairable (state which of the reasons apply). ✓ The only premise I can think of that would even make the argument strong is something like "Almost anyone who votes to give more money to people on welfare doesn't care about working people." And I know that's false. So the argument is unrepairable, right?

Right! Excellent work. You've clearly got the idea here. I'm sure you can do more of these now if you'll just remember that sometimes the correct answer is that the argument is unrepairable. Review those conditions on p. 94.

Analyze Exercises 6–31 by answering these questions:

Argument? (yes or no)
Conclusion (if unstated, add it):
Premises:
Additional premises needed to make it valid or strong (if none, say so):
Classify (with the additional premises): valid strong ———— weak

Good argument? (Choose one and give an explanation.)
- It's good (passes the three tests).
- It's valid or strong, but you don't know if the premises are true, so you can't say if it's good or bad.
- It's bad because it's unrepairable (state which of the reasons apply).

6. Dr. E is a teacher. All teachers are men. So Dr. E is a man.
7. George walks like a duck. George looks like a duck. George quacks like a duck. So George is a duck.
8. If you're so smart, why aren't you rich?
9. You caught the flu from me? Impossible! I haven't seen you for two months.
10. You caught the flu from me? Impossible! You got sick first.
11. Suzy: I just got 23 new Twitter followers! I must be really popular.
12. Mary Ellen just bought a Mercedes. So Mary Ellen must be rich.
13. All great teachers are tough graders. So Dr. E is a great teacher.
14. No cat barks. So Ralph is not a cat.
15. You're blue-eyed. So your parents must be blue-eyed.
16. Dick: When you're out, can you stop at the grocery and buy a big bag of dog food?
    Zoe: You know I'm riding my bike today.
17. Cheap horses are rare. Rare things are expensive. Therefore, cheap horses are expensive.
18. Flo is taller than when I saw her three months ago. So she's grown.
19. Suzy is taller than when I saw her yesterday. So she's grown.
20.

21. Dick: Harry got into college because of affirmative action.
    Suzy: Gee, I didn't know that. So Harry isn't very bright.
22. These exercises are impossible. How do they expect us to get them right? There are no right answers! They're driving me crazy.

23. These exercises are difficult but not impossible. Though there may not be a unique right answer, there are definitely wrong answers. There are generally not unique best ways to analyze arguments you encounter in your daily life. The best this course can hope to do is make you think and develop your judgment through these exercises.

24. —That masked man saved us.
    —Did you see he has silver bullets in his gunbelt?
    —And he called his horse Silver.
    —Didn't he call his friend Tonto?
    —He must be the Lone Ranger.

25. What!? Me sexually harass her? You've got to be kidding! I never would have asked her out for a date. Look at her—she's too fat, and, besides, she smokes. I'm the boss here, and I could go out with anyone I want.

26. Tom: Suzy was diagnosed with strep throat. I've been around her for weeks. My throat feels sore in the same way it did the last time I had strep. So I have strep too.

27. (From the Associated Press, July 8, 1999, about a suit against tobacco companies for making "a defective product that causes emphysema, lung cancer, and other illnesses.")
    The industry claimed there is no scientific proof that smoking causes any illness and that the public is well aware that smoking is risky.

28. This book will be concerned exclusively with abstract decision theory and will focus on its logical and philosophical foundations. This does not mean that readers will find nothing here of practical value. Some of the concepts and methods I will expound are also found in business school textbooks. Michael Resnik, *Choices*

29. Lee: Boring professors make students fall asleep in class.
    Tom: So Professor Zzzyzzx is boring.

30. 

31. This happened in broad daylight and that means that somebody saw something that can help catch the person responsible for this killing before there is any more violence.
    Pasadena Interim Deputy Police Chief Mike Korpal, March 11, 2010

32. a. Make up an argument against the idea that lying is a good way to convince people.
    b. Convert your argument in (a) to show that reasoning badly on purpose is not effective or ethical.

D. Reasoning with Prescriptive Claims

Example 18 Dr. Wibblitz: The university should stop doing dissection experiments on monkeys.

Analysis This is a prescriptive claim. Suzy agrees because she thinks that monkeys have souls and we shouldn't hurt animals with souls. But Lee disagrees because he believes that AIDS experiments on monkeys are important. Dr. Wibblitz thinks that such experiments are important, too, yet he thinks they're too expensive because of the new National Science Foundation regulations. Unless they can agree on a standard by which they mean to judge the claim, they cannot resolve their disagreements.

Debates about prescriptive claims should be about either the standard assumed or whether the claim follows from the standard.

Example 19 You shouldn't eat the fat on your steak. Haven't you heard that cholesterol is bad for you?

Analysis The conclusion is the first sentence. But what are the premises? The speaker's question is rhetorical, meant to be taken as an assertion: "Cholesterol is bad for you." But that alone won't give us the conclusion. We need something like "Steak fat has a lot of cholesterol" plus the obvious standard for that "should": "You shouldn't eat anything that's bad for you." Premises like these are so well known that we don't bother to say them.

Example 20 I totally don't support prohibiting smoking in bars—most people who go to bars do smoke and people should be aware that a bar is a place where a lot of people go to have a drink and smoke. There are no youth working or attending bars and I just don't believe you can allow people to go have a beer but not to allow people to have a cigarette—that's a person's God-given right.

Gordy Hicks, city councilor, Socorro, N.M.,
reported in *El Defensor Chieftain*, July 24, 2002

Analysis The conclusion here has to be stated: "Smoking should not be prohibited in bars." *That prescriptive claim needs some standard*. The unstated one here seems to be that society should not establish sanctions against any activity that doesn't corrupt youth or create harm to others who can't avoid it. The argument is just as good without the appeal to God, so we can ignore that. If it turns out that Hicks really does think the standard is theological, then the argument he gave isn't adequate.

Example 21 Smoking destroys people's health. So we ought to raise the tax on cigarettes.

Analysis The premise, a descriptive claim, is true. But the conclusion doesn't follow without some prescriptive premise such as "We should tax activities that are destructive of people's health." The issue then is why we should believe that.

You can't get "ought" from "is" You can't get a prescriptive conclusion from only descriptive premises.

Example 22 ARF High should require students to wear uniforms in order to minimize gang signs.

Analysis This is really two prescriptive claims: "ARF High should require students to wear uniforms" and then a reason why, "We should minimize gang signs (in school)."

Example 23 Maria (to Zoe and Tom): Parking is still difficult on campus. From 9 a.m. to 4 p.m. every weekday it's impossible to find a parking place—I've spoken with all my friends, and it takes us more than 15 minutes, often more. And that's when we already have a parking sticker that we paid $25 for just to get a spot. Without that you could look forever or park on the street and hope not to get a ticket, 'cause it always takes more than an hour to go to class and come back. The school should build more parking lots.

Analysis Everything Maria says is true and obvious to Zoe and Tom—except her conclusion. Zoe, who rides her bike to campus every day, just asks "So?" There are lots of ways those claims could be true and Maria's conclusion false: the university doesn't want to encourage more people to drive to campus; the university has no money to build parking lots; the university has an agreement with the city not to build more parking. Some general prescriptive claim is needed as premise.

Exercises for Section D

1. What do we mean when we say that you can't get "ought" from "is"?

Here's one of Tom's exercises on prescriptive reasoning.

Our government is broke. We should raise the tax on millionaires.

Argument? (yes or no) Yes.

Conclusion (if unstated, add it): We should raise the tax on millionaires.

Premises: Our government is broke.

Additional premises needed to make it valid or strong (if none, say so):

Something's needed—I guess you'd call it a standard, you know, some prescriptive claim. Isn't that what you mean by you can't get "ought" from '"is"?

Good argument? (Choose one and give an explanation.)

- It's good (passes the three tests).
- It's valid or strong, but you don't know if the premises are true, so you can't say if it's good or bad.
- It's bad because it's unrepairable (state which of the reasons apply). ✓

> I can think of lots of ways to repair it, like saying we should tax rich people more than poor ones, or that the rich owe us. But adding those would be putting words in this guy's mouth, cause I can't imagine what he thinks is a good standard. So I think it's unrepairable.
>
> *Very good work! Wow! You've got the idea really well. But note that those standards you suggested wouldn't really repair the argument because they seem to demand some further justification, like a claim about equality being important in society, or everyone should pay his fair share. Or maybe "From each according to his ability, to each according to his need" —look that one up.*

Analyze the following exercises by answering these questions:

Argument? (yes or no)
Conclusion (if unstated, add it):
Premises:
Additional premises needed to make it valid or strong (if none, say so):
Classify (with the additional premises): valid strong ———— weak
Good argument? (Choose one and give an explanation.)

- It's good (passes the three tests).
- It's valid or strong, but you don't know if the premises are true, so you can't say if it's good or bad.
- It's bad because it's unrepairable (state which of the reasons apply).

2. Flo has always wanted a dog, but she's never been very responsible. She had a fish once, but it died after a week. She forgot to water her mother's plants, and they died. She stepped on a neighbor's turtle and killed it.

3. They shouldn't execute that guy tomorrow, even if he is a murderer. It's wrong to kill anyone.

4. Zoe: I want to make a lot of money.
Zoe's mother: So you should go to law school.

5. Capital punishment executes innocent people, and it disproportionately affects minorities. States with capital punishment do not have lower murder rates than states without capital punishment. So capital punishment should be abolished.

6. Dick: We shouldn't leave the lights on when we're away.
Zoe: Why?
Dick: Because we should do all we can to conserve energy.

7. Zoe: We should go to Suzy's dinner party tonight.
Dick: Why?
Zoe: She invited us and she'll be very unhappy if we don't come.
Dick: But I always have a miserable time at her dinner parties.
Zoe: Look, we should go because she's our friend, and we shouldn't make our friends unhappy.

E. Inferring and Implying

Example 24 Maria: Why did you write up this exercise? It wasn't assigned.
Lee: Dr. E said that all his best students hand in the optional exercises for extra credit.
Maria: I better do one, too.

Analysis Dr. E hasn't said that his students should hand in extra work to get a good grade. But Lee and Maria have inferred that; they think he's implied it.

> ***Implying and inferring*** When someone leaves a conclusion unsaid, he or she is *implying* it. When you decide that an unstated claim is the conclusion, you are *inferring* it.
>
> We can also say that someone is implying a claim if in context it's clear that he or she believes it. In that case we infer that the person believes the claim.

Example 25 If Lee complains to the department head that Dr. E is demanding more than he asked on the syllabus, Dr. E could reply that Lee was jumping to his own conclusions. Dr. E might say, "I've observed that my best students hand in extra-credit work—that's all I was saying. I had no intention of asking for extra assignments." Lee, however, could say that in the context in which Dr. E made the remark it was fairly obvious he was implying that if Lee wanted him to believe he's a good student, he should hand in extra work. Implying and inferring can be risky.

Example 26 When Suzy was home for vacation, her father said to her before she went out Saturday night, "Don't forget we're going to be leaving very early for the beach tomorrow." Suzy got home at 3:30 a.m., and the next morning her father was livid when she said that she was too tired to help with the driving. "I *told* you we were leaving very early," he said. To which Suzy replied, "So?" Her father believes he clearly implied, "You should get home early and rest enough to help with the driving." Suzy says he should have made that clear.

The trouble is, we aren't always explicit; we often leave the conclusion unstated because it seems so obvious. And what is obvious to you may not be obvious to someone else. One person's intelligent inference is another's jumping to a conclusion.

Examples What's being implied? What's being inferred?

Example 27 Harry: I'm not going to vote, because no matter who becomes mayor, nothing is going to get done to repair roads in this part of town.

Analysis An unstated claim is needed to make sense of what Harry said: "If no matter who becomes mayor nothing is going to get done to repair roads in this part of town, then you shouldn't vote for mayor." We infer this from what he said; Harry has implied it.

Example 28 Lee is working in the computer lab at school. He's been there for an hour and a half. He looks up and notices that all the students who have come in lately are wearing raincoats and are wet. He figures it must be raining outside.

Analysis We can say that Lee inferred "It is raining outside." But where's the argument? This is the kind of inferring that psychologists and scientists and lawyers do all the time. They have evidence but not stated verbally, and they proceed as if they had an argument.

We often infer from our experience, but we can't analyze those inferences or discuss them with others until we've verbalized them.

Example 29 Lee's teacher makes a sexual innuendo the first day of class. He figures she must have meant something harmless, and he just didn't get it. But it happens again. And again. Lee starts taking notes on all the remarks. Finally, after four weeks Lee is fed up and goes to the head of the department. He says, "My teacher is making sexually suggestive remarks in class. It's not an accident. It's intentional."

Analysis The argument Lee would need to make to the department head might be "My teacher made many remarks over a long period of time that could be taken sexually. This could not be an accident because it happened too often. Therefore, she intended to make sexually suggestive comments."

This may or may not be a strong argument, depending on exactly what the teacher said. It has a subjective claim as a conclusion, one Lee inferred from the teacher's actions.

Example 30 A member of Pakistan's parliament stood his ground in August, defending news reports from his Baluchistan province that five women had been shot and then buried alive as tribal punishment for objecting to their families' choosing husbands for them. A defiant Israr Ullah Zehri told the Associated Press, "These are centuries-old traditions, and I will continue to defend them," despite condemnation by Zehri's colleagues. "Only those who indulge in immoral acts should be afraid," Zehri said.

New York Daily News-AP, August 30, 2008

Analysis We can infer from what Zehri said that he believes if an act is in accord with a centuries-old tradition, it is morally acceptable. He has implied that.

Exercises for Section E

1. Suzy says, "I find fat men unattractive, so I won't date you."
   a. What has Suzy implied?
   b. What can the fellow she's talking to infer?

2. The following conversation is ascribed to W. C. Fields at a dinner party. What can we say he implied?

   W. C. Fields: Madame, you are horribly ugly.

   Lady: Your behavior is inexcusable. You're drunk.

   W. C. Fields: I may be drunk, but tomorrow I'll be sober.

3. Dr. E: I always keep about 10 pounds extra on me because I heard that women are intimidated by a man with a perfect body.

   What can we infer that Dr. E believes?

4. (Advertisement on a billboard) Wendy's. Our beef is fresh. Never frozen.

   What's implied here?

5. In July 2002, the famous race-car driver Al Unser, Jr. was arrested on allegations by his girlfriend that very late one night he hit her and forced her out of the car in a deserted area. His uncle, Bobby Unser, was quoted in the *Albuquerque Journal* as saying:

   > What Little Al and Gina Sota did that night was the most nothing thing I've ever heard of . . . . He didn't use a gun or a knife or a stick. What's the big deal about that? This girl is a topless dancer. She's been down that road 100 times.

   What can we infer that Bobby Unser believes?

6. [State Senator Manny Aragon] has complained that New Mexico's population is 42 percent Hispanic but the state has no Hispanic representative in Congress.

   That sentiment was echoed Thursday by State House Majority Whip James Taylor, an Albuquerque Democrat, who, like Aragon, represents the South Valley in Bernalillo County. "It's embarrassing that New Mexico currently has no Hispanic representative in Congress, especially being a majority-minority state," Taylor said in an interview, meaning that the sum of all non-Anglo residents is larger than the Anglo population. "We need to make sure all people of the state are represented."

   Associated Press, June 1, 2001

   What has James Taylor implied?

7. Michael Hauptman is a civil libertarian, period. . . . Hauptman defends those he wants to defend, no matter what anyone else thinks. He has been the lawyer for witch doctors, the homeless, the outspoken civil rights loner Hosea Williams, and, as described by the *Atlanta Constitution*, "a parade of candidates for the electric chair."

   Hauptman puts it this way: "I've represented all kinds of bad people . . . . I even once represented an insurance company and a bank."

   Nat Hentoff, *Free Speech for Me—But Not for Thee*

   What can we infer from Hauptman's remarks?

8. Give a recent example where you inferred a claim. Were you justified?

Summary Most arguments we encounter are flawed. But they aren't necessarily bad. They can often be repaired by adding claims that are common knowledge.

By reflecting on the conditions for us to enter into a rational discussion, we can formulate a guide for how to repair apparently defective arguments. We assume the other person is knowledgeable about the subject, is able and willing to reason well, and is not lying. So we add premises that make the argument stronger or valid and that are plausible to us and to the other person.

Of course, not everyone can reason well or wishes to reason well. And lots of arguments can't be repaired, which is something we can discover when we try to add premises. That, too, helps us evaluate arguments.

Our actions, as well as our words, can lead people to think we believe some claims. People imply claims by their actions or words, and others infer claims from them.

Key Words		
	unstated premise	suspend judgment
	unstated conclusion	unrepairable argument
	The Principle of Rational Discussion	irrelevant premise
	mark of irrationality	inferring
	The Guide to Repairing Arguments	implying

Further Study To follow up on the idea that rational discussion is necessary for a democracy, you can read Plato's *Gorgias* in which Socrates castigates those who would convince without good arguments.

An article about the moral and the utilitarian values of reasoning well, especially for how that may or may not be a "Western" value, is "East and West: The Reach of Reason," by Amartya Sen in the *New York Review of Books*, vol. XLVII, no. 12 (July 20, 2000).

A fuller discussion of rationality, both in terms of arguments and inferring beliefs from actions, can be found in "Rationality" in my book *Prescriptive Reasoning*.

Writing Lesson 5

Write an argument in outline form either for or against the following:

No one should receive financial aid his or her first semester at this school.

- Just list the premises and the conclusion. You can include definitions, too. Nothing more.
- Your argument should be at most one page long.
- Check whether your instructor has chosen a different topic for this assignment.

Remember that with a prescriptive conclusion you need at least one prescriptive premise that establishes the standard.

To give you a better idea of what you're expected to do, I've included here Manuel's argument on a different issue.

Manuel Luis Andrade y Castillo de Pocas
Critical Thinking
Section 2
Writing Lesson 5

Issue: The chance of contracting AIDS through sexual contact can be significantly reduced by using condoms.

Definition: "AIDS" means "Acquired Immunodeficiency Syndrome"
"significantly reduced" means by more than 50%
"using condoms" means using a condom in sexual intercourse rather than having unprotected sex

Premises:

- AIDS can only be contracted by exchanging blood or semen. *A*
- In unprotected sex there is a chance of exchanging blood or semen.
- Condoms are better than 90% effective in stopping blood and semen.*
- 90% is bigger than 50%.
- AIDS has never been known to have been contracted from sharing food, using a dirty toilet seat, from touching, or from breathing in the same room with someone who has AIDS. *B*
- If you want to avoid contracting AIDS you should use a condom. *C*

Conclusion: The chance of contracting AIDS through sexual contact can be significantly reduced by using condoms.

*I'm not sure of the exact figure, but I know it's bigger than 90%.

Good. Your argument is indeed valid. But it could easily be better. You don't need "only" in A, which is what makes me uneasy in accepting that claim. And without a reference to medical literature, I'm not going to accept B. But you don't need it. You can delete it and your argument is just as good.

And the last claim, C, is really irrelevant—delete it. This isn't an editorial: You're not trying to convince someone to do something; you're trying to convince them an objective claim is true.

Cartoon Writing Lesson B

Here's a chance to reason as you might in your everyday life, drawing conclusions from what you see.

For each cartoon, write the best argument you can that has as its conclusion the claim that accompanies the cartoon. List only the premises and conclusion. If you believe there is no good argument, explain why by describing a likely way the conclusion could be false even if everything we see in the cartoon is true. Refer back to Cartoon Writing Lesson A on p. 56 for suggestions about how to do this lesson.

Remember that with subjective claims, you'll need to have a premise that links actions to thoughts, beliefs, or feelings.

To give you a better idea of what you're expected to do, I've included Maria's writing lesson for a different cartoon.

Name Maria Schwartz Rodriguez Section 6

In New Mexico, cars are required to have only one license plate, in the rear.

1. Some of the cars don't have license plates in the front.
2. All of the cars have license plates in the back.
3. So probably the rear license plate is required, and no front plate is required in New Mexico since it is pretty unlikely all the front plates just fell off.

You've only proved part of the conclusion with your argument. How do you know these are New Mexico cars?

First, this is a restaurant parking lot, so these are normal cars, not cars for sale in a used car lot where, of course, many of them wouldn't have license plates.

Second, the restaurant is advertising New Mexico's best chile, and so it must be in New Mexico. It would be absurd for a restaurant to advertise like that in another state.

Third, if the restaurant is in New Mexico, it's likely that most of the cars there are from New Mexico—not certain, but likely.

Now you can use the argument you gave to get the conclusion. But you could have gotten a much stronger argument using the following general claim:

> *It would be extremely unlikely for <u>three</u> drivers at the same time and place to have lost their front plates <u>and</u> to risk a serious penalty for not having a front plate.*

Overall, this is pretty good. You're only using what you see, not making up a story. But you're not using enough of what you see—remember to prove all of the conclusion. Also, it's really good how you put in the glue, the last part of #3 that shows how you got from what you saw to the conclusion. But #3 is two claims, not one, as you recognized by using that indicator word "since." Be sure to list each claim separately so you can judge the plausibility of each and see how it links to the others.

1.

These girls are friends.

2.

Dr. E shaved his beard.

3.

The dog is trying to catch the Frisbee.

4.

The mother is scolding her child for breaking the flower pot.

5. 

Spot is afraid of being punished.

6. 

Suzy hit Puff with the car.

6 Counterarguments

A. Raising Objections

Everyone should ride a bicycle for transportation. *1*
Cars are expensive to buy and maintain and cause a lot of pollution. *2*
A bicycle is better for your health and also for everyone else's. *3*
Bicycles also look better than cars. *4*

When asked to evaluate this argument, most students think it's good—to which I respond, "Why do you drive a car?" Remember, it's irrational to say that an argument is good and then deny its conclusion.

Some students, rather than evaluating the argument directly, raise objections:

Bicycles aren't good for people who are handicapped or weak. *5*
Bikes aren't useful for carrying groceries or lots of kids. *6*

Then they say that the argument is bad. They have good reason not to believe the conclusion, *1*.

Raising objections is a standard way to show that an argument is bad. In doing so, we're making another argument that either calls into question one of the premises or shows that an unstated premise is dubious, or illustrates why the argument is weak.

In this example, *5* shows that *3* is dubious, while *6* makes us doubt the unstated premise needed to make the argument good: "Anything that's cheaper to buy and maintain than a car, causes less pollution than a car, and is better for your health and everyone else's should be the form of transportation for everyone." (We might as well ignore *4* since it's subjective and there's no sense to debate it.)

Raising objections is common.

Dick: Zoe, we ought to get another dog.
Zoe: What's wrong with Spot?
Dick: Oh, no, I mean to keep Spot company.
Zoe: Spot has us. He doesn't need company.
Dick: But we're gone a lot. And he's always escaping from the yard 'cause he's lonely. And we don't give him enough time. He should be out running around more.
Zoe: But think of all the work! We'll have to feed the new dog. And think of all the time necessary to train it.
Dick: I'll train him. We can feed him at the same time as Spot, and dog food is cheap. It won't cost much.

Dick is trying to convince Zoe to believe "We should get another dog." But he has to answer her objections.

We ought to get another dog.
    (*objection*) We already have Spot.
The other dog will keep Spot company.
    (*objection*) Spot already has us for company.
We're gone a lot. (*answer*)
He's always escaping from the yard. (*answer*)
He's lonely. (*answer*)
We don't give him enough time. (*answer*)
He should be out running around more. (*answer*)
    (*objection*) It will be a lot of work to have a new dog.
    (*objection*) We'll have to feed the new dog.
    (*objection*) It will take a lot of time to train the new dog.
Dick will train him. (*answer*)
We can feed him at the same time as Spot. (*answer*)
Dog food is cheap. (*answer*)

Argument. Counterargument. Counter-counterargument. This is how we reason every day. Objections are raised: someone puts forward a claim that, if true, makes one of our claims false or at least doubtful. We then have to answer that challenge to sustain our argument. *Knocking off an objection is a mini-argument within your argument—if it's not a good (though brief) argument, it won't do the job.*

But reasoning well isn't about winning. You could say, "I hadn't thought of that. I guess you're right." Or, "I don't know, I'll have to think about that."

In making an argument of your own, you'll want to make it strong. You might think you have a great one. All the premises seem obvious, and they glue together to get the conclusion. But if you imagine someone objecting, you can see how to give better support for doubtful premises. And answering counterarguments in your own writing allows the reader to see you haven't ignored obvious objections. All you have to do, as in the earlier writing lessons, is make a list of the pros and cons. Then either answer the other side, or change your argument.

B. Refuting an Argument

1. Refuting directly

It's useless to kill flies. The ones you kill will be the slowest, because the fast flies will evade you.
So you will be killing off the slowest ones and the fastest ones will remain. Over time, then, the genes for being fast will predominate.
Then with super-fast flies, it will be impossible to kill them anyway. So it's useless to kill flies.

Zoe can't let it pass. But how do you refute an argument?

Zoe might object to one of the premises, saying Dick won't be killing the slowest but only the ones that happen to come into their house.

Or she could agree with the premises but note that "over time" could be thousands of years, so the conclusion doesn't follow.

Or she could attack the conclusion, saying that it's not useless to kill flies because she does it all the time and it keeps their home clean.

All the ways that we can show an argument is unrepairable are useful in refuting an argument. We pick out three as fundamental.

> ***Direct ways of refuting an argument***
> - Show that at least one of the premises is dubious.
> - Give an example to show that the argument isn't valid or strong.
> - Show that the conclusion is false.

2. Refuting indirectly

Sometimes we can't point to any one premise that's false or dubious, but we know there's something wrong with the premises. They might get the conclusion that's argued for, but they get a lot more—so much more that we can see the premises are inconsistent or lead to an absurdity.

Example 1 Tom: Everyone in the U.S. should have to speak English. Everyone's got to talk the same, so we can communicate easily. And it'll unify the country.

Lee: Sure. But I have real trouble understanding people from New York. So we should make everyone speak just like me, from Iowa.

Analysis Lee isn't directly refuting Tom's argument. Rather, starting with the same premises as Tom, he gets a claim that he knows Tom won't accept.

> ***Reducing to the absurd*** To reduce to the absurd is to show that at least one of several claims is false or dubious, or collectively they are unacceptable, by drawing a false or unwanted conclusion from them.

If a valid argument has a false conclusion, one of the premises is false. If a strong argument has a false conclusion, one of the premises is very likely false. If the conclusion is absurd, the premises aren't what you want. But *you have to be sure the argument you use to get the false or absurd conclusion is really strong or valid and doesn't use any other dubious claims*. Only then is there good reason to believe that there's a problem with the original collection of claims.

Example 2 Zoe: I can't believe you're eating those *Baken-ets* fried pork skins. I thought you wanted to lose weight.

Dick: Right, and the package says on the front in big letters "0 g Net Carbs."

Analysis Dick believes he's refuted the unstated claim that fried pork skins are fattening. But his refutation rests on an assumption that's false: if a food has no carbohydrates, it's not fattening.

One particular form of reducing to the absurd is ***refuting by analogy***: use the crucial premises in a different situation to get an absurd conclusion.

Example 3

LOOK, YOUR ARGUMENT AGAINST KILLING FLIES IS BAD. I COULD USE THE SAME ARGUMENT AGAINST KILLING BACTERIA, OR AGAINST KILLING CHICKENS FOR DINNER FROM AUNT MARGERY'S HENHOUSE. THOSE CONCLUSIONS WOULD BE ABSURD.
BUZZ BUZZ

Example 4 You say we should leave you alone and let you cockfight because it's a tradition of your New Mexican Hispanic culture? Well, arranged marriages for 12-year-old girls were a tradition in some parts of this country. So was wife beating. We stopped those because, like cockfighting, they're cruel.

Analysis This refutation by analogy goes further by suggesting a general claim that would sanction the opposite of the conclusion: we should stop traditions that are cruel.

3. Attempts to refute that are bad arguments

Some attempts to refute are just bad arguments.

In Chapter 4 we looked at ***phony refutations***. They're bad versions of reducing to the absurd: here's the conclusion, here's what the speaker believes, they're contradictory, so the argument is bad.

Then there's ***ridicule***.

Example 5 Dr. E: I hear that your department elected a woman as chairman.

Prof. Zzzyzzx: Jah, jah, dat is right. Und now ve is trying to decide vot ve should be calling her—"chairman" or "chairvoman" or "chairperson."

Dr. E: "Chairperson"? Why not use a neutral term that's really appropriate for the position, like "chaircreature"?

Analysis No argument has been given for why the title "chairman" shouldn't be replaced by "chairperson," though Dr. E thinks he's shown the idea is absurd.

In rational discussion, ridicule is a worthless device: it ends arguments, belittles the other person, and makes enemies. In theory there's a big difference between reducing to the absurd and ridicule. But in practice it's difficult to distinguish them. Often, not enough of an argument is given to see how the absurd conclusion follows, so it sounds like ridicule. *If someone wants us to see his or her comments as an argument, it's his or her responsibility to make that clear*. Otherwise, let's classify it as ridicule.

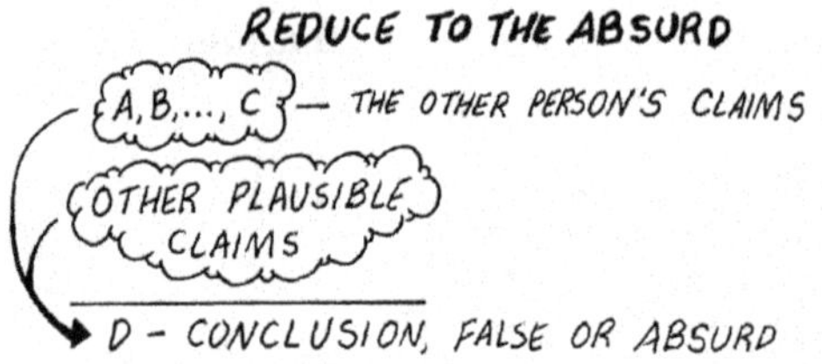

When judging whether something is ridicule, an attempt to reduce to the absurd, or an unwillingness to acknowledge distinctions because they're a bit vague, think less of rejecting what the other person says and more of taking his or her comments as a challenge to make your own ideas clearer.

The worst of the bad ways to refute is to attack an argument the other person didn't even say. When someone makes a claim, and the other person tries to refute it by putting words in that person's mouth, that's a ***strawman*** (because it's easier to knock down). It often shows up in political discourse:

The incumbent congressman is against gun control. Clearly, he doesn't care about violence on the streets.

Excuse me? What's the connection here? The congressman never said he wasn't against violence in the streets.

The only reasonable response to a strawman is to say calmly that that isn't what you said:

Tom: Unless we allow the logging of old-growth forests in this county, we'll lose the timber industry and these towns will die.
Dick: So you're saying that you don't care what happens to the spotted owl and to our rivers and the water we drink?
Tom: I said nothing of the sort. You've misrepresented my position.

Note that Tom didn't say, "You've misrepresented my position, you jerk." Let's keep alive some hope of reasoned discussion.

Summary When we make an argument, we should be prepared to defend it. Think ahead and imagine what objections might be raised, then answer them.

There are direct ways to refute an argument: show a premise is false, show the argument isn't valid or strong, or show the conclusion is false.

We can also refute an argument by showing that a false or absurd conclusion follows from the premises. To do that, we must be sure that any other claims we use to get the false or absurd conclusion are plausible and that the argument we give is strong or valid. But remember, refuting an argument does not show that the conclusion is false.

There are bad ways to reason that imitate reducing to the absurd: phony refutation and ridicule. And then there's a strawman— which is just putting words in someone's mouth.

Key Words

direct ways of refuting
reducing to the absurd
refuting by analogy
ridicule
strawman

Exercises for Chapter 6

1. In my first comment after the argument about bicycling on p. 114, I challenge the student. Have I shown the argument is bad? Explain.
2. What is a counterargument?
3. If you show an argument is bad, what have you shown about its conclusion?
4. How should you respond to a counterargument?
5. a. Why are counterarguments useful in your own writing?

b. Give three phrases you can use to introduce objections to your own argument in your writing.

6. Find an article in which the author answers a counterargument.

7. Find an article where a comment posted after it is an attempt to refute the conclusion.

8. Explain the role of each claim in the following discussion.

Zoe: I think sex is the answer to almost everyone's problems.
Dick: How can you say that?
Zoe: It takes away your tension, right?
Dick: Not if you're involved with someone you don't like.
Zoe: Well, anyway, it makes you feel better.
Dick: Not if it's against your morals. Anyway, heroin makes you feel good, too.
Zoe: But it's healthy and natural, just like eating and drinking.
Dick: Sure, and you can catch terrible diseases. Sex should be confined to marriage.
Zoe: Is that a proposal?

9. Write a short argument against drinking alcohol that acknowledges why some people want to drink alcohol.

10. If you can start with a collection of claims and can make a valid or strong argument with a false conclusion, what does that tell you? Explain.

11. What is reducing to the absurd?

12. Which of the ways of refuting an argument is best? Why?

13. What's the difference between ridicule and reducing to the absurd?

14. Why isn't a phony refutation really a refutation of an argument?

15. a. What is a strawman?
    b. Bring in an example.

Evaluate the attempts to refute arguments in Exercises 16–31 by answering the following questions:

Method of refutation?
Is the refutation a good argument? (Explain)

16. Lee: I'm going to vote for that initiative to eliminate discrimination against transgender people in hiring and getting places to live. They should be treated like everyone else. They deserve a chance to get jobs and homes.
    Tom: Are you kidding? I'm voting against it. You should, too. They don't deserve any preference over the rest of us.

17. Some say government healthcare would compete unfairly with private companies and amount to socialism. But the same people who object passionately to "socialized health care" don't block their 911 service, or disconnect themselves from socialized sewers, or avoid interstate highways, or reject Medicare when they're old.

18. Zoe: You should eat less red meat. Red meat has lots of cholesterol, which blocks up the arteries and leads to an increased risk of heart disease.

    Dick: Mankind has been eating red meat since the dawn of time, and we have still survived as a species. If we stopped eating everything that was bad for us, we would be left with nothing to consume but small, white, tasteless pills, which would later be discovered to cause a new type of deadly cancer.

19. Look, I agree with you. We have too much violence in the streets, too many drug pushers, too little respect for the law. But our prisons are overflowing, and that's costing us a fortune. So we've got to reduce our prison population. Yet you say we should be even tougher on crime. The answer is simple: institute a lottery among all convicted felons in jail and execute one of them every month—no appeals. That'll instill a real fear of being arrested. And it'd be fair, too.

20. Mary Ellen: Yes, yes, Dr. E. Raw food is best for you. I eat only raw food. Cooking destroys all the goodness in the food.

    Dr. E: There goes 2,000,000 years of evolution.

21. Zoe: I can't believe you're eating all those spicy almonds. I thought you were trying to lose weight. They're really fattening.

    Dick: Not if you don't chew them.

22. (Complete letter to the editor from Vern Raburn, CEO, Eclipse Aviation, in *Crosswinds Weekly*, July 11, 2002, in response to an article "Eclipse Aviation's Money Troubles.")

    Should you decide you are interested in supplying your readers with something other than lies and bullshit, I suggest you spend more time fact checking for yourself. This will help prevent you from the embarrassment of propagating others' inaccuracies.

23. Columnist George Will wrote in *Newsweek* last year that a dime placed on the edge of a 4-foot by 6-foot dinner table would represent the relative portion of the refuge that would be opened for drilling.

    I could use Will's analogy to compare the size of a bullet through your heart with the size of your body and draw the mistaken conclusion that very little damage would result. Unfortunately for the refuge, the area proposed for drilling has been described (by the Republican Reagan administration, no less) as its "biological heart."

    "America's Arctic National Wildlife Refuge" by N. K. Whiton
    Albuquerque Tribune, May 7, 2003

24. Maria: You say that life begins at conception, right?

    Tom: Yes. Suzy and I believe that.

    Maria: So a person conceived in the U.S. should be a citizen—that's where his or her life began. So an Iranian mullah whose mother was in the U.S. from the whole time between eleven and seven months before he was born should be able to claim citizenship in the U.S., since he was surely conceived while she was here. But you're dead set against letting more people who were born and raised outside the U.S. into the country. So the solution is that we should make sure that all women coming to the U.S. don't have sex while they're here.

25. Maria: Really, it was Einstein's wife who was the great genius. She was the one who had the ideas that went into those early papers "he" wrote about relativity. They were working together. But he got the honors because he was a man. And she had the child and had to keep the house.
    Harry: Look, there weren't two geniuses like Einstein. That's beyond probability. And after those earlier papers, he continued to make incredible scientific breakthroughs. He would have been considered one of the greatest minds of all time for just the work that came after those early papers, while his wife never did anything scientifically important again.
    Maria: That was because she was keeping house, 'till that chauvinist pig divorced her.
    Harry: I don't doubt that she had some input into those early works, maybe even did equal work with him at the beginning. But it was Einstein who saw the ideas through and made them real to people and who continued to do great work. It wasn't his wife.

26. I have heard people talk of the "scientific" extermination of the Jews in Germany. There was nothing scientific about it. It was only thorough. There was no question of making observations and then checking them in order to determine something.

    Richard Feynman, *The Meaning of It All*

27. Tom: I'm going to the animal shelter to adopt a big dog, like a German shepherd.
    Maria: But your place is too small.
    Tom: I don't like small dogs. You can get more exercise with a big dog.
    Maria: Why don't you get a pony then? I'm sure you'd get into great shape with that.

28. Lee: Sure Tom gets it wrong sometimes, and he can be really hardheaded. But you've got to admire how he's consistent in his opinions.
    Maria: So was Hitler.

29. Harry: There's no reason to think the Nazca lines were made by aliens. The art is similar to Nazca pottery. Wooden posts have been found next to the lines, showing they used ground-based techniques to draw them.
    Wanda: Since no one knows for sure whether aliens exist, it's really up to the individual to decide whether they do or not.

30. Suzy: Suicide and euthanasia are wrong because no person should play God. That's taking over the right to decide life and death, which belongs only to God.
    Manuel: But then I shouldn't push someone out of the way if a car is coming fast at her. I'd be taking over the right to decide life and death, playing God like you say.

31. Wanda: I want to have a baby. They're so cute, so small and cuddly. And I could dress it up with those adorable outfits they have. And they love you totally, without complaining.
    Maria: Get a chihuahua instead. It'll be cheaper and you won't have to save for its college education.

Refute the following arguments. Say whether you are showing a premise is dubious, attacking an unstated premise, showing the argument is weak, or reducing to the absurd.

32. Mrs. Wang is a great marriage therapist. She really cares about her clients.

33. Multiple-choice examinations are the best way to examine students. The grading is completely objective. Students know how to prepare for them. And professors don't have to spend a lot of time grading them.

34. You should keep a gun in your home. This is a dangerous neighborhood, and a gun is the best protection you can get. Think of what could happen if someone broke in.

35. Single parents should get special assistance from the government. After all, a two-parent family has two paychecks and twice the attention to give to their children. Some single-parent families end up having to use the welfare system because they can't afford child care. Therefore, the government should give free child care to single-parent families.

36. There should be more extra credit available in this course because it's a hard course.

37. Evaluate the following argument. Indicate what argument is being refuted and how each part of it is challenged. Say whether the refutation is good or not.

    The State's primary claim is that death is a necessary punishment because it prevents the commission of capital crimes more effectively than any less severe punishment. The first part of this claim is that the infliction of death is necessary to stop the individuals executed from committing further crimes. The sufficient answer to this is that if a criminal convicted of a capital crime poses a danger to society, effective administration of the State's pardon and parole laws can delay or deny his release from prison, and techniques of isolation can eliminate or minimize the danger while he remains confined. The more significant argument is that the threat of death prevents the commission of capital crimes because it deters potential criminals who would not be deterred by the threat of imprisonment. The argument is not based upon evidence that the threat of death is a superior deterrent. Indeed, as my Brother [Justice] Marshall establishes, the available evidence uniformly indicates, although it does not conclusively prove, that the threat of death has no greater deterrent effect than the threat of imprisonment.

    From Justice Brennan's opinion in *Furman v. Georgia,* 408 U.S. (1972)

Writing Lesson 6

You've learned about filling in unstated premises, about indicator words, about what counts as a plausible premise, and how to evaluate the strength or validity of an argument. And now you know that you should include the other side when arguing for a controversial claim. Argument, counterargument, counter-counterargument. Remember that to knock off an objection you need a mini-argument that will be judged by the same standards as any argument.

Write an argument either for or against the following:

Peer-to-peer downloading of songs on the internet is theft.

Check whether your instructor has chosen a different topic for this assignment.

In order to improve your new skills, this assignment has an extra step.

First page: List just the premises and conclusion. Nothing more.

Second page: Write the argument as an essay with indicator words.

We should be able to see at a glance from the list of premises whether your argument is good. The essay form should read just as clearly, if you use indicator words well. Remember, there should be no claims in the essay that aren't listed as premises.

> For this issue, and generally, there is often a trade-off:
>
> You can make your argument very strong but only at the expense of a rather dubious premise. Or you can make all your premises clearly true but leave out the dubious premise that's needed to make the argument strong. Given the choice, *opt for making the argument strong*. If it's weak, no one should accept the conclusion. And if it's weak because of an unstated premise, it's better to have that stated so it can be the object of debate.

Tom is so embarrassed about his last writing assignment that he's asked me not to include any more. But he's doing much better now, and I'm sure he'll do well in the course. Maria has done such a good job, though, that I'm including her essay on a different issue.

Maria Schwartz Rodriguez
Critical Thinking, Section 6
Writing Lesson 6

Issue: If a woman has a baby, then she should not work outside the home until the child reaches the age of four.

Definition: I take "work outside the home" to mean the woman takes a job that requires her to be away from her home and child at least 15 hours/week.

Premises:

1. Some women who have a child under the age of four are single mothers.

2. Some women who have a child under the age of four have husbands who do not earn enough money to support them and the child.

3. Some women who have children have careers from which they cannot take time without stopping them permanently or for a very long time from advancing.

4. Some women who have children do not have extended families or lots of friends.

5. A woman who has only her family can go stir-crazy if she is just with her child all the time.

6. A woman who is going stir-crazy, or who is too poor to provide for her child, or who is unsatisfied because her child is stopping her from getting along in her career will make a bad mother and companion for her child who is under four.

7. Mothers who are not with their children do not deserve to have children.

8. Whether they deserve to have them or not, they do have them.

9. Children who are not with their mothers will not develop proper intellectual and emotional skills.

10. What studies I have seen contradict that claim. Until reliable studies are produced for it, we should not accept it.

11. Day care can be dangerous.

12. The mother can screen day-care providers, and besides, a bitter, unsatisfied mother can be dangerous, too.

Conclusion: Under some circumstances it is acceptable for a woman to work outside the home when she has a child under the age of four.

Maria Schwartz Rodriguez
Critical Thinking, Section 6
Writing Lesson 6, page 2

Under some circumstances it is acceptable for a woman to work outside the home when she has a child under the age of four. After all, some women who have a child under the age of four are single mothers. And other women who have a child under the age of four have husbands who do not earn enough money to support them and the child. We can't forget women who have children and have careers from which they cannot take time without stopping them permanently or for a very long time from advancing. And think of the women who have children who do not have extended families or lots of friends. She could go stir-crazy if she is just with her child all the time. These women should be allowed to take work outside the home, for a woman who is going stir-crazy, or who is too poor to provide for her child, or who is unsatisfied because her child is stopping her from getting along in her career will make a bad mother and companion for her child who is under four.

But lots of people say that mothers who are not with their children do not deserve to have children. Well, whether they deserve to have them or not, they do have them.

But children who aren't with their mothers will not develop proper intellectual and emotional skills, it is said. Well, what studies I have seen contradict that claim. Until reliable studies are produced for it, we should not accept it.

One objection is that mothers who work outside the home often need day care.*A* And day care can be dangerous. But the mother can screen day-care providers, and besides, a bitter, unsatisfied mother can be dangerous, too.

So despite the obvious objections, we can see that under some circumstances it is acceptable for a woman to work outside the home when she has a child under the age of four.

This is very, very good. But there are a few points where you could improve:

You must include the definition in the essay, right after the first sentence giving the conclusion.

The grammar on premise (3) is not right.

You missed a possible response to (8) that the state or a church should take the child, and you'd need to come up with a response to that.

Some variety in putting in the objections might be good—for example, stating (9) as a question.

<u>We don't know what studies say that you've seen in</u> (10)—cite them or delete that part.

You left A out of your list of premises. And (12) is two premises, not one.

I see you avoided entirely the issue of welfare. Have you asked other students to look at your paper to see if they can think of objections or support because of that?

If you can write like this in your other courses, you'll do great all through college!

Review Chapters 1–6

Let's review what we've done.

We began by saying we would study attempts to convince. But that was too broad, so we restricted ourselves to convincing through arguments: collections of claims used to show a particular claim is true.

We said a claim was any declarative sentence used in such a way that it is true or false. But to be able to use that definition took practice. We learned to recognize sentences that pose as claims but are ambiguous or too vague for us to deliberate. Definitions are one way to clear up confusions, and we saw how to evaluate and make them. We differentiated among claims, noting that unstated standards could make a claim objective or subjective and that for most prescriptive claims some standard is needed.

We saw that there are three tests for an argument to be good. There should be good reasons to believe the premises, and we looked at criteria for when we're justified in accepting a claim that isn't supported by evidence. And the premises should be more plausible than the conclusion. But even if the premises are plausible, it might not be enough to give us good reason to believe the conclusion. The conclusion should follow from the premises. We decided that means the argument must be either valid or strong.

Often there's a gap between the premises and conclusion. We need a guide for when it's reasonable to repair an argument and when an argument is unrepairable. We based our guide on the assumptions we need in order to deliberate with someone. Along the way, we also saw various kinds of bad arguments that are common mistakes in reasoning.

Counterarguments are useful in our own writing because they help us see what assumptions we may have missed. Looking at counterarguments led us to consider the ways we can refute an argument: directly or by reducing to the absurd. We also saw bad ways to attempt to refute an argument.

You should now be able to analyze an attempt to convince.

Steps in evaluating an argument

- Is this an argument?
- What's the conclusion?
- What are the premises?
- Are any further premises needed?
- Is it valid? If not, where is it on the scale from strong to weak?
- Is it a good argument?
- Can it be repaired?

You'll get a lot more practice in analyzing arguments in the following chapters. The review exercises here are designed to make sure you know the definitions. You can't apply ideas you only half-remember.

> ***Steps in understanding a definition***
> - Know what the words mean and be able to recall the definition.
> - Know an example of the definition.
> - Know an example of something that doesn't fit the definition.
> - Practice classifying with the exercises.
> - Relate the definition to other concepts you've learned.

The last step is crucial in putting this material together. You may have learned the definition of "valid" and know how to recognize whether an argument is valid, but you don't really understand that definition until you know how it relates to other terms such as "strong argument" and "good argument."

Review Exercises for Chapters 1–6

1. What is an argument?
2. What is a claim?
3. a. What is an objective claim?
   b. Give an example of an objective claim.
   c. Give an example of a subjective claim.
4. Can a vague sentence be a claim? Explain.
5. a. What is a prescriptive claim?
   b. Give an example.
   c. What standard, if any, is presupposed by your example?
6. Is a definition a claim? Explain.
7. a. What is a persuasive definition?
   b. Give an example.
8. What is the drawing the line fallacy?
9. What three tests must an argument pass for it to be good?
10. a. What is a valid argument?
    b. Give an example of a valid argument that is good.
    c. Give an example of a valid argument that is bad.
11. a. What does it mean to say an argument is strong?
    b. Give an example of a strong argument that is good.
    c. Give an example of a strong argument that is bad.

12. Is every weak argument bad? Give an explanation or example.

13. How do you show an argument is weak?

14. If a strong argument has eight true premises and one false premise, should we accept the conclusion? Explain.

15. If an argument is bad, what does that tell us about its conclusion?

16. Is every valid or strong argument with true premises good? Give an explanation or example.

17. Should we always prefer valid arguments to strong arguments? Give an explanation or example.

18. What is our most reliable source of information about the world?

19. What three choices can we make about whether to believe a claim?

20. Give five criteria for accepting an unsupported claim.

21. Give two criteria for rejecting an unsupported claim.

22. When should we suspend judgment on a claim?

23. What does it mean to say that someone is arguing backwards?

24. What does it mean to say that someone is mistaking the person for the argument?

25. When are we justified in rejecting a claim because of who said it?

26. When are we justified in rejecting an argument because of who said it?

27. What is a phony refutation?

28. State the Principle of Rational Discussion.

29. What is the Mark of Irrationality?

30. State the Guide to Repairing Arguments.

31. List the circumstances in which we shouldn't bother to try to repair an argument.

32. What does it mean to say that you can't get "ought" from "is"?

33. a. What is an indicator word?
    b. Is an indicator word part of a claim?

34. Why is it a good idea to include a counterargument to an argument that you are writing?

35. What are the three ways of directly refuting an argument?

36. When you use the method of reducing to the absurd to refute an argument, does it show that one of the premises is false? Explain.

37. How does ridicule differ from reducing to the absurd?

The STRUCTURE of ARGUMENTS

7 Compound Claims

A. Consider the Alternatives

1. Compound claims and "or" claims

Some words can link two or more claims together to make a new, compound claim whose truth-value depends on the truth-values of the claims that are part of it. For example, suppose your neighbor says,

> "I'll return your lawn mower or I'll buy you a new one."

Has he promised to return your lawn mower? No. Has he promised to buy you a new lawn mower? No. He's promised to do one or the other. We have one claim, not two.

> ***Compound claim*** A compound claim is a claim that is composed of other claims but has to be viewed as just one claim.

In this chapter we'll look at different kinds of compound claims and see how to reason with them. To start, we can link two claims to make a compound with "or":

Either a Democrat will win the election or a Republican will win.
Either some birds don't fly or penguins aren't birds.
Columbus landed in South Carolina or on some island near there.

Each is just one claim, though made up of two claims. The last one, for instance, contains:

Columbus landed in South Carolina.
Columbus landed on some island near South Carolina.

Alternatives Alternatives are the claims that are part of an "or" claim.

Example 1 Dick or Zoe will go to the grocery to get eggs.
Analysis This is an "or" claim with alternatives "Dick will go to the grocery to get eggs" and "Zoe will go to the grocery to get eggs."

Example 2 Lee will pass his exam because he studied so hard.
Analysis This is not a compound claim: "Because" is an indicator word that tells us this is an argument. *Not every sentence with two or more claims is a compound claim.*

2. A contradictory of a claim

Because a compound claim is made up of other claims, it's easy to get confused about how to say it's false.

Contradictory of a claim A contradictory of a claim is a claim that must have the opposite truth-value.

Example 3 Spot is barking.
Analysis A contradictory of this is "Spot is not barking."

Example 4 Dick isn't a student.
Analysis A contradictory of this is "Dick is a student." A contradictory needn't have "not" in it.

Example 5 Maria got the van or Manuel won't go to school.
Analysis A contradictory of this is "Maria didn't get the van, and Manuel will go to school."

In order to discuss the forms of compound claims, let's use the letters A, B, C, D, . . . to stand for any claims, and "not A" to stand for a contradictory of a claim.

Contradictory of an* or *claim *A or B* has contradictory *not A and not B*.

Example 6 Tom or Suzy will pick up Manuel for class today.

Analysis One contradictory of this is "Tom will not pick up Manuel for class today, and Suzy will not pick up Manuel for class today." Another is, "Neither Tom nor Suzy will pick up Manuel for class today." We can use "neither . . . nor . . ." for a contradictory of an "or" claim.

Using "and" to join two claims creates a compound, but it's simpler to consider each claim independently.

Example 7 Pigs can catch colds, and they can pass colds on to humans.

Analysis When is this true? Exactly when both "Pigs can catch colds" is true and "Pigs can pass colds on to humans" is true. So in an argument we'd have to treat each of those claims separately anyway.

Example 8 Pigs can catch colds, but dogs can't.

Analysis This is true when both parts are true. So we might as well view each claim independently, as if the sentence were just a list of claims. "But" works the same as "and" in an argument—it's just a stylistic variation.

To contradict this example we have to say that one or the other of the parts is false: pigs can't catch colds, or dogs can catch colds.

Contradictory of an* and *claim *A and B* has contradictory *not A or not B*.

Example 9 Suzy and Dick both like cats.

Analysis We can rewrite this as an "and" claim, "Suzy likes cats and Dick likes cats." A contradictory is "Suzy doesn't like cats, or Dick doesn't like cats."

Exercises for Sections A.1 and A.2

1. What is a compound claim?
2. What do we call the parts of an "or" claim?
3. What is a contradictory of a claim?
4. How can you say a contradictory of "A or B"?
5. How can you say a contradictory of "A and B"?
6. Why can we take both A and B to be premises when someone says "A and B"?

For each of the following, write a contradictory of the claim. If it's an "or" claim, identify the alternatives.

7. Inflation will go up, or interest rates will go up.

8. Maria or Lee will pick up Manuel after classes.
9. Neither Maria nor Lee has a bicycle.
10. You're either for me or against me.
11. You'd better stop smoking in here or else!
12. AIDS cannot be contracted by touching or by breathing air in the same room as a person infected with AIDS.
13. Maria will go shopping, but Manuel will cook.
14. Zoe (to Dick): Will you take the trash out, or do I have to?
15. Inflation will be less than 3% this year.

3. Reasoning with "or" claims

Often we can determine that an argument is valid or weak by looking at the role a compound claim plays in it. For example,

> Either there is a wheelchair ramp at the school dance, or Manuel stayed home.
> But there isn't a wheelchair ramp at the school dance.
> Therefore, Manuel stayed home.

The argument is valid: there's no possible way for the premises to be true and the conclusion false at the same time.

This is just one example of lots of arguments that have the same form and are valid. In order to illustrate that form in a diagram, let's use an arrow (⟶) to stand for "therefore" and the symbol "+" to indicate an additional premise.

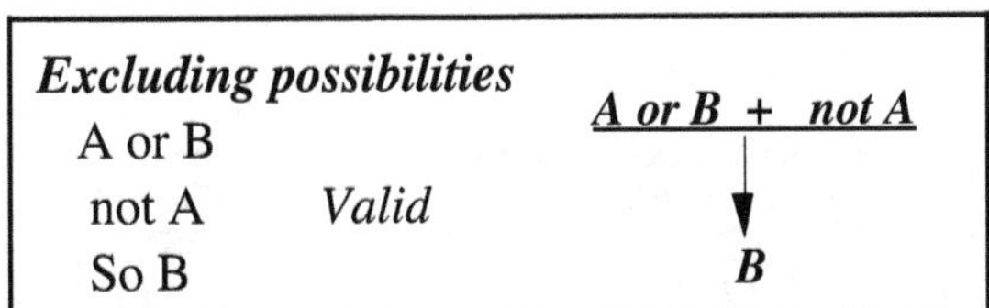

This form of argument is sometimes called the *disjunctive syllogism* or reasoning by *process of elimination*.

We also have the valid argument form: A or B, not B, therefore A. Or there may be more than two alternatives.

Example 10 Somebody's cat killed the bird that always sang outside. *1*
Either it was Sarah's cat or the neighbor's cat or some stray. *2*
Sarah says it wasn't her cat, *3* because hers was in all day. *4*
My neighbor says her cat never leaves the house. *5*
So it must have been a stray. *6*

Analysis From *3* and *4* we get:

Sarah's cat didn't kill the bird. *a*

(Lowercase letters mark claims that are added to an argument.) And from *5* we get:

My neighbor's cat didn't kill the bird. *b*

With *2* rewritten as "Either Sarah's cat killed the bird, or the neighbor's cat killed the bird, or some stray cat killed the bird," we now have:

A or B or C
not A, not B
Therefore C.

Example 11 Dr. E: Either these psychics are charlatans, or they are misguided fools, or there's some truth to their claims about ESP, or there's been a statistical fluctuation in the universe to cause these results.

Prof. Aloxmani: There's no statistical fluctuation that can account for these results, and I know both of the authors and they aren't charlatans.

Dr. E: So they're misguided fools or there is some truth to their claims about ESP.

Analysis The argument is valid because some of the possibilities given in Dr. E's first claim are eliminated. But even if Dr. E's first claim is true (that is, it really lists all the possibilities), all we get from this argument is another "or" claim—we've reduced the possibilities.

A or B or C or D
not A, not C
Therefore, B or D.

Arguments like this are valid, too.

4. False dilemmas

Zoe has made a valid argument but not a good one. She's posed a false dilemma. "You're either going to have to stop smoking those nasty expensive cigars, or we'll have to get rid of Spot" is false. Dick could respond that Zoe could get a cheaper phone plan that doesn't allow for unlimited data transfer. Excluding possibilities is a valid form of argument. But valid arguments need not be good. We get a bad argument when the "or" claim doesn't list all the possibilities.

> ***False dilemma*** A false dilemma is a bad use of excluding possibilities where the "or" claim is false or dubious. Sometimes just a dubious "or" claim by itself is called "a false dilemma."

Example 12 Society can choose high environmental quality but only at the cost of lower tourism or more tourism and commercialization at the expense of the ecosystem, but society must choose. It involves a tradeoff.

Robert Sexton, *Exploring Economics*

Analysis The alternatives are claimed to be mutually exclusive. But Costa Rica has created a lot of tourism by preserving almost 50% of its land in parks. When you see a *versus*-claim, think, "Is this a false dilemma?"

Example 13 The question is whether the Taliban are ready to help build a 21st century Afghanistan or whether they just want to kill people.

Secretary of Defense Robert Gates, *Bloomberg News*, January 23, 2010

Analysis This would be a false dilemma if "a 21st century Afghanistan" weren't too vague for this to be a claim.

To avoid false dilemmas, we have to imagine the possibilities.

Exercises for Section A

1. Give an "or" claim that you know is true, though you don't know which of the alternatives is true.
2. a. State the form of valid arguments called "excluding possibilities."
   b. Give two other forms of valid arguments that use "or" claims.

3. What is a false dilemma?

4. Give three examples of *either-or* sayings that if stated as claims would be false dilemmas. (Example: You're either part of the solution or you're part of the problem.)

5. Why is using a false dilemma so good at making people do what you want them to do? Is it a good way to convince?

6. Show that the argument about Manuel going to the dance on p. 136 is a false dilemma.

7. Sometimes a false dilemma is stated using an "if . . . then . . ." claim:

   If you don't stop smoking, you're going to die.
   (Either you stop smoking or you will die.)

   Mommy, if you don't take me to the circus, then you don't really love me.
   (Either you take me to the circus or you don't love me.)

   If you can't remember what you wanted to say, it's not important.
   (Either you remember what you want to say or it's not important.)

   Give two examples of false dilemmas stated using "if . . . then . . .".
   Trade with a classmate to rewrite them as "or" claims.

8. A particular form of false dilemma is the *perfectionist dilemma,* which assumes:

   Either the situation will be perfect if we do this, or we shouldn't do it.
   (*All or nothing at all.*)

   Dick: I'm voting for raising property taxes to pay for improvements to the schools.
   Tom: Don't be a fool. No matter how much money they pour into the schools, they'll never be first-rate.

   a. Give the unstated premise that shows that this argument is a false dilemma.
   b. Give an example of a perfectionist dilemma you've heard or read—or made.

Analyze the exercises below by answering these questions:

Argument? (yes or no)

Conclusion (if unstated, add it):

Premises:

Additional premises needed to make it valid or strong (if none, say so):

Classify (with the additional premises): valid strong ———————— weak

Good argument? (Choose one and give an explanation.)

- It's good (passes the three tests)
- It's valid or strong, but you don't know if the premises are true, so you can't say if it's good or bad.
- It's bad because it's unrepairable (state which of the reasons apply).

9. Tom: Look, either you'll vote for the Republican or the Democratic candidate for president.
   Lee: No way I'll vote for the Democrat.
   Tom: So you'll vote for the Republican.

10. Lee: Manuel and Tom went to the basketball game if they didn't go to the library.
 Maria: I know they're not at the library because I was just there.
 Lee: So they must have gone to the basketball game.

11. Tom: Both Lee and I think they should allow logging on Cedar Mountain. You do, too—don't you, Dick?
 Dick: Actually, no, . . .
 Tom: I didn't know you were one of those environmentalist freaks.

12. Dick: Somebody knocked over our neighbor's trash can last night. Either our neighbor hit it with her car again when she backed out, or a raccoon got into it, or Spot knocked it over.
 Zoe: Our neighbor didn't hit it with her car because she hasn't been out of her house since last Tuesday.
 Dick: It wasn't a raccoon because Spot didn't bark last night.
 Zoe: Spot! Bad dog! Stay out of the trash!

13. Zoe: We should get rid of Spot. He keeps chewing on everything in the house.
 Dick: But why does that mean we should get rid of him?
 Zoe: Because either we train him to stop chewing or we get rid of him. And we haven't been able to train him.
 Dick: But I love Spot. We can just make him live outdoors.
 (Evaluate what Zoe says as an argument. Consider Dick's answer in doing so.)

B. Conditionals

1. Conditionals and their contradictories

Suppose your instructor says to you:

> If you do well on the final exam, then I'll give you an A in this course.

This is *one* claim. If it shows up in an argument, we don't say one premise is "You do well on the final exam" and another is "I'll give you an A in this course." Rather *if* you do well, *then* your instructor will give you an A in this course. There is no promise to give you an A, only a *conditional* promise. If you do poorly on the final exam, your instructor is not obligated to give you an A.

> ***Conditional claim*** A conditional claim is a claim that is either in the form *If A, then B* or is equivalent to one in that form. The claim A is the ***antecedent*** and the claim B is the ***consequent***.

Example 14 If Spot ran away, then the gate was left open.

Analysis This is a conditional with antecedent "Spot ran away" and consequent "The gate was left open." The consequent need not happen later.

Example 15 I'll meet you at the cafeteria if they're not serving beef stroganoff.

Analysis Here the order of the parts is reversed. The antecedent is "They're not serving beef stroganoff," and the consequent is "I'll meet you at the cafeteria."

Example 16 Bring me an ice cream cone and I'll be happy.

Analysis There's no "if" and no "then," but this is a conditional because it's equivalent to "If you bring me an ice cream cone, then I'll be happy." Generally, we say that two claims are ***equivalent*** if the one is true exactly when the other is true.

Example 17 A mammal is an ungulate if it has hoofs.

Analysis This is not a conditional or compound. It's a definition, using "if" in place of "means that."

How do we form a contradictory of a conditional? Yesterday Manuel said, "If Maria called in sick today, then Lee had to go to work." To decide whether this is true, we ask whether Lee was obligated to work if Maria called in sick. He wasn't. She called in sick, and he didn't have to go to work.

Contradictory of a conditional *If A then B* has contradictory *A but not B*.

Zoe: I'm so worried. Spot got out of the yard. If he got out of the yard, then the dogcatcher got him, I'm sure.

Suzy: Don't worry. I saw Spot. He got out of the yard, but the dogcatcher didn't get him.

A contradictory of a conditional is not another conditional.

Sometimes, when we reason about how the world might be, we use a conditional with a false antecedent:

If cats had no fur, they would not give people allergies.

We could form a contradictory as for any conditional. But more commonly we use words like "although" or "even if":

Even if cats had no fur, they would still give people allergies.

"Even if" does *not* make a conditional. "Even if" is used in much the same way as "although" or "despite that."

Exercises for Section B.1

1. a. What is a conditional?
   b. Is a conditional a compound claim?
2. Make a conditional promise to your instructor that you believe you can keep.
3. What is the antecedent of a conditional?
4. Make up five examples of conditional claims that don't use the word "if" or don't use the word "then." At least one should have the consequent first and antecedent last. Exchange with a classmate to identify the antecedents and consequents.
5. What is a contradictory of a claim?
6. How can you make a contradictory of "If A, then B"?
7. a. Give a contradictory of:

   (*) If Suzy studies hard, then she'll pass Dr. E's class.

   Show that each of (b)–(d) is not a contradictory of (*) by giving a possibility where both it and (*) could be true or both false at the same time.

   b. If Suzy doesn't study hard, then she'll pass Dr. E's class.
   c. If Suzy doesn't study hard, then she won't pass Dr. E's class.
   d. If Suzy studies hard, then she won't pass Dr. E's class.
8. Make up two conditionals and two "or" claims. Exchange them with a classmate to write the contradictories.

Here are two examples of Tom's homework on conditionals.

> **Getting an A in critical thinking means that you studied hard.**
> *Conditional*? (yes or no) Yes.
> *Antecedent*: You get an A in critical thinking.
> *Consequent*: You studied hard.
> *Contradictory*: You got an A in critical thinking, but you didn't study hard.
> (or Even though you got an A in critical thinking, you didn't study hard.)
> *Good work.*
>
> **Spot loves Dick because Dick plays with him.**
> *Conditional*? (yes or no) No.
> *Antecedent*: Spot loves Dick. *No*
> *Consequent*: Dick plays with him. *No*
> *Contradictory*: Spot loves Dick but Dick doesn't play with him. *No*
> *You're right—it's not a conditional. The word "because" tells you it's an argument. But if it's not a conditional, then there's no antecedent and no consequent. And there can't be a contradictory of an argument.*

For each exercise below, fill in the following:

Conditional? (yes or no)
Antecedent:
Consequent:
Contradictory:

Remember that even though it might not be a conditional, it could still have a contradictory.

9. If Spot barks, then Puff will run away.
10. Lee will take care of Spot next weekend if Dick will help him with his English exam.
11. If you don't apologize, I'll never talk to you again.
12. Flo's mother won't go to the movie if she can't get someone to watch Flo.
13. Loving someone means you never throw dishes at them.
14. Since 2 times 2 is 4, and 2 times 4 is 8, I should be ahead $8, not $7.
15. Get me some cake mix at the store, and I'll bake a cake.
16. Tuna is good for you even though they say you shouldn't eat it more than once a week.
17. Tom: Being late for football practice will make the coach really mad.
18. If it's really true that if Dick takes Spot for a walk Dick will do the dishes, then Dick won't take Spot for a walk.
19. If Manuel went to the basketball game, then he either got a ride with Maria or he left early to wheel himself over there.
20. Drop the gun and no one will get hurt.

21. When there's a raccoon in the yard, you can be sure that Spot will bark.
22. Lee didn't go to the lecture because he knew Maria would take notes.
23. With good ratings, the series will be renewed.

2. Necessary and sufficient conditions

We can rewrite a conditional to get an equivalent conditional, where two claims are equivalent means that the one is true exactly when the other is true.

> ***Contrapositive*** The contrapositive of *If A, then B* is *If not B, then not A*. The contrapositive of a claim is equivalent to the original claim.

Example 18 If Zoe does the dishes, then Dick will walk Spot.
Contrapositive If Dick doesn't walk Spot, then Zoe didn't do the dishes.

Sometimes it's easier to understand a conditional via its contrapositive.

Example 19 If you get a speeding ticket, then a policeman stopped you.
Contrapositive If a policeman didn't stop you, then you didn't get a speeding ticket.

Another kind of equivalence comes with "only if"-claims.

Example 20 Dick will go into the army only if there is a draft.
Analysis This example is equivalent to "If there is no draft, then Dick will not go into the army."

Example 21 Harry will get into graduate school only if his grades place him in the top 10% of his graduating class.
Analysis This example is equivalent to "If Harry's grades don't place him in the top 10% of his graduating class, then he won't get into graduate school." It does not mean the same as "Harry will get into graduate school if his grades place him in the top 10% of his graduating class"—after all, he could do badly on the Graduate Record Exam.

A only if B is equivalent to *If not B, then not A*. But that's just the contrapositive of "If A, then B."

> ***"Only if"*-claims** *A only if B* is equivalent to *If A, then B*. "Only if" does not mean the same as "if."

So the following are equivalent:

- You'll get a speeding ticket only if you're going over the speed limit.
- If you're not going over the speed limit, then you won't get a speeding ticket.
- If you get a speeding ticket, then you went over the speed limit.

Conditionals are crucial for understanding what we mean by necessary or sufficient conditions. For example, what's necessary for getting a driver's license? Well, you've got to pass the driving exam. That is, if you don't pass the driving exam, you won't get a driver's license. There's no way you'll get a driver's license if you don't pass the driver's exam.

What's sufficient for getting money at the bank? Cashing a check there will do. That is, if you cash a check at the bank, then you'll get money at the bank.

A is ***necessary*** for B means that *If not A, then not B* is true.
A is ***sufficient*** for B means that *If A, then B* is true.

Example 22 Passing an eye test is necessary but not sufficient for getting a driver's license.
Analysis This is the same as saying: "If you don't pass an eye test, you can't get a driver's license" is true, but "If you pass an eye test, then you get a driver's license" is false.

Example 23 You can pass calculus only if you study hard.
Analysis This isn't the same as "If you study hard, you can pass calculus." Rather, studying hard is necessary, required to pass calculus; it's not sufficient. The example is equivalent to "If you pass calculus, then you studied hard." Confusing "only if " with "if " is confusing a necessary with a sufficient condition.

Example 24 Manuel: It's just wrong that Betty didn't make the basketball team.
Lee: Yeah. I watched the tryouts, and she was great. She hit a couple 3-pointers, and she can really jump.
Manuel: And the coach chose only girls who could jump well and hit 3-pointers.
Lee: She had everything you need to get on the team.
Analysis Lee thinks that jumping well and hitting 3-pointers are sufficient for getting on the team. But what Manuel said is that they're necessary. Lee's got it backwards. This kind of mistake is easy enough to avoid if you translate statements about necessary or sufficient conditions into conditionals.

Example 25 (Heard on National Public Radio)

Interviewer: So, will we continue to see home schooling in America?
Interviewee: As long as there are parents who love their kids and are willing to work hard, yes.

Analysis The last person has said that love and willingness to work hard are enough for home schooling to continue. That may be necessary, but it's certainly not sufficient. Also needed are laws allowing home schooling, a cultural climate encouraging it, and much more.

Exercises for Section B.2

1. State the contrapositive of:
   a. If Flo plays in the mud with Spot, then she has to take a bath.
   b. If Manuel doesn't get his wheelchair fixed by Wednesday, he can't attend class Thursday.
   c. If Maria goes with Manuel to the dance, then Lee will be home alone on Saturday.
2. For each (a)–(e) state which of the following are correct:

   (i) is necessary for (ii) | (i) is both necessary and sufficient for (ii)
   (i) is sufficient for (ii) | (i) is neither necessary nor sufficient for (ii)

   a. (i) Dr. E had his annual physical examination.
   (ii) Dr. E had an appointment with his physician.
   b. (i) Manuel opened a checking account. (ii) Manuel wrote his first check.
   c. (i) Zoe won $47 at blackjack. (ii) Zoe was gambling.
   d. (i) Maria is divorced. (ii) Maria has an ex-husband.
   e. (i) Suzy is over 21. (ii) Suzy can legally drink in this state.
3. We often say that one condition is necessary or sufficient for another, as in "Being over 16 is necessary for getting a driver's license." That means that the general conditional is true: "If you can get a driver's license, then you're over 16."
   For each of (a)–(d) state which of the following are correct:

   (i) is necessary for (ii) | (i) is both necessary and sufficient for (ii)
   (i) is sufficient for (ii) | (i) is neither necessary nor sufficient for (ii)

   a. (i) visiting City Hall (ii) leaving home
   b. (i) having the ability to fly (ii) being a bird
   c. (i) being a U.S. citizen (ii) being allowed to vote in the U.S.
   d. (i) losing at the lottery (ii) buying a lottery ticket
   e. (i) being hired (ii) being fired
4. What is a necessary condition for there to be a fire?
5. What is a sufficient condition for you to be happy? Is it necessary?
6. We know that the following are equivalent claims:
   - If Dick went to the movies, then he got home before 6 p.m.
   - If Dick didn't get home before 6 p.m., then he didn't go to the movies.
   - For Dick to go to the movies, it's necessary for him to get home before 6 p.m.

Rewrite each of (a)–(c) in two ways (using "necessary" or "sufficient" as appropriate)

a. Suzy will go with Tom to the library if he gets out of practice by 6.

b. For Dick to take Spot for a walk, it's necessary that it not be raining.

c. If Spot got out of the yard, then the gate was unlatched.

7. Rewrite each of the following as an "if . . . then . . ." claim if that is possible. If it's not possible, say so.

   a. Paying her library fines is required in order for Zoe to get a copy of her transcript.

   b. Dick: Since I'm on the way to the store anyway, I'll pick up some dog food.

   c. Suzy loves Puff even though he isn't housetrained.

   d. Of course, Suzy loves Tom despite the coach suspending him for a game.

   e. For Tom to get back on the team, he has to do 200 push-ups.

8. Rewrite each of the following as a conditional and as a statement of a necessary or sufficient condition.

   a. Maria will buy a new dress only if she gets a bonus this month.

   b. Flo will go over to play with Spot only if her mother lets her.

   c. Lee: Only if Tom is back on the team can we win this weekend.

9. We know that "A only if B" is equivalent to "if A, then B." So we have:

   A *if and only if* B means *if* A, *then* B; *and if* B, *then* A.

   We use "if and only if" to mean that each of two claims is both necessary and sufficient for the other. For example,

   Suzy will marry Tom if and only if he remains faithful to her until graduation.

   This means it's necessary for Tom to stay faithful to Suzy for her to marry him. But it's also sufficient for Tom to stay faithful to Suzy to ensure that she will marry him.

   Give an example of an "if and only if " claim from your own life that you know is true.

C. Valid and Weak Forms of Arguments with Conditionals

If Spot barks, then Dick will wake up.
Spot barked.
So Dick woke up.

That's valid. It's impossible for the premises to be true and the conclusion false.

If Suzy calls early, then Dick will wake up.
Suzy called early.
So Dick woke up.

This is valid, too.

These two arguments have the same *form*, as you can see in the diagram on the next page.

If Spot barks, *then* Dick will wake up.
A B

Spot barked.
A

So Dick woke up.
B

If Suzy calls early, *then* Dick will wake up.
A B

Suzy called early.
A

So Dick woke up.
B

Any argument of this form is valid—though not necessarily good since a premise could be implausible.

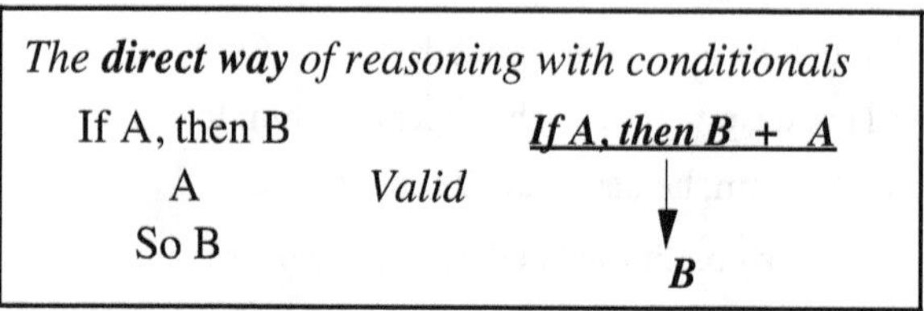

This way of reasoning is sometimes called *modus ponens*.

We can also reason:

If Spot barks, then Dick will wake up.
Dick didn't wake up.
So Spot didn't bark.

That's valid. After all, if Spot had barked, Dick would have woken up. Similarly:

If Suzy calls early, *then* Dick will wake up.
A B

Dick didn't wake up.
not B

So Suzy didn't call early.
not A

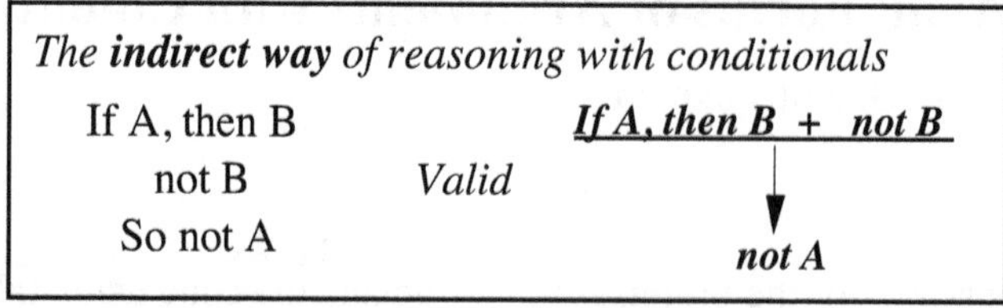

This way of reasoning is sometimes called *modus tollens*. Here, again, "not A" and "not B" are shorthand for "a contradictory of A" and "a contradictory of B." For example, this argument also uses the indirect way:

If Suzy doesn't call early, then Zoe won't go shopping.
Zoe went shopping.
So Suzy called early.

Recognizing this form can be hard if "not" occurs in the antecedent or consequent or if their order is reversed. For example, this uses the indirect way:

Zoe won't go shopping if Dick comes home early.
Zoe went shopping.
So Dick didn't come home early.

<u>Zoe won't go shopping</u> *if* <u>Dick comes home early</u>.
B A

<u>Zoe went shopping</u>.
not B

So <u>Dick didn't come home early</u>.
not A

To help us see how reasoning with conditionals involves possibilities, let's look at what Dick has to face every morning:

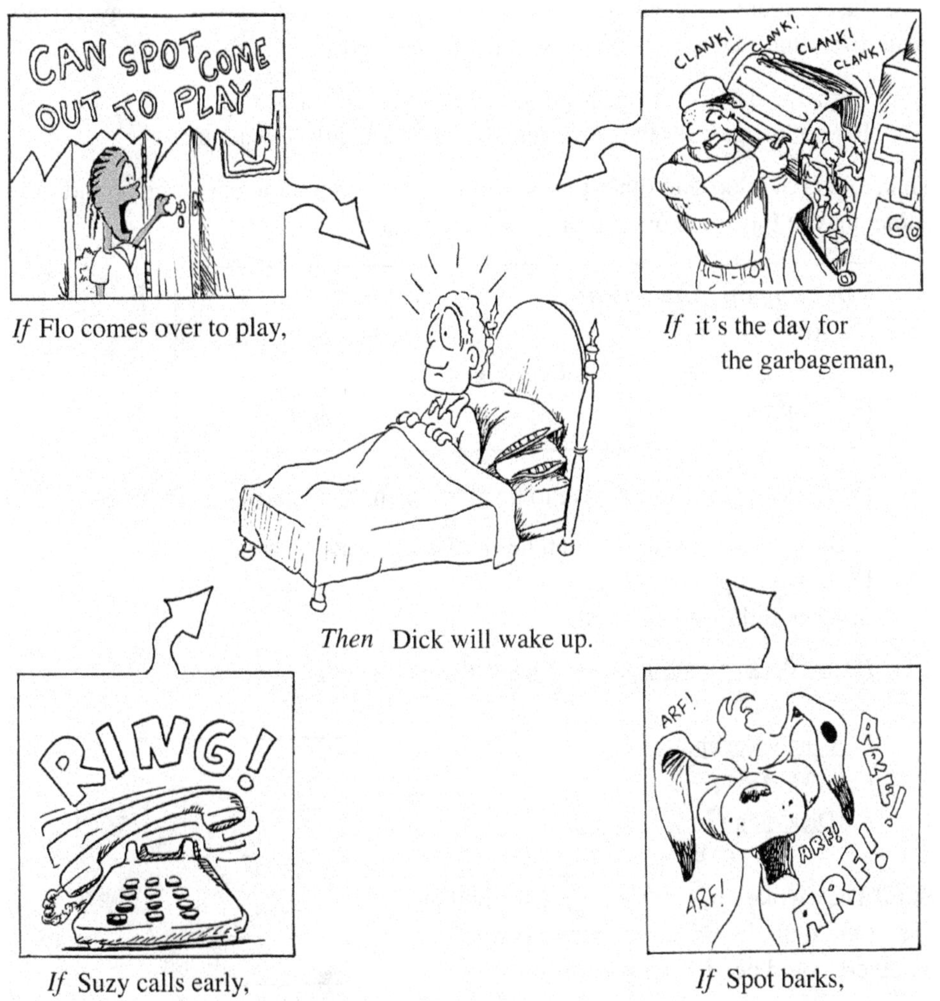

If Flo comes over to play,

If it's the day for the garbageman,

Then Dick will wake up.

If Suzy calls early,

If Spot barks,

There are many ways that Dick could be woken up. And if he doesn't wake up, then we know that none of those happened.

But it's wrong to reason that if Dick did wake up, then Spot barked. Maybe Suzy called early. Or maybe Flo came over to play. It's reasoning backwards, overlooking possibilities, to reason: If A, then B; B; so A. Yet it's easy to get confused and use this way of reasoning as if it were valid because it's so similar to the direct way of reasoning with conditionals.

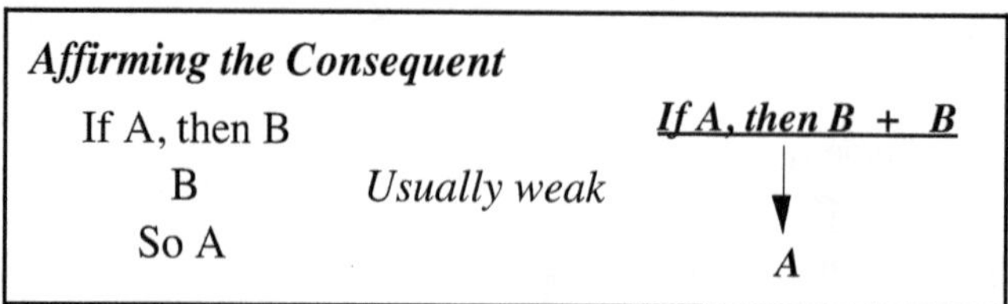
Affirming the Consequent

If A, then B
B
So A

Usually weak

If A, then B + B
↓
A

Just as there's a weak form that's easy to confuse with the direct way, there's a weak form that's easy to confuse with the indirect way.

If it's the day for the garbageman, then Dick will wake up.
It's not the day for the garbageman. So Dick didn't wake up.

This, too, is overlooking other possibilities. Even though the garbageman didn't come, maybe Flo came over to play, or Spot barked.

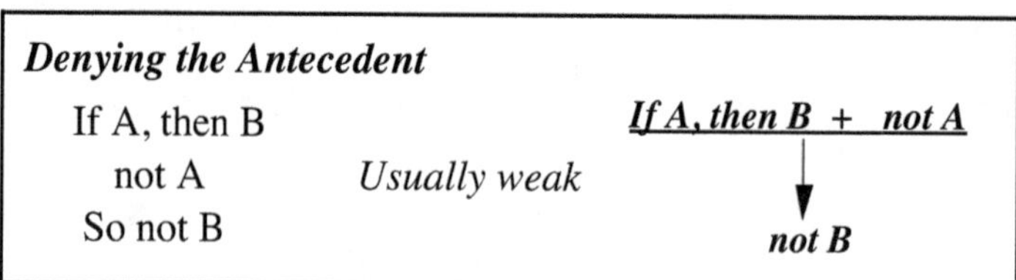
Denying the Antecedent

If A, then B
not A
So not B

Usually weak

If A, then B + not A
↓
not B

With this form, too, we have to be alert when "not" shows up in the conditional.

If Dick doesn't wake up, then he'll miss his class.
Dick woke up.
So Dick didn't miss his class.

If Dick doesn't wake up, *then* Dick will miss his class.
A — B

Dick did wake up.
not A

So Dick didn't miss his class. *not valid*
not B

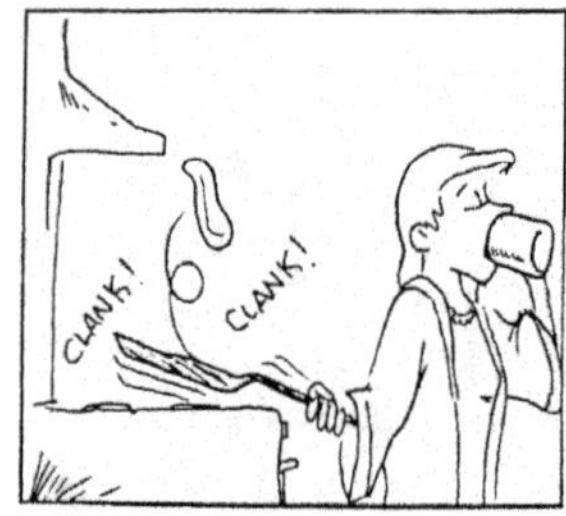

But if Dick woke up, can't we at least say that one of the four claims in the picture is true? No, there could be another possibility.

Here's a chart to summarize the valid and weak forms we've seen.

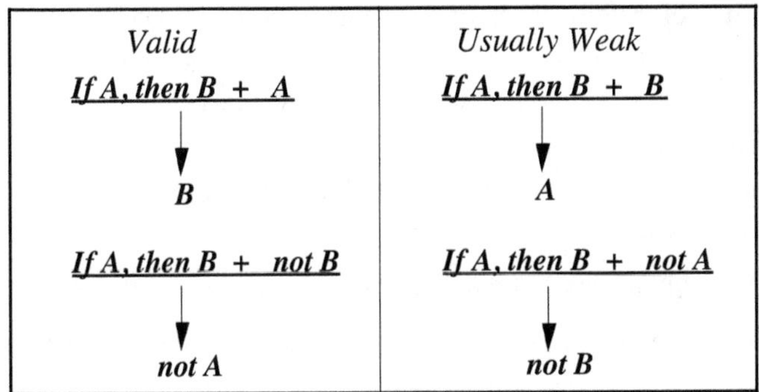

These weak forms of arguing with conditionals are confusions with valid forms, mistakes a good reasoner doesn't make. *When you see one, don't bother to repair the argument.* For example, suppose you hear:

Maria: If Suzy called early, then Dick woke up.
Lee: So Dick didn't wake up.

The obvious premise to add is "Suzy didn't call early," and probably Lee knows that. But it makes the argument weak. So Lee's argument is unrepairable.

Exercises for Section C

1.

If Dick and Zoe get another dog,

If Dick spends more time with Spot,

Then Spot will be happy!

If Dick buys Spot a juicy new bone,

If Spot finally learns how to catch field mice,

Assume that all the conditionals represented in the picture are true. Using them:

a. Give two examples of the direct way of reasoning with conditionals.
b. Give two examples of the indirect way of reasoning with conditionals.
c. Give two examples of affirming the consequent. Explain why each is weak in terms of other possibilities.
d. Give two examples of denying the antecedent. Explain why each is weak in terms of other possibilities.

2. Give an example (not from the text) of the direct way of reasoning with conditionals.
3. Give an example (not from the text) of the indirect way of reasoning with conditionals.
4. Give an example (not from the text) of affirming the consequent. Show that it is weak.
5. Give an example (not from the text) of denying the antecedent. Show that it is weak.

For Exercises 6–11, if there's a claim you can add to make the argument valid according to one of the forms we've studied, add it. If the argument is unrepairable, say so.

6. If Flo comes over early to play, then Spot will bark. So Spot barked.
7. Whenever Flo comes over to play, Spot barks. So Flo didn't come over to play.
8. Tom: Suzy will fail Dr. E's class for sure if she doesn't study hard.
   Harry: So she'll have to repeat that class, right?
9. Zoe will wash the dishes if Dick cooks. So Dick didn't cook.
10. Suzy: Dr. E won't give an exam today if he doesn't finish grading by this afternoon.
    Maria: So Dr. E will give an exam today.
11. If Flo does her homework, then she can watch TV. So Flo did her homework.
12. Here's another valid form of reasoning with conditionals:

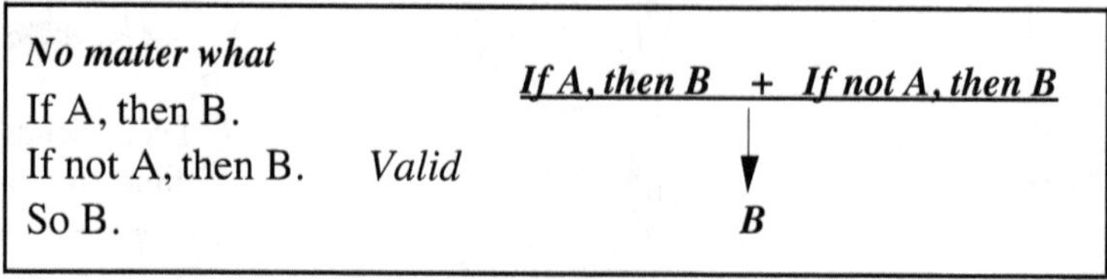

Dick: If I study for my math exam this weekend, we won't be able to have a good time at the beach.

Zoe: But if you don't study for your exam, you'll worry about it like you always do, and we won't be able to have a good time at the beach. So it looks like this weekend is shot.

Give another example of a no-matter-what argument.

D. Reasoning in a Chain and the Slippery Slope

Suppose we know that if Dick takes Spot for a walk, then Zoe will cook dinner. And if Zoe cooks dinner, then Dick will do the dishes. Then we can conclude that if Dick takes Spot for a walk, he'll do the dishes. We can set up a chain of reasoning, a chain of conditionals.

Here's another example:

If Manuel's wheelchair isn't fixed tomorrow, then he can't go to classes.
If Manuel can't go to classes, then Lee will have to take notes for him.
If Lee takes notes for Manuel, then Manuel will have to cook dinner.
So if Manuel's wheelchair isn't fixed tomorrow, then Manuel will have to cook dinner.

The conclusion is another conditional.

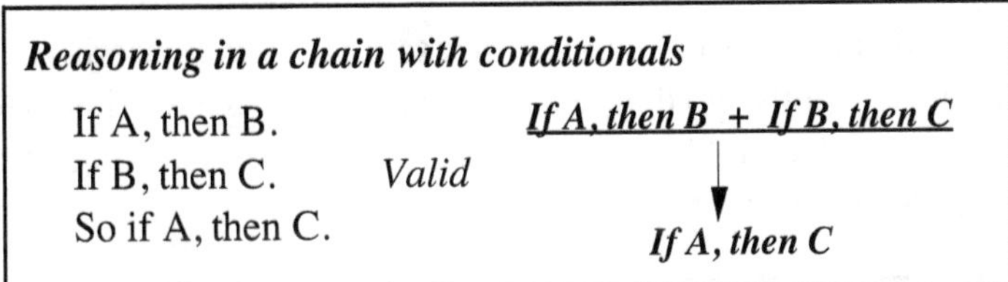
Reasoning in a chain with conditionals

If A, then B.
If B, then C.
So if A, then C.

Valid

Reasoning in a chain is important: We go by little steps. Then if A is true, we can conclude C.

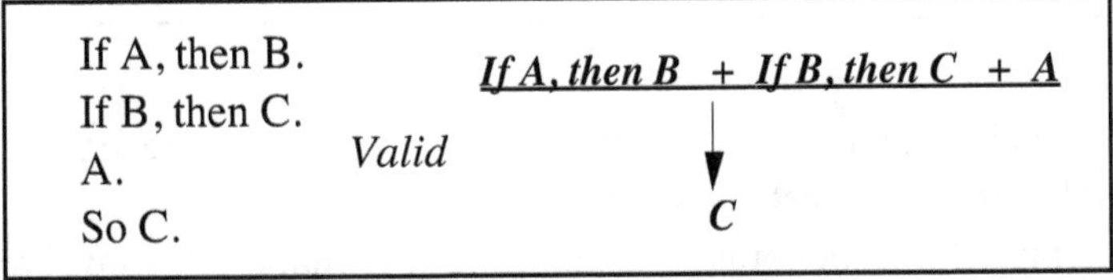
If A, then B.
If B, then C.
A.
So C.

Valid

But this valid form of argument can be used badly.

> When Tan began to date, her mother offered this hardly reassuring advice: "Don't ever let boy kiss you. You do, you can't stop. Then you have baby. You put baby in garbage can. Police find you, put you in jail, then you life over, better just kill youself."
>
> from a *New York Times* review of Amy Tan's memoir, *The Opposite of Fate*, November 23, 2003

This isn't a series of conditionals, but it's easy to rewrite it as one. Then it will be valid. But it's not a good argument. If you take the first step (accept the antecedent of the first conditional), the chain of conditionals forms a slippery slope for you to slide all the way to the conclusion. But you can stop the slide: just point out that one of the conditionals is dubious. The second one is a good candidate. Or perhaps each one is only a little dubious, but your reason to believe the conclusion becomes thinner and thinner as the doubt of each one adds to the doubt of the previous ones.

> ***Slippery slope argument*** A slippery slope argument is a bad argument that uses a chain of conditionals, at least one of which is false or dubious.

E. Reasoning from Hypotheses

Lee: I'm thinking of doing a nursing degree.
Maria: That means you'll have to take summer school.
Lee: Why?
Maria: Look, you're in your second year now. To finish in four years like you told me you need to, you'll have to take all the upper-division biology courses your last two years. And you can't take any of those until you've finished the three-semester calculus course. So you'll have to take calculus over the summer in order to finish in four years.

Maria has not shown that Lee has to go to summer school. Rather, Maria has shown that on the assumption (hypothesis) that Lee will do a nursing degree, Lee will have to go to summer school. That is, Maria has proved: if Lee does a nursing degree, then he'll have to go to summer school.

> ***Reasoning from hypotheses*** The following are equivalent:
> - Start with an hypothesis A and make a good argument for B.
> - Make a good argument for *If A, then B*.

Summary Some claims are made up of other claims. We need to recognize that such claims must be treated as just one claim.

We looked at two kinds of compound claims in this chapter that involve possibilities for how things could be: "or" claims and conditionals. There are lots of issues to master with conditionals: how to say they are false; what counts as a necessary or sufficient condition; how to recognize valid and weak forms. We need to do that work because conditionals are the way we talk about how things could turn out under certain conditions.

We found that compound claims are an important way to construct valid arguments. We can reason with "or" claims by excluding possibilities. We can reason with conditionals using the direct or indirect way or using a chain of conditionals. We can reason from hypotheses.

There are typical mistakes people make using these valid forms. Some use dubious or false premises, like false dilemmas or slippery slope arguments. Others overlook possibilities by affirming the consequent or by denying the antecedent.

Key Words

compound claim
"or" claim
alternative
contradictory of a claim
excluding possibilities
false dilemma
conditional
equivalent claims
antecedent
consequent
contrapositive
necessary condition
sufficient condition
direct way of reasoning with conditionals
indirect way of reasoning with conditionals
affirming the consequent
denying the antecedent
reasoning in a chain with conditionals
slippery slope argument
reasoning from hypotheses

Exercises for Chapter 7

1. What does it mean to say someone is reasoning in a chain with conditionals?
2. What is a slippery slope argument?
3. Make a list of the valid argument forms we studied in this chapter.
4. Make a list of the weak argument forms we studied in this chapter.
5. Make a list of the bad argument types we studied in this chapter.
6. Why won't a slippery slope argument do as a way to reduce to the absurd?
7. Rewrite the argument on p. 153 to show that it is reasoning in a chain.
8. Make flash cards to practice recognizing the forms of arguments we saw in this chapter.
   - On the back of a card, put the form (for example, If A then B; not A; so not B).
   - Write whether it's valid or weak.
   - On the front, put an example of that form that you've made up.
   - Make three cards for each form, each card showing a different example. Some of the examples should have a conditional that isn't already in "if . . . then . . ." form.
   - Practice with your own cards.
   - Trade with a classmate.
   - If you're not sure that your examples illustrate the forms, ask your instructor.
9. Assume that all of the conditionals in the picture on the next page are true. Using them:
   a. Write a contrapositive for each.
   b. Write a contradictory of each.
   c. Give an example of each of the valid and weak forms of arguments using conditionals, except for reasoning in a chain.

d. State which claims are sufficient for which others.

e. State which claims are necessary for which others.

If Dr. E wins the lottery,

If Dr. E marries a rich woman,

Then Dr. E will be rich.

If Dr. E's book sells a million copies,

Here are some more of Tom's homework along with Dr. E's comments.

Suzy: If you apologize to Zoe, I'm sure she'll help you look for Spot.
Dick: It's her fault he got loose. I won't apologize.
Suzy: Then she won't help you look for Spot.

Argument? (the whole dialogue) (yes or no) Yes.

Conclusion (if unstated, add it): Zoe won't help Dick look for Spot.

Premises: If you apologize to Zoe, she'll help you go look for Spot.
It's Zoe's fault Spot got loose. Dick won't apologize to Zoe.

Additional premises needed (if none, say so): None.

Classify (with the additional premises): Valid.

Form: It's the direct way of reasoning with conditionals.

Good argument? (yes or no, with an explanation) Good.

No. It's a case of denying the antecedent. The premises are true, all right, but Zoe did go help Dick. She felt guilty.

If you don't give to charity, you're selfish. If you pay all your bills on time with nothing left over, you can't give to charity. Since you don't want to be selfish, you shouldn't pay all your bills on time.

Argument? (yes or no) Yes.

Conclusion (if unstated, add it): You shouldn't pay all your bills on time.

Premises: If you don't give to charity, you're selfish. If you pay all your bills on time with nothing left over, you can't give to charity. You don't want to be selfish.

Additional premises needed (if none, say so): When you pay your bills, you have nothing left over.

Classify (with the additional premises): Valid.

Form: Reasoning in a chain and indirect way.

Good argument? (yes or no, with an explanation) It looks O.K. if the premises apply to the person, but something seems wrong.

Good. You recognized the form, and you're getting good at spotting what unstated premises are needed. What's wrong here is that "selfish" is too vague. The first premise isn't true. What is true, perhaps, is "If you don't give to charity when you have more money than you need for your essentials, then you're selfish."

Analyze Exercises 10–36 by answering these questions:

Argument? (yes or no)
Conclusion (if unstated, add it):
Premises:
Additional premises needed to make it valid or strong (if none, say so):
Classify (with the additional premises): valid strong ———— weak
One of the forms we studied in this chapter? (state which one)

Good argument? (Choose one and give an explanation.)

- It's good (passes the three tests).
- It's valid or strong, but you don't know if the premises are true, so you can't say if it's good or bad.
- It's bad because it's unrepairable (state which of the reasons apply).

10. If Suzy breaks up with Tom, then she'll have to return his letter jacket. But there is no way she'll give up that jacket. So she won't break up with Tom.

11. Steve Pearce is a congressman who meets with his constituents regularly. If someone is a good congressman, he meets with his constituents regularly. So Rep. Pearce is a good congressman.

12. To take issue with current Israeli policy is to criticize Israel. To criticize Israel is to be anti-Israel. To be anti-Israel is to be anti-Semitic. So if you take issue with current Israeli policy, you're an anti-Semite.

13. When Johnny comes marching home again, the girls will all laugh and shout. Johnny died in the war. So the girls didn't laugh and shout.

14. Dr. E (on an exam day): If students don't like me, they won't show up. But all of them showed up today. So they must really like me.

15. Manuel: Look here in the paper. People in Uganda are dying of some fever where they hemorrhage a lot.
    Maria: If people in Uganda are dying of hemorrhagic fever, it must be the ebola virus.
    Manuel: So it's the ebola virus!

16. Maria: Professor, professor, why wouldn't you answer my question in class?
    Professor Zzzyzzx: Questions in my class I do not allow. If one student I am allowing to ask a question, then others I must allow. Und then I will have lots und lots of questions to answer. Und time I won't have for mine lecture.

17. Maria: Lee will take care of Spot Tuesday if Dick will help him with his English paper.
    Manuel: (*later*) Dick didn't help Lee with his English paper, so I guess Lee didn't take care of Spot on Tuesday.

18. Dick: If Freud was right, then the only things that matter to a man are fame, riches, and the love of beautiful women.
    Zoe: But Ralph is poor, single, never married, and uninterested in women. And he's certainly not famous. Yet he's happy. So Freud was wrong.

19. Only if Columbus landed in a place with no people in it could you say that he discovered it. But the Americas, especially where he landed, were populated. He even met natives. So Columbus didn't discover America. He just discovered a route to America.

20. Tom: If Dick loves Zoe, he'll give her an engagement ring.
    Harry: But Dick loves Spot a lot more than Zoe.
    Suzy: So Dick won't give Zoe an engagement ring.

21. Zoe's mother to Zoe: Don't get a credit card! If you do, you'll be tempted to spend money you don't have. Then you'll max out on your card. Then you'll be in real debt. And you'll have to drop out of school to pay your bills. You'll end up a failure in life.

22. Every criminal either is already a hardened repeat offender or will become one because of what he'll learn in jail. We don't want any hardened criminals running free on our streets. So if you lock up someone, he should be locked up forever.

23. Mary Ellen: If I go on this workout and diet plan from this magazine, I'll lose weight.
    Suzy: *(later)* Did you see how much weight Mary Ellen lost?
    Zoe: She must have gone on that workout and diet plan.

24. Zoe: Don't go out with a football player.
    Suzy: Why not?
    Zoe: You're crazy about football players, and if you go out with one you're sure to sleep with him.
    Suzy: So?
    Zoe: Then you'll get pregnant. And you'll marry the guy. But those guys are such jerks. You'll end up cooking and cleaning for him while he and his buddies watch football on TV. In twenty years you'll have five kids, no life, and a lot of regrets.
    Suzy: Gosh. I guess you're right. I'll go out with a basketball player instead.

25. Dick: If the car's bumper isn't crumpled, Lee wasn't speeding.
    Tom: So Lee didn't get a ticket.

26. Dick: I heard that Tom's going to get a pet. I wonder what he'll get?
    Zoe: The only pets you're allowed in this town are dogs or cats or fish.
    Dick: Well, I know he can't stand cats.
    Zoe: So he'll get a dog or fish.
    Dick: Not fish. He isn't the kind to get a pet you just contemplate.
    Zoe: So let's surprise him and get him a leash.

27. Mom: For a marriage to work, people have to have a lot in common.
    Zoe: Wrong! I know lots of miserable marriages where the people had a lot in common.

28. Lee: If Maria's paycheck comes in on time, she can pay the rent this month.
    Manuel: I saw Maria at the bank this afternoon. She said she was depositing her paycheck.
    Lee: Great! So the rent will be paid!

29. You say you want to raise tuition again? Why not raise the parking fees, too? And the dorm contracts. And raise prices at the cafeteria, while you're at it. Or maybe even charge students for using the library. You could balance the school's budget for sure that way.

30. Aid to third-world countries? Why should we care more about starving children there than here?

31. Zoe: You look depressed.
    Dick: I feel really low.
    Zoe: You should eat some chocolate—that always makes me feel better.
    Dick: (looking into the cupboard) Hey! There are no chocolate bars here. You must have been really depressed last week.

32. Zoe: I can't believe you let Spot run away on your walk.
    Dick: We'll just have to wait for him to come home. I searched everywhere for him.
    Zoe: (*later*) Did you let Spot back in the yard?
    Dick: No.
    Zoe: So someone else must have let him in. The gate's latched.
    Dick: Maybe he got back in by himself.
    Zoe: No. If he could get in, he could get out. And if he could get out, he would because he loves to run around the neighborhood. But he never gets out anymore when the gate is latched.

33. Gun control should not be allowed. If laws requiring registration of all guns are passed, then they'll start investigating people who have guns. They'll tap our phones. They'll look at what we check out of the library. They'll tap our internet records. They'll come gunning for us. It'll be a police state.

34. I'm suspicious of this theory that thirteen-year-old kids are intrinsically messed up. If it's physiological, it should be universal. Are Mongol nomads all nihilists at thirteen? I've read a lot of history, and I don't think I've seen a single reference to this supposedly universal fact before the twentieth century. Teenage apprentices in the Renaissance seem to have been cheerful and eager. They got in fights and played tricks on one another of course (Michelangelo had his nose broken by a bully), but they weren't crazy.
    Paul Graham, "Why Are Nerds Unpopular?"

35. To take issue with the assumptions of evolution is to be a creationist. To be a creationist is to be a theist and to reject science. To reject science is to be irrational. So to take issue with the assumptions of evolution is to be irrational.

36. Maria: Listen to this argument I read in Steen's *Practical Philosophy for the Life Sciences,* "If the population density of a species is high in some area, then the species will not reproduce in that area. If a species doesn't reproduce in some area, it will go extinct in that area. Therefore, if the population density of a species is very high in some area, it will go extinct in that area."
    Lee: Gosh, that explains why there aren't any alligators in New York. There used to be too many of them.

37. Assume that all of the conditionals in the picture on the next page are true. Using them:
    a. Write a contradictory of each "if . . . then . . ." claim.
    b. Write the contrapositive of each "if . . . then . . ." claim.
    c. Give an example of each of the valid and weak forms of arguments using conditionals, except for reasoning in a chain.
    d. State which claims are sufficient for which others.
    e. State which claims are necessary for which others.

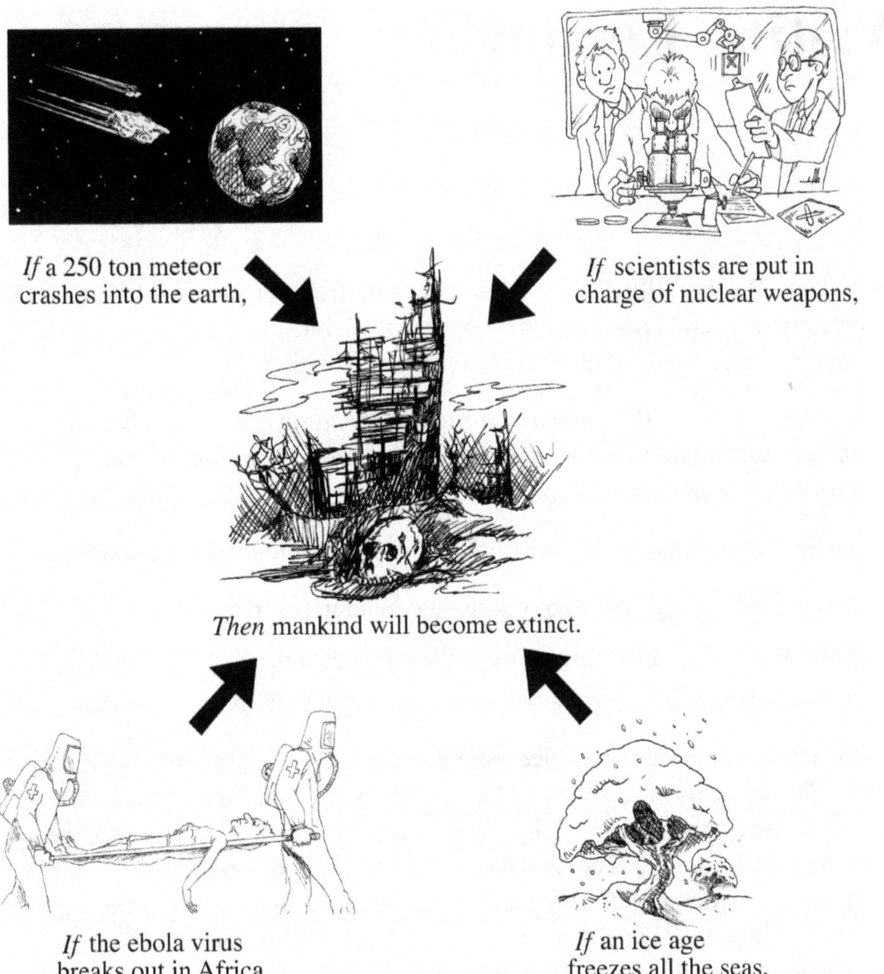
If a 250 ton meteor
crashes into the earth,
If scientists are put in
charge of nuclear weapons,
Then mankind will become extinct.
If the ebola virus
breaks out in Africa,
If an ice age
freezes all the seas,

38. You've worked hard enough. Take some time off. Go to a bar or a party or a church social, or . . . Listen. And bring back examples of the valid and weak forms of reasoning we studied in this chapter.

Further Study Propositional logic is the study of how to analyze arguments solely in terms of their structure as composed of compound claims using "and," "or," "not," "if . . . then . . .". For a short introduction see the *Truth-Tables Supplement* free on our website at www.AdvancedReasoningForum.org/CT/supplements. For a full presentation, see *An Introduction to Formal Logic*, also published by the Advanced Reasoning Forum.

Writing Lesson 7

You've learned about filling in unstated premises, indicator words, what counts as a plausible premise, and reasoning with compound claims.

Write an argument either for or against the following:

> *For any course at this school, if a student attends every class, takes all the exams, and hands in all the assignments, then the professor should give the student a passing mark.*

Check whether your instructor has chosen a different topic for this assignment.

Just as for Writing Lesson 6, you should hand in two pages:

First page A list of premises and the conclusion.

Second page The argument written as an essay with indicator words.

We should be able to see at a glance from the list of premises whether your argument is good. The essay form should read just as clearly if you use indicator words well. Remember, there should be no claims in the essay that aren't listed as premises.

Note that the topic is a conditional. You need to understand how to form a contradictory in order to make up your pro and con lists and to write your argument. Be very clear in your mind about what you consider to be necessary as opposed to sufficient conditions to get a passing mark.

To show you some of the problems students have, I'm including Suzy's argument on a different topic, and I'm also including Tom's. He's doing better now and has agreed to let folks see his work. Lee wrote a better one, so I've included his, too.

Suzy Queue
Critical Thinking

Issue: If a professor's colleagues do not consider his exams to be well written, then marks for the course should be given on a curve, not on percentage.

Premises:
1. A grade on a test reflects just how students are doing on that subject. If a test is not clearly understood, then the reflection of the scores will be lower.

2. Every student deserves to be treated fairly if the test is not clearly written the opportunity is not equal.

3. Due to the unclear test, the grading should start with the highest scored test in the class and the other test scores behind that.

4. Unclear tests should not be given in the first place, so to compensate for the strain on your brain for trying to decipher the test, grades should be curved to compensate.

5. The test is a direct reflection of how the teacher is getting through to his students, so in order to have an accurate idea, grading on the curve would show him the relation of all the students scores together.

Conclusion: Teachers who give poorly written exams should grade on the curve.

The essay's on the next page like you asked.

Suzy Queue
page 2

A grade on a test reflects just how students are doing on that subject. If the test is not clearly understood, then the reflection of the scores will be lower. Every student deserves to be treated fairly if the test is not clearly written the opportunity is not equal. Due to the unclear test, the grading should start with the highest scored test and the other test score behind that. Unclear tests should not be given in the first place, so to compensate for the strain on your brain for trying to decipher the test, grades should be curved to compensate. The test is a direct reflection of how the teacher is getting through to his students, so in order to have an accurate idea, grading on a curve would show him the relation of all the students scores together. Teachers who give poorly written exams should grade on the curve.

Some problems here. For (1) on the previous page, what does "reflect" mean? And "clearly understood"? By whom? That's the point. Besides, it's not one premise—it's two claims. For (2) you apparently have two claims, but it's incoherent. Your (4) is an argument (that word "so" is the clue), not a premise. And (5) is two claims, too.

You almost proved the conclusion you've stated. But you missed the point. It's a lot easier to prove what you stated than the issue you were supposed to write on. Who decides what "poorly written" means? Where is anything about who counts as his colleagues?

It's pretty clear to me that you wrote the essay first and then tried to figure out what you said.

Tom Wyzyczy
Critical Thinking
Section 4
Writing Lesson 7

Issue: Every student should be required to take either critical thinking or freshman composition, but not both.

Definition: I'll understand the issue as "University students should be required to take either a freshman course on critical thinking or freshman composition, but not both."

Premises:

Critical thinking courses teach how to write. ***1***

Freshman composition teaches how to write. ***2***

Critical thinking courses teach how to read an essay. ***3***

Freshman composition teaches how to read an essay. ***4***

Credit should not be given for taking two courses that teach roughly the same material. ***5***

If credit shouldn't be given for taking a course, students shouldn't be required to take it. ***6***

Conclusion: Every student should be required to take either critical thinking or freshman composition, but not both.

continued on next page

This is sloppy work compared to what you've done in the past. You've shown, more or less, that a student should not have to take both courses. But you haven't shown that he should take one or the other, which is also part of the issue [(A or B) and not C]. So you've established neither the original claim nor its contradictory.

You need a claim that links 1–4 with 5 and 6, like "Freshman composition and critical thinking courses teach the same material." (I see on the next page you do have that claim.)

But worse is that 6 is at best dubious: How about those students who have to take remedial math for which no credit is given? And 1 and 2 are too vague. Both courses teach "how to write," but quite different aspects of that. Ditto for 3 and 4.

Tom Wyzyczy, Writing Lesson 7, page 2

Both critical thinking courses and freshman composition courses teach how to write. Both critical thinking courses and freshman composition courses teach how to read an essay. Since they both teach roughly the same material, they shouldn't both be required, because credit should not be given for taking two courses that teach roughly the same material. And if credit shouldn't be given for taking a course, students shouldn't be required to take it.

Good use of indicator words. It was O.K. to put two claims together in the first sentence as you did, since you recognized in your list of premises that they were two claims.

But you did what I specifically asked you not to do. You added a claim here you didn't have on the previous page: "Both courses teach roughly the same material."

The argument looks good when it's written this way, but the previous page shows its weaknesses.

You should re-do this whole assignment.

Lee Hong-Nakamura O'Flanagan

Issue: If critical thinking were not a required course, a lot fewer people would take it.

Definition: I assume that "a lot fewer" is purposely vague.

Premises: ‡ Critical thinking is required of all students now.
‡ Critical thinking is one of the harder core requirement courses.
‡ A lot of students prefer to take easy courses, rather than learn something.
‡ Students in engineering and architecture have more courses to take than they can finish in four years.
‡ Students don't want to spend more time at their studies than they have to. 1
‡ Money is a problem for many students. 2
‡ For most students, if they have more courses to take than they can finish in four years, they will not take courses that aren't required. 3
‡ Students think they already know how to think critically. 4
‡ If critical thinking weren't required, then students who prefer easy courses and students who want to finish as quickly as they can, which are a lot of students, will not take it.

Conclusion: If critical thinking were not a required course, a lot fewer people would take it.

Critical thinking is required of all students now. And critical thinking is one of the harder core requirement courses. A lot of students prefer to take easy courses, rather than learn something. So many of them won't take critical thinking. 5 Besides, students in engineering and architecture have more courses than they can finish in four years. Why would they take critical thinking if they didn't have to? After all, we all know that students don't want to spend more time at their studies than they have to. After all, money is a problem for most students. So for most students, if they have more courses to take than they can finish in four years, they will not take courses that aren't required. Anyway, students think they already know how to think critically. Thus we can see that if critical thinking weren't required, then students who prefer easy courses and students who want to finish as quickly as they can, which are a lot of students, will not take it. That is, if critical thinking were not a required course, a lot fewer people would take it.

This is good, but there are a few problems. 1 isn't tied into 3, though the unstated premise is reasonably clear. But 2 definitely needs to be tied into 3 better. And 4 is left dangling—what's the connection you intend? Finally, you use 5 and it should be on the list of premises. Nonetheless, this is pretty good work.

But it was supposed to be on 2 pages! I guess once in my life I can be a good guy and give you credit anyway.

Cartoon Writing Lesson C

For each cartoon, write the best argument you can that has as its conclusion the claim that accompanies the cartoon. List only the premises and conclusion. If you believe the best argument is only weak, explain why. Refer back to Cartoon Writing Lesson A (p. 56) for suggestions about how to do this lesson.

1.

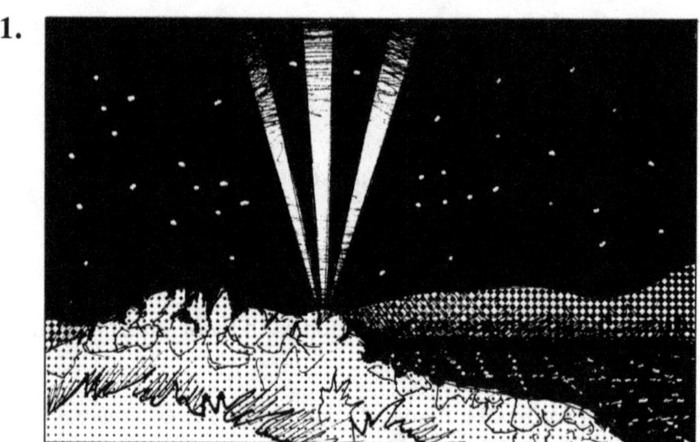

There are searchlights behind the hill.

2.

Someone has walked here since the snow began falling.

3.

Spot took the steak.

4.

Spot escaped by digging a hole under the fence.

5.

Birds ate Farmer Hong's corn.

6.

The fellow standing between Harry and Manuel is or was in the military.

8 General Claims

A. General Claims and Their Contradictories

We need to know how to reason with claims that assert something about all or a part of a collection, which we call ***general claims***. For example,

> All good teachers give fair exams.
> Prof. Zzzyzzx gives fair exams.
> So Prof. Zzzyzzx is a good teacher.

This may seem valid, but it's not. The premises could be true, yet Prof. Zzzyzzx could be a terrible teacher and give fair exams from an instructor's manual.

> Some dogs like cats.
> Some cats like dogs.
> So some dogs and cats like each other.

This seems valid, too. But it's not. It could be that all the dogs that like cats are abhorred by the cats as too wimpy.

These arguments sound right, but they're bad. How can we avoid getting lured into belief? We first need to be clear about what "all" and "some" mean.

"All" means "every single one, no exceptions." But then is the following true?

> All polar bears in Antarctica can swim.

There are no exceptions: there's not one polar bear in Antarctica that can't swim. There also aren't any polar bears in Antarctica that can swim. There aren't any polar bears at all in Antarctica.

Some people say the claim is false: there has to be at least one thing for us to be right when we say "all" in ordinary conversation. Others say the claim is true.

There's disagreement about "some," too. Consider:

Dr. E: At the end of this term, some of my students will get an A.

At the end of the term one student in all of Dr. E's classes got an A. Was Dr. E right? If you don't think so, then how many is "some students"? At least 2? At least 8? At least 10%? More than 18%? "Some" is purposely vague. We use it when we can't or don't want to be precise. When we say "some," we're only guaranteeing that there is at least one.

Dr. E: Some of my students will pass my next exam.

All Dr. E's students pass the exam. Was Dr. E right? For this claim to be true, don't some students also have to fail? With "some" we usually mean "at least one, but not all." But not always. "Some" and "all" can be ambiguous.

> ***All*** means "Every single one, no exceptions." Sometimes *all* is meant as "Every single one, and there is at least one." Which reading is best may depend on the context.
>
> ***Some*** means "At least one." Sometimes *some* is meant as "At least one, but not all." Which reading is best may depend on the context.

There are lots of different ways to say "all" in English. For example, the following are equivalent claims:

All dogs bark.	Dogs bark.
Every dog barks.	Everything that's a dog barks.

There are lots of ways to say "some" in the sense of "at least one." For example, the following are equivalent claims:

Some foxes are affectionate.	At least one fox is affectionate.
There is a fox that's affectionate.	There exists an affectionate fox.

There are also lots of ways of saying that nothing or no part of a collection satisfies some condition. For example, the following are equivalent claims:

No dog likes cats.	Nothing that's a dog likes cats.
All dogs do not like cats.	Not even one dog likes cats.

To clarify the meaning of "not," and for other analyses in this chapter, let's use the letter S, P, Q, R for parts of a sentence.

No "No *S* is *P*" means "Not even one *S* is *P*," "every single *S* is not *P*."

Another word used in general claims is "only." For example:

Only postal employees deliver U.S. mail.
Laurie is a postal employee.
So Laurie delivers U.S. mail.

This is not valid. Only postal employees deliver U.S. mail does not mean that all postal employees deliver U.S. mail. It means that anyone who delivers U.S. mail has to be a postal employee.

Only "Only S are P" means "All P are S."

It's easy to get confused about a contradictory of a general claim. Recall that a *contradictory* of a claim is one that has the opposite truth-value no matter what the circumstances are. For example, here's an advertisement that's on TV:

Zocor is a cholesterol medicine. Zocor is not right for everyone.

Why are they advertising medicine that no one should use? They've got the contradictory of "Zocor is right for everyone" wrong. It should be "Zocor is not right for some people."

And a contradictory of "All dogs bark" isn't "All dogs don't bark." Both claims are false. A contradictory is "Some dogs don't bark."

A contradictory of "Some students are athletes" isn't "Some students are not athletes." Both of those claims are true. Rather, it's "Not even one student is an athlete," or "All students are not athletes," or better still, "No student is an athlete."

Here are some examples of claims and their contradictories:

Claim	*Contradictory*
All dogs bark.	Some dogs don't bark.
Some dogs bark.	No dog barks.
Some dogs don't bark.	All dogs bark.
No women are philosophers.	Some women are philosophers.
Every Mexican likes vodka.	Some Mexicans don't like vodka.
Some Russians like chile.	No Russian likes chile.
Some whales eat fish.	Not even one whale eats fish.

A contradictory of "Only S are P" can be made in two ways:

Some P are not S.
Not every P is S.

So "Only postal employees deliver mail" is contradicted by "Some people who deliver mail are not postal employees." If we want to say that just exactly postal employees and no one else delivers U.S. mail, we should say that. Or we can say:

All postal employees and only postal employees deliver U.S. mail.
Contradictory Either some postal employees don't deliver U.S. mail, or some people who deliver U.S. mail aren't postal employees.

Because there are so many ways we can make general claims, it's hard to give set forms for contradictories. With some practice you ought to be able to use your common sense to get a correct one. As an aid, here's a rough guide:

Claim	*Contradictory*
All S are P.	Some S are not P. Not every S is P.
Some S are P.	No S are P. All S are not P. Not even one S is P.
Some S are not P.	All S are P.
No S is P.	Some S are P.
Only S are P.	Some P are not S. Not every P is S.

Exercises for Section A

1. Give two other ways to say "All dogs eat meat."
2. Give two other ways to say "Some cats can swim."
3. Give two other ways to say "All computers are powered by electricity."
4. Give two other ways to say "Some state governors are women."
5. Give another way to say "Only birds fly."
6. Give two other ways to say "No police officer is under 18 years old."
7. Give another way to say "Everything that's a dog is a domestic canine, and everything that's a domestic canine is a dog."
8. Give two other ways to say "No pig can fly."
9. Judging from your experience, which of the following claims are true? Be prepared to defend your answer.

a. Only dogs bark.
b. All blondes are dumb.
c. Some textbooks are designed to fall apart after one semester.
d. Crest toothpaste is not for sale in all stores.
e. Some English professors are women.
f. Dictionaries are the only way to learn the meaning of new words.
g. No student can register for this course after the first week of classes.

10. For each of the following, give a contradictory claim.
    a. All students like to study.
    b. No women are construction workers.
    c. Every CEO of a Fortune 500 company is a man.
    d. This book is used in all sections of critical thinking.
    e. No exam is suitable for all students.
    f. Not all drunk drivers get into accidents.
    g. Donkeys eat carrots.
    h. Only the good die young.
    i. All teachers and only teachers are allowed to grade exams.
    j. Nothing both barks and meows.
    k. Tom will start every football game if he's not injured.
    l. If some football player is a vegetarian, his coach will hate him.
    m. All decisions about abortion should be left to the woman and her doctor.
    n. The Lone Ranger was the only cowboy to have a friend called "Tonto."

11. There are general claims about time, too. Give a contradictory for each of the following:
    a. Dr. Wallace always gives an exam when he is irritated with his students.
    b. It never rains in Seattle in July.
    c. Sometimes Spot will not chase Puff.
    d. Only during the winter are there flocks of birds along the river.

B. Some Valid and Invalid Forms

Recall the first argument in this chapter:

> All good teachers give fair exams.
> Prof. Zzzyzzx gives fair exams.
> So Prof. Zzzyzzx is a good teacher.

We saw it's weak: Prof. Zzzyzzx could be among the bad teachers who give fair exams. This diagram summarizes that analysis:

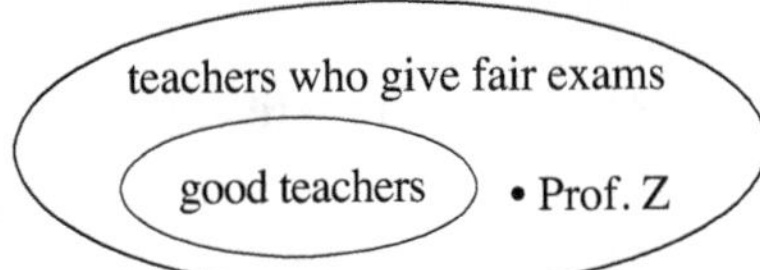

This argument sounds good because it's similar to a valid form of argument. Schematically, where "a" stands for the name of someone or something:

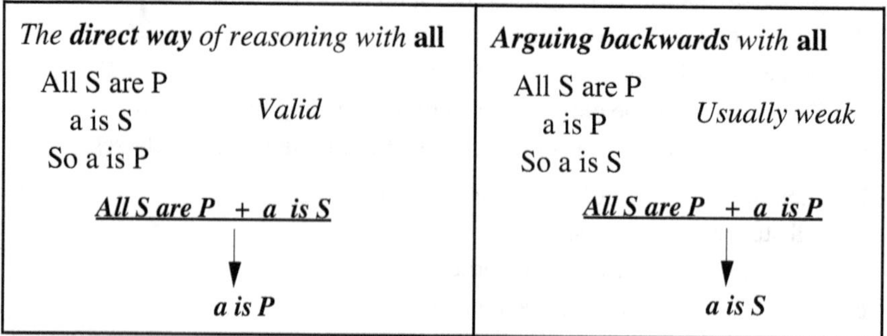

The direct way of reasoning with all
All S are P
a is S
So a is P
Valid
All S are P + a is S
a is P
Arguing backwards with all
All S are P
a is P
So a is S
Usually weak
All S are P + a is P
a is S

Valid: All dogs bark.
Ralph is a dog.
So Ralph barks.

Weak: All dogs bark.
Ralph barks.
So Ralph is a dog.

The argument on the right is overlooking possibilities. One way to be something that barks is to be a dog, but there may be other ways (seals and foxes).

Example 1 All mortgage brokers are honest. Ralph is a mortgage broker. So Ralph is honest.
Analysis This is valid, an example of the direct way of reasoning with "all." But though valid, it's not good because the first premise is false, as we learned in the financial crash of 2008.

Example 2 All stockbrokers earn more than $50,000. Earl earns more than $50,000. So Earl is a stockbroker.
Analysis This is weak, arguing backwards with "all." Earl could be a basketball player or a mortgage broker.

The diagram on the previous page is an example of a way to check whether certain kinds of arguments that use general claims are valid.

Checking for validity with diagrams

- A collection is represented by an enclosed area.
- If one area is entirely within another, then everything in the one collection is also in the other.
- If one area overlaps another, then there is something that is common to both collections.

- An “a” or a dot in an area marks that a particular object is in that collection
- Draw the areas to represent the premises as true while trying to represent the conclusion as false. If you can, then the argument is invalid. If there’s no way to represent the premises as true and the conclusion as false, the argument is valid.

For example, we can use diagrams to check whether the following is valid:

All dogs bark. Everything that barks is a mammal.
So all dogs are mammals.

We first draw the diagram to represent the premises as true.

The “dogs” area is completely inside the “things that bark” area: All dogs bark.

The “things that bark” area is completely inside the “mammals” area: All things that bark are mammals.

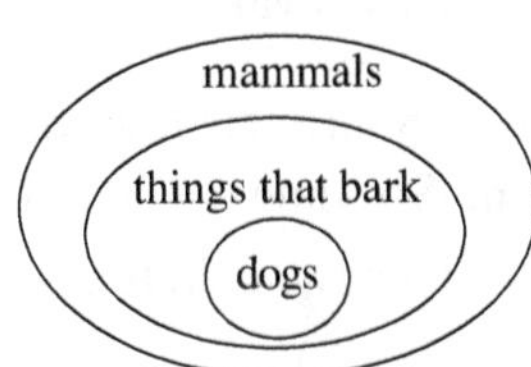

So the “dogs” area ends up being inside the “mammals” area. There’s no way it couldn’t be. That represents that all dogs are mammals. So if we represent the premises as true, we are forced to represent the conclusion as true. The argument is valid.

Compare that to a similar argument:

Some kangaroos are tame. Some creatures that are tame live in New Zealand. So some kangaroos live in New Zealand.

Is the argument valid? What do we need to have in a diagram?

The “kangaroos” area must overlap the “tame” area: Some kangaroos are tame.

The “tame” area must overlap the “New Zealand” area: Some creatures that are tame live in New Zealand.

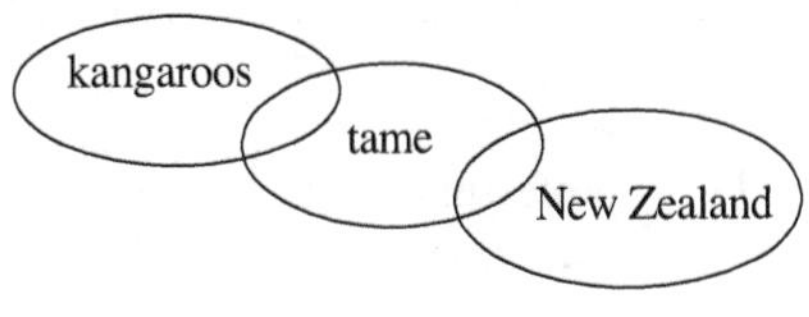

We’re able to draw the diagram to represent both premises as true, yet there’s no overlap between the “kangaroos” area and the “New Zealand” area, so the conclusion is false: it’s possible that no kangaroos live in New Zealand. Thus, the argument is invalid. Even though its conclusion is true (there are some kangaroos in zoos there), it’s weak.

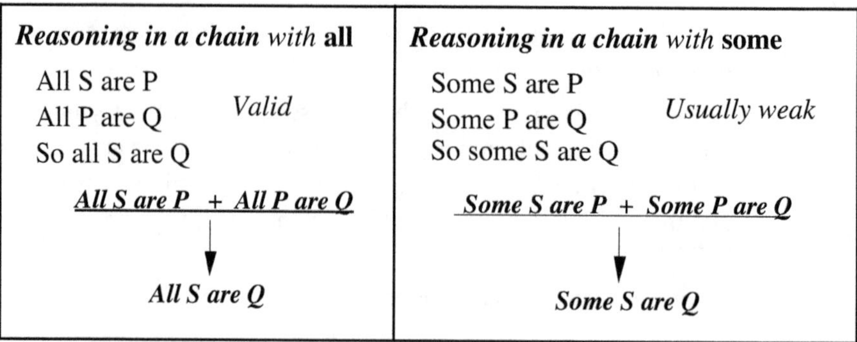

Example 3 Every newspaper the vice-president reads is published by an American publisher. All newspapers published by an American publisher are biased against Muslims. So the vice-president reads only newspapers biased against Muslims.
Analysis This is valid, reasoning in a chain with "all."

Example 4 Some cats like ice cream. Some things that like ice cream will bark for ice cream. So some cats will bark for ice cream.
Analysis This is weak, reasoning in a chain with "some."

Here's an argument with "no":

All dogs bark.
No professor is a dog.
So no professor barks.

How do we check if this is valid? We do what we've always done: look for all the possible ways the premises could be true. Only now we can use diagrams to represent those possibilities. We know that the "dogs" area must be entirely within the "things that bark" area (All dogs bark). So we just have to figure out where to put the "professors" area. We know that there must be no overlap of the "professors" area and the "dogs" area (No professor is a dog). Here are three possibilities:

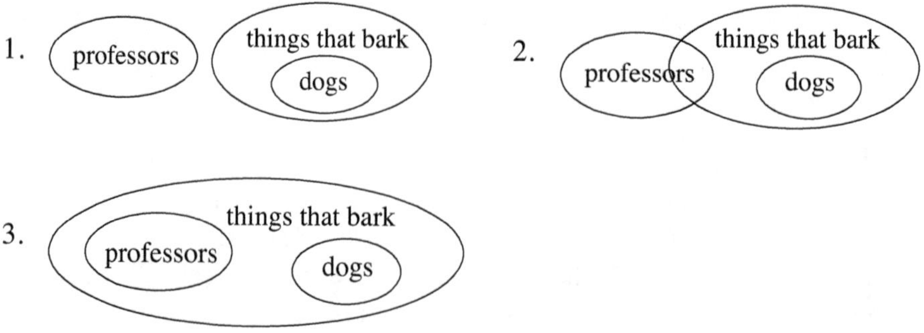

These (schematically) represent all the ways the premises could be true. Yet in both (2) and (3) the conclusion is represented as false. It's possible for there to be a professor who barks, even though he (she?) isn't a dog. Arf, arf. The argument is invalid. It mimics a valid form of argument.

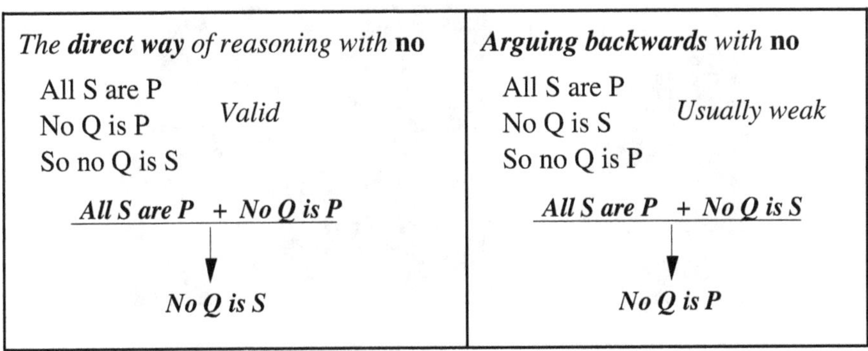

The **direct way** of reasoning with **no**
All S are P
No Q is P
So no Q is S
Valid
All S are P + No Q is P
No Q is S
Arguing backwards with **no**
All S are P
No Q is S
So no Q is P
Usually weak
All S are P + No Q is S
No Q is P

Example 5 All corporations are legal entities. No computer is a legal entity. So no computer is a corporation.
Analysis This is valid, the direct way of reasoning with "no."

Example 6 All nursing students take calculus in their freshman year. No heroin addict is a nursing student. So no heroin addict takes calculus in their freshman year.
Analysis This is weak, arguing backwards with "no."

Here are three examples of how Maria and Lee have been using diagrams to check for validity.

AND NO PHILOSOPHY PROFESSOR IS A POLITICIAN...

SO WE DRAW THE POLITICIANS AWAY FROM THE PHILOSOPHY PROFESSORS.
POLITICIANS
REASONS WELL
PHILOSOPHY PROFESSOR

SO THE CONCLUSION FOLLOWS– NO POLITICIAN REASONS WELL.
POLITICIANS
NO– SURE YOU CAN DRAW THE PICTURE THAT WAY...

BUT WE WANT TO SHOW THE CONCLUSION IS FALSE, AND I SEE HOW WE CAN.

WE CAN DRAW IT THIS WAY.

THAT MAKES THE PREMISES TRUE AND THE CONCLUSION FALSE. SO IT'S INVALID.
REASONS WELL
PHILOSOPHY PROFESSORS
POLITICIANS

Only cats claw their owners.
Puff is a cat.
So Puff claws its owner.
THIS ONE'S EASY.

claws owners
cats
puff
IT'S VALID.

ARE YOU SURE? LET'S CHECK.
CRITICAL THINKING

NO. SEE? "ONLY S ARE P" MEANS THE SAME AS "ALL P ARE S".

YEAH-ONLY CATS...

cats
claws owners
x puff
SO IT'S INVALID.

Some students don't have jobs.
Everyone who has a job works hard.
So some students don't work hard

WE START WITH THE FIRST PREMISE - BUT THERE ARE LOTS OF WAYS TO DRAW THAT.

SO LET'S START WITH THE SECOND ONE - THERE'S ONLY ONE WAY.

works hard
has a job

SO WHERE DO WE DRAW "STUDENTS"?
WE'RE TRYING TO MAKE THE CONCLUSION FALSE— SO CAN WE MAKE THE STUDENTS ENTIRELY INSIDE THE "WORKS HARD" AREA?

?
?
SURE, I'VE GOT IT.

BUT THAT'S RIDICULOUS. WE KNOW THERE ARE STUDENTS WHO DON'T WORK HARD.
works hard
has a job
students
SURE. BUT IT'S POSSIBLE THAT ALL STUDENTS WORK HARD. SO IT'S INVALID

Drawing diagrams to check for validity is just another way to look for possibilities that make the premises true and the conclusion false. The method works for some arguments that use general claims, but not for all. Even the simple argument we began the chapter with about dogs that like cats can't be analyzed using diagrams this way. You'll have to think your way through the ways the premises could be true when you do some of the exercises.

Exercises for Section B

Which of the argument forms in Exercises 1–6 are valid? Justify your answer. Then give an argument of that form.

1. All S are P.
   No Q is S.
   So some Q aren't P.

2. All S are P.
   a is S.
   So *a* is P.

3. Some S are P.
   All P are Q.
   So some S are Q.

4. Only S are P.
   a is S.
   So *a* is P.

5. Some S aren't P.
   So no P are S.

6. All S are P.
   No Q is P.
   So no Q is S.

Exercises 7–14 are simple examples for you to develop some skill in analyzing general claims. For each, select the claim that makes the argument valid—you're not asked to judge whether the claim is plausible, just whether it makes the argument valid.

7. All turtles can swim. So turtles eat fish.
   a. Anything that eats fish swims.
   b. Fish swim and are eaten by things that swim.
   c. Anything that swims eats fish.
   d. None of the above.

8. Anyone who plagiarizes is cheating. So Ralph plagiarizes.
   a. Ralph wrote three critical thinking essays in two days.
   b. Ralph cheated last week.
   c. Both (a) and (b).
   d. None of the above.

9. Pigs are mammals. So pigs eat apples.
   a. Anything that eats apples is a mammal.
   b. Pigs don't eat meat.
   c. Anything that is a mammal eats apples.
   d. None of the above.

10. All professional dancers cannot hold a day job. So no lawyer is a professional dancer.
   a. Lawyers don't usually like to dance.
   b. Dancers aren't interested in making money.
   c. Being a lawyer is a day job.
   d. Professional dancers can't write essays.
   e. None of the above.

11. Every voter must have a legal residence. So no sex-offender has a legal residence.
   a. No sex-offender is a voter.
   b. No sex-offender can register to vote.
   c. If you're a sex-offender, then no one will want to live near you.
   d. None of the above.

12. Some cats chase songbirds. So some songbirds are eaten by cats.
   a. Some cats catch songbirds.
   b. Some things that chase songbirds eat them.
   c. Some songbirds attack cats.
   d. None of the above.

13. Every dog chases cats. So Spot chases Puff.
   a. Spot is a dog.
   b. Puff is a cat.
   c. Puff irritates Spot.
   d. Both (a) and (b).
   e. None of the above.

14. Manuel is sweating. So he must be hot.
   a. Manuel sweats when he is hot.
   b. Anyone who is hot sweats.
   c. Only Manuel sweats when he is hot.
   d. Only people who are hot sweat.
   e. None of the above.

Which of Exercises 15–33 are valid arguments? You're not asked to determine whether the argument is good, only whether it is valid. Check by doing *one* of the following:

- Give a possible way in which the premises could be true and the conclusion false to show it's invalid.
- Draw a diagram.
- Point out that the argument is in one of the forms we have studied.
- Explain why it's valid.

15. Not every student attends lectures. Lee is a student. So Lee doesn't attend lectures.

16. No professor subscribes to *Rolling Stone* magazine. Maria is not a professor. So Maria subscribes to *Rolling Stone* magazine.

17. No professor subscribes to *Rolling Stone* magazine. Lou subscribes to *Rolling Stone* magazine. So Lou is not a professor.

18. Some dogs bite postal workers. Some postal workers bite dogs. So some dogs and postal workers bite each other.

19. Everyone who is anxious to learn works hard. Dr. E's students work hard. So Dr. E's students are anxious to learn.

20. All CEOs of Fortune 500 companies earn more than $400,000. Ralph earns more than $400,000. So Ralph is a CEO of a Fortune 500 company.

21. All students who are serious take critical thinking in their freshman year. No one who smokes marijuana every week is a serious student. So no one who smokes marijuana every week takes critical thinking his or her freshman year.

22. No student who cheats is honest. Some dishonest people are found out. So some students who cheat are found out.

23. Only ducks quack. George is a duck. So George quacks.

24. Everyone who likes ducks likes quackers. Dick likes ducks. Dick likes cheese. So Dick likes cheese and quackers.

25. No dogcatcher is kind. Anyone who is kind loves dogs. So no dogcatcher loves dogs.

26. Some things that grunt are hogs. Some hogs are good to eat. So some things that grunt are good to eat.

27.

28. All dogs chase cats. All cats chase songbirds. So all dogs chase songbirds.

29. Some paraplegics can't play basketball. Belinda is a paraplegic. So Belinda can't play basketball.

30. Every dog loves its master. Dr. E has a dog. So Dr. E is loved.

31. Only managers can close out the cash register. Juan is a manager. So Juan can close out the cash register.

32. Dogs are mammals. Cats are mammals. Some dogs hate cats. Therefore, some dogs hate mammals.

33. Everything made with chocolate is delicious. No liquor is delicious. So no liquor is made with chocolate.

34. The argument forms for conditionals and the argument forms for general claims are related. For example, we can rewrite:

All dogs bark.		If anything is a dog, then it barks.
Ralph barks.	as	Ralph barks.
So Ralph is a dog.		So Ralph is a dog.

Rewrite the following claims as *conditionals*:

a. All cats cough hair balls.

b. Every donkey eats hay.

c. Everything that's made of chocolate is good to eat.

d. Ducks like water.

C. Between One and All

1. Precise generalities

There are a lot of quantities between one and all. For example,

> 72% of all students who take critical thinking from Dr. E think he's the best teacher they've ever had. Harry took Dr. E's critical thinking course last year. So Harry thinks Dr. E is the best teacher he's ever had.

This is not valid. Where does it land on the strong–weak scale? We can say exactly: there's a 28% chance the premises could be true and the conclusion false. So it's not strong. If the percentages are very high or very low, though, we can get a strong argument, assuming we know nothing more about the people or things involved:

> 95% plus or minus 2% of all cat owners have cat-induced allergies. Dr. E's ex-wife has a cat. So Dr. E's ex-wife has cat-induced allergies.

> Only 4 of the 123 students who take Dr. E's classes failed his final exam. Mary Ellen took Dr. E's class. So Mary Ellen passed Dr. E's final exam.

2. Vague generalities

There are a lot of ways we talk about all or a part of a collection without specifying a precise number:

> *All* dogs bark.
>
> *Almost all* dogs bark.
>
> *Many* students at this school will vote.

Most dogs bark.

A lot of students at this school will vote.

Some students study hard.

A few students study hard.

Very few students dislike Dr. E.

Though the words "all" and "some" can be ambiguous, we've seen that we can analyze whether arguments using them are valid. We have enough precision.

The rest of these quantity words are too vague to figure in valid arguments. Most of them are too vague even to be used in a claim. How could we tell if "A few students dislike Dr. E" is true? Or whether "A lot of students will vote" is true?

There are two vague generalities, though, that we can use in *strong* arguments:

Almost all parakeets are under 2 feet tall.
So the parakeets at Boulevard Mall are under 2 feet tall.

Very few dogs don't bark.
Spot is a dog.
So Spot barks.

The premises give us good reason to believe the conclusion of each—if we don't know anything more about those parakeets or dogs—even though the conclusion doesn't follow with no exceptions. The following are the "almost all" versions of the forms for "all."

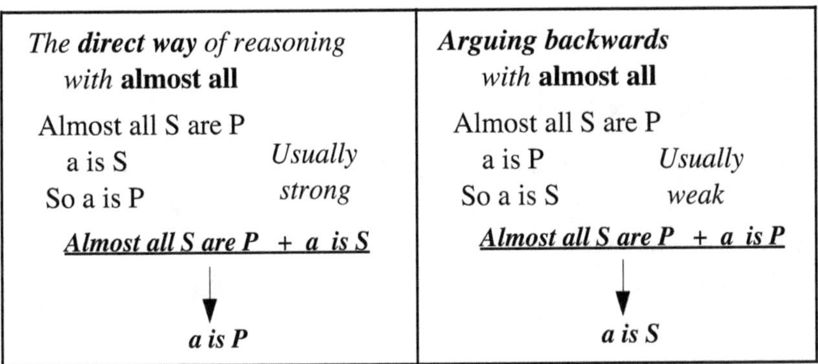

The direct way of reasoning with almost all
Almost all S are P
a is S
So a is P
Usually strong
Almost all S are P + a is S
a is P
Arguing backwards with almost all
Almost all S are P
a is P
So a is S
Usually weak
Almost all S are P + a is P
a is S

But reasoning in a chain with "almost all" is usually weak. For example:

Almost all dogs like peanut butter.
Almost all things that like peanut butter don't bark.
So almost all dogs don't bark.

The premises are true and the conclusion false.

Reasoning in a chain *with* **almost all**	
Almost all S are P Almost all P are Q So almost all S are Q	*Usually weak*

An argument of this form might be strong if you could specify exactly which S aren't P and which P aren't Q. But that's just to say you need further premises

Exercises for Section C

1. Give two other ways to say "Almost all teenagers listen to pop music."
2. Give two other ways to say "Only a few adults listen to classical music."

Which of the argument forms in Exercises 3–6 are strong? Justify your answer, and give an example.

3. Very few S are P.
   a is S.
   So *a* is not P.
4. Very few S are P.
   a is P.
   So *a* is not S.
5. Most S are P
   Most P are Q.
   So most S are Q.
6. Almost all S are P.
   Every P is Q.
   So almost all S are Q.

Which of the following arguments are strong? Check by doing one of the following:

- Give a not unlikely possible way in which the premises are true and the conclusion false to show the argument is weak.
- Point out that the argument is in one of the forms we have studied.
- Explain why it's strong or weak.

7. Very few college students use heroin. Zoe is a college student. So Zoe doesn't use heroin.
8. Almost no students read *The New York Review of Books*. Martha reads *The New York Review of Books*. So Martha is not a student.
9. Only a very few dogs like cats. Almost no cats like dogs. So virtually no dogs and cats like each other.
10. No student who cheats is honest. Almost all dishonest people are found out.
    So almost all students who cheat are found out.

11. Almost all people who are vegetarians like pizza. Almost all vegetarians will not eat eggs. So all but a few people who like pizza will not eat eggs.
12. Most newspaper columnists have a college degree. Almost everyone who has a college degree is not self-employed. So most newspaper columnists are not self-employed.
13. Very few paraplegics can play basketball. Belinda is a paraplegic. So Belinda can't play basketball.
14. All but a few members of Congress have a college degree. Mr. Ensign is a member of Congress. So Mr. Ensign has a college degree.
15. Almost every dog loves its master. Dr. E has a dog. So Dr. E is loved.

Summary General claims are how we assert something about all or part of a collection. We studied ways to use "all," "some," "no," and "only" in arguments. We first tried to get clear about how to understand those words and then noted that there are lots of equivalent ways to say them and to form their contradictories. Then we looked at a few valid and invalid forms of arguments using those words. We also saw that we could sometimes use diagrams to decide if an argument is valid.

Other precise general claims that lie between "one" and "all" normally don't figure in valid arguments, but we saw that sometimes they can figure in strong arguments.

Then we looked at vague generalities. Most don't figure in good arguments. Most don't even belong in claims. But "almost all" and "a few" can be used in strong arguments. We looked at some strong and weak argument forms using them.

Key Words

all	reasoning in a chain with "some"
some	direct way of reasoning with "no"
no	arguing backwards with "no"
only	precise generalities
contradictory	vague generalities
direct way of reasoning with "all"	direct way of reasoning with "almost all"
arguing backwards with "all"	arguing backwards with "almost all"
reasoning in a chain with "all"	reasoning in a chain with "almost all"

Further Study *An Introduction to Formal Logic*, also published by ARF, is an introduction to the role of general claims in valid arguments.

Writing Lesson 8

Write an argument either for or against the following:

No one should be allowed to ride in the back of a pickup truck.

Check whether your instructor has chosen a different topic for this assignment.

Just as for Writing Lessons 6 and 7, you should hand in two pages:

First page A list of premises and the conclusion.

Second page The argument written as an essay with indicator words.

We should be able to see at a glance from the list of premises whether your argument is good. The essay form should read just as clearly, if you use indicator words well. Remember, there should be no claims in the essay form that aren't listed as premises.

The issue is simple. There's nothing subtle that you're supposed to do here that you haven't done on the previous assignments. You just need to know how to argue for or against a general claim. And for that you must be able to form a contradictory of it.

By now you should have learned a lot about writing arguments. You don't need more examples, just practice using the new ideas presented in the chapters. As a guide you can use the section *Composing Good Arguments* at the end of this book, which summarizes many of the lessons you've learned.

Review Chapters 7 and 8

In Chapters 1–6 we established the fundamentals of critical thinking. In this part we looked at the structure of arguments.

Compound claims have their own structure. We saw that a compound claim, though made up of other claims, has to be viewed as just one claim. We saw that some arguments are valid and others typically weak due to their form relative to the compound claims in them. For example, excluding possibilities is a form of valid argument using "or" claims. But if the "or" claim doesn't list all the possibilities, we get a bad argument, a false dilemma.

Conditionals took more care. We saw how to form their contradictories and considered how conditionals that are always true express necessary or sufficient conditions.

We noted the direct and indirect ways to make valid arguments using conditionals. Two forms are similar to valid conditional arguments but are usually weak: affirming the consequent and denying the antecedent. We decided that any argument using those shouldn't be repaired. Reasoning in a chain with conditionals is valid, too. But if some of the conditionals are false or enough of them are dubious, the result can be a bad argument, a slippery slope.

General claims are how we assert something about all or a part of a collection. They can create a lot of confusion in reasoning. We made sure how to understand the words "all," "some," "no," and "only." Then we considered how to form contradictories of general claims. We looked at a few valid and weak forms using general claims, finding that sometimes we can use diagrams to check for validity. But with vague generalities we have less scope. They don't figure in valid arguments, and only "almost all" and "a very few" seem to yield strong argument forms.

You should now be able to use the methods of these chapters to analyze arguments that have more complicated structures. In the next part we'll work on spotting bad arguments. Then you can try your hand at evaluating lots of real arguments.

Review Exercises for Chapters 7 and 8

1. What is an argument?
2. What are the tests for an argument to be good?
3. What is a valid argument?
4. What does it mean to say an argument is strong?
5. Is every valid argument good? Explain.

6. How do you show an argument is weak?
7. Is every valid or strong argument with true premises good? Explain.
8. What is a compound claim?
9. Give a conditional, and then rewrite it three ways.
10. a. What is a contradictory of a claim?
    b. Give an example of an "or" claim and its contradictory.
    c. Give an example of a conditional and its contradictory.
11. Give an example of arguing by excluding possibilities. Is it valid?
12. What is a false dilemma? Give an example.
13. Give an example of the direct way of reasoning with conditionals. Is it valid?
14. Give an example of the indirect way of reasoning with conditionals. Is it valid?
15. Give an example of affirming the consequent. Is it valid?
16. Give an example of denying the antecedent. Is it valid?
17. Is every argument that uses reasoning in a chain with conditionals good? Explain.
18. a. What does it mean to say that A is a necessary condition for B?
    b. Give examples of claims A and B such that:
       i. A is necessary for B, but A is not sufficient for B.
       ii. A is sufficient for B, but A is not necessary for B.
       iii. A is both necessary and sufficient for B.
       iv. A is neither necessary nor sufficient for B.
19. How does a slippery slope argument differ from reducing to the absurd?
20. Give an example of an "all" claim and a contradictory of it.
21. Give an example of a "some" claim and a contradictory of it.
22. Give an example of a "no" claim and a contradictory of it.
23. Give an example of arguing backwards with "all." Is it valid?
24. Give an "only" claim, and then rewrite it as an "all" claim.
25. Give an example of a strong method of reasoning with vague generalities.
26. Give an example of a weak method of reasoning with vague generalities.
27. List the valid forms of arguments we studied in Chapters 7 and 8.
28. List the weak forms of argument in Chapters 7 and 8 that we said indicated that an argument is unrepairable.

AVOIDING

BAD ARGUMENTS

9 Concealed Claims

A. Where's the Argument?

Someone tries to convince us by a choice of words rather than by an argument— the subtleties of rhetoric in place of reasoned deliberation.

We've already seen an example: persuasive definitions. Someone tries to close off the argument by making a definition that should be the conclusion. If someone defines "abortion" to mean "the murder of an unborn child," he's made it impossible to debate whether abortion is murder and whether a fetus is a human being. Those conclusions are built into the definition.

There are lots of ways we conceal claims through our choice of words. Collectively we call them ***slanters***. Slanters are bad because they can get us to believe a dubious claim without reflecting on it. Let's look at some.

B. Loaded Questions

"When are you going to stop drinking and driving?"

Don't answer. Respond, instead, by pointing out the concealed claim: "What makes you think I've been drinking and driving?"

> ***Loaded question*** A loaded question is a question that conceals a dubious claim that should be argued for rather than assumed.

Example 1 Lee: Why can't cats be taught to follow?
Suzy: What makes you think that cats can't be taught to follow?

Analysis Lee poses a loaded question. Suzy answers it by pointing out and challenging the concealed claim. *The best response to a loaded question is to point out the concealed claim and begin discussing that.*

Example 2 Dick: Why do all women like to shop?
Zoe: We don't.

Analysis Zoe has answered Dick's loaded question by denying his concealed claim.

Example 3 *What Do Dogs Dream About?*

The title of a book on sale at a supermarket checkout counter

Analysis Sometime it's not so easy to see that a dubious claim has been concealed if we're ready to believe it.

C. What Did You Say?

1. Making it sound nasty or nice

Dysphemism (dis´-fuh-mizm) A dysphemism is a word or phrase that makes something sound worse than a neutral description.

Euphemism (yoo´-fuh-mizm) A euphemism is a word or phrase that makes something sound better than a neutral description.

Example 4 The freedom fighters attacked the convoy.

Analysis "Freedom fighters" is a euphemism, concealing the claim that the guerillas are good people fighting to liberate their country and give their countrymen freedom.

Example 5 The terrorists attacked the convoy.

Analysis "Terrorists" is a dysphemism, concealing the claim that the guerillas are bad people, inflicting violence on civilians for their own partisan ends without popular support. *A concealed claim may be true.* The guerillas may be fighting for freedom. Or they may be terrorists. Or they may be neither. But strong language doesn't prove it.

Example 6 The merciless slaughter of seals for their fur continues in a number of countries.

Analysis "Merciless slaughter" is a dysphemism; "harvesting" would be a euphemism; "killing" would be a neutral description.

Example 7 The home page of the website of Los Alamos National Laboratory has the following links you can click: Science and Technology, Working with LANL, Organization, Community, Education & Internships, Life@LANL, International.

Analysis The home page is a euphemism by ***misdirection***. If you didn't already know that LANL is the main center for nuclear weapons research in the United States, you might think from this that the lab is devoted solely to scientific research and its applications for the betterment of humanity.

The descriptions in the personals ads are full of euphemisms, like "full-figured" or "mature." But not every description involves a euphemism. One man described himself as "attractive, fun, and fit." He may have lied, but he didn't use a nice word in place of a neutral one. Nor is every euphemism bad. We don't want to get rid of every pleasant or unpleasant description in our writing and speech. We just want to be aware of misuses where we're being asked to buy into dubious concealed claims.

Sometimes people use complicated sounding terms to make their work sound more "scientific." In *Nursing Process and Nursing Diagnosis* the authors talk about "diversional activity deficit"—when you read on, you realize they mean "boredom."

2. Downplayers and up-players

Example 8 Zoe: Hey Mom. Great news. I managed to pass my first French exam.
Mom: You only just passed?

Analysis Zoe has up-played the significance of what she did, concealing the claim "It took great effort to pass" with the word "managed." Her mother downplayed the significance of passing by using "only just," concealing the claim "Passing and not getting a good grade is not commendable."

A ***downplayer*** is a word or phrase that minimizes the significance of a claim, while an ***up-player*** exaggerates the significance.

> "Yes, I have cheated in a class although it has never been off someone else. Just crib notes." *U. The National College Magazine*, November 1996

The extreme version of an up-player is called ***hyperbole*** (hi-purr´-buh-lee):

> Maria: I'm sorry I'm late for work. I had a terrible emergency at home.
> Boss: Oh, no. I'm so sorry. What happened?
> Maria: I ran out of mousse and had to go to the store.

One way to downplay is with words that restrict or limit the meaning of others, what we call ***qualifiers***—as in my promise that if you buy this book you will certainly pass this course.*

Example 9 The city will install stop signs this week for a four-way stop at the corner of St. George Boulevard, attempting to cut down accidents and to prepare motorists for a stoplight at the intersection.

* Purchaser must agree to study this material at least five hours per day during the term.

"The city has recorded six accidents at the intersection in the past four months, and there may have been more that were not reported," said city traffic engineer Aron Baker.

The Spectrum, September 23, 1996

Analysis What did he say? Were there more accidents? No. There *may have been* more. But then there may not have been more. Or aliens may have landed at that intersection. The qualifiers "may" and "might" allow someone to suggest what he's not willing to say. In a badly written history book you'll find those words too often, with sentences like "Thomas Jefferson may have thought that . . .".

Example 10 Maria (to her boss): I am truly sorry that it has taken so long for you to understand what I've been saying.

Analysis Maria isn't sorry at all. A ***weaseler*** is a claim that's qualified so much that the apparent meaning is no longer there.

Example 11 Zoe: She got her "degree" from a beauty school.

Analysis People also downplay by using quotation marks or a change in voice. The hidden claim here is "A degree from a beauty school is not really something worth calling a degree."

3. Where's the proof?

Example 12 Dr. E to Suzy: Cats can't reason. It's obvious to any thinking person. Being around them so much must have convinced you of that. Of course, some people are misguided by their emotions into thinking that felines have intelligence.

Analysis Dr. E didn't prove that cats can't reason, though he made it sound as if he were proving something. He was just repeating the claim, trying to browbeat Suzy into believing it with the words "obvious," "must have convinced," "some people are misguided."

> ***Proof substitute*** A proof substitute is a word or phrase that suggests the speaker has a proof, but no proof is actually offered.

Example 13 Suzy: Cats can so reason. It's been shown over and over that they can.

Analysis Unless Suzy can point to some studies, this is a proof substitute, too. "I know it 'cause I read it somewhere" shouldn't be convincing, even to yourself.

Example 14 When a dog is offered a choice between a full dish and a half-full dish of the same food, doesn't it spontaneously pick the larger meal? Acting otherwise would be devastatingly irrational. Choosing the larger of two amounts of food is probably one of the preconditions for the survival of any living organism. Evolution has been able to conceive such complex strategies for food gathering, storing, and predation, that it should not be astonishing that an operation as simple as the comparison of two quantities is available to so many species.

Stephen Dehaene, *The Number Sense*

Analysis Rather than being browbeaten by this author's proof substitute, I thought of my own experience with dogs over the years. I've seen that they don't choose more rather than less. They choose what is more accessible or comes to their notice (noses) first; they will almost always eat first a few bits of dry dog food that are spread on the ground instead of a mound of dog food in a dish. This is an armchair psychology conjecture hardened by proof substitutes into an assertion.

I always say that I prefer a student who asks questions. It's better to be thought dumb and learn something than to sit on your ignorance. If someone tells you it's obvious or conceals a lack of proof with flowery language, don't be cowed—ask for the proof.

Ridicule, which we looked at before, is a particularly nasty form of proof substitute: that's so obviously wrong it's laughable.

> Dr. E: Cats can reason? Sure, and the next thing you know you'll be inviting them over to play poker.

Another way to conceal that you have no support for your claim is to ***shift the burden of proof***.

> Suzy: Cats can reason.
> Dick: You've got to be joking.
> Suzy: O.K. then mister smarty-pants, tell me why you think they can't.

Example 15 Tom: The university should lower tuition.
Maria: Why?
Tom: Why not?

Analysis Tom hasn't given any reason to think his claim is true. He's only invited Maria to say why she thinks it's false, so he can attack that—which is easier than supporting his position.

The burden of proof is on the person making the claim. "I don't have to support my claim; you have to show it's not true" is just wrong.

Example 16 Why wouldn't you want laws against where sexual predators can live?

Analysis Often an attempt to shift the burden of proof is given as a question that assumes a default judgment.

4. Innuendos

Any concealed claim is an ***innuendo***. But usually we use that term for concealed claims that are really unpleasant.

> Zoe: Where are you from?
> Harry: New York.
> Zoe: Oh, I'm sorry.

Innuendos imply nasty claims, as politicians know well: "I agree. My opponent is telling the truth this time."

You may be tempted to use slanters in your own writing. Don't. Slanters turn off those you want to convince, so you'll only be preaching to the converted. Worse, though they may work for the moment, they don't stick. Without a real argument, the other person will remember only the joke or jibe. A good argument can last and last—the other person can see the point clearly and reconstruct it. And if you use slanters, your opponent can destroy your points not by facing your real argument but by pointing them out.

If you reason calmly and well, you will earn the respect of others and may learn that others merit your respect, too.

When evaluating someone else's reasoning, acknowledge that he or she may have been a bit emotional. Get rid of the noise—ignore the slanting, interpret the claims neutrally, and see if there is a good reason to believe.

Summary We want to recognize slanters. Labels and classifications like "downplayer," "weaseler," and "innuendo" are aids to help you learn how to recognize that something bad is going on when someone's trying to convince. Often not just one but two or more labels apply. You know the material in this chapter when you can take an argument and point out the concealed claims in it, rewriting to eliminate slanted language. The labels are just shorthand for explanations you can give in your own words.

Key Words

slanter
loaded question
euphemism
dysphemism
misdirection
downplayer
up-player
hyperbole
qualifier
weaseler
proof substitute
burden of proof
innuendo

> To recite from a Pentagon press release that an Iraqi division has been "degraded by 70 percent" is an astounding abdication of journalistic responsibility. A journalist these days must not just report the facts, but also explain the news, give it color and significance. The graphic reality of "degradation" is a large pile of dismembered bodies. . . .
>
> Russell Smith, "The New Newspeak,"
> *The New York Review of Books*, May 29, 2003

Exercises for Chapter 9

1. Come up with a loaded question you might pose to an instructor to try to make him or her give you a better grade.
2. Give a loaded question you might ask a police officer who stops you.
3. Give an example of "politically correct" language and rephrase it in neutral language.
4. Give a euphemism and a dysphemism for each of the following. Be sure your word or phrase can be used in a sentence in place of the original.
   a. Used car.
   b. Sexually explicit books.
   c. Mentally handicapped person.
   d. Unemployed person.
5. Find an example of a euphemism from a news broadcast.
6. Find an example of a dysphemism from a news broadcast.
7. Find an example of a downplayer. Say what the hidden claim is.
8. Find an example of hyperbole from a news broadcast.
9. Typical proof substitutes are "obviously" and "everyone knows that . . .". List six more.
10. Find an example from *another* textbook in which it sounds like the author is giving an argument but there's really no proof.
11. Find an example from a political speech in which it sounds like the speaker is giving an argument but there's really no proof.
12. Rewrite the following actual quotes in neutral language:
    a. "Our operatives succeeded with the termination with extreme prejudice." (Reported by the CIA)
    b. "There was a premature impact of the aircraft with the terrain below." (Announced by the FAA)
13. Write a neutral description of someone you know well, one that someone else could use to recognize him or her. Now write a slanted version by replacing the neutral terms with euphemisms or dysphemisms, adding downplayers or up-players.

14. Bring to class an article from a respected website. Read it to the class. Then replace all the slanters and read it again.

Say what, if anything, is wrong in the following and make any concealed claim explicit.

15. When are you going to start studying in this course?

16. New Mexico surveys show 60 percent of high schoolers have had sex before graduating, and only 12 percent remain abstinent until marriage.
Albuquerque Journal, January 13, 2005

17. Scientists have discovered a cure for baldness.

18. E-mail us and we'll do our best to get back to you within 12 hours.
Ticketmaster's "contact us" web page

19. New Mexico had fewer than one in five—about 18 percent—of its total population living in poverty last year, while the United States remained level at about 12.5 percent.
Sean Olson, *Albuquerque Journal*, August 27, 2008

20. Dick: That was really rotten, making me wait for an hour.
Zoe: I'm sorry you feel that way.

21. The study of history is not expected to yield any framework in which successful predictions can be made. From time to time, schools of thought arise which claim this ability, but their record makes even economists seem like skilled clairvoyants.
Paul Ormerod, *The Death of Economics*

22. Knowing the law, and being perhaps a respectable, religious person, he is anxious to abstain from all appearance of evil. *The Shepherd's Life*, W. H. Hudson, 1921

23. The Army Corps of Engineers will begin its work on swamp reclamation next month.

24. Thousands of words from U.S. officials, it appears, have proved no match for the last week's news, which produced a barrage of pictures of wounded Afghan children and of Israeli tanks rolling into Palestinian villages.
"Talking heads just can't compete," a Western diplomat in Cairo said. "The images touch emotions, and people in this part of the world react according to their emotions."
New York Times News Service, October 19, 2001

25. (from the front of a Simple Truth Almond Milk carton)
Free from 101+ artificial preservatives & ingredients*
[there is no note for the asterisk]
(from the back of Simple Truth Almond Milk)
INGREDIENTS: Almond milk (filtered water, almonds), Evaporated Sugar Cane, Tricalcium Phosphate, Sea Salt, Gellan Gum, Dipotassium Phosphate, Xanthan Gum, Sunflower Lecithin, Vitamin A Palmitate, Vitamin D2, D-Alpha-Tocopherol

26. "In a way, we're a kind of a Peace Corps."
A training director of the Fort Bragg Green Beret Center, 1969

27. Tom: This book *Esperanza's Box of Saints* by Maria Escandón is great. It's so good that if I didn't know better I would have thought it was written by a man.

28. Though France is one of the most atheistic nations on earth—surpassed only by Japan, China, and, oddly, the Czech Republic—it has always revered political messiahs: Napoleon, Boulanger, Pétain, De Gaulle, Mitterand.
    Mark Lilla,"The Strangely Conservative French," *New York Review of Books*, 2015

29. [In the Business Outlook section of the *Albuquerque Journal*, July 18, 2011, there was an article by Jerry Pacheco about businesses in northern Mexico exporting to the U.S.] Only 18 percent of the companies surveyed that had operations in Mexico said that they had experienced supply chain disruption due to security issues.

30. How many years in prison should someone get for sending a virus out on the internet that infects thousands of machines?

31. It seems fairly safe to assume that foreign-exchange dealers are human and hence more intelligent than ants. We may occasionally have our doubts, but broadly speaking this is true.
    Paul Ormerod, *Butterfly Economics*

32. U.S. Air Force Colonel David Opfer, air attaché in Cambodia, complained to reporters about their coverage of the Vietnam War, "You always write bombing, bombing, bombing. It's not bombing; it's air support."

33. Students should be required to wear uniforms in high schools. It has been well documented that wearing uniforms reduces gang violence.

34. Despite the fact that [Benjamin] Franklin was out of touch with the centers of European thought, his ideas on electricity were truly original and fundamental.
    Gordon S. Wood, *The New York Review of Books*, September 26, 2003

35. Maria: Wanda's so sad. She doesn't even want to get out of bed anymore. It looks like she's in another bout of blues.

36. The gaming industry in Nevada recorded another record year of profits.

37. (In a review of a book that contains descriptions of leaders of the Soviet Union) Even for politicians, they spend a disproportionate amount of their time drinking, plotting, lying, swearing, and insulting one another.
    Robert Cottrell, *The New York Review of Books*, May 1, 2003

38. Manuel: Hey, Dr. E, I read in the *New Scientist* that in Queensland, Australia, you can buy free-range eggs endorsed by the Australian humane society, where the egg boxes say, "These eggs come from hens that are: Free from hunger and thirst; Free from pain, injury and disease; Free from fear and distress; Free from discomfort; Free to express themselves."
    Dr. E: Great. I should apply for a job as a free-range hen.

39. The U.S. economy shed 1.4 million jobs over the 12 months ended in March.
    USA Today, March 24, 2002

40. "We didn't turn him down. We didn't accept him." President of Springdale Country Club (Princeton, N.J.), concerning an African-American applicant for membership.

41. That corporation wants to erect a hotel in an unspoiled wilderness area.

42. The proposed ban on bulk shipments [of tequila to the United States] would not take place until January 2005, and Greisser said the year's delay was to provide Mexican companies time to expand their bottling plants.

 "This proposal could have a grave effect on consumers worldwide through higher prices, fewer choices and the significant potential for serious product shortages," said Peter Cressy, president of the Distilled Spirits Council of the United States.

Albuquerque Journal, Sept. 26, 2003

43. [Malcolm] Sharbutt [co-star of the current production and two-year veteran] attributes the staying power [of the Vortex theater] to the plays on the program. "It's because we offer a different venue than the other places in town," he says. "You can see 'Arsenic and Old Lace' or a play by Neil Simon anywhere in town, but we're going to do plays about junkies and rape and bad families. We try to keep it real."

Albuquerque Tribune, January 10, 2003

44. (from the front of a bottle of Equate Clear Hand Soap in large type)
Washes away germs and bacteria**
 (from the back in small type)
** Washing hands helps wash away bacteria and germs.

45. At last our government has decided to give compensation to the Japanese who were resettled in internment camps during World War II.

46. *Blondes aren't dumb—they're just slow*
BERLIN—Blonde women are not dumber than brunettes or redheads, a reassuring study shows—they are just slower at processing information, take longer to react to stimuli and tend to retain less information for a shorter period of time than other women.

 "This should put an end to the insulting view that blondes are airheads," said Dr. Andrea Stenner, a blond sociologist who studied more than 3,000 women for her doctoral research project. *Weekly World News,* October 15, 1996

47. Dr. Rajendra K. Pachauri, the chairman of the United Nations Intergovernmental Panel on Climate Change (IPCC), compared Bjørn Lomborg, Danish statistician and author of *The Skeptical Environmentalist*, to Adolf Hitler in an interview with *Jyllandsposten*, a leading Danish newspaper (April 21). Pachauri said, "What is the difference between Lomborg's view of humanity and Hitler's? You cannot treat people like cattle. You must respect the diversity of cultures on earth. Lomborg thinks of people like numbers. He thinks it would be cheaper just to evacuate people from the Maldives, rather than trying to prevent world sea levels from rising so that island groups like the Maldives or Tuvalu just disappear into the sea. But where's the respect for people in that? People have a right to live and die in the place where their forefathers have lived and died. If you were to accept Lomborg's way of thinking, then maybe what Hitler did was the right thing." Cooler Heads Coalition, April 28, 2004
<http://www.globalwarming.org/article.php?uid=637>

48. (in large type from the front of a package of Purina Dog Chow Complete)
50 lb. BONUS SIZE 4 lbs. free

49. *Viviscal Man*
    Scientifically formulated for men who want to nourish thinning hair and promotes existing hair growth* from within
    [there is no note for the asterisk]
    Clinically Researched Formula
    Viviscal is grounded in 25 years of continuous research and development. The efficacy of Viviscal is supported by 7 clinical studies.

50. Wages for the same kind of labor are lower in the South than in the North. Also, wages are lower in Puerto Rico than in the United States. How can a northern employee protect his wage level from the competition of lower-wage southern labor? And how can a laborer in the United States protect his job (and higher wage rate) from Puerto Rican labor? One device would be to advocate "equal pay for equal work" in the United States, including Puerto Rico, by legislating minimum wages higher than the prevailing level in the South and Puerto Rico. It should come as no surprise to learn that in the United States support for minimum-wage laws comes primarily from northerners who profess to be trying to help the poorer southern laborers.
    A. Alchian and W. Allen, *University Economics*

Further Study Courses on rhetoric and on advertising spend a lot of time looking at slanters in nonargumentative persuasion.

10 Too Much Emotion

Emotions do and should play a role in our reasoning. We can't even begin to make good decisions if we don't consider their significance in our lives. But that doesn't mean we have to be swayed entirely by our emotions.

An ***appeal to emotion*** in an argument is just a premise that says you should believe or do something because you feel a certain way. Often we call the entire argument in which such a premise appears an appeal to emotion.

For example, last night Suzy and Tom were watching TV:

> Suzy: Did you see that ad? It's so sad, I cried. That group says it will help those poor kids. We should send them some money.

To construe this as a good argument, we need to add "If you feel sorry for poor kids, you should give money to any organization that says it will help them." That's an ***appeal to pity***. It's implausible: some drug cartels help kids, too.

Compare that to what Zoe said to Dick last week:

> We should give to the American Friends Service Committee. They help people all over the world help themselves, and they don't ask the people they help whether they agree with them. They've been doing it well for nearly a century now, and they have very low overhead—almost all the money they get is used for projects to help people. All those people who don't have running water or health care deserve our help. Think of those poor kids growing up malnourished and sick. We've got enough money to send them $50.

This argument requires an unstated premise appealing to pity, too. But it isn't just "Do it because you feel sorry for someone." What's needed is something like "If you feel sorry for people, *and* you have a way to help them that is efficient and morally upright, *and* you have enough money to help, then you should send the organization money." That seems plausible, though whether this is the best use of Zoe and Dick's money needs to be considered, too.

Appealing to fear is one way politicians and advertisers manipulate people. For example, on the cover of a free three-minute video mailed to voters' homes in Las Vegas is a picture of a bearded young man in a sweatshirt pointing a gun directly at the reader, with the following text.

> At 14 Years Old He Stole A Car.
> At 16 He Raped.
> At 17 He Killed.
> And He Still Doesn't Have A Record.
> We Cannot Continue To Allow Violent Criminals To Terrorize Our Neighborhoods.

Las Vegas Review Journal Tuesday, June 25, 1996 Living in Fear "*. . . By many measures, the threat of youth related crime and its fallout are on the rise in Las Vegas Valley . . .*"	Reuter News Service Friday, June 18, 1996 Nevada Rated Most Dangerous State "*. . . Nevada is the most dangerous state in the nation this year . . .*" *according to an independent midwest research firm.*	Reno Gazette Journal Sunday, July 14, 1996 Youth-Crime Increase Alarms Officials "*The rise in violent crime young people commit is the most serious issue confronting the juvenile system today . . .*"

> Elect COBB Nevada State Senate

This is an argument. The unstated conclusion is "You should vote for Cobb." The only reason it gives for electing Cobb is fear. And in this particularly egregious example it doesn't even link the fear to the conclusion. An appeal to fear is bad if it substitutes one legitimate concern for all others, clouding our minds to alternatives.

Often it requires some thought to see whether an appeal to fear is good. Consider the advertisement:

> A lonely road. Your car breaks down. It's dark. Aren't you glad you have a Dorkler interactive alert system that can contact our office with your location!

The implicit argument here is "Because your car might break down at night on a lonely road, you should buy a Dorkler interactive alert system." What's needed to make it a strong argument is a premise like "A Dorkler brand interactive alert system will save you from the dangers of the night." That's not so implausible. But it isn't enough. Also needed is "Your only consideration in deciding whether to buy *this* brand of interactive alert system is your concern about your safety." That's implausible.

Sometimes, though, an appeal to fear can be the sole legitimate factor in making a decision, as in the next example.

Zoe: You shouldn't drive so fast in this rain.
Dick: Why not?
Zoe: The roads are very slippery after the first rain of the season, and we could get into a serious accident.

This argument appeals to Dick's fears—but appropriately so. The unstated and quite plausible appeal to emotion is "You should slow down driving in the rain if you are afraid of getting into a serious accident."

An ***appeal to spite***, the hope of revenge, is invariably rejected as bad by some people on moral grounds. In some cultures, though, it's not only acceptable but a moral imperative to "get even," to preserve one's "honor." We encounter this kind of argument often enough:

Dick: Hi, Tom. What's wrong with your car?
Tom: The battery's dead. Can you help me push it? Harry will steer.
Dick: Sure.
Zoe: (whispering) What're you doing, Dick? Don't you remember that Tom wouldn't help you fix the fence last week?

What Zoe said isn't an argument, but we can construe it as one: "You shouldn't help Tom start his car because he wouldn't help you last week." The premise needed to make this a strong argument is "You shouldn't help anyone who has refused to help you (recently)." You decide whether that's plausible.

An appeal to spite often invokes the "principle" that ***two wrongs make a right***. For example, when a new national monument was declared in Utah just before the 1996 presidential election, some who were opposed to it complained there was no consultation before the decision, no "due process." Here's what the Southern Utah Wilderness Alliance, strong lobbyists for the monument, said in its November 1996 *Bulletin*:

Q: What about due process?
A: Due process meant nothing to Utah politicians last year when they tried to ramrod their anti-wilderness proposal down the throat of not only Utahns, but all Americans; their intransigence only proved to the President that rational negotiation on land protection issues in southern Utah is not possible.

This principle is used a lot in justifying or excusing atrocities in war. On November 22, 2012, a representative of the Syrian coalition fighting the government in Syria was asked on the BBC if he condemned the execution of Syrian soldiers held prisoner by his coalition fighters. He responded by citing all the horrible things the Syrian government had done. That's a sure way for everyone's behavior to sink to the lowest level.

An argument that ***calls in your debts*** appeals to the opposite of spite: "You should believe or do something if you owe someone a favor." For example, yesterday Lee said to Dick:

> How can you go to the movies with Harry and not watch the game with me? Don't you remember how I helped you wash your car last week?

Calling in your debts as a motive is often nothing more than milking guilt.

It isn't only negative emotions that are played on in trying to convince. A ***feel-good argument*** is one that appeals to our wanting to feel good about ourselves. Yesterday Suzy said to Dr. E,

> I really deserve a passing grade in your course. I know that you're a fair grader, and you've always been terrific to everyone in the class. I admire how you handle the class, and I've enjoyed your teaching so much that it would be a pity if I didn't have something to show for it.

"Gee," Dr. E thinks, "I guess I should pass her . . . No, wait, she hasn't given me any reason to change her grade." The premise that's missing is "You should give a passing mark to anyone who thinks you're a great person." This ***apple polishing*** is an ***appeal to vanity***.

But not every comment on what seems to be vanity is a bad argument:

> *To Have and to Hold*
> Get healthy, shiny hold with Pantene® Pro-V® Hairspray. The pro-vitamin formula penetrates to make your hair strong and your shine last. Now, spray your way to all-day hold and all-day shine. With Pantene Pro-V Hairsprays.
> PANTENE PRO-V For Hair So Healthy It Shines

This attempt to convince you to buy hairspray requires an unstated premise that you want to look good with shiny, well-kept hair. That may be true. Whether to believe the other claims, though, and whether to believe the unstated premise that this hairspray is the best to satisfy your desire to look good, are the real issues.

Yet sometimes invoking our wish to feel good is all that's needed. As Zoe said to Dick:

> We should go to the Zoe Austen movie tonight. I've always liked her novels, and I'm sure I'll enjoy it, and you said it was my turn to pick.

After all, what besides feeling good is there in making a choice of which movie to see?

Finally, there's the ***appeal to tradition***: if it was good enough for father, it's good enough for me.

> In September, despite an increasing chorus of complaints, Peruvians celebrated the annual Gastronomic Festival of the Cat in a village just south of Lima, serving a variety of feline delicacies (fried cat strips, cat stew, grilled cat with spicy huacatay). For the most part, according to a *Chicago Tribune* report, the dishes are made with specially bred cats rather than street prowlers, and are consumed for their health benefits, though centuries-old tradition is the likeliest explanation. Said one Peruvian, such cultural events "are our roots and can't be forgotten."
> *Chicago Tribune*, October 15, 2008

Each appeal to emotion we've looked at has a prescriptive conclusion: each is an attempt to convince someone that he or she should do something.

> An appeal to emotion in an argument with a *prescriptive* conclusion can be good or can be bad. Being alert to the use of emotion helps clarify the kinds of premises needed in such an argument so we can more easily analyze it.

Bad arguments that appeal to emotion aren't bad just because they appeal to emotion. They're bad for the same reasons other arguments are bad: they have a false premise, or are weak, or assume dubious unstated premises. If Flo says, "I shouldn't have to eat vegetables because I hate 'em," she's making a bad argument: the unstated premise "Flo should eat only what she likes" is dubious, for then she'd eat only ice cream and lollipops.

Labeling an argument as an appeal to emotion, then, is not an analysis of the argument but only a helpful start to seeing whether the argument is good or bad. Except in some cases, . . .

This is an appeal to emotion with a *descriptive* conclusion, an example of ***wishful thinking***. It's bad. Why should we believe some description of the world is true just because we are moved by our emotions? Wanting it so doesn't make it so.

> Any appeal to emotion with a *descriptive* conclusion is bad if the appeal cannot be deleted as premise.

Key Words

appeal to emotion	calling in your debts
appeal to pity	feel-good argument
appeal to fear	appeal to vanity
appeal to spite	appeal to tradition
two wrongs make a right	wishful thinking

Exercises for Chapter 10

1. Write a *bad* argument in favor of affirmative action whose only premises appeal to pity.

2. Find an advertisement that uses apple polishing. Is it a good argument?

3. Find an advertisement that uses an appeal to fear. Is it a good argument?

4. Make up an appeal to some emotion for the next time a traffic officer stops you.

5. Report to your class on a "calling in your debts" argument you've heard.

6. Give an example of an appeal to spite that invokes what someone believes. (Hint: Look at political speeches.) Is it a good argument?

7. Give an example of an *appeal to patriotism*. Is it a good argument?
   (Samuel Johnson: "Patriotism is the last refuge of a scoundrel.")
   (Ambrose Bierce: "Patriotism is the first refuge of a scoundrel.")

For each of the following, decide if it is an argument. If it is, decide if it is an appeal to an emotion and, if so, which emotion(s). Then decide whether it's a good argument.

8. Zoe: We should stop all experimentation on animals right now. Imagine, hurting those poor doggies.
   Dick: But there's no reason why we shouldn't continue experimenting with cats. You know how they make me sneeze.

9. Vote for Senator Wong. He knows how important your concerns are.

10. Before you buy that Japanese car, ask whether you want to see some Japanese tycoon get rich at your expense or whether you'd prefer to see an American kid get a meal on his plate next week.

11. Dear Dr. E,
    I was very disappointed with my grade in your critical thinking course, but I'm sure that it was just a mistake in calculating my marks. Can I speak with you this Tuesday, right before I have lunch with my uncle, Dr. Jones, the Dean of Liberal Arts, where we plan to discuss sexual harassment on this campus?
    Sincerely, *Elizabeth Burnstile*

12. Mom: Go ahead, Zoe. Live with your boyfriend, Dick. Who am I to say no? I'm just your mother. Break my heart.

13. Sunbathing does not cause skin cancer. If it did, how could I enjoy the beach?

14. Democracy is the best form of government. Otherwise this wouldn't be the greatest country in the world.

15. Smoking can't cause cancer, or I would have been dead a long time ago.

16. Dear Senator:
    Before you make up your mind on how to vote on the abortion bill, I'd like to remind you that those who support abortion rights usually have small families. A few years from now, all my six children, and the many children of my friends, all of whom believe abortion is morally wrong, will be voting.

17. You mean that after we flew you here to Florida, paid for your lodging, showed you a wonderful time—all for free—you aren't going to buy a building site from us?

18. You shouldn't vote for gun control. It'll just make it easier for violent criminals to take advantage of us.

19. Wanda: I know this diet's going to work because I have to lose 20 pounds by the end of this month.

20. In Dr. E's class, if a student has to miss an exam, then he or she has to petition to be excused. If the petition is granted for a midterm, then the final counts that much more. If the petition is denied, the student fails the exam. Here's an excuse petition from one of his students, written before the exam. Is it a good argument? Should Dr. E grant it?

    October seventeenth through the twenty-first I will be out of town due to a family function. I am aware that my philosophy midterm falls on the 17th and, unfortunately, my flight leaves at 7 a.m. that morning. I am asking to please be excused from the midterm.

    My boyfriend of two and a half years is standing as the best man in his brother's wedding. Being together for two years, I have become as much a part of his family as he is. This wedding is a once in a lifetime event and I want to be there to share it with him.

    I am a 100% devoted student and would never intentionally miss an exam. However, this is something beyond my control. I understand that if my request is granted I will have to put forth extra effort and prepare myself for the final. With the only other alternative being to drop the course, I am fully prepared to do whatever it takes.

    I have attached a copy of my flight reservation as well as a copy of the wedding invitation for verification. I am aware that many teachers would not even give me the opportunity to petition to be excused when the midterm is the case, but I would more than appreciate it if you would grant my request.

Further Study *Descartes' Error: Emotion, Reason, and the Human Brain* by Antonio R. Damasio is a good discussion of how emotions are essential to good reasoning.

11 Fallacies

A summary of bad arguments

A. What Is a Fallacy?

We've seen lots of bad arguments. Each fits *at least* one of the conditions for an argument to be unrepairable (p. 94), or else directly violates the Principle of Rational Discussion. We've labeled a few kinds of these as the sort that typically are unrepairable.

> ***Fallacy*** A fallacy is a bad argument of one of the types that we've agreed are typically unrepairable.

For some fallacy types, every single argument of that type is bad; for others, most, though not all, are bad. Even taking shortcuts in analyzing arguments requires judgment. Let's review ones we've seen by classifying them into three kinds: structural fallacies, content fallacies, and violations of the Principle of Rational Discussion.

B. Structural Fallacies

Some arguments are bad just because of their form. It doesn't matter if they're about dogs and cats, or numbers, or truth and beauty. The form alone tells us the person isn't reasoning well. These are the bad arguments we learned about when we studied compound claims and general claims. Each, unless there are other claims as premises, is weak and unrepairable.

Fallacy type	***Similar type of valid or strong argument***
affirming the consequent If A, then B. B. Therefore, A.	*direct way of reasoning* If A, then B. A Therefore, B.
denying the antecedent If A, then B. not A. Therefore, not B.	*indirect way of reasoning* If A, then B. not B Therefore, not A.
arguing backwards with all All S are P. a is P. Therefore, a is S.	*direct way of reasoning with* all All S are P. a is S. Therefore, a is P.
reasoning in a chain with some Some S are P. Some P are Q. Therefore, some S are Q.	*reasoning in a chain with* all All S are P. All P are Q. Therefore, all S are Q.
arguing backwards with no All S are P. No Q is S. Therefore, no Q is P.	*direct way of reasoning with* no All S are P. No Q is P. Therefore, no Q is S.
arguing backwards with almost all Almost all S are P. a is P. Therefore, a is S.	*direct way of reasoning with* almost all Almost all S are P. a is S. Therefore, a is P.
reasoning in a chain with almost all Almost all S are P. Almost all P are Q. Therefore, almost all S are Q.	

When someone presents an argument that fits one of these fallacy types, we assume that he or she is confused about how to reason. We don't try to repair it.

C. Content Fallacies

Many arguments are bad because they use or require for repair a false or dubious premise. Usually we have to spend some time analyzing the argument, isolating the dubious premise.

But some arguments look like ones we're always suspicious of. When we spot one of those, we look for the *generic premise* that the argument uses or needs for repair. An argument that uses one of those isn't necessarily bad. Sometimes the premise is plausible or even clearly true. *The argument is a fallacy only if the premise is dubious and can't be deleted.*

- ***Drawing the line***
  If you can't make this difference precise, there's no difference.
- ***Subjectivist fallacy***
  If there's a lot of disagreement about this claim, it's subjective.
- ***Mistaking the person (group) for the claim***
  (Almost) anything that _____ says about _____ is (probably) false.
- ***Mistaking the person (group) for the argument***
  (Almost) any argument that _____ gives about _____ is bad.
- ***Bad appeal to authority***
  (Almost) anything that _____ says about _____ is (probably) true.
- ***Bad appeal to common belief***
  If (almost) everyone else (in this group) believes (or does) _____ , then it's true.
- ***Phony refutation***
  1. _____ has done or said _____, which shows that he or she does not believe the conclusion of his or her own argument.
  2. If someone does not believe the conclusion of his or her own argument, then the argument is bad.
- ***False dilemma***
  (This is the use of any "or" claim that is false or dubious. Sometimes an equivalent conditional is used.)
- ***Slippery slope***
  (This is reasoning in a chain with conditionals where at least one of them is false or dubious.)
- ***Appeal to emotion***
  You should believe or do _____ because you feel _____ .
  (This is always bad if the conclusion is a descriptive claim.)
- ***Appeal to tradition***
  You should believe or do _____ because it's a tradition.

D. Violating the Principle of Rational Discussion

Sometimes it seems the other person doesn't understand how to reason well or is intending to mislead. And sometimes there's not even an argument.

- ***Begging the question***
  The point of an argument is to convince that a claim is true. So the premises of an argument have to be more plausible than the conclusion.
- ***Strawman***
  It's easier to knock down someone's argument if you misrepresent it, putting words in the other person's mouth.
- ***Shifting the burden of proof***
  It's easier to ask for a disproof of your claim than to prove it yourself.
- ***Relevance***
  Sometimes people say a premise or premises aren't relevant to the conclusion. But that's not a category of fallacy, just an observation that the argument is so weak you can't imagine any way to repair it.

There are two other bad ways to try to convince that we've considered. Though they aren't arguments, and so aren't fallacies, they're worth noting as violations of the Principle of Rational Discussion.

- ***Slanters***
  Concealing claims that are dubious by a misleading use of language.
- ***Ridicule***
  Making someone or something the butt of a joke in order to convince.

E. Is This Really a Mistake?

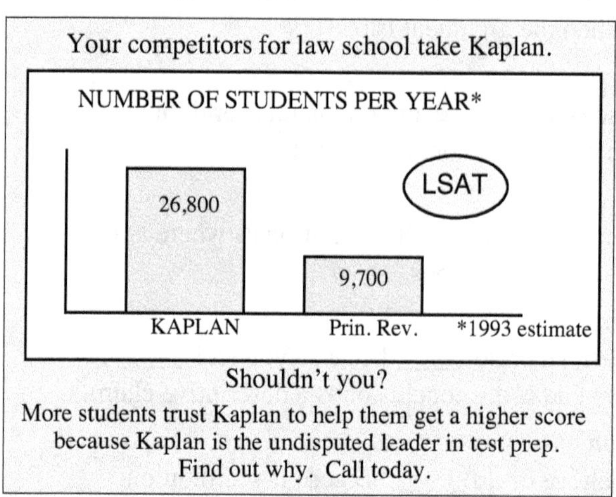

Your competitors for law school take Kaplan.
NUMBER OF STUDENTS PER YEAR*
LSAT
26,800
9,700
KAPLAN
Prin. Rev.
*1993 estimate
Shouldn't you?
More students trust Kaplan to help them get a higher score because Kaplan is the undisputed leader in test prep.
Find out why. Call today.

This advertisement is an attempt to convince. Its unstated conclusion is "If you plan to take the LSAT, you should enroll at Kaplan."

It can be seen as a bad appeal to fear, with an unstated premise: "If you are afraid that your competitors will gain an advantage by enrolling at Kaplan, then you should enroll at Kaplan."

Or it can be seen as a bad appeal to common practice: "If this is the most popular way to prepare for the LSAT, and you wish to prepare for the LSAT, then you should enroll at Kaplan."

Either way the unstated premise is dubious. So the argument is bad. It's a fallacy no matter which analysis you use.

Often an unstated premise is needed to make an argument valid or strong, and the sketchiness of most arguments will allow for various choices. The argument is a fallacy only if for *each* obvious choice of premise, the premise is one of the generic kind and is clearly false or dubious. *There's no reason to think that a bad argument is bad in only one way.*

Sometimes an argument can be one of the types we call a fallacy while there is still a more or less obvious premise that will save it. But that's so rare we feel confident that arguments of the types we've labeled here are normally unrepairable.

The labels you've learned here are like names that go on pigeonholes. This bad argument can go in here. That argument there. This one fits into perhaps two or three of the pigeonholes. This argument, no, it doesn't fit into any, so we'll have to evaluate it from scratch. If you forget the labels, you can still remember the style of analysis, how to look for what's going wrong. That's what's important. *If you can describe what's wrong, then you understand.* The labels are just shorthand for doing the hard work of explaining what's bad in an argument.

F. So It's Bad, So What?

You've learned a lot of labels and can manage to make yourself unbearable to your friends by pointing out the bad arguments they make. That's not the point.

We are seekers of wisdom—or at least we're heading in that direction. We want to learn, to exchange ideas, not to stifle disagreements. We want to convince and educate, and to that end we must learn to judge bad arguments.

Some arguments are so bad there's no point trying to repair them. Start over.

Some arguments are bad because the other person intends to mislead you. In that case the Principle of Rational Discussion is violated. There's no point continuing the discussion, except perhaps to point out the other person's failings. These labels and analyses are then prophylactics against being taken in.

But often enough the person making the bad argument isn't aware that he or she has changed the subject or brought in emotions where they don't belong. Be gentle. Point out the problem. Educate. Ask the other person to fill in the argument, to add more claims. Then you can, perhaps, learn something, and the other person can, too.

Key Words	fallacy	generic premise
	structural fallacy	violating the Principle of Rational Discussion
	content fallacy	

Exercises for Chapter 11

The exercises here are a review of this chapter and some of the basic parts of earlier ones. Your real practice in using this material will come in evaluating the arguments for analysis that follow in the next section.

1. What are the three tests an argument must pass to be good?
2. State the Guide to Repairing Arguments.
3. State the conditions under which an argument is unrepairable.
4. Is every valid or strong argument with true premises good? Give an explanation and/or counterexample.
5. If a very strong argument has twelve true premises and one dubious one, should we accept the conclusion?
6. What does a bad argument tell us about its conclusion?
7. What is our most reliable source of information about the world?
8. Why isn't a slippery slope argument classified as a structural fallacy?
9. Why isn't a false dilemma classified as a structural fallacy?
10. How can we distinguish between ridicule and an attempt to reduce to the absurd?
11. Give an example of affirming the consequent.
12. Give an example of denying the antecedent.
13. Give an example of arguing backwards with "all."
14. Give an example of arguing backwards with "almost all."
15. Give an example of reasoning in a chain with "some." Is it valid?
16. Give an example of arguing backwards with "no."
17. Give an example of confusing objective and subjective. Is it a bad argument?
18. Give an example of drawing the line. Is it a bad argument?
19. Give an example of mistaking the person for the claim. Is it a bad argument?
20. Give an example of mistaking the person for the argument. Is it a bad argument?
21. Give an example of an appeal to authority that is *not* a bad argument.
22. Give an example of a phony refutation. Is it a bad argument?

23. Give an example of a false dilemma. Is it a bad argument?
24. Give an example of an appeal to pity. Is it a bad argument?
25. Give an example of an appeal to fear. Is it a bad argument?
26. Give an example of an argument that uses the generic premise of one of the types of content fallacies but which is *not* a bad argument.
27. Give an example of begging the question. Is it a bad argument?
28. Give an example of an argument that someone might criticize as having an irrelevant premise or premises.
29. What is a strawman? Give an example.
30. Why are slanters included in this chapter on fallacies?

Writing Lesson 9

Here is your chance to show that you have all the basic skills to write an argument. Compose an argument either for or against the following:

Cats should be legally prohibited from roaming freely in cities.

Check whether your instructor has chosen a different topic for this assignment.

This time write only a (maximum) one-page argument. It should be clear and well structured, since you will have written out the premises and conclusion for yourself first. You can recognize slanters and fallacies, so don't use any in your argument. And you know to include possible objections to your argument.

By now you should have learned a lot about writing arguments. You don't need more examples, just practice. As a guide you can use the section *Composing Good Arguments* (p. 372), which summarizes many of the lessons you've learned.

Cartoon Writing Lesson D

For each cartoon, write the best argument you can that has as its conclusion the claim that accompanies the cartoon. List only the premises and conclusion. If you believe the best argument is only weak, explain why. Refer back to Cartoon Writing Lesson A (p. 56) for suggestions about how to do this lesson.

1.

Manuel is in an Olympic race for the handicapped.

2.

Flo is lying.

3. 

Professor Zzzyzzx hit the wasps' nest.

4. 

An adult who is not a city employee opened the fire hydrant.

5.

Spot made the boy go away.

6.

The professor is boring.

ARGUMENTS for ANALYSIS

Short Arguments for Analysis

Here's a chance for you to put together all the ideas and methods of the previous chapters. Below are short passages you might hear or read any day. Before you start analyzing them, take a look at how Tom is doing.

Dick: I can't stand Siamese cats. Ugh. They have those strange blue eyes.
Suzy: Mary Ellen has a kitten with blue eyes. I didn't know it was Siamese.

Argument? (yes or no) Yes.
Conclusion (if unstated, add it): Mary Ellen's cat is a Siamese.
Premises: Siamese cats have blue eyes. Mary Ellen's cat has blue eyes.
Additional premises needed to make it valid or strong (if none, say so): None.
Classify (with the additional premises): valid strong ————X– weak
Good argument? (yes or no, with an explanation—possibly just the name of a fallacy) No. It's just arguing backwards with "all."

Excellent!

I hear that Brigitte Bardot is campaigning for animal rights. But she's the one who used to do advertisements for fur coats.

Argument? (yes or no) Yes—when rewritten.
Conclusion (if unstated, add it): You shouldn't listen to Brigitte Bardot about animal rights.
Premises: Brigitte Bardot used to do advertisements for fur coats.
Additional premises needed to make it valid or strong (if none, say so): Don't listen to anything Brigitte Bardot says about fur coats.
Classify (with the additional premises): valid strong ————X– weak
Good argument? (yes or no, with an explanation—possibly just the name of a fallacy) No. I think it's mistaking the person for the argument.

At least you spotted that something was wrong. But the premise you added was just restating the conclusion. That would have made it valid, all right, but it also would have been begging the question.

This is an example of mistaking the person for the claim. Review that.

—Kelly is a moron.
—Why do you say that?
—Because she's so stupid.

Argument? (yes or no) Yes.
Conclusion (if unstated, add it):
Premises:
Additional premises needed to make it valid or strong (if none, say so):
Classify (with the additional premises): valid strong ————X– weak
Good argument? (yes or no, with an explanation—possibly just the name of a fallacy) This is just begging the question and a bad argument. Do I really need to fill in all the blanks in your form when it's this obvious?

No, you don't need to fill in all the steps—as long as you're sure you've got it right. And you almost do. It's begging the question, all right, but that's valid. You've confused "bad argument" with "weak argument."

Wash your car? Sure, and the next thing you know you'll want me to vacuum the upholstery, and fill up the gas tank, and maybe even make a car payment for you.

Argument? (yes or no) Yes.
Conclusion (if unstated, add it): I shouldn't wash your car for you.
Premises:
Additional premises needed to make it valid or strong (if none, say so):
Classify (with the additional premises): valid strong ————X– weak
Good argument? (yes or no, with an explanation—possibly just the name of a fallacy) This is a bad argument. I could rewrite it as a slippery slope, but it's pretty clear that the premises aren't plausible. It's really almost ridicule.

Good.

Here are the questions you should consider in evaluating each of the following arguments.

Argument? (yes or no)

Conclusion (if unstated, add it):

Premises:

Additional premises needed to make it valid or strong (if none, say so):

Classify (with the additional premises): valid strong ———— weak

Good argument? (Choose one and give an explanation.)

- It's good (passes the three tests).
- It's valid or strong, but you don't know if the premises are true, so you can't say if it's good or bad.
- It's bad because it's unrepairable (state which of the reasons apply).

To make it easier to answer these, use the formatted versions of them which you can find at www.AdvancedReasoningForum.org/CT5/exercises.

1. Wanda: I'm going to go on that paleo diet. It's got to be safe and effective, with so many people doing it now.

2. Suzy: I know that there is ESP.
   Dick: How?
   Suzy: If there wasn't, there'd be too much left unexplained.

3. Suzy: I can't believe Dr. E got so angry about Ralph getting his essay from the internet. Next thing you know, he's going to tell us we can't work on our homework together.

4. 

5. Dan was clever, but he couldn't go to college. His father disappeared leaving lots of debt, and his mother was ill. So Dan had to take care of his mother and work full time.

6. Of course it's good for you—it's got all natural ingredients.

7. Lee: Maria and Manuel and I are thinking about getting a pet. What do you think?
   Dick: Get a dog.
   Tom: Get one of those small pigs. They're very intelligent animals. They make great pets. They learn to do tricks as well as any dog can. They can be house-trained too. And they're affectionate since they like to cuddle. Pigs are known as one of the smartest animals there are. And if you get bored with it or it becomes unruly, you can eat it.
   Dick: Don't listen to him. The only pet he ever had was a turtle, and it died after two weeks. Kaput. Unless you call Suzy a pet.
   Tom: Geez, Dick, you're harsh. Zoe get on you about the dishes again?

8. Mom: Your profile picture on Facebook is just not proper. Your Aunt Alice and everyone else in the family think it's inappropriate.
   Zoe: You and Aunt Alice are just jealous that you can't wear clothes like that anymore.

9. Manuel: Where's Maria? I'm counting on her for a ride to my early class.
   Lee: She must be asleep.
   Manuel: Then her alarm didn't go off.

10. Unprotected sex is O.K. I know lots of people who do it, and what's the worst that can happen? You get pregnant.

11. From an interview with Vladimir Putin, president of Russia, on Russian national television, as reported in *The New York Review of Books,* May 25, 2000:

Putin: We had a dog, true it was a different one . . . unfortunately, it died, run over by a car. . . . But the kids wanted a little dog, and they finally convinced me. Now it's not clear whose dog it is more—mine, my wife's, the kids' . . . . The dog just sort of lives here on its own.

Interviewer (*jokingly*): Like a cat.

Putin: (*not laughing at the joke, coldly*) No, no, don't insult our dog. It doesn't work as a cat. A dog is a dog. We really love it.

12. Candidate for the Senate: My opponent doesn't even believe that inflation is a serious risk in this country. So how is he going to protect you from it?

13. Why am I preaching that we should become nudists? We could all zip through airport security. Nudists don't know how rich someone is because everyone is dressed the same. Nudists listen to each other because at a clothing-optional beach, everyone makes eye contact. A final thought: nudity is truly our most natural state.

    Robert Denker, *Newsweek* letter, June 17, 2007

14. Where do correct ideas come from? Do they drop from the skies? No. Are they innate in the mind? No. They come from social practice, and from it alone; they come from three kinds of social practice, the struggle for production, the class struggle and scientific experiment. It is man's social being that determines his thinking. Once the correct ideas of the advanced class are grasped by the masses, these ideas turn into a material force which changes society and changes the world. In their social practice, men engage in various kinds of struggle and gain rich experience.

    Mao Tse-Tung, "Where do correct ideas come from?", 1963

15. Zoe: We shouldn't go to the fair this year. You always get sick and I never have any fun. So what if it is a tradition?

16. Zoe: Dick, I can't believe you got some goldfish at the fair. No goldfish from the fair will live longer than two weeks. So don't bother to buy a bowl for them.

17. Maria: Some of these cookies were baked by Mary Ellen.
    Zoe: And I know that some of the stuff Mary Ellen bakes is awful. So, thanks, but I won't eat any.

18. Dick: I've got to find a lawyer about that accident where the lady rear-ended me.
    Tom: Check out Mr. Abkhazian. He's been doing accident cases for 20 years.

19. I'd rather believe in God than that I developed from a rock and am without a soul and my life (and everyone's) is without meaning or consequence.

    Comment on a 2011 *Baltimore Sun* article

20. Suzy: Why don't you do something about Dick's smoking?
    Zoe: I don't want to give him a hard time.
    Suzy: The difference between you and me is that I care about people.

21. Reggie: Look, I deserve at least a C in this course. Here, I did all my homework and contributed in class, just like you said. I know I only got a D+ on the final, but our other work was supposed to be able to outweigh that.

Ms. F: Perhaps I did say that, but I can't go back and change your grade. I'd have to change a lot of grades.

Reggie: That's unfair and unethical. I'll take it to the department head.

(*Later in the head of department's office*)

Ms. F: So this student is going to come in and see you to complain about his grade. He thinks that just because he showed up regularly and handed in some homework he should get a good grade.

22. Psychiatrist: You are suffering from delusions of grandeur.

Dr. E: What? What? There's nothing wrong with me.

Psychiatrist: It is not normal to think that you are the smartest man in the world.

Dr. E: But I am.

Psychiatrist: Certainly you think so.

Dr. E: Look, if Arnold Schwarzenegger came in and said he was the strongest man in the world, would you think he's crazy?

Psychiatrist: Crazy? I did not say you were crazy. You are suffering from delusions of grandeur.

Dr. E: O.K. Would Arnold Schwarzenegger be suffering from delusions of grandeur?

Psychiatrist: Possibly not.

Dr. E: So someone has to be the smartest person in the world.

Psychiatrist: That's true.

Dr. E: Why not me?

Psychiatrist: Because you are not.

Dr. E: How do you know?

Psychiatrist: Trust me.

Dr. E: You can't even define "delusions of grandeur," can you?

Psychiatrist: I am trained to spot it when it occurs.

23. Dick: Now you're in for it. I told you the police would stop you if you didn't slow down.

Zoe: Oh, no. If that police officer gives me a ticket, I'll get three points taken off my driver's license. And I'll lose my license if I get more than two points taken off.

Dick: So let's hope you get off with a warning. Because if that police officer gives you a ticket, I'll have to drive you everywhere.

24. Lee: Hey! Our neighbors have a kid! I just saw Mrs. Goldenstone with a brand-new baby, really tiny. She says its name is Louis.

Maria: What? I never saw her pregnant. They must have adopted the child.

25. Tom: Everyone I know who's passed the critical thinking course has really liked it.

Dick: Suzy liked that course.

Harry: So she must have passed it. Amazing.

26. Israeli troops used Palestinian civilians as human shields and forced them to participate in dangerous military operations during the Israeli sweep through a refugee camp in Jenin last month, according to a report released Friday by Human Rights Watch. . . .

"When the Israeli army decided to go into this densely populated refugee camp, they had an obligation under international law to take all possible precautions to protect the civilian population," said [Peter] Bouckaert [senior researcher for HRW]. "Clearly the Israeli army failed to take the necessary precautions during its attack."

Israel disputes that conclusion, noting that 23 of its own soldiers died in the fiercest urban warfare the [Israeli Defense Forces] has experienced in 30 years. "The extent of Israeli casualties and the duration of the combat are proof of the great efforts made by the IDF to conduct the operation carefully in an effort to bring to an absolute minimum the number of Palestinian civilian casualties," said an IDF statement.

CNN, May 4, 2002

27. Manuel: Did you hear? Larry just got back from the Dead Kittens concert in Buffalo.
    Maria: Buffalo? Last month he went to Florida to hear them. And Wanda says he's planning to go to Atlanta next week for their big show there.
    Manuel: He must really like their music.

28. Lee: My calculus course is killing me. There's so much homework.
    Maria: Everyone who takes calculus complains about too much homework.
    Manuel: So Wanda must be taking calculus.

29. You should take your cousin to the dance because she's shy and doesn't go out much, and she's really sad since her dog died. It would make her feel good.

30. The U.S. attorney general said that there was no need to investigate the president's business deals. So the president didn't do anything wrong.

31. *Saudi official blames Jews for Sept. 11 attack*
    The Saudi police minister [Nayef] has claimed Jews were behind the Sept. 11 attacks on the United States because they have benefited from subsequent criticism of Islam and Arabs, according to media reports.

    Interior Minister Prince Nayef made the remarks in the Arabic-language Kuwaiti daily *Assyasah* last month. The latest edition of Ain al-Yaqueen, a weekly internet magazine devoted to Saudi issues, posted the *Assyasah* interview and its own English translation.

    In the interview, Nayef said he could not believe that Osama bin Laden and his network, including Saudi participants, worked alone.

    He was quoted as saying he believed terrorist networks have links to "foreign intelligence agencies that work against Arab and Muslim interests, chief among them is the Israeli Mossad [intelligence agency]." *Albuquerque Tribune,* November 5, 2002

32. You're good at numbers. You sort of like business. You should major in accounting—accountants make really good money.

33. Said by the CEO of a tobacco company at a U.S. Senate hearing questioning whether tobacco is a drug: "Would you prefer to be in a plane with a pilot who just drank or one who just smoked?"

34. Lee: Amazing. Did you see that Maria got a tattoo?
    Manuel: You're kidding. Well, if she did, then she must have gone to a professional. She's railed at the crazy kids who do it to each other.
    Lee: I've got to get the name of the guy she went to.

35. Dick: If Suzy doesn't pass her critical thinking class, she can't be a cheerleader unless she goes to summer school.
    Zoe: She's going to fail that course for sure.
    Dick: Looks like she'll be going to summer school.

36. Dick: Is this plate clean?
    Zoe: It's been through the dishwasher, so yes, it's clean.

37. BART [San Francisco Bay Area Rapid Transit] spokesman Linton Johnson, an African-American who said his own aunt had been roughed up by a Los Angeles cop years ago, defended the agency's police force. "They care about the public and they've done a wonderful job keeping BART safe for everyone," he said. "There have been only five officer-involved shootings resulting in injury or death in BART's 36 years. The officers do a hell of a job protecting the public."
    Patrick May, *The Mercury News*, Jan. 8, 2009

38. Tom: Either Suzy shows up in 10 minutes, or I'll have to go to the game alone.
    Lee: I just saw her sitting with Zoe at the Dog & Duck coffeehouse on Third Street.
    Tom: Looks like I'm going to the game alone.

39. Wanda: There is no life on other planets. If there were, then there'd be some evidence.
    Suzy: Many people have evidence of UFOs—pictures, videos, all that stuff.
    Wanda: Then I was wrong. There must be life on other planets.

40. Lee: Our kids should be allowed to pray in schools.
    Maria: What? If they're not allowed to pray, maybe God won't exist?

41.

42. Dick: The stupid ball went over the fence, Spot. Let's ask Harry to let us in. He's a tenant there, and I know that only tenants have a key to that gate.

43. Suzy: Either Dr. E doesn't like me or he misgraded my test, because I got a D.

44. Maria: I read that some of the cheerleaders were invited to try out for a movie they're going to film in that little town north of here.
    Lee: Tom said that some of the people at the auditions are going to get a real contract. Big money—like $900 a week.
    Maria: So maybe Suzy can finally pay me that $50 she's owed me since October. She'll get a part, or she can borrow it from one of her friends on the squad.

45. Maria: Dr. E's course is just great.
    Suzy: It's easy for you to say—you just got an A on the midterm.

46. Sixty-two of Utah's 134 credit unions—46 percent—are led by women CEOs, many of whom began their careers in entry-level positions and lack formal business education. . . .

By comparison, none of the three-dozen banking companies operating in Utah have women CEOs, although women do hold numerous high-level positions within those organizations. . . .

"Diversity is a priority for banks as it is with credit unions," said Howard Headlee, president of the Utah Bankers association. "But too few women meet the stringent qualifications boards of directors and banking regulators demand in top-level banking executives at publicly held companies," he said.

"The regulatory environment does not allow a bank to look past safety and soundness issues for the sole purposes of achieving diversity," Headlee said.

The Salt Lake Tribune, August 12, 2001

47. Adolescents who are emotionally unprepared engage in sex with serious consequences for their ability to form normal attachments later in life. Young people who are ignorant of sexually transmitted diseases risk not only their immediate health but their lives by engaging in sexual intercourse. Over half of young women in America become pregnant before they are 20. For these reasons we should not only teach the mechanics of sexuality but also encourage young people to refrain from sexual intercourse.

48. How can you doubt Dan's advice about getting a Jeep? He's only 25, and he already has an income over $150,000 a year.

49. (Contributed by a student)
Student athletes should not be given special leniency in assigning course marks. Student athletes who do receive special leniency turn out to be failures. They are not given the mental challenge that regular students are given. All student athletes that I have ever met or seen that have received special leniency have not graduated from college. In order to make something of yourself, you must first graduate from college. Everyone that I have ever met or seen wants to make a good living and make something of themselves. On the other hand, all of the student athletes I know that do not receive special leniency have graduated and have been successful in life. Therefore, student athletes that want to be successful in life must not receive special leniency.

50. Smoking is disgusting. It makes your breath smell horrid. If you've ever kissed someone after they smoked a cigarette, you feel as though you're going to vomit. Besides, it will kill you.

51. Lee: Every computer science major is a nerd.
Maria: None of the cheerleaders are majoring in computer science.
Lee: Exactly—none of them are nerds.

52. I resent that. Our company is not racist. We give a donation to the NAACP every year.

53. Suppose this patient really does have hepatitis. Well, anyone who has hepatitis will, after a week, begin to appear jaundiced. Yellowing of the eyeballs and skin will proceed dramatically after two weeks. So if he has hepatitis now, since he's been feeling sick for two weeks, he should be jaundiced. But he isn't. So he doesn't have hepatitis.

54. (Summarizing a discussion heard on National Public Radio)
An experiment is being conducted to study temperature changes in the ocean using very

low-frequency sound waves that will be generated in the South Pacific and picked up near the Arctic Circle. The sound waves will be generated two times a day for ten years.

The interviewer, speaking to one of the people involved in the experiment, said that perhaps we shouldn't do this since we don't know the effect of the sound on whales. The experimenter replied that the ocean is already so full of sound, if you count all the acousticians versus all the supertankers, the supertankers would win hands down.

55. Zoe: (*Monday*) If you eat that candy bar, then you'll gain weight.
Dick: (*Friday*) I gained weight again this week.
Zoe: So you ate that candy bar on Monday.

56. Lee: It's odd. None of the bartenders here have ever been women.
Zoe: But this is a union shop—all of them have been union members. So it looks like the union won't accept women.

57. Zoe: If you don't start helping around the house, doing the dishes and cleaning up, then you don't really understand what it means to be a part of a couple.
Dick: O.K., O.K., look, I'm vacuuming. I'll do the dishes tonight.
Zoe: So you do understand what it means to be part of a couple.

58. Zoe: Boy, is Suzy down about her fight with Tom. If she goes out tonight, she'll get drunk. Why not call her and invite her for dinner?
Dick: Too late. Manuel told me on the phone that she's already blotto.
Zoe: So she did go out.

59. Professor Zzzyzzx: A dentist I am needing. My teeth they are killing me. That Dr. Bears, he is O.K., no? I read his advertising all the time.
Dr. E: Don't go to him. I went to get a chipped front tooth fixed, and he kept me waiting an hour in the chair, and then he wanted to sell me teeth whitening and a very expensive cap for the tooth. I got up and left. I ended up going to Dr. Hay, and he just filed the tooth down and it cost $60. It's been just fine.

60. Lee: Every cat sheds hair on its master's clothes. No question about it.
Suzy: Dr. E doesn't have a cat. So he doesn't have cat hair shed on his clothes.

61. Lee: All felines cough up hairballs.
Manuel: But ferrets don't cough up hairballs.
Lee: Which is just what I thought. Ferrets aren't felines. They're more like dogs.

62. Manuel: There's Sam. Let's ask him to get us a drink.
Maria: Only bartenders and managers are allowed behind the bar in this restaurant.
Manuel: But Sam's a manager, so he's allowed behind the bar.

63. Tom: I can't believe you're an hour late!
Suzy: What are you talking about?
Tom: You said you'd meet me here at 7 to work on the English assignment.
Suzy: I am not late.
Tom: It's almost 8.
Suzy: I said I'd be here a little after 7.

64. Maria: That's awful. How can you eat a steak?
    Suzy: Huh?
    Maria: You should be a vegetarian. I've been to those factory farms where they "raise" cattle and pigs. They're awful.
    Suzy: But I like steak. I just won't visit any factory farms.

65. You should not take illegal drugs. They can kill you. If you overdose, you can die. If you share a needle, you could get AIDS and then die. If you don't die, you could end up a vegetable or otherwise permanently incapacitated. By using drugs you run the risk of getting arrested and possibly going to jail. Or at least having a hefty fine against you. Although some think the "high" from drugs is worth all the risks, the truth is that they are addicted and are only trying to justify supporting their habit.

66. Beer has lots of vitamins and protein, so it can't be bad for my liver.

67. Lee: I read that almost all people who graduate from college end up earning more than $38,000 per year.
    Tom: So the guy in charge of maintenance who gets such a great salary must have graduated from college.

68. To some Afghan commanders, the recent U.S. offensive against the Al-Qaida fighters in eastern Afghanistan failed because most of them got away. . . .

    "Operation Anaconda . . . is an incredible success," said Maj. Bryan Hilferty, spokesman of the 10th Mountain Division. "It took only 20 terrorists to kill 3,000 of the world's citizens in the World Trade Towers. We've killed hundreds and that means we've saved hundreds of thousands of lives. This is a great success."

    Kathy Gannon, Associated Press, March 17, 2003

69. Mom: Well, what do you think? Did man evolve from cells and apes, or did God create man?
    Zoe: I don't know.
    Mom: Come on. You've got to have thought about it.
    Zoe: Oh, I guess I have, just never very hard. Beats me.
    Mom: You've got to believe one side or the other. Which is it?

70. *Proof that God does not exist*

    (Several philosophers have become famous for their proofs that God exists. All those proofs have been theoretical. Here is a practical proof supplied by Dr. E that God does not exist. It can be repeated—try it yourself!)

    I go into the Sahara Hotel and Casino in Las Vegas, Nevada. I go up to the Megabucks slot machine at which you can win at least five million dollars on a $3 bet if you hit the jackpot. I put in three $1 coins. I pull the handle. I win nothing, or just a little, and when I continue, I lose that, too. Therefore, God does not exist.

Analyzing Complex Arguments

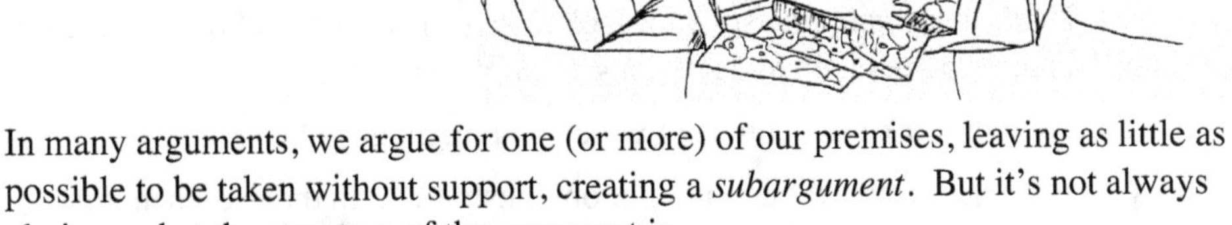

In many arguments, we argue for one (or more) of our premises, leaving as little as possible to be taken without support, creating a *subargument*. But it's not always obvious what the structure of the argument is.

Example 1 Whatever you do, don't take the critical thinking course from Dr. E. *1* He's a really tough grader, *2* much more demanding than the other professors who teach that course. *3* You could end up getting a bad grade. *4*

Analysis I've numbered every sentence or clause that might be a claim. But *1* isn't a claim, so we rewrite it as "You shouldn't take the critical thinking course from Dr. E." We can rewrite *3* as "He's much more demanding than the other professors who teach that course." Now what is the structure of this argument? There aren't any indicator words.

It seems that *1* is the conclusion. Why? Someone who believed *2*, *3*, and *4* would have some reason to believe *1*. Not an awfully good reason, since some unstated premise(s) is needed to make the argument strong or valid. But it makes sense to say, "You shouldn't take the critical thinking course from Dr. E *because* he's a really tough grader," while it seems silly to say, "You shouldn't take the critical thinking course from Dr. E, *therefore* he's a really tough grader."

Even with the conclusion identified, we still have two ways to interpret the argument:

(X) Dr. E is more demanding than the other professors who teach that course.
Therefore, he's a really tough grader.
Therefore, you could end up getting a bad grade.
Therefore, you shouldn't take the critical thinking course from Dr. E.

(Y) Dr. E is more demanding than the other professors who teach that course, and he's a really tough grader.
Therefore, you could end up getting a bad grade.
Therefore, you shouldn't take the critical thinking course from Dr. E.

To choose between these, we can use the Guide to Repairing Arguments to make the argument valid or strong. For (X) we'd need an unstated premise like:

(Almost) anyone who's more demanding than other professors who teach critical thinking is a really tough grader.

That's plausible. For (Y) we'd need something like:

If you take critical thinking from someone who's more demanding than other professors who teach that course and who is a really tough grader, then you could end up getting a bad grade. *a*

(We use numbers for claims in the original argument and lowercase letters for claims we add.) That's a lot more plausible. It looks like (Y) is a better choice, though we still need a prescriptive claim to get from *4* to *1*. We can use:

You shouldn't take any course in which you might get a bad grade. *b*

That's what we need, even though it's not obviously true. In the end, then, this argument is only as good as the unsupported prescriptive premise *b*.

Even if there's no one right way to interpret this argument, that doesn't mean there aren't wrong ways. If you said that *4* supports *2*, that would be wrong.

> *When there are no indicator words ask*:
> - If I believed this claim, would I have more reason to believe that one?
> - Can I put *therefore* or *because* between these two claims?

If it's not clear which claim is meant to support which, that's a fault of the argument.

Example 2

1. CATS SMELL BAD.
2. CATS URINATE IN THE HOUSE.
DO YOU MIND!
3. CATS KILL SONG BIRDS.
4. CATS BARF UP HAIRBALLS.
HACK!
5. SO ALL IN ALL, CATS ARE UNPLEASANT CREATURES

Analysis Sometimes people use several premises hoping the combined weight of them will somehow bring about the conclusion. But someone who likes cats could just say "So?" after each of *1* through *4*. Compare:

Cats smell bad. *1*
Anything that smells bad is unpleasant. *a*
Cats kill songbirds. *3*

Anything that kills songbirds is nasty. *b*
Thus, cats are nasty and unpleasant creatures. *5*

Here it's not just piling up "facts" to support the conclusion. Claim *a* is the glue that links *1* to the conclusion; claim *b* is the glue that links *3* to the conclusion.

Some people think it's fine to give an argument with many separate premises supporting the conclusion. Here are lots of reasons to believe the conclusion—if you don't like this one, take that one. I've got a bag full of 'em. That may convince some folks, but it shouldn't convince you. You're sharp enough to spot that after each premise that's not linked to the conclusion you should ask "So?" When someone keeps piling up reasons with no glue, it just means you have to ask "So?" more often. It doesn't make the argument strong.

Example 3

Pet owners need to take responsibility for their animals. *1* Not only is it unsafe for these pets to wander, *2* it is very inconsiderate to other neighbors. *3* Many of us are tired of the endless, nauseating piles we have to shovel from our lawns and dead flowers caused by dogs passing by. *4* Children in our neighborhoods cannot walk to a friend's house to play for fear of aggressive dogs. *5* Pets should be in a fenced yard or on a leash, *6* not just to protect pets, *7* not just out of consideration for your neighbors, *8* but also because it is the law. *9* Claudia Empey, *The Spectrum,* 1996

Analysis I've labeled every clause that might be a claim.

First we need to identify the conclusion, though there's no indicator word. The choice seems to be between *1* and *6*. Looking at all the other claims, it seems they best support *6*. If we believed all the others, we'd have more reason to believe *6*. Indeed, *1* supports *6*, though weakly.

We have the conclusion, but that doesn't give us the structure. First, let's see if there's any noise or problematic sentences.

Sentence *2* is ambiguous: does it mean "unsafe for the pets" or "unsafe for people"? Those two readings are made separately in *5* and *7*, so we can ignore *2*. Also *3* and *8* are the same, so let's ignore *8*.

What do we have? Just lots of independent premises. But the weight of them doesn't give the conclusion. We are missing the glue. Why should we care about our neighbors? Why protect the pets? Each of these needs some further premise to help us get *6*. I'll let you finish this analysis by trying to repair the argument.

Here's how Tom analyzed the structure of two arguments in his homework.

The dogcatcher in this town is mean. *1* **He likes to kill dogs.** *2* **He is overzealous, picking up dogs that aren't really strays.** *3* **Some people say he beats the dogs.** *4* **So the position of dogcatcher should be eliminated.** *5*

Argument? (yes or no) Yes.

Conclusion: The position of dogcatcher should be eliminated.

Additional premises needed? If someone likes to kill dogs, picks up dogs that aren't really strays, and beats dogs, then he is mean. *a*

If someone is mean, he shouldn't be dogcatcher. *b*

Identify any subargument: *2*, *3*, and *4* are independent and support *1*. Then *1* supports the conclusion, *5*.

Good argument? Looks good to me.

You haven't been critical enough. The argument is really pretty bad. First, I agree that 2, 3, and 4 are independent. You can say they support 1, but 1 is vague and no improvement on 2, 3, and 4. I think it's too vague to be a claim. We do need something like your a. But for that we need a further premise, one you're always overlooking: "If people say that the dogcatcher beats dogs, then he does beat dogs." And that's pretty dubious. So instead of a, let's take: "If someone likes to kill dogs and picks up dogs that aren't strays, then he should not be a dogcatcher." That's true. But that doesn't get you the conclusion. What you then need is "If the person who is now dogcatcher shouldn't be dogcatcher, then the position of dogcatcher should be eliminated." And that is implausible. — Still, it's just your first try.

Today, education is perhaps the most important function of state and local governments. *1* **Compulsory school attendance laws and the great expenditures for education both demonstrate our recognition of the importance of education to our democratic society.** *2* **It is required in the performance of our most basic public responsibilities, even service in the armed forces.** *3* **It is the very foundation of good citizenship.** *4* **Today it is a principal instrument in awakening the child to cultural values, in preparing him for later professional training, and in helping him to adjust normally to his environment.** *5* **In these days, it is doubtful that any child may reasonably be expected to succeed in life if he is denied the opportunity of an education.** *6* **Such an opportunity, where the state has undertaken to provide it, is a right which must be made available to all on equal terms.** *7*

From Justice Warren's opinion in *Brown v. Board of Education* 347 U.S. 483 (1954), ending racial segregation in public schools

Argument? (yes or no) Yes.

Conclusion: When the state undertakes to provide education, it must be made available to all on equal terms.

Additional premises needed? Something like "If 1, 2, 3, 4, 5, 6, then 7."

Identify any subargument: 1, 2, 3, 4, 5 and 6 are independent and support the conclusion, 7.

Good argument? All the premises look plausible, and it's valid with the new premise. So it's good. Anyway, it was good enough for the Supreme Court.

A good job of rewriting the conclusion to make it clear. But these premises aren't all independent. Here 2, 3, 4, and 5 are meant to support 1, and they need an additional premise like "If school attendance is mandatory and a lot of money is spent on education, and if education is the foundation of good citizenship, and if it is a principal instrument in awakening the child to cultural values and preparing him for professional training and adjusting him to his environment, then education is the most important function of state and local governments." It pays to write out the additional premise in full to see if it's really plausible. Don't get lazy when the argument gets long—that's a sure way to get conned.

That argument for 1 is pretty good. But how does he get from 1 to 7? Well, he adds 6. Then 6 + 1, together with some glue will get him 7. But what does he need? Something like "If education is the most important function of state and local government, and if it is doubtful that any child may reasonably be expected to succeed in life if he is denied the opportunity of an education, then when the state undertakes to provide education, it must be made available to all on equal terms." That isn't obvious. But you can see how Justice Warren supported that claim with the 14th Amendment in the full decision at <http://www.nationalcenter.org/brown.html>.

Exercises

For each exercise below, analyze the structure by answering the following:

Argument? (yes or no) If an argument, number each part that might be a claim.

Conclusion:

Additional premises needed?

Identify any subargument:

Good argument?

1. My neighbor should be forced to get rid of all the cars in his yard. People do not like living next door to such a mess. He never drives any of them. They all look old and beat up and leak oil all over the place. It is bad for the neighborhood, and it will decrease property values.

2. I'm on my way to school. I left five minutes late. Traffic is heavy. Therefore, I'll be late for class. So I might as well stop and get breakfast.

3. Las Vegas has too many people. There's not enough water in the desert to support more than a million people. And the infrastructure of the city can't handle more than a million: the streets are overcrowded, and traffic is always congested; the schools are overcrowded, and new ones can't be built fast enough. We should stop migration to the city by tough zoning laws in the city and county.

4. Dr. E: I took my dogs for a walk last night in the fields behind my house. It was very dark. They started to chase something—I could hear it running in front of them. It

seemed like it was big because of the way the bushes were rustling, and they came back towards where I was in a U-turn, which suggests it wasn't a rabbit. Rabbits almost always run in more or less one direction. I think they killed it because I heard a funny squeaky "awk" sound. It didn't sound like a cat, but it didn't sound like a big animal either. And I don't think rabbits make that kind of sound. I'm puzzled what it was, but one thing I am sure of after the dogs returned: It wasn't a skunk.

The steps in analyzing complex arguments

1. Read the entire passage and decide if it's an argument. If so, identify the conclusion, then number every sentence or clause that might be a claim.
2. For each numbered part:
   a. Is it ambiguous or too vague to be a claim?
   b. If it's vague, could we clear that up by looking at the rest of the argument? Are the words implicitly defined?
   c. If it's too vague, scratch it out as noise.
   d. If it uses slanters, reword it neutrally.
3. Identify the claims that lead directly to the conclusion.
4. Identify any subarguments that are meant to support the claims that lead directly to the conclusion.
5. See if the obvious objections have been considered.
   a. List ones that occur to you as you read the passage.
   b. See if they have been answered.
6. Note which of the claims in the argument are unsupported, and evaluate whether they are plausible.
7. Evaluate each subargument as valid or on the scale from strong to weak.
   a. Note if the argument is a valid type or fallacy we've seen.
   b. If it's not valid or strong, can it be repaired?
   c. If it can be repaired, do so and evaluate any added premises.
8. Evaluate the entire argument as valid or on the scale from strong to weak.
   a. Note if the argument is a valid type or fallacy we've seen.
   b. If it is not valid or strong, can it be repaired?
   c. If it can be repaired, do so and evaluate any added premises.
9. Decide whether the argument is good.

That's a lot to do. But not all the steps are always needed. If you spot that the argument is one of the bad types we've discussed, you can dismiss it. If key sentences are too vague for the conclusion or crucial parts to be claims, you can dismiss the argument. But often you will have to go through all these steps.

Before you start analyzing complex arguments, look at how Maria used this method.

Morass of value judgments
Well-intentioned DUI law chips away at individual rights
Editorial, *Las Vegas Review-Journal*, October 1, 1995

When a new state law goes into effect today, police will be allowed to use "reasonable force" to obtain blood samples from first-time drunken driving suspects who refuse to take a breath test. ***1***

Defense attorneys plan to challenge this law, citing the potential for unnecessary violence resulting from attempts to enforce it. ***2*** The law's proponents say it is necessary to obtain adequate evidence to lock up violators of drunken driving laws and force is already allowed against repeat offenders. ***3*** One supporter of the law was quoted on television recently saying that people who are suspected of driving drunk give up their rights. ***4***

There is a hidden danger with laws that chip away at the Fourth Amendment prohibition against unreasonable searches and seizures. ***5***

Yes, we need to vigorously fight drunken driving, take away driver's licenses of those who refuse breath tests, and lock up repeat offenders who are obviously impaired according to eyewitness testimony. ***6*** But our hard-won individual rights, freedoms, and protections should not be flippantly squandered, even in the name of public safety. ***7***

The danger is that once we begin to buy into the concept that the rights of society as a whole are superior to the rights of the individual, then we begin to slide into a morass of value judgments. ***8*** If it is more important for society to stop drunken driving than for the suspected driver to be free from unreasonable search of his blood veins and seizure of his blood, then might it not be argued that it is more important for elected officials and sports heroes to get organ transplants than mere working stiffs? ***9***

If rights can be weighed against societal imperatives, what next? ***10*** Our rights against self incrimination? ***11*** Freedom of religion? ***12*** Speech? ***13*** Fair trial? ***14*** The vote? ***15***

Having personally experienced the heavy hand of tyranny, the Founding Fathers wrote, "The right of the people to be secure in their persons, houses, papers, and effects, against unreasonable searches and seizures, shall not be violated, and no Warrants shall issue, but upon probable cause, supported by Oath or affirmation, and particularly describing the place to be searched, and the person or things to be seized." ***16***

Rather than slug it out in the courts, we would hope that our various police forces would give a second thought or more before resorting to constitutionally questionable exercises. ***17*** What difference is there between a hypodermic needle and a battering ram? ***18***

If we vigilantly guard and revere the rights of individuals, society in general will be better off. ***19***

Conclusion: Police should not be allowed to use reasonable force to obtain blood samples from first-time drunken driving suspects who refuse to take a breath test.

Premises: 1. This is just stating the background. The editor uses a downplayer in putting quotes around "reasonable force."

2. I suppose this is true. It shows that someone other than the editors think there's a problem. But so what?

3. Gives the other side. Counterargument.

4. Big deal. So one nut said that. Doesn't really contribute to the argument. He'd have to show that a lot of people thought that. Otherwise it's probably a strawman.

5. "Chip away" is a slanter. Dysphemism. Anyway, he hasn't shown that this law goes against the Fourth Amendment. Apparently the lawmakers didn't think so. If it does, it'll be declared unconstitutional, and that's that. Doesn't really help his conclusion. Waving the flag, sort of.

6. Sets out his position. Sort of a counterargument to the supporters of the bill. Shows he's not unreasonable. Giving a bit to the other side, I guess. Doesn't seem to help get to his conclusion.

7. "Hard-won" is there without proof. Perhaps it was hard-won. Possibly adds to the argument by adding a premise "Whatever is hard-won should not be given up." But that's false. "Flippantly squandered" is a dysphemism, and he hasn't shown that they are flippantly squandered. But worst is when he talks about rights, protections, etc. It's not clear what "right" he is talking about. If it's the one in the Fourth Amendment, he's got to prove that this law is giving that up, which he hasn't. Otherwise he's just waving the flag.

8. He's got to prove this. It's crucial to his argument.

9. This is supposedly support for 8, but it doesn't work. I think the answer is "No." He's got to show it's "Yes." And 10 is just a question, not a claim.

11.–15. These are rhetorical questions, too. As premises they seem very dubious. Altogether they're a slippery slope.

16. The first part is just there like "hard-won" was before. Quoting the Fourth Amendment doesn't make it clear to me that this law violates it.

17. "Slug it out in the courts" is a dysphemism. He hasn't shown that the law is constitutionally questionable.

18. Another rhetorical question with a stupid comparison. My answer is "Plenty." He's got to convince me that there's no difference. The old slippery slope again.

19. Vague and unproved. Can't be support for the conclusion, and it's not the conclusion, either. Does nothing.

It's a bad argument. Too many slanters, and there's really no support for the conclusion.

Very, very good. Only you need to expand on why it's a bad argument. What exactly are the claims that have any value in getting the conclusion?

First, in 1 it's not a downplayer. It's a quote. It might also show that he doesn't believe the words have a clear meaning.

All that 2 elicits is "So?" We can't guess what the missing premise is that could save this support. He doesn't knock off 3 (perhaps 4 is intended to do that, sort of reducing to the absurd?). The support for 8 is a worthless slippery slope (9–15), plus one person's comments that we'd have to take to be exemplary of lots of people (there's a missing premise like "If one person said this on television, then lots of people believe it" — which is very dubious). Number 16 is crucial, but he hasn't shown that 7 follows from it. That's the heart of the argument that he's left out (as you noted): He's got to show that this law really violates the Fourth Amendment and, for 19, that it isn't a good trade-off of personal rights vs. society's rights. So there's really no support for his conclusion. That's why it's bad. <u>The use of slanters is bad, but it doesn't make the argument bad.</u> We can eliminate them and then see what's wrong. I'd give B+/A- for this. Incorporate this discussion in your presentation to the class, and you'll get an A.

Now it's time for you to try your hand at analyzing complex arguments. Find some on the internet, or in your local newspapers, or in your textbooks and bring them in to challenge your classmates.

REASONING

from EXPERIENCE

12 Reasoning by Analogy

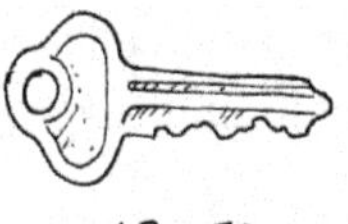

A. What Is Reasoning by Analogy?

We have a desire to be consistent in our lives, to see and apply general principles. "Why shouldn't I hit you? You hit me," says the first-grader, invoking the principle that whatever someone does to me that's bad, I'm justified in doing back to her.

Since it was O.K. there, it should be O.K. here. This situation is like that one. Since we concluded here, we can conclude there. That's arguing by analogy.

> We should legalize marijuana. After all, if we don't, what's the rationale for making alcohol and tobacco legal?

Alcohol is legal. Tobacco is legal. Therefore, marijuana should be legal. They're sufficiently similar.

> DDT has been shown to cause cancer in rats. Therefore, there is a good chance DDT will cause cancer in humans.

Rats are like humans. So if rats get cancer from DDT, so will humans. That's arguing by analogy.

Reasoning by analogy starts with a comparison. But not every comparison is an argument.

> ***Reasoning by analogy*** A comparison becomes reasoning by analogy when it is part of an argument: on one side of the comparison we draw a conclusion, so on the other side we should conclude the same.

"My love is like a red, red rose" is a comparison. Perhaps your English teacher called it an analogy. But it's not an argument—what conclusion is being drawn by Robert Burns?

Analogies, as we'll see, are often only suggestions for arguments. But they have to be taken seriously, for they are used in science, law, and ethics. You use them yourself every day—how often have you heard or said, "But last time . . ." ?

How can we tell if an analogy is good?

B. An Example

Example 1 (Country Joe McDonald was a rock star who wrote songs protesting the war in Vietnam. In 1995 he was interviewed on National Public Radio about his motives for working to establish a memorial for Vietnam War soldiers in Berkeley, California, his home and a center of anti-war protests in the '60s and '70s. Here is what he said.)

"Blaming soldiers for war is like blaming firemen for fires."

Analysis This is a comparison. But it's meant as an argument:

We don't blame firemen for fires.
Firemen and fires are like soldiers and wars.
Therefore, we should not blame soldiers for war.

This sounds pretty reasonable.

But in what way are firemen and fires like soldiers and wars? They have to be similar enough in some respect for Country Joe's remark to be more than suggestive. We need to pick out important similarities that we can use as premises.

Firemen and fires are like soldiers and war.
wear uniforms
answer to chain of command
cannot disobey superior without serious consequences
fight (fires/wars)
work done when fire/war is over
until recently only men
lives at risk in work
fire/war kills others
firemen don't start fires—soldiers don't start wars
usually drink beer

That's stupid: Firemen and soldiers usually drink beer. So?

When you ask "So?" you're on the way to deciding if the analogy is good. It's not just any similarity that's important. There must be some crucial, important way that firemen fighting fires is like soldiers fighting wars, some similarity that can account for why we don't blame firemen for fires that also applies to soldiers and war. Some similarities listed above don't seem to matter. Others we can't use because they trade on an ambiguity, like saying firemen "fight" fires.

We don't have any good guide for how to proceed—that's a weakness of the original argument. But if we're to take Country Joe McDonald's remark seriously, we have to come up with some principle that applies to both sides.

The similarity that seems most important is that both firemen and soldiers are involved in dangerous work, trying to end a problem/disaster they didn't start. We don't want to blame someone for helping to end a disaster that could harm us all.

(‡) Firemen are involved in dangerous work.
Soldiers are involved in dangerous work.
The job of a fireman is to end a fire.
The job of a soldier is to end a war.
Firemen don't start fires.
Soldiers don't start wars.

But even with these premises added to the original argument, we don't get a good argument for the conclusion that we shouldn't blame soldiers for wars. We need a general principle, some glue. And we know it has to be prescriptive:

> You shouldn't blame someone for helping to end a disaster that could harm others if he didn't start the disaster.

This claim, this general principle seems plausible, and it yields a valid argument.

But is the argument good? Are all the premises true? This is the point where the differences between firemen and soldiers might be important.

The first two premises of (‡) are clearly true, and so is the third. But is the job of soldiers to end a war? And do soldiers really not start wars? Look at this difference:

> Without firemen there would still be fires.
> Without soldiers there wouldn't be any wars.

Without soldiers there would still be violence. But without soldiers—any soldiers anywhere—there could be no organized violence of one country against another ("What if they gave a war and nobody came?"—an anti-war slogan of the 1960s).

So? The analogy shouldn't convince. The argument has a dubious premise.

We did not prove that soldiers *should be* blamed for wars. As always, *when you show an argument is bad, you haven't proved the conclusion false*. You've only shown that you have no more reason than before for believing the conclusion.

Perhaps the premises at (‡) could be modified, adding that soldiers are drafted for wars. But that's beyond Country Joe's argument. If he meant something more, then it's his responsibility to flesh it out. Or we could use his comparison as a starting place to decide whether there is a general principle, based on the similarities, for why we shouldn't blame soldiers for war.

C. Judging Analogies

Why was the example of firemen and soldiers so hard to analyze? Like many analogies, all we had was a sketch of an argument. *Just saying one side of the analogy is "like" the other is too vague to use as a premise.* Unless the analogy is very clearly stated, we have to survey the similarities and guess the important ones in order to find a general principle that applies to both sides. Then we have to survey the differences to see if there's some reason that the general principle might not apply to one side.

Example 2 Magic Johnson was allowed to play in the National Basketball Association, and he was HIV-positive. So people who are HIV-positive should be allowed to remain in the military.

Analysis This doesn't seem very convincing. What has the NBA to do with the military? We can list similarities (uniforms, teamwork, orders, winning, penalties for disobeying orders) and differences (great pay/lousy pay, game/not a game), but none of these matter unless we hit on the basis of the argument.

> The only reason for eliminating someone from a job who is HIV-positive is the risk of contracting HIV for others who work with that person.
> Magic Johnson was allowed to play basketball when he was HIV-positive.
> So in basketball the risk of contracting HIV from a fellow worker is considered insignificant.
> Basketball players have as much chance of physical contact and contracting HIV from one another as soldiers do (except in war).
> Therefore, the risk of contracting HIV from a fellow soldier should be considered insignificant.
> Therefore, people with HIV should be allowed to remain in the military.

Here it is not the similarities between basketball players and soldiers that are important. Once we spot the general principle (the first premise, which in this case is prescriptive), it is the differences that support the conclusion (basketball players sweat and bleed all over one another every day, soldiers normally do not, except in war). Whether the analogy is good depends on whether these premises are true, but the argument is certainly a lot better than it seemed at first glance.

Example 3 Suzy: This candy bar is really healthy. Look, on the label it says "All natural ingredients."

Dick: Lard is all natural, too.

Analysis Suzy has made an argument for the conclusion "This candy bar is really healthy." It has one premise: The label says "All natural ingredients." Dick shows it's bad by showing that another argument "just like" hers has a conclusion that we would consider absurd: Lard is healthy. Whatever general principle that makes his argument work must also apply in the other case. So Dick has refuted Suzy—though that doesn't mean her conclusion is false.

An analogy of one argument to another can be a powerful way to refute. See also Zoe's refutation of Dick's argument about killing flies on p. 117.

Example 4 It's wrong for the government to run a huge deficit—just as it's wrong for any family to overspend its budget.

Analysis The unstated assumption behind this analogy is that what's good for a person or family is also what's good for a country. Without more premises, though, this is unconvincing. There are big differences between a family and a country: A family doesn't have to repair roads. It can't put up tariffs. It can't print money.

The ***fallacy of composition*** is to argue that what is true of the individual is therefore true of the group, or what is true of the group is therefore true of the individual. The differences between a group and an individual are typically too great for such an analogy to be good.

Example 5 For at least three years in California, about every third teacher hired was brought aboard under an emergency permit, a provisional license that enables people who possess college degrees, but no teaching credentials, to work.

"We wouldn't allow a brain surgeon to learn on the job," says Day Higuchi, president of the United Teachers Los Angeles, a 41,000-member teachers union. "Why is it OK to let someone who doesn't know what they're doing teach our kids?"

USA Today, August 30, 1999

Analysis This is an argument with conclusion (stated as a rhetorical question) that it isn't OK to let someone teach who isn't trained as a teacher. Higuchi, however, needs another premise like "If someone doesn't have a teacher's credential, then they don't know what they're doing teaching," which is not so clearly true. The comparison of a brain surgeon with a teacher has too many dissimilarities to be convincing. A teacher saying "Oops" is nothing like a brain surgeon saying "Oops." But remember, that the argument is bad doesn't mean that the conclusion is false.

Example 6 According to a Food and Drug Administration statement, "the question of a relationship between brain tumors and aspartame was initially raised when the agency began considering approval of this food additive in the mid-1970s."

However, aspartame was approved for use in 1981. Since it is an effective insecticide and rodenticide, I can't see any justification for human consumption.

Ask the Bugman, Richard Fagerlund, *Albuquerque Journal*, May 9, 2009

Analysis This is an analogy from the ill effects of a chemical on animals and insects to the ill effects on humans. But what are the similarities between the animals and humans that matter, and why don't the differences matter? We can refute this argument by noting that chocolate will kill dogs, but it's fine (actually great!) for humans.

Evaluating an analogy

1. Is this an argument? What is the conclusion?
2. What is the comparison?
3. What are the premises? (one or both sides of the comparison)
4. What are the similarities?
5. Can we state the similarities as premises and find a general principle that covers the two sides?
6. Does the general principle really apply to both sides? Do the differences matter?
7. Is the argument valid or strong?

D. Analogies in the Law

Most analogies are not made explicit enough to serve as good arguments. But in the law, analogies are presented as detailed, carefully analyzed arguments, with the important similarities pointed out and a general principle stated.

Laws are often vague, or situations come up which no one ever imagined might be covered by the law. For instance, do the laws for verbal threats apply to online harassment? Similarities or differences have to be pointed out, general principles enunciated. Then those principles have to be respected by other judges. That's the idea of precedent or common law.

> The basic pattern of legal reasoning is reasoning by example. It is reasoning from case to case. It is a three-step process described by the doctrine of precedent in which a proposition descriptive of the first case is made into a rule of law and then applied to a next similar situation. The steps are these: similarity is seen between cases; next the rule of law inherent in the first case is announced; then the rule of law is made applicable to the second case.
>
> Edward H. Levi, *An Introduction to Legal Reasoning*

But why should a judge respect how earlier judges ruled? Those decisions aren't actually laws.

Imagine getting thrown in jail for doing something that's always been legal, yet the law hadn't changed. Imagine running a business and suddenly finding that something you did, which before had been ruled safe and legal in the courts, now left you open to huge civil suits because a judge decided differently this week. If we are to live in a society governed by laws, the law must be applied consistently. It's rare that a judge can say that past decisions were wrong.

Only a few times has the Supreme Court said that all rulings on one issue, including rulings the Supreme Court made, are completely wrong. *Brown v. the*

Board of Education said that segregation in schools, which had been ruled legal for nearly a hundred years, was now illegal. *Roe v. Wade* said that having an abortion, which had been ruled illegal for more than a century, was now legal. Such decisions are rare. They have to be. They create immense turmoil in the ways we live. We have to rethink a lot. And we can't do that regularly.

So what does a judge do when he's confronted by fifteen cases that were decided one way, the case before him falls under the general principle that was stated to cover those cases, yet his sense of justice demands that he decide this case the other way? He looks for differences between this case and those fifteen others. He tweaks the general principle just enough to get another principle that covers all those fifteen cases but doesn't include the one he's deciding. He makes a new decision that now must be respected or overthrown.

Example 7 The Supreme Court has decided that it is a constitutional right for a doctor to terminate medical treatment that prolongs the life of a terminally ill or brain-dead person, so long as the doctor acts according to the wishes of that person (*Cruzan vs. Director*, *Missouri Department of Health*, 497 U.S. 261). Therefore, the Supreme Court should decide that assisting someone to commit suicide, someone who is terminally ill or in great suffering, as Dr. Kevorkian does, is a constitutionally protected right (*Compassion in Dying vs. State of Washington*).

Analysis The question here is whether the two situations are similar. The court should decide with respect to the actual incidents in these cases. The court can decide narrowly, by saying this new case is not sufficiently like *Cruzan*, or broadly, by enunciating a principle that applies in both cases or else distinguishes between them. Or it can bring in more cases for comparison in trying to decide what general principle applies. (In the end the court was so divided that it ruled very narrowly, sidestepping the whole issue. You can look it up on the internet.)

Summary Comparisons suggest arguments. When we draw a conclusion from a comparison, we say we are reasoning by analogy: we can use the similarities to draw conclusions, so long as the differences don't matter.

Analogies are usually incomplete arguments. Often they are best treated as motive for finding a general principle to govern our actions or beliefs by surveying similarities and differences between two cases. When a general principle is made explicit, an analogy can be a powerful form of argument. When no general principle is made explicit, an analogy can be a good place to begin a discussion.

Exercises for Chapter 12

1. Some words and phrases that suggest an analogy is being used are "like," "just as," and "for the same reason." List three more.
2. What do you need to make a comparison into reasoning by analogy?
3. Are analogies typically complete arguments? Explain.
4. What should you do first in evaluating an analogy? Second?

Lee is having trouble evaluating analogies. Here's what Dr. E said about one of his exercises.

> **Just as you and I need eight hours of sleep to feel well, Spot does, too.**
> *Argument*? (yes or no) Yes.
> *Conclusion* (if unstated, add it): Spot needs 8 hours of sleep to feel well.
> *Comparison*: Spot and us.
> *Premises*:
> *Similarities*:
> *Additional premises* (make the comparison explicit, add a general principle):
> *Classify* (with the additional premises): valid strong ———— weak
> *Good argument*? (look for differences or ways the general principle could be false) They're too different, so it's weak.
>
> *Of course they're different, otherwise it wouldn't be an analogy. But they're similar too. We need food; Spot needs food. We need water; Spot needs water. Why do the differences matter for sleep? If it's weak, you should show that by pointing out the differences that matter, why there's no obvious general principle that covers both sides.*

Tom, though, has caught on to the idea of how to evaluate analogies pretty well. Here are some of the exercises he did along with Dr. E's comments.

> **You should treat dogs humanely. How would you feel if you were caged up all day and experimented on? Or if you were chained to a stake all day? Or someone beat you every time you did something wrong?**
> *Argument*? (yes or no) Yes.
> *Conclusion* (if unstated, add it): You should treat dogs humanely.
> *Comparison*: I'm not certain, 'cause they stated most of it as questions. But it seems they're comparing being a dog and being treated badly with you being treated badly, like getting caged up all day, or chained to a stake all day, or someone beating you every time you did something wrong.

Wrong

Wrong

Premises: Most of this is unstated. We're just supposed to put down what's actually said here, which I guess would be:

You shouldn't cage up a person all day.

You shouldn't chain a person to a stake all day.

You shouldn't beat someone every time she does something wrong.

People are like dogs.

So you shouldn't do any of that to dogs.

Similarities: I know we're supposed to pick out ones that'll give us a general principle. I've got to figure out how dogs and humans are similar. Well, dogs and humans are both mammals.

Additional premises (make the comparison explicit, add a general principle):

Dogs and humans are both mammals. You shouldn't mistreat any mammal.

Classify (with the additional premises): valid strong ———— weak

Good argument? (look for differences or ways the general principle could be false) I don't know. I guess the added premises are O.K. So probably it's pretty good.

Good. You've got the basis of the analogy right. You understand the method. You've picked out a general principle. But is it true? Isn't it too broad? After all, hyenas are mammals—does that mean we should treat them humanely? There's one clue you overlooked. They said, "How would you feel . . ." I can imagine how it would feel to
be a dog and be mistreated, just as I can (sort of) imagine how it would feel to be you and be mistreated. How about:

We can imagine what it would be like to be a dog and be mistreated.

We should treat humanely any creature that we can imagine what it would feel like to be mistreated.

That's more plausible because it rules out bats. And it might include fish, which some people think should be treated humanely. But really, you did O.K. We're unsure how to repair the original argument because it's too sketchy.

NICE CARTOONS!

It is easier for a camel to go through the eye of a needle than for a rich man to enter into the kingdom of God.

Argument? (yes or no) This is from the Bible, right? I think it's supposed to make us think that being rich is bad. But I'm not sure. I can't figure out a conclusion, so I better say it's not an argument.

Conclusion (if unstated, add it):

Comparison:

Premises:

Similarities: *Good work!*

Critical thinking is like learning to drive a car. It requires practice—you can't just learn it as theory. That's why I give you so many messy arguments to analyze.

Argument? (yes or no) Yes, but just barely.

Conclusion (if unstated, add it): You should have lots of messy arguments to analyze in doing critical thinking.

Comparison: Critical thinking isn't at all like driving a car. Driving a car is a kind of physical skill, like playing football. Critical thinking is something you strain your brain over. Sure you need practice on hard stuff till it gets routine. But I don't see how messy arguments are anything like driving a car.

Premises:

Similarities:

Additional premises (make the comparison explicit, add a general principle):

Classify (with the additional premises): valid strong ———— weak

Good argument? (look for differences or ways the general principle could be false) I think it's pretty bad. I can't figure out what general principle you'd want.

Good—you jumped to the punch line. There may be something in this comparison, but it's not clear yet, and you're justified in stopping here.

Exercises 5–27 are comparisons for you to evaluate. Note that there may be more than one argument in an exercise. To analyze them, fill in the following for each:

Argument? (yes or no)

Conclusion (if unstated, add it):

Comparison:

Premises:

Similarities:

Additional premises (make the comparison explicit, add a general principle):

Classify (with the additional premises): valid strong ———— weak

Good argument? (look for differences or ways the general principle could be false)

- It's good (passes the three tests).
- It's valid or strong, but you don't know if the premises are true, so you can't say if it's good or bad.
- It's bad because it's unrepairable (state which of the reasons apply).

Remember: It's easier to do these exercises if you use the formatted versions of them, which you can find at www.AdvancedReasoningForum.org/CT5/exercises.

5. You wouldn't buy a kitten at a pet store to give to your dog. Why, then, do you consider it acceptable to buy white rats for your boa constrictor?

6. All the world's a stage, and all the men and women merely players.—Shakespeare

7. Zoe: (*while driving*) Don't throw that banana peel out the window.
   Dick: Don't worry, it's biodegradable.
   Zoe: So is a newspaper.

8. Dick: Zoe, let's get married.
   Zoe: I've told you before, Dick, I won't get married until we sleep together.
   Dick: But that would be wrong. I won't sleep with you before we get married.
   Zoe: Would you buy a car without a test drive?
   Dick: Why buy the cow when the milk's free?

9. Dick: Congratulations on getting away with the shoplifting.
   Zoe: What are you talking about?
   Dick: Didn't you just install Adobe Acrobat on your computer from Tom's copy?

10. If killing is wrong, why do you punish murderers by killing them?

11. [Concerning the suggestion that the government should do nothing to rescue the big automakers Chrysler and General Motors from going bankrupt in 2008.]
    It's easy to demonize the American auto industry. It has behaved with the foresight of a crack addict for years. But even when people set their own house on fire, we still dial 9-1-1, hoping to save lives, salvage what we can and protect the rest of the neighborhood. Bob Herbert, *The New York Times*, November 15, 2008

12. From an article in *Smithsonian*, vol. 32, no. 11, 2002, about irrigation of small farms in New Mexico:
    The practice of trading in water as a commodity, observes one activist, is like "selling sunshine."

13.

14. Tom: Colleges should be run like a business. Then they'd be more efficient, would cost less, and the education would be better because competition would be rewarded and bad teaching would be penalized.

15. Downloading computer software from someone you don't know is like accepting candy from a stranger.

16. Maria: Suppose someone came up to you and offered you a sure-fire method for finding $100 bills on the street, for which he'd charge you only $5.95. You'd be crazy to buy it from him. After all, he could just as easily pick up the $100 bills himself. Besides, we know there aren't any $100 bills lying around the street, since any time there's a $100 bill floating free you can be sure someone will pick it up immediately. So why pay money to a stock analyst?

17. Flo's mother: It's just so hard raising Flo.
    Dick: How hard can it be to raise a kid? After all, I've trained two dogs.

18. When it emerged that the Salahis had managed to get through security [to a party with the Obamas at the White House] without being on the guest list, blame fell on the Secret Service, which has admitted failures, but also on the social office, which didn't have staff stationed at the checkpoints—a departure from past administrations.

    "I mean, come on, even Wal-Mart has a greeter," Rep. Loretta Sanchez, D-Calif., told Politico.com.

    Associated Press, 2010

19. Tom: I can't believe you're out demonstrating against the U.S. fighting in Afghanistan.
    Dick: I'm against war—all wars. I'm a pacifist.
    Tom: So, if someone came up to you on the street and hit you from behind, you wouldn't turn and hit him back?

20. When a trout rising to a fly gets hooked on a line and finds himself unable to swim about freely, he begins with a fight which results in struggles and splashes and sometimes an escape. Often, of course, the situation is too tough for him.

    In the same way the human being struggles with his environment and with the hooks that catch him. Sometimes he masters his difficulties; sometimes they are too much for him. His struggles are all that the world sees and it naturally misunderstands them. It is hard for a free fish to understand what is happening to a hooked one.

    Karl A. Menninger, *The Human Mind*

21. "Violent video games are like peanut butter," said Christopher J. Ferguson, of Texas A&M International University. "They are harmless for the vast majority of kids but are harmful to a small minority with pre-existing personality or mental health problems."

    "More Studies Show that Violent Video Games Aren't a Problem for Kids," Reuters, June 9, 2010

22. Tom: Seat belts cause accidents.
    Dick: Are you crazy? Seat belts save lives. Everyone knows that.
    Tom: No, they cause accidents. They may prevent serious injury in some accidents, but there are more accidents now because people use seat belts.
    Dick: Why's that?
    Tom: The threat of getting killed or seriously injured in an accident is much less if you're wearing a seat belt. Because people reckon they are safer, they're less careful and drive faster. So they get into more accidents. Some guy at the University of Chicago looked at the numbers in the 1970s and found that there were fewer deaths per accident, but more accidents, so that the actual number of people getting killed remained about the same after seat belts were required.

Dick: Well, if that's the case, we better not make any more improvements on cars. And we certainly shouldn't require motorcycle riders to wear helmets.

23. We should take claims about extrasensory perception seriously. Look, suppose no one in the world had a sense of smell except one person. He would walk along a country road where there is a high stone wall and tell his friend, "There are roses there." Or he would walk into a home and say, "Someone cooked onions here yesterday." These would seem extraordinary extrasensory perceptions to his friends and acquaintances. Similarly, just because we don't understand and can't imagine a mechanism that would explain extrasensory perception, we shouldn't stop the investigation.

24. Zeke: Boy, did you screw up.
    Dick: That is so unnecessary.
    Zeke: So is ice cream. But if it gives you pleasure, why not do it?

25. Dick: Our diet should be similar to that of cavemen—that's what our genes are programmed for.
    Zoe: You're nuts. Besides, it's *cave dwellers*, not "cavemen."

26. I know I can't really feel a pain you have. But because we're so much alike in so many ways, I'm sure that you feel physical pain in roughly the same way I do.

27. God must exist. The way everything works together in nature—the adaptation of means to ends, the beauty—resembles, but far exceeds, what humans do. Everything works together as a fine piece of machinery, like a watch. So there must be some maker with intelligence behind all of nature. That is, God exists and is similar to human mind and intelligence.

28. a. Suppose that good, highly reliable research is announced showing that oil derived from eyes removed without anesthetic from healthy cats when applied to human skin reduces wrinkles significantly. Would it be justifiable to do further research and manufacture this oil?
    b. Same as (a) except that the oil is drunk with orange juice and significantly reduces the chance of lung cancer for smokers.
    c. Same as (a) except the oil is mixed with potatoes and eaten and significantly reduces the chance of heart disease and lengthens the lives of women.
    d. Same as (a) except that when drunk, the oil kills off all viruses harmful to humans.

29. Do Exercise 28 reading "dogs" for "cats."

Further Study Analogies are discussed in courses in criminal justice, ethics, and health sciences. The exercise Tom did about how we justify treating dogs humanely is typical of the sort of problem and reasoning you'd encounter in a course on ethics. Some philosophy classes on reasoning or philosophy of science look at the nature of analogies more deeply.

Writing Lesson 10

Now you understand what reasoning by analogy is. So write an argument *using an analogy* either for or against the following:

> *Just as alcohol and tobacco are legal, we should legalize the use of marijuana.*

Check whether your instructor has chosen a different topic for this assignment.

There are roughly three ways you can argue:

- Marijuana is no worse than alcohol or tobacco, so we should legalize it. (Arguing from similarities.)
- Marijuana is worse than alcohol and tobacco, so we should not legalize it. (Arguing from differences.)
- Marijuana is no worse than alcohol or tobacco, but it is a mistake to have those legal, and we should not make the situation worse by legalizing marijuana.
  (Arguing from similarities.)

Make your general principle clear and argue for it if it's not clearly plausible. Be sure to make explicit what prescriptive premises you are using.

Write your argument as a maximum *one page* essay. It should be clear and well structured since you will have written out the claims first for yourself. You shouldn't have to do major research for this assignment, but at least be sure your premises are plausible.

13 Numbers?

In this chapter we'll look at some ways you can get confused about numbers in claims. If your eyes are starting to glaze, if your mind is going blank with talk of numbers, relax. Numbers don't lie.

> Florida has over 250,000 Arab-Americans now—enough to be a swing vote given how close Florida elections are:

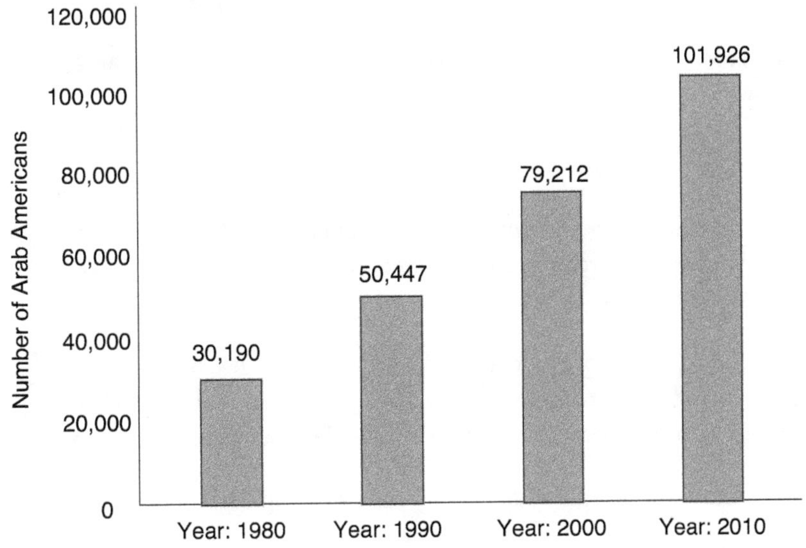

Juan Cole, Informed Consent, July 7, 2012 at <http://readersupportednews.org>

A. Percentages

Example 1 Maria: I don't know what I'm going to do. I don't have enough money to buy groceries and pay my car loan. I guess I'll have to go to Rooney-Díaz Dollars for Checks to get a loan.

Lee: How does that work?

Maria: They give me $100 and I give them a check for $110 that they cash when my paycheck comes in—7 days from now.

Lee: That sounds good—only 10% interest.

Harry: Not! It's a 520% interest rate.

Lee: Huh?

Harry: 52 weeks in a year, so if they charged you $10 for each week, you'd owe them $520 by the end of the year. Interest rates are for the year.

Maria: That's crazy—I only need the money for a week. I'll pay it back then.

Harry: And if you don't, they'll let you roll the loan over and charge you the same $10 for the next week. And pretty soon you'll owe a fortune for that $100.

- Percentages are used to present a summary of numbers.
- A percentage is a fraction of 100.

percent	*fraction*	*ratio*
26%	26/100	26 out of 100
92%	92/100	92 out of 100
18.1%	18.1/100	181 out of 1,000
0.2%	0.2/100	2 out of 1,000

Sometime percentages greater than 100 are used to indicate an increase.

400%	400/100	4 times as much
115%	115/100	1.15 times as much

Example 2 52 out of 217 students failed Calculus I last year.

To calculate the percentage of students who failed, take 52/217 = 24%, rounded to the nearest percentage.

Example 3 Of 81,173 women tested, 41,829 were allergic to cats.

In percentages, 41,829/81,173 = 51.53% were allergic to cats, rounding to the nearest hundredth of a percent. Or 52% rounded to the nearest whole percent.

Example 4 Last year Ralph's Pet Supply sold 412 dog collars. This year they sold 431.

To calculate the *increase* as a percentage of the previous year's sales, which is the *base*, take the difference and divide by the previous year's number: $(431–412)/412$ = 4.6% increase in the sale of dog collars, rounding to the nearest tenth of a percent.

Example 5 Last month Piotr Adamowicz's Car Repair took in $59,031 in total receipts. This month it took in $51,287.

To calculate the *decline* in gross receipts as a percentage of last month's sales, which is the base of the comparison, take the difference in gross receipts and divide by the base $(59{,}031–51{,}287)/59{,}031$ = 13.1%, rounding to the nearest tenth percent.

Example 6 Ralph's Pet Supply buys dog collars from a wholesaler for $3.21 and sells them for $6.95.

Their *markup* is $3.74, which as a percentage of the price it pays is $3.74/3.21$ = 117%, rounding to the nearest percent. Their *cost* as a percentage of what they sell them for is $3.21/6.95$ = 46%.

Example 7 Last month out of the 47 rats used in Dr. Wibblitz's experiments, 17 died. This month 24 out of 52 rats died.

The death rate last month was $17/47$ = 36.2% to the nearest tenth of a percent.

The death rate this month is $24/52$ = 46.2% to the nearest tenth of a percent.

The *increase* in the death rate was $(46.2–36.2)/36.2$ = 27.6% to the nearest tenth of a percent.

Example 8 Tom sees a stock for $60 and thinks it's a good deal. He buys it. A week later, it's at $90, so he sells. He made $30—a 50% gain! His friend Wanda hears about it and buys the stock at $90; a week later it goes down to $60, so she panics and sells the stock. Wanda lost $30—that's a $33^1/_3$% loss. The same $30 is a different percentage depending on where you start (the *base* of the comparison):

$$50\% \uparrow \begin{bmatrix} \$90 \\ \\ \$60 \end{bmatrix} \downarrow 33\frac{1}{3}\%$$

B. Averages

"It ought to be safe to cross here. I heard that the average depth is only 2 feet."

Beware: The average is not the maximum or most likely depth.

Mean, median, mode

- The ***mean*** or ***average*** of a collection of numbers is obtained by adding the numbers and then dividing by how many items there are.
- The ***median*** is the midway mark: the same number of items ranked by number above as below.
- The ***mode*** is the number most often attained.

Example 9 For the numbers 7, 9, 37, 22, 109, 9, 11,

The *average* or *mean* is calculated:

Add 7 + 9 + 37 + 22 + 109 + 9 + 11 = 204

Divide 204 by 7 (the number of items) = 29.14

The *median* is 11.

The *mode* is 9.

Example 10 The average weight of the children in Ms. Al-Wazedi's fifth-grade class is 103.7 pounds.

Analysis Are most of the children at about that weight, or are there a lot of skinny kids and a few obese ones? Or mostly obese kids and just a few skinny ones? More informative would be the median. Better yet, with fewer than 30 children the actual numbers can be given along with the median as a summary. *An average is a useful figure to know only if there isn't too much variation in the figures.*

Example 11 The median weight of the children in Mr. Humbert's fifth-grade class this year is 91 pounds, and last year it was 88 pounds.

Analysis To allow for a comparison, we need to summarize the numbers, which is best done in this case with the medians.

Example 12 The average weight of children in New York City's fifth grade classes is 101.72 pounds.

Analysis Again, the median would be more informative. But with this large a number of children, the mode could tell us a lot, too.

Get your class to stand up. Look around. Do you think the average height is the same as the median height? How can you tell? Come up with a *physical* way to determine the median height and the mode of the heights.

Suppose your class had just eight players from the men's basketball team and five women gymnasts. Do you think the median and the average would be the same?

Example 13 Here are the marks Dr. E gave in his course last semester:

score	52	55	57	62	75	90	92	94	95
number of students	2	4	5	4	1	4	1	7	3

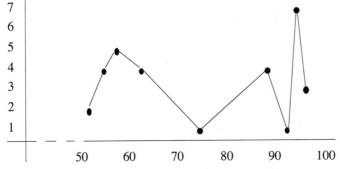

The grading scale was: 90–100 = A
80–89 = B
70–79 = C
60–69 = D
59 and below = F

When Dr. E's department head asked him how the teaching went, he told her, "Great, just like you wanted, the average mark was 75%, a C."

But she knows Dr. E too well to be satisfied. She asks him, "What was the median score?" Again Dr. E can reply, "75." As many got above 75 as below 75.

But knowing how clever Dr. E is with numbers, she asks him what the mode score was. Dr. E flushes, "Well, 94." Now she knows something is fishy. When she said that she wanted the average score to be about 75, she was thinking of a graph that looked like:

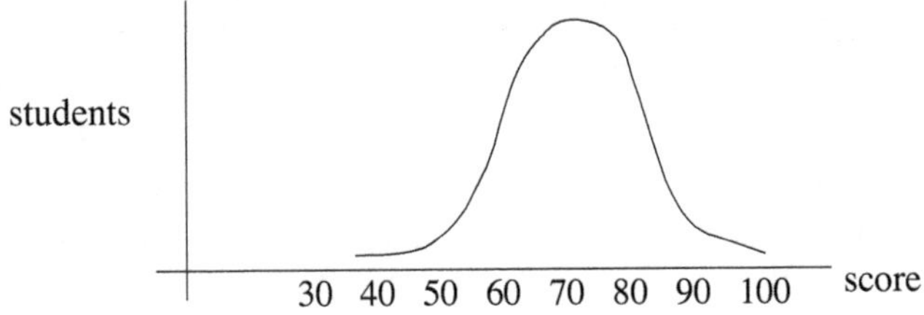

The distribution of the marks should be in a bell shape, clustered around the median.

Unless you have good reason to believe that the average is pretty close to the median and that the distribution is more or less bell-shaped, the average doesn't tell you anything important.

Sometimes people misuse the word "average" by confusing it with the mode or with "most" as in "The average American enjoys action movies."

C. What Numbers?

Numbers can be misleading or just plain nonsense.

Example 14 *Roadway Congestion*

Cities with highest and lowest roadway congestion index.
A value greater than 1.0 indicates significant congestion.

Highest	*Index*	*Lowest*	*Index*
Los Angeles	1.57	Bakersfield, Calif.	0.68
Washington	1.43	Laredo, Texas	0.73
Miami-Hialeah	1.34	Colorado Springs	0.74
Chicago	1.34	Beaumont, Texas	0.76
San Francisco	1.33	Corpus Christi, Texas	0.78

USA Today, April 13, 1999

Analysis What are they talking about? What does a "road congestion index" measure? These figures are meaningless to us.

Example 15 Breast-feeding is up 16% from 1989.

—heard on a National Public Radio news broadcast

Analysis How could they know? Who was looking in all those homes? A survey? Who did they ask? Women chosen randomly? But lots of them don't have infants. Women who visited doctors? But lots of women, lots of poor ones, don't visit a doctor. What does "breast feeding" mean? Does a woman who breast-feeds one day and then gives it up qualify as someone who breast-feeds? Or one who breast-feeds two weeks? Six months? Maybe NPR is reporting on a reliable survey, but what they said is so vague and open to doubt as to how they could know it that we should ignore it as noise. Always ask *how could they know those numbers*?

Example 16 [From a glossy brochure "Why do I need a water softener?" by Pentair Water Treatment] The Bureau of Statistics found that between 17 and 20.8 cents of every dollar are spent on cleaning products. . . . The bottom line? Soft water can save you thousands of dollars.

Analysis What dollars are they talking about? When you consider the billions of dollars spent by the government on debt and the military—which aren't for cleaning products—you can see that what they say can't be right. And there's no reason to believe that so much money is spent on cleaning products by individuals. Worse, there's no government agency called "The Bureau of Statistics."

Example 17 New Mexico Department of Health statistics estimate that of the 115,000 New Mexicans with diabetes, 37,000 don't know they have it.

El Defensor Chieftain, Socorro, NM, November 9, 2005

Analysis If they don't know they have diabetes, how does the Department of Health know? There may be a good way the department got this number, but we should suspend judgment about whether it's right unless we're willing to believe everything the Department of Health says.

D. Misleading Comparisons

Zoe has 4 apples and Dick has 2 oranges. Who has more?

More *what*? An ***apples and oranges*** comparison is one that compares different kinds of things where there's no common basis for comparison.

When numbers are used, it looks exact, but a vague or meaningless comparison gets no better by having a few numbers in it.

Example 18 There were twice as many rapes as murders in our town.

Analysis So? This is an apples and oranges comparison.

Example 19 Prisons are getting worse as breeding grounds for disease in this state. There were 8% more cases of TB among prison inmates this year than last.

Analysis This is a misleading comparison. If the prison population increased by 16%, then it would be no surprise that the number of cases of TB is going up, though the rate (how many per 1,000 inmates) might be going down.

Example 20 Paid attendance at Learn Your Way Out of Debt seminars is up more than 50% this year!

Analysis This sounded impressive to Lee until he found that last year 11 people paid for the seminars, and this year 17 did.

> ***Two times zero is still zero*** A two-times-zero-is-still-zero comparison is one in which the base of the comparison is not given.

Example 21 A clothing store advertises "Sweaters at 25% off."

Analysis Zoe expects the price now to be $15, since it used to be $20. But the store means 25% off the suggested retail price of $26, so now it's $19.50.

Example 22 Identity Theft. Prevention & Repair Kit.

The fastest growing white-collar crime in the US!

Publication of the Attorney General's Office of New Mexico, 2007

Analysis So it went from 5 cases to 10? Or from 5,000 to 6,000?

Example 23 A report on the radio says unemployment is up 10%.

Analysis This does not mean unemployment is *at* 10%. It means if unemployment was 10%, it's now 11%, a big increase. But if unemployment was 2%, it's now 2.2%, a very small increase. Unless we know what the unemployment rate was before, the comparison is meaningless.

Example 24 *UNM athletes continue to win in the classroom*
Once again, University of New Mexico student-athletes have made the grade. And then some.

The overall grade-point average for the school's 21 sports was 3.05 in the fall semester, according to the UNM registrar's office. That surpasses the previous best of 3.04, set in the spring of 2003. Mark Smith, *Albuquerque Journal*, Feb. 23, 2005

Analysis This is a two-times-zero-is-still-zero comparison. The base of the comparison should be the grade-point average for all students, which isn't given. With grade inflation, it might be 3.0; so student athletes aren't better than average. Or maybe student athletes were taking easy courses—what's the grade-point average for the courses they were taking?

Example 25 Last term 22.857% of all Dr. Aloxomani's students failed his organic chemistry class.

Analysis This is a case of ***phony precision***. It's accurate but misleading, suggesting that there was a huge sample when it was just 8 out of 25.

Even when all the numbers are accurate, and it's all clear, *the interpretation of them can be skewed.*

Example 26 Harry: Did you hear that new applications for unemployment have fallen since last month and also from this month last year?

Dick: At last the economy is picking up.

Analysis Or perhaps there are so many people already out of work that there aren't many left to be fired. *Imagine the possibilities.*

> *The don't-drop-the-other-shoe technique*
> Another "statistic" widely quoted in feminist literature comes from the Society for the Advancement of Women's Health. It says that "only 14% (of the National Institutes of Health clinical trials funding) goes to research 52% of the population." In other words, "women-predominant" diseases, such as breast cancer, get the short end of the stick. Sounds terrible, discriminatory, unfair! But wait a minute. At least 76% of NIH clinical trial grants go to diseases that affect both sexes, such as heart disease and lung cancer. Since 76 + 14 equals 90, whether Washington lobbying groups like it or not, that means that "men-predominant" diseases are getting no more than 10% of the research money while women-predominant diseases get 14%.
>
> It is just such techniques that caused Benjamin Disraeli, 130 years ago, to say that mendacity comes in only three forms, 'lies, damn lies, and statistics.'
>
> John Steele Gordon, *USA Today*, May 21, 1999

E. Graphs

Graphs summarize lots of number claims. When they're done well, as in this example, they allow for easy, visual comparisons.

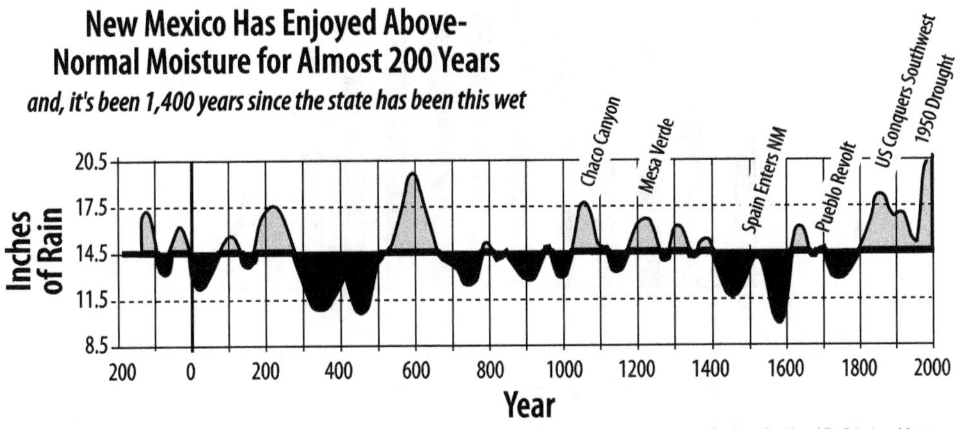

Enchantment Magazine, published by rural electric co-operatives, 2005

Graphs can be useful in making comparisons clearer. But we have to be careful when we look at them because they can conceal claims, mislead, or just be wrong.

Example 27

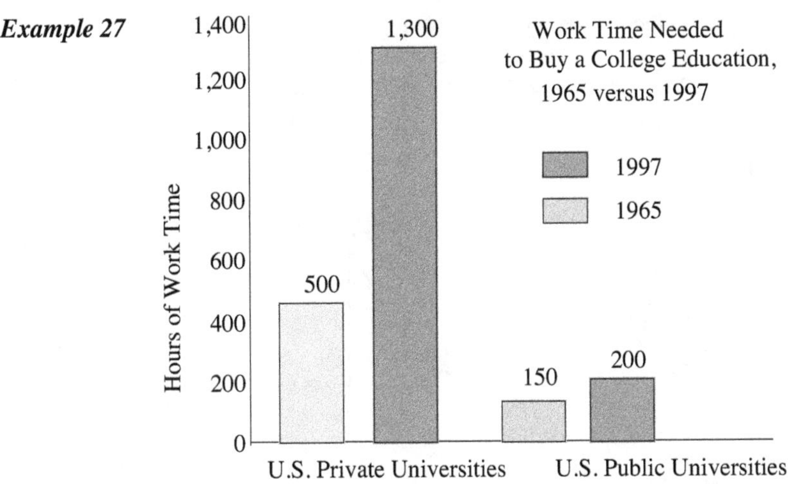

W. Baumol and A. S. Blinder, *Economics: Principles and Policy*

Analysis You should check the information in a graph against your personal experience. The authors of this economics textbook say that the average hourly wage is about $13. So according to the graph the (average?) cost of a college education in 1997 at a U.S. public university was about $13/hour x 200 hours = $2,600. But that was unlikely to be enough for tuition and books for that one year, much less housing and board—and certainly not for four years.

Example 28

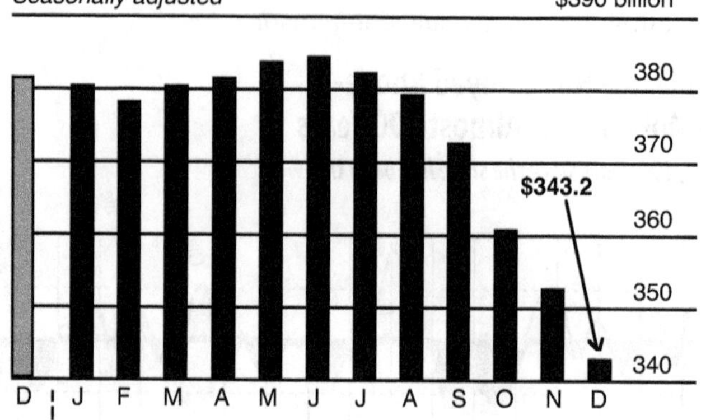

Source: Department of Commerce, Associated Press, January 15, 2009

Analysis The graph lies. The decrease from the highest sales in July to the lowest sales in December is about 11%. But the graph makes it look like a decrease of 90% because of the height of the bars. Visually the difference appears even greater because we're comparing areas instead of lengths.

When a graph doesn't show the baseline—the base of the comparison—it exaggerates increases and decreases.

Example 29

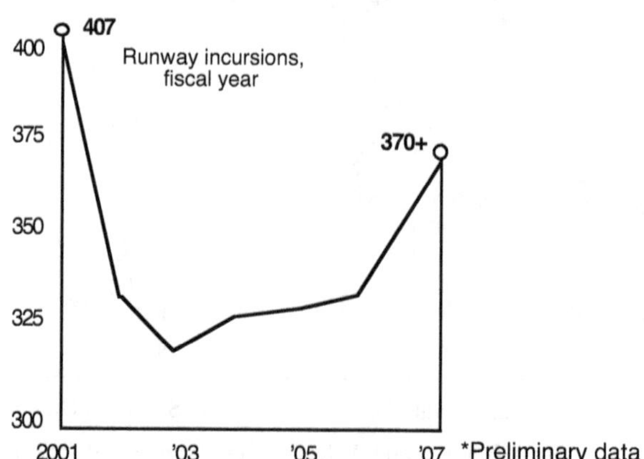

Note: An incursion is any aircraft, vehicle or person that enters space reserved for takeoff and landing.

Source: Federal Aviation Administration Associated Press, December 6, 2007

Analysis The figures are all there, the source is reliable, the graph is easy to read, but a 12% increase in runway incursions is depicted as a 150% increase in the heights of the points.

Example 30

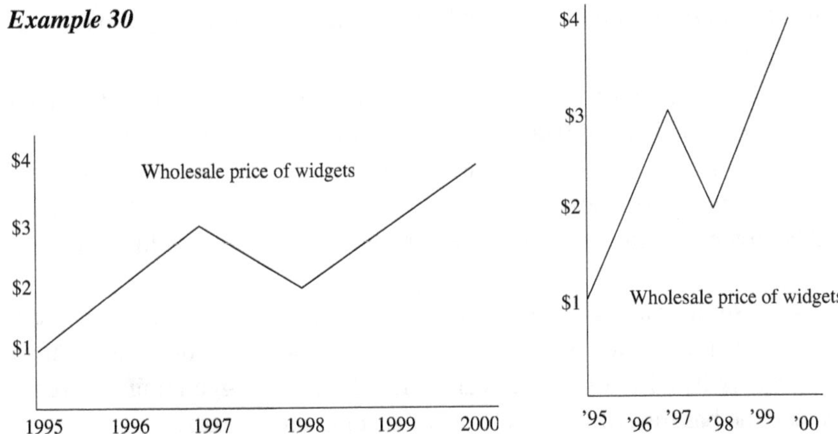

Analysis Here we can see how the angle, the sharpness of increase and decrease, can be exaggerated by the spacing of the scales on the axes. And that affects our perception of the volatility and the amount of increase or decrease of prices.

> *A graph can create misleading comparisons by the choice of how the measuring points on the axes are spaced.*

Example 31

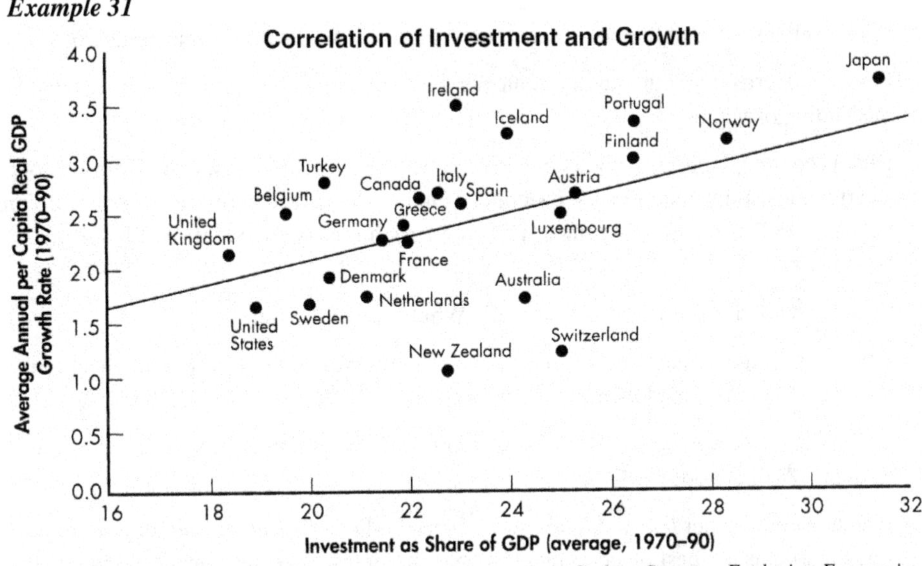

Robert Sexton, *Exploring Economics*

Analysis By drawing the line in this graph, the author is asserting that investment and growth are correlated: both rise together. His premises are the data plotted as points. But the picture doesn't obviously support that. Unless you know why and how the author is justified in drawing this line, the implicit argument here should be seen as only an appeal to the author's authority.

A graph is a summary of one or more claims or sometimes a whole argument, which we should evaluate by the standards we already have.

Summary Numbers are our way of measuring. They're important in our reasoning. But it's easy to be misled or use them badly. A vague sentence doesn't get any better by using numbers. Both sides of a comparison must be made clear. The numbers must represent quantities someone could actually know and the base of the comparison should be given. Often it's not the average that's significant but the median or the mode.

Graphs can summarize lots of claims about numbers, and sometimes they can summarize a whole argument. When done well they illustrate relationships that are hard to grasp otherwise. But often they can be misleading, exaggerating differences by not showing the baseline or by the choice of spacing on the axes.

Key Words	base of a comparison	average
	apples and oranges	mean
	two times zero is still zero	median
	phony precision	mode

Exercises for Chapter 13

1. Find an advertisement that uses a sentence with percentages that is misleading or vague.
2. Find an advertisement that uses a sentence with numbers other than percentages that is misleading or vague.
3. Dick is contemplating getting a new printer. It's faster than his old one. He prints out a cartoon and finds that it takes 7 seconds. On his old printer it took 10.5 seconds. Tom tells him he'll save 1/3 of his time. Dick says no, he'll save about 50% of his time. Who is right?
4. "The birth control pill is 97% effective." What does this mean?
5. Find the average, mean, median, and mode of the scores of Dr. E's students who took his critical thinking final exam: 92, 54, 60, 86, 62, 76, 88, 88, 62, 68, 81.
6. Estimate the average age of students in your class. Do you think it's the same as the median? As the mode?
7. Wanda's grandfather listened to all those experts who say that over the long term the stock market is the best place to invest. So he put most of his retirement money in stocks. He just turned 70 and needs cash to retire. But the market went down 8% last week and 15% since the beginning of the year. How should he evaluate those experts' advice now?

For Exercises 8–21, point out any use of numbers that is vague, misleading, or wrong.

8. [Advertisement] Our employees have a combined 52 years of experience!

9. [Advertisement for *3 Musketeers*® candy bars]
   The sweetest part is finding out how little fat it has.
   (45% less fat than the average of the 25 leading chocolate brands, to be exact.)*
   *Not a low-fat food. 8 fat grams per serving for single bar vs. 15 gram average for leading chocolate brands.

10. [On a box of Texmati® rice]
    Serving size 1/4 cup (45g)
    Servings Per Package about 22

Amount per serving	
Calories 150	%DV*
Total Fat 0.5g	1%
Sodium 0mg	0%
Total Carb. 34g	11%
Protein 3g	

* Percent Daily Values are based on a 2,000 calorie diet.

11. Dick: Gee, cars are really expensive now. My uncle said he bought a new Ford Mustang in 1968 for only $2,000.

12. [On the box of a fan made by Lasco™]
    NEW WIND RING™ 30% MORE Air Velocity

13. [Concerning the way the U.S. Census Bureau operates] In 1990, 65% of the questionnaires that were mailed were filled out and returned. Census counters went back to every household that didn't mail back a form. Even then, the bureau was able to count only 98.4% of the U.S. population. *USA Today,* April 15, 1998

14. Less than 10% of women who get breast cancer have the gene for breast cancer. Therefore, if you have the gene, there's only a 10% chance you'll get breast cancer.

15. The two-year study by the Pathways to Prosperity Project at the Harvard University Graduate School of Education notes that, while much emphasis is placed in high school on going on to a four-year college, only 30 percent of young adults in the United States successfully complete a bachelor's degree. Huffington Post, February 2, 2011

16. 

17. *Cattle herds shrivel in face of drought*
    A widespread drought that's forcing ranchers in New Mexico and across the country to sell off animals has helped shrink the nation's cattle herd to its smallest in at least four decades.

    The National Agricultural Statistics Service reports that the number of cattle and calves in the United States totaled 97.8 million head as of July. That's 2 percent less than a year ago. Beef cattle numbers were down 3 percent at 30.5 million head counted, while dairy cows remained unchanged at 9.2 million.

Albuquerque Journal, July 24, 2012

18. Dick: Which section of English Lit should I take, Zoe, Professor Zzzyzzx's or Professor Øllebød's?

    Zoe: It doesn't really matter. You can't understand either, and the department info on the sections said the average mark in both their classes was a C.

19. [Advertisement] Mitsubishi is the fastest growing Japanese car company in America.

20. According to Camille Scielzi, who coordinates the program, out of approximately 17,000 people who live in this county, 33 percent must exist solely on Social Security benefits that average $600 a month and 19 percent of the county residents live at or below the poverty level. Scott Turner, "Socorro Storehouse seeks volunteers, donors", *El Defensor Chieftain*, November 12, 2015

21. *S. Korea declares war on leftovers*

    Because of the feeling of bounty and plenty that it gives, Koreans routinely cook more at home than they can eat, and restaurants serve more than any customer could reasonably consume. . . . "Koreans are used to thinking 'the more, the better,'" said Koh, the restaurant manager. It's a philosophy the government is battling to change. In the latest round, the government announced Dec. 6 that it will make a major push in 1997 to cut food waste by half. Many Koreans say they are careful at home to eat leftovers the next day. But restaurant waste, which the government says accounts for 42 percent of food garbage, is a tougher problem. . . .

    The government says the country's 45 million people throw away nearly 48,000 metric tons of garbage a day. Pauline Jelinek, Associated Press, November 23, 1996

Which of the following should be trusted to give you a good idea of the population as a whole? For which would you prefer to know the median or mode? Explain.

22. The average wage in the U.S. is $28,912.
23. The average wage in one rural county of Utah was $14,117.
24. The average wage of concert pianists in the U.S. is less than the average wage of university professors.
25. The average number of people in a household in Las Vegas is 2.1.
26. The average income of a woman in the U.S. was only 82% that of a man.

For exercises 27–31, point out what is misleading, or if the graph is good, say so.

27.

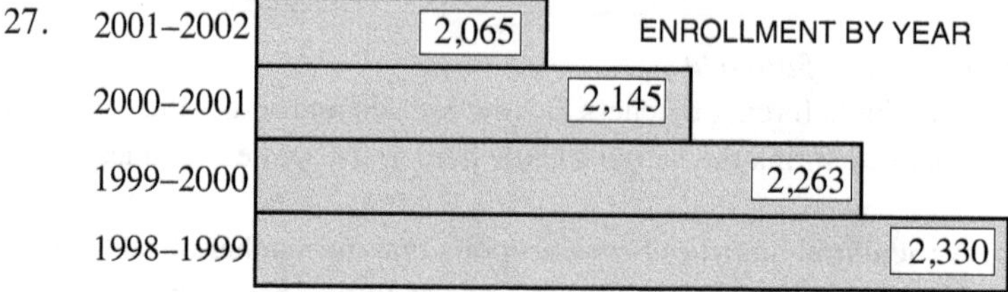

Socorro, N.M. Consolidated Schools Accountability Report, 2000–2001

28.

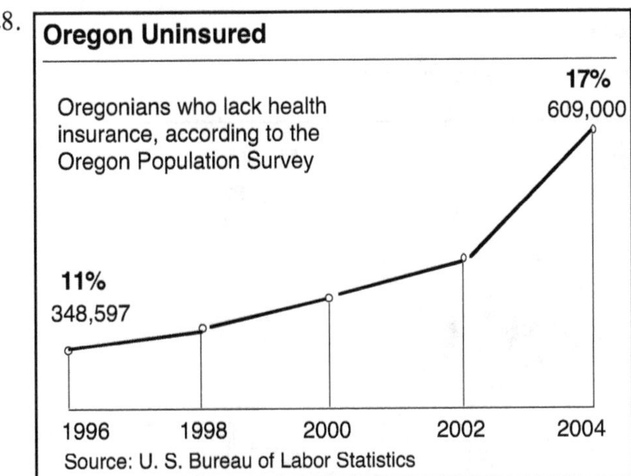

ERIC BAKER/THE OREGONIAN August 15, 2005

29.

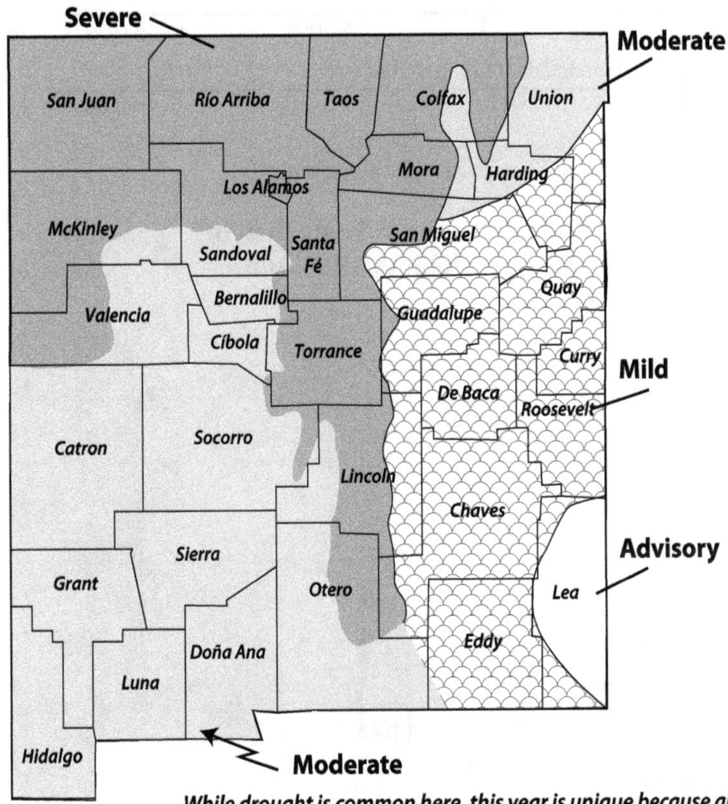

Ted Sammis in *Enchantment Magazine*,rural electric cooperatives, 2005

30. 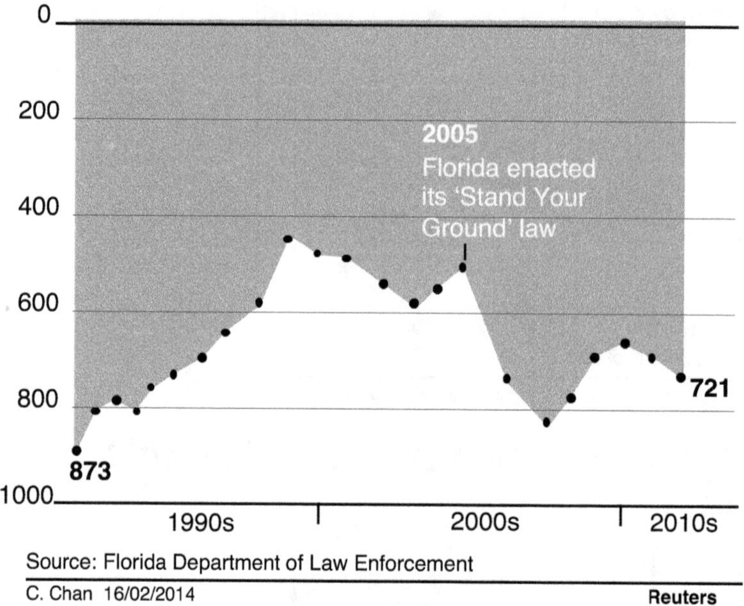

31. List all the claims that are summarized in this graph.

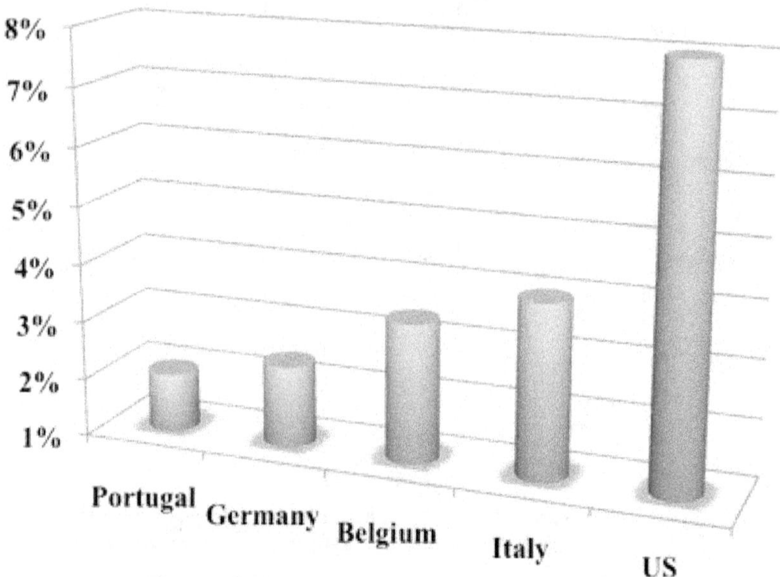

David Morris, at <http://www.ilsr.org/the-real-american-exceptionalism/>

14 Generalizing

A. Generalizing

I think I'll get a border collie. Every one I've met has been friendly and loyal.

I'd better not visit your home. You've got a cat, and every time I've been around a cat I get a terrific sneezing fit and asthma.

We generalize every day, arguing from a claim about some to a claim about more. It's how we make sense of our world. What's happened before is likely to happen again. My experience is typical, until I learn otherwise. As we experience more, we can generalize better because we have more examples from which to generalize.

But it's not only our own experience. Poll takers and scientists generalize when they say that the president's approval rating is 54% or they report that 28% of all people who smoke get cancer. Those are generalizations from the groups of people who were interviewed or studied.

> ***Generalizations*** A generalization is an argument in which we conclude a claim about a group, called the ***population***, from a claim or claims about some part of it, the ***sample***. Sometimes just the conclusion is called the *generalization*. Plausible premises about the sample are called the ***inductive evidence*** for the generalization.

To evaluate whether a generalization is good, we need to see it as an argument. Strong arguments with plausible premises will be the best we're likely to get, since there's always be the possibility that there's an exception to a generalization.

Examples Are the following generalizations? If so, what is the sample? What is the population?

Example 1 I should build my house with the bedroom facing this direction to catch the morning sun.

Analysis We believe we know where the sun will rise in the future based on where we've see it rise in the past. The sample is all the times in the past when the sun rose. We know that the point where the sun rises varies slightly from season to season but is roughly east. The population is all times the sun has risen or will rise, which we think will be in roughly the same direction.

Example 2 Of potential customers surveyed, 72% said they liked "very much" the new green color that Yoda plans to use for its cars. So about 72% of all potential customers will like it.

Analysis The sample is the group of potential customers interviewed, and the population is all potential customers.

Sometimes the generalization we want and we're entitled to isn't "all" but "most" or "72%": the same proportion of the whole as in the sample will have the characteristic. This is a ***statistical generalization***.

Example 3 The doctor tells you to fast from 10 p.m. Then at 10 a.m. she gives you glucose to drink. Forty-five minutes later, she takes some of your blood and has it analyzed. She concludes you don't have diabetes.

Analysis The sample is the blood the doctor took. It's a very small sample compared to the amount of blood you have in your body, but the doctor is confident that it is like the rest of your blood.

Example 4 Maria goes to the city council meeting with a petition signed by all the people who live on her block requesting that a streetlight be put in. Addressing the city council, she says, "Everyone on this block wants a streetlight here."

Analysis Maria is not generalizing. There's no argument from some to more, since the sample equals the population.

Example 5 In a study of 816 people who owned sport utility vehicles in Cincinnati, Rigochi owners expressed the lowest satisfaction with their SUVs. So Rigochi owners are less satisfied with their cars than other SUV owners.

Analysis Here we know about the 816 people who were surveyed in Cincinnati—they are the sample. The conclusion is about all SUV owners everywhere, and they constitute the population.

Is the generalization good? That is, is the argument good? Unstated premises are needed about how the study was conducted. Is there any reason that we should think that these 816 people are like all SUV owners everywhere?

Exercises for Section A

Here's some of Tom's work on identifying generalizations, with Dr. E's comments.

Every time I've gone to Luigi's, it's taken over 30 minutes to get our pizza. So let's not go there tonight because we're in a hurry.

Generalization? (yes/no) Yes.
Sample: Every time the guy has gone to Luigi's and ordered a pizza.
Population: All the times anyone orders a pizza at Luigi's. *Good work!*

You shouldn't go out with someone from New York. They're all rude and pushy.

Generalization? (yes/no) Yes.
Sample: All the New Yorkers the person has met.
Population: All New Yorkers.

You're too generous. How do you know if the speaker has ever met a New Yorker? Maybe he's just spouting off a prejudice he acquired from his friends. Don't treat it as a generalization if you can't identify the sample.

Should we try the new Mexican restaurant on Sun Street? I heard it was pretty good.

Generalization? (yes/no) Yes.
Sample: People who told him it was good.
Population: It will be good food for him, too.

A generalization is an argument, right. But the sample and the population aren't claims—they're groups. The sample here is the times that other people have eaten there (and reported that it was good). The population is all times anyone has or will eat there. It's an implicit past to future generalization.

For Exercises 1–13 answer the following questions:

Generalization? (yes/no)
Sample:
Population:

1. German shepherds have a really good temperament. I know because lots of my friends and my sister have one.

2. Maria: Look! That dry cleaner broke a button on my blouse again. I'm going to go over there and complain.

3. Suzy: I hear you got one of those cell phones from Hirangi.
   Maria: Yeah, and I wish I'd never gotten one. It's always breaking down.
   Suzy: Well, I won't get one then, since they're probably all the same.

4. Maria to Suzy: Don't bother to ask Tom to do the dishes. My brother's a football player, and no football player will do the dishes.

5. Suzy: Guys are such nitwits.
   Zoe: What do you mean?
   Suzy: Like, they can't even tell when you're down. Emotionally, they're clods. Besides, they just want a girl for her body.
   Zoe: How do you know?
   Suzy: Duh, it's like a cheerleader like me isn't going to have a lot of dates?

6. Lee: Are you taking Spot for a walk?
   Dick: No. I'm getting the leash because I have to take him to the vet, and it will be hard to get him to go. Every time I take him there he seems to know it before we get in the car.

7. Manuel: Are those refried beans?
   Maria: Yes.
   Manuel: I can't believe you'd cook those for dinner. Don't you remember I had terrible indigestion the last time you made them?

8. Maria: Do you know of a good dry cleaner other than Ricardo's?
   Zoe: The one in the plaza north of campus is pretty good. They've always done O.K. with the stuff I take them.

9. Don't go to Seattle in December. It rains there all the time then.

10. Dogs can be trained to retrieve a newspaper.

11. I want to marry a Japanese guy. They're hardworking and really family-oriented.

12. You don't have to worry about getting the women's gymnastic team in your van. I saw them at the last meet, and they're small enough to fit in.

13. From our study it appears that bald men are better husbands.

14. Write down three examples of generalizations you've heard or made in the last week and one example of a claim that sounds like a generalization but isn't. See if your classmates can pick out the one that isn't. For the generalizations, ask a classmate to identify the sample and the population.

B. What's a Good Sample?

1. How you can go wrong

Tom's sociology professor has assigned him to conduct a survey to find out the attitudes of students on campus about sex before marriage. "That's easy," Tom thinks, "I'll just ask some of my friends. They're typical, aren't they?"

So he asks all his friends he can reach on Tuesday whether they think sex before marriage is a great idea or not. Twenty of the 28 say "Yes," while 8 say "No." That was easy.

Tom takes the results to his professor, and she asks why he thinks his friends are typical. "Typical? I guess they are," Tom responds. But aren't they mostly your age? And the same sex as you? How many are gay? How many are married? And is 28 really enough to generalize from? And what about that question "Is sex before marriage a *great* idea or not?" A bit biased?

O.K., it wasn't such a good job. So Tom brainstorms with some of his friends and figures he'll ask 100 students as they leave the student union one question, "Do you approve of sexual intercourse before marriage?"

He goes to the student union at 4 p.m. on Wednesday, asks the students, and finds that 83 said "No," while 17 said "Yes." That's different from what he expected, but what the heck, this is science, and science can't be wrong. There was no bias in the question, and surely those 100 students are typical.

Tom presents the results to his professor, and she suggests that perhaps he should find out what was going on at the student union that day. . . . It seems the campus Bible society was having a big meeting there that let out about 4 p.m. Maybe this survey won't give a good generalization.

So Tom and two friends get together, and at 9 a.m., 1 p.m., and 6 p.m. they station themselves outside the student union, the administration offices, and the big classroom building. Each is to ask the first 20 people who come by just two questions: "Are you a student here?" and "Do you approve of sexual intercourse before marriage?"

They get 171 people saying they are students, with 133 saying "Yes" and 38 saying "No" to the second question. That's a lot of responses with no evident bias in the sampling. Tom's sure his professor will be happy this time.

Tom tells his professor what they've done, and she asks, "Why do you think your sample is representative? Why do you think it's big enough?"

Tom's puzzled. It's big enough. Surely 170 out of 20,000 students is a lot, isn't it? How many could she expect us to interview? We're just human.

And representative? What does she mean? "We didn't do anything to get a bias," he says. "But are those students typical?" she asks. "Is not doing anything to get a bias enough to ensure your sample is representative?"

2. Representative samples

Tom's first two attempts to survey students about their attitudes towards sex before marriage used clearly unrepresentative samples. But his third attempt? Do we have good reason to think he got a sample that's like the population, a representative one?

> ***Representative sample*** A sample is representative if no one subgroup of the whole population is represented more than its proportion in the population. A sample is ***biased*** if it is not representative.

Tom's method was ***haphazard sampling***: choosing the sample with no *intentional* bias. Perhaps the sample is representative. Maybe not. But we don't have any good reason to believe that it's representative. There is, however, a way we can choose a sample that is very likely to get us a representative sample.

> ***Random sampling*** A sample is chosen randomly if at every choice there is an equal chance for any one of the remaining members of the population to be picked.

If you assign a number to each student, write the numbers on slips of paper, put them in a fishbowl, and draw one number out at a time, that's probably going to be a random selection. But there's a chance that slips with longer numbers will have more ink and fall to the bottom of the bowl when you shake it. Or the slips aren't all the same size. So typically to get a random selection, we use tables of random numbers prepared by mathematicians. There are many online programs that generate tables of random numbers. For Tom's survey he could get a list of all students; if the first number on the table is 413, he'd pick the 413th student on the list; if the second number is 711, he'd pick the 711th student on the list; and so on, until he has a sample that's big enough.

Why is random sampling better? Suppose that of the 20,000 students at your school, 500 are gay males. Then the chance that *one* student picked at random would be a gay male is $^{500}/_{20,000} = {}^{1}/_{40}$. If you were to pick 300 students at random, the chance that half of them would be gay is very small. It is very likely, however, that 7 or 8 ($^{1}/_{40}$ of 300) will be gay males.

Or suppose that roughly 50% of the students at your school are female. Then each time you choose a student at random, there's a roughly 50% chance the person will be female. And if you randomly choose a sample of 300 students, the chance is very high that about 50% will be female.

The ***law of large numbers*** says, roughly, that if the probability of something occurring is X percent, then over *the long run* the percentage of times that happens will be about X percent. For example, the probability of a flip of a fair coin landing heads is 50%. So, though you may get a run of 8 tails, then 5 heads, then 4 tails, then 36 heads to start, in the long run, repeating the flipping, if the coin is fair, eventually the number of heads will tend toward 50%.

IT'S COME UP RED 12 TIMES IN A ROW. IT'S BOUND TO COME UP BLACK SEVERAL TIMES IN A ROW NOW.

Don't bet on it. The times it comes up red and the times it comes up black will even out in the *long run*. But if it came up red 100 times in a row, black could even out by coming up just one more time than red every 100 spins for the next 10,000 spins. The ***gambler's fallacy***: A run of events of a certain kind makes a run of contrary events more likely in order to even up the probabilities.

If you choose a large sample randomly, the chance is very high that it will be representative. That's because the chance of any one subgroup being over-represented is small—not nonexistent, but small. It doesn't matter if you know anything about the composition of the population in advance. After all, to know how many homosexuals there are, and how many married women, and how many Muslims, and how many . . . you'd need to know almost everything about the population in advance. But that's what you use surveys to find out.

With a big enough random sample we have good reason to believe the sample is representative. A sample chosen haphazardly may give a representative sample—but you have no good reason to believe it will be representative.

Weak Argument	***Strong Argument***
Sample is chosen *haphazardly*. Therefore, The sample is representative.	Sample is chosen *randomly*. Therefore, The sample is representative.
Lots of ways the sample could be biased.	Very unlikely that the sample is biased.

The classic example that haphazard sampling needn't work, even with an enormous sample, is the poll done in 1936 by *Literary Digest*. The magazine mailed out 10,000,000 ballots asking who the person would vote for in the 1936 presidential election. They received 2,300,000 back. With that huge sample the magazine confidently predicted that Alf Landon would win. Roosevelt received 60% of the vote, one of the biggest wins ever. What went wrong? The magazine selected its sample from lists of it own subscribers and telephone and automobile owners. In 1936 that was the wealthy class. And the wealthy folks preferred Alf Landon. The sample wasn't representative of all voters.

In any case, we can't always get a perfectly representative sample. Of 400 voters in Mississippi who are chosen randomly, 6 are traveling out of the state, 13 have moved with no forwarding address, . . . you can't locate them all. Like being vague, the right question to ask is: does the sample seem *too* biased to be reliable?

Exercises for Section B

1. What is a representative sample?
2. Explain why a good generalization is unlikely to be valid.
3. a. What is the law of large numbers?
   b. How does it justify random sampling as giving unbiased samples?
4. Which of the following seem too biased to be reliable, and why?
   a. To determine the average number of people in your city who played tennis last week, interview women only.
   b. To determine what kind of cat food is purchased most often, interview only people who are listed in the telephone directory.
   c. To determine what percentage of women think that more women should be doctors, poll female students as they leave their classes at your school.
   d. To determine whether to buy grapes at the supermarket, pick a grape from the bunch you're interested in and taste it.
5. a. Suppose you want to find out whether people in your city believe that there are enough police officers. Give four characteristics of people that could bias the survey. That is, list four subgroups of the population that you would not want to have represented out of proportion to their actual percentages in the population.
   b. Now list four characteristics that you feel would not matter for giving bias.
6. A professor suggested the best way to get a sample is to make sure that for the relevant characteristics—for example, gender, age, ethnicity, income—we know that the sample has the same proportion as in the population as a whole. Why won't that work?
7. One of Dr. E's students was a blackjack dealer at a casino and heard a player say, "I ran a computer simulation of this system 1,000 times and made money. So why didn't I win today playing for real?" Can you explain it?
8. Is every randomly chosen sample representative? Explain.

C. When Is a Generalization Good?

1. Sample size

> I know a couple of Chinese students in my classes. They're both hardworking and get good grades. All Chinese must be like that.

That's generalizing from *too small a sample*—the way stereotypes begin. It's a ***hasty generalization*** using ***anecdotal evidence***.

But how big does a sample have to be? To estimate what percentage of students at your school approve of sex before marriage, is it enough to ask 5? 25? 150? Why is it that opinion polls regularly extrapolate to the preferences of all voters in the U.S. from sampling 1,500 or fewer people?

Roughly, the idea is to measure how much more likely it is that your generalization is going to be accurate as you increase the number in your sample. If you want to find out how many people in your class of 300 sociology students are spending 12 hours a week on the homework, you might ask 15 or 20. If you interview 30, you might get a better picture, but there's a limit. After you've asked 100, you probably won't get a much different result if you ask 150. And if you've asked 200, do you really think your generalization will be different if you ask 250? It hardly seems worth the effort.

Often you can rely on common sense when small numbers are involved. But when we generalize to a very large population, say 2,000, or 20,000, or 200,000,000, how big the sample should be cannot be explained without at least a mini-course on statistics. In evaluating statistical generalizations, you have to expect that the people doing the sampling have looked at enough examples, which is reasonable if it's a respected organization, a well-known polling company, physicians, or a drug company that has to answer to the Food and Drug Administration. Surprisingly, 1,500 is typically adequate for the sample size when surveying all adults in the U.S.

2. Is the sample studied well?

Choosing a large enough representative sample is important, but it's not enough. The sample has to be investigated well.

The doctor taking your blood to see if you have diabetes won't get a reliable result if her test tube is contaminated or if she forgets to tell you to fast for 12 hours before. You won't find out the attitudes of students about sex before marriage if you ask a biased question. Picking a random sample of bolts won't help you determine if the bolts are O.K. if all you do is inspect them visually, not with a microscope or a stress test.

Questionnaires and surveys are particularly problematic. Questions need to be formulated without bias.

Example 6 A "Grassroots Survey of Democratic Leaders" in 2005 from the Democratic National Committee asked 14 questions. Among them was:

Do you support new tax cuts targeted at working families?
—Yes, with our economy struggling, working families need a tax break.
—No, additional tax cuts at this time will only worsen the federal deficit.

Analysis There's no reason to believe any generalization from a survey that uses such biased questions.

Even if questions are formulated without bias, we have to rely on respondents answering truthfully. Surveys on sexual habits are notorious for inaccurate self-reporting. Invariably, the number of times that women in the U.S. report they engaged in sexual intercourse with a man in the last week, or month, or year is much lower than the reports that men give of sexual intercourse with a woman during that same time. The figures are so different that it would be impossible for both groups to be answering accurately.

Example 7 More than four million people younger than 21 drove under the influence of drugs or alcohol last year, according to a government report released Wednesday. That's one in five of all Americans aged 16 to 20. Associated Press, December 30, 2004

Analysis We don't know whether they used an anonymous questionnaire, so we have no reason to accept their generalization.

3. Three premises needed for a good generalization

A generalization is an argument. You need to examine it as you would any argument: Does the argument rely on slanted or vague language? What unstated premises are missing? Do you have good reason to believe the premises? Does the conclusion follow from the premises? For some generalizations you will have to rely on "the experts" to decide whether to believe the premises, which include "The sample is representative," "The sample is big enough," "The sample was studied well," whether stated or not. Even if you have a degree in statistics, you will rarely have access to the information necessary to evaluate those premises.

Premises needed for a good generalization
- The sample is representative.
- The sample is big enough.
- The sample is studied well.

But you could choose a big enough representative sample, study it well, get a trustworthy generalization, and still have a lousy argument.

Example 8 Dick: A study I read said people with large hands are better at math.
Suzy: I guess that explains why I can't divide!

Analysis You don't need a study to know that people with large hands do better at math: babies have small hands and they can't even add. The collection of all people is the wrong population to study.

4. The margin of error and confidence level

It's never reasonable to believe exact statistical generalizations: 37% of the people in your town who were surveyed wear glasses, so 37% of all people in your town wear glasses. No matter how many people in your town are surveyed, short of virtually all of them, you can't be confident that exactly 37% of all of them wear glasses. Rather, "37%, more or less, wear glasses" would be the right conclusion.

That "more or less" can be made fairly precise according to a theory of statistics. The ***margin of error*** (or *confidence interval*) tells us the range within which the actual number for the population is likely to fall. How likely is it that they're right? The ***confidence level*** measures that.

Example 9 The opinion poll says that when voters were asked their preference, the incumbent was favored by 53% and the challenger by 47%, with a margin of error of 2% and a confidence level of 95%. So the incumbent will win tomorrow.

Analysis From this survey, the pollsters are concluding that the percentage of *all* voters who favor the incumbent is between 51% and 55%, while the challenger is favored by between 45% and 49%. The confidence level is 95%. That means there's a 95% chance it's true that the actual percentage of voters who prefer the incumbent is between 51% and 55%. If the confidence level were 60%, then the survey wouldn't be very reliable: there would be a 4-out-of-10 chance that the conclusion is false, given those premises.

The confidence level *measures the strength of the generalization as an argument*. Typically, if the confidence level is below 95%, the results won't even be announced. To summarize in this example:

> Margin of error ± 2% gives the range around 53% in which it is likely that the population value lies. It is part of the conclusion: Between 51% and 55% of all voters favor the incumbent.
>
> Confidence level of 95% says how likely it is that the population value lies in that range. It tells you how strong the generalization is.

The bigger the sample, the higher the confidence level and the lower the margin of error. The problem is to decide how much it's worth in extra time and expense to increase the sample size in order to get a better argument.

So will the incumbent win? The generalization that a majority of voters at the time of polling favor the incumbent is strong. But to conclude the incumbent will win depends on what happens from the time of the polling to the voting. It depends on how fixed people are in their opinions and on a lot of other unstated premises.

5. Variation in the population

Dick: It takes me forever to download anything on the internet.
Tom: But you've got a computer just like mine.

Dick: Yeah, but I've got service through El Rooney Internet.
Tom: Get on to that high-speed service that Beene Internet is providing. I've got it and it's super fast. I can download a song from the Apple site in less than 8 seconds.

Tom is generalizing. His conclusion is that any other computer like his on the same kind of internet connection will be as fast. Isn't that a hasty generalization? No. Tom's generalization is good because any other computer like his (that's in running order) with the same internet connection should perform exactly as his. They're all supposed to be the same.

How big the sample has to be depends on how much ***variation*** there is in the population. If there is very little variation, then a small sample chosen haphazardly will do. Lots of variation demands a very large sample, and random sampling is the best way to get a representative sample.

6. Selective attention

Beware of ***selective attention***: It seems that buttered toast always lands the wrong side down because we notice—or remember—when it does.

We remember what is especially bad: our horror of plane crashes we read about, even though driving a car is statistically much more dangerous. We remember what is especially good—how clever we were last week and how rarely we make mistakes. Our memory often isn't a good guide to picking out a representative sample.

7. Risk

With a shipment of 30 bolts, inspecting 15 of them and finding all of them O.K. would allow you to conclude that all the bolts are O.K. But if they're for the space shuttle, where a bad bolt could doom the spacecraft, you'd want to inspect each and every one of them.

On the other hand, suppose you eat a kumquat for the first time. Two hours later you get a stomachache, and that night and the next morning you have diarrhea. You probably wouldn't eat a kumquat again. But the argument from this one experience to the conclusion that kumquats will always do this to you is weak— it could have been something else you ate, or a 24-hour flu, or . . . .

> *Risk doesn't change how strong an argument you have, only how strong an argument you want before you'll accept the conclusion.*

8. Analogies and generalizations

The analysis of analogies usually ends in our trying to come up with a general claim that will make a valid or strong argument. This car is like that one; they both have bad suspension; here's another from the same manufacturer, which the owner says has bad suspension; so if you buy one of these cars, it will have bad suspension. From two or three or more examples, you figure that the next one will be the same. That's an analogy, but it's also a generalization, for the unspoken general claim that needs to be proved is: (almost) all cars from this manufacturer have bad suspension.

Summary We generalize all the time. From a few instances (the sample) we conclude something about a bigger group (the population). Generalizations are arguments. They need three premises to be good: the sample is representative; the sample is big enough; the sample is studied well.

Often we can figure out whether these premises are true. But it's harder for large populations with a lot of variation. The best way to ensure that a sample is representative is to choose it randomly. Haphazardly chosen samples are often used, but we have no reason to believe that a haphazardly chosen sample is representative.

With polls and scientific surveys we usually have to decide whether to believe the experts. They should tell us the margin of error and confidence level. We can develop some sense of when a generalization is good or bad. Our best guide is to remember a generalization is an argument, so that all we've learned about analyzing arguments applies.

Key Words

	generalization	random sampling
	population	law of large numbers
	sample	gambler's fallacy
	inductive evidence	hasty generalization
	statistical generalization	anecdotal evidence
	representative sample	margin of error
	biased sample	confidence level
	haphazard sampling	selective attention

> The popularity of American therapy movements might also explain why all the books mentioned in this review base much of their thinking on interviews and personal stories, or "narratives," as though American readers can no longer follow abstract arguments from ethical or economic or statistical premises. As

a result, instead of constructive social policy based on statistical data, we have endless testimonials, diatribes, and spurious science from people who imagine that their personal experience, the dynamics of their particular family, sexual taste, childhood trauma, and personal inclination constitute universals.
Diane Johnson, "What Do Women Want?"
The New York Review of Books, November 28, 1996

Exercises for Chapter 14

1. Your candidate is favored by 56% to 44%, with a margin of error of 5% and a confidence level of 94%. What does that mean?
2. You read a poll that says the confidence level is 71%. Is the generalization reliable?
3. a. What do we call a weak generalization from a sample that is obviously too small?
   b. Can a sample of one ever be enough for a strong generalization?
4. The larger the ____________ in the population, the larger the sample size must be.
5. What premises do we need for a good generalization?
6. a. You're at the supermarket trying to decide which package of strawberries to buy. Describe and evaluate your procedure as a sampling and generalizing process (of course, you're not allowed to actually taste one).
   b. Now do the same supposing the package is covered everywhere but on top.
7. Why does the phone ring more often when you're in the shower?
8. Suppose you're on the city council and have to decide whether to put a bond issue for a new school on the next ballot. You don't want to do it if there's a good chance it will fail. You decide to do a survey but haven't time to get a polling agency to do it. There are 7,200 people in your town. How would you go about picking a sample?
9. The president of your college would like to know how many students approve of the way she is handling her job. Explain why no survey is going to give her any useful ideas about how to improve her work.
10. The mayor of a town of 8,000 has to decide whether to spend town funds on renovating the park or hiring a part-time animal control officer. She gets a reputable polling organization to do a survey.
    a. The results of the survey are 52% in favor of hiring an animal control officer and 47% in favor of renovating the park, with 1% undecided, and a margin of error of 3%. The confidence level is 98%. Which choice will make the most people happy? Should she bet on that?
    b. The results are 61% in favor of hiring an animal control officer and 31% in favor of renovating the park, with 8% undecided, and a margin of error of 9%. The confidence level is 94%. Which choice will make the most people happy? Should she bet on that?
11. A "Quality of Education Survey" was sent out to all parents of students at Socorro High School (Socorro, NM) for the school year 2000–2001. Of 598 forms sent out, 166 were returned. For one of the issues the results were:

My child is safe at school 6% (10 forms) strongly agreed, 42.8% (71) agreed, 28.9% (48) disagreed, 13.9% (23) strongly disagreed, 7.8% (13) did not know, and 0.6% (1) left the question blank.

What can you conclude?

12. 
I TALKED TO ALL THE PEOPLE WHO LIVE ON THIS STREET AND EVERYONE WHO HAS A DOG IS REALLY HAPPY. SO IF I GET MY MOM A DOG, SHE'LL BE HAPPY, TOO.

How should Dick explain to Flo that she's not reasoning well?

Here are some of Harry's attempts to use the ideas from this chapter.

Maria: Every time I've seen a stranger come to Dick's gate, Spot has barked. So Spot will always bark at strangers at Dick's gate.

Generalization (state it; if none, say so): Spot will bark at every stranger who comes to the gate.

Sample: All the times Maria has seen a stranger come to the gate.

Sample is representative? (yes or no) Who knows?

Sample is big enough? (yes or no) No.

Sample is studied well? (yes or no) Yes—Maria knows if Spot barked when she was there.

Additional premises needed:

Good generalization? No. The sample isn't good.

You almost got it. The generalization shouldn't convince you—that's right. But the problem isn't that the sample isn't "good" but that Maria hasn't given any reason to believe that it's big enough and representative. Is "every time" once? Twice? 150 times? And are those times representative? It's enough that you have no reason to believe that the sample is representative to make this a bad generalization, that is, a bad argument.

In a study of 5,000 people who owned pets in Anchorage, Alaska, dog owners expressed higher satisfaction with their pets and their lives. So dog owners are more satisfied with their pets and their own lives.

Generalization (state it; if none, say so): Dog owners are more satisfied with their pets and their own lives.

Sample: The people surveyed.

Sample is representative? No.

Sample is big enough? Don't know.

Sample is studied well? Not sure—I don't know what questions were asked.

Additional premises needed:

Good generalization? No. The sample isn't good.

Right. Once you note that the sample isn't representative, you know immediately that the argument isn't good.

Every time the minimum wage is raised, there's squawking that it will cause inflation and decrease employment. And every time it doesn't. So watch for the same worthless arguments again this time.

Generalization (state it; if none, say so): Raising the minimum wage won't cause inflation and decrease employment.

Sample: Every time in the past that the minimum wage was raised.

Sample is representative? Yes.

Sample is big enough? Yes—it was all the times before.

Sample is studied well? Yes—assuming she knows what she's talking about.

Additional premises needed: None.

Good generalization? Yes.

The sample is big enough since it can't get any bigger. But is it representative? Is there any reason to think that the situation now is like the situations in the past when the minimum wage was raised? It's like an analogy: This time is like the past times. Until the speaker fills that in, we shouldn't accept the conclusion.

Maria has asked all but three of the 36 people in her class whether they've ever used heroin. Only two said "yes." So she concluded that almost no one in the class has used heroin.

Generalization Almost no one in Maria's class has used heroin.

Sample: The 33 people Maria asked.

Sample is big enough? Yes.

Sample is studied well? Yes.

Additional premises needed:

Good generalization? Yes.

Do you really think everyone who's used heroin is going to admit it to a stranger? The sample isn't studied well—you'd need anonymous responses at least. So the generalization isn't good.

Evaluate Exercises 13–31 by answering the following:

Generalization (state it; if none, say so):

Sample:

Sample is representative? (yes or no)

Sample is big enough? (yes or no)

Sample is studied well? (yes or no)

Additional premises needed:

Good generalization?

13. Socialized medicine in Canada isn't working. I heard of a man who had colon cancer and needed surgery. By the time doctors operated six months later, the man was nearly dead and died two days later.

14. Lee: Every rich person I've met invested heavily in the stock market. So I'll invest in the stock market, too.

15. Don't take a course from Dr. E. I know three people who failed his course last term.

16. In a test of 5,000 cattle from Manitoba, none of them were found to be infected with mad cow disease. So it's pretty likely that no cattle in Canada have mad cow disease.

17. Everyone I've met at this school is either on one of the athletic teams or has a boyfriend or girlfriend on one of the athletic teams. Gosh, I guess just about everyone at this school is involved in sports.

18. Dick: Hold the steering wheel.
    Zoe: What are you doing? Stop! Are you crazy?
    Dick: I'm just taking my sweater off.
    Zoe: I can't believe you did that. It's *so* dangerous.
    Dick: Don't be silly. I've done it a thousand times before.

19. According to the National Pork Producers Council (www.nppc.org), average hog market weight is 350 pounds, and it takes about 3.5 pounds of feed to produce 1 pound of live hog weight.

20. In 2015, Public Policy Polling asked 532 Republican primary voters across the U.S. if they supported or opposed bombing Agrabah: 30% supported bombing, 13% opposed bombing, and 57% said they were not sure.

21. Manuel to Maria: Lanolin is great for your hands—you ought to try it. It's what's on sheep wool naturally. How many shepherds have you seen with dry, chapped hands?

22. Lee: When I went in to the health service, I read some women's magazine that had the results of a survey they'd done on women's attitudes towards men with beards. They said that they received over 10,000 responses from their readers to the question in their last issue, and 78% say they think that men with beards are really sexy! I'm definitely going to grow a beard now.

23. My grandmother was diagnosed with cancer seven years ago. She refused any treatment that was offered to her over the years. She's perfectly healthy and doing great. The treatments for cancer are just a scam to get people's money.

24. Tom: Can you pick up that pro basketball player who's coming to the rally today?
Dick: I can't. Zoe's got the car. Why not ask Suzy?
Tom: She's got a Yoda hatchback. They're too small for someone over 6 foot tall.

25. (Overheard at a doctor's office) I won't have high blood pressure today because I got enough sleep last night. The last two times you've taken my blood pressure I've rested well the night before, and both times it was normal.

26. We recruited participants at six busy locations in Zurich, Switzerland. Eligible participants were randomly approached and asked whether they would agree to take part in the study. We approached 272 pedestrians, and 185 (68%) were willing to take part. . . .

In this sample, Swiss citizens did not know more than a third of MMK [minimum medical knowledge]. We found little improvement from this low level within groups with medical experience (personal or professional), suggesting that there is a consistent and dramatic lack of knowledge in the general public about the typical signs of and risk factors for important clinical conditions.

"Do citizens have a minimum medical knowledge? A survey"
L. Bachmann, F. Gutzwiller, M. Puhan, J. Steurer, C. Steurer-Stey, and G. Gigerenzer, *BMC Medicine*, vol. 5, no. 14, 2007

27. Give the baby his pacifier so he'll stop crying. Every time I give him the pacifier, he stops crying.

28. We will be late for church because we have to wait for Gina. She's always late. She's been late seven Sundays in a row.

29. Every time I or anyone else has looked into my refrigerator, the light is on. Therefore, the light is always on in my refrigerator.

30. Every time I or anyone I know has seen a tree fall in the forest, it makes a sound. Therefore, anytime a tree falls in the forest it makes a sound.

31. *Biology breeds grumpy old men*

Men lose brain tissue at almost three times the rate of women, curbing their memory, concentration and reasoning power—and perhaps turning them into "grumpy old men" —a researcher said Wednesday.

"Even in the age range of 18 to 45, you can see a steady decline in the ability to perform such (attention-oriented) tasks in men," said Ruben C. Gur, a professor of psychology at the University of Pennsylvania.

Gur said shrinking brains may make men grumpier because some of the tissue loss is in the left frontal region of the brain, which seems to be connected to depression.

"Grumpy old men may be biological," Gur, who is continuing to study whether there is a connection, said Wednesday. However, one researcher not affiliated with the study said Wednesday that other recent studies contradict Gur's findings on shrinkage.

The findings, which augment earlier research published by Gur and colleagues, are the result of his studies of the brain functions of 24 women and 37 men over the past decade. He measured the brain volume with an MRI machine and studied metabolism rates.

From young adulthood to middle age, men lose 15% of their frontal lobe volume,

8.5% of their temporal lobe, he said. Women, while they have "very mild" shrinkage, lose tissue in neither lobe. For the brain overall, men lose tissue three times faster.

Gur found that the most dramatic loss was in men's frontal lobes, which control attention, abstract reasoning, mental flexibility and inhibition of impulses, and the temporal lobe [which] governs memory. Associated Press, April 11, 1996

32. How would you explain to the author of this letter what's wrong with his reasoning?

This letter is in response to "Bugman's" letter from Corrales (*El Defensor Chieftain*, Sept. 29).

First of all, the recent poll that stated that 66 percent of New Mexicans oppose cockfighting is misleading because I am a New Mexican and no one polled me. So that statement in itself is misleading. In a recent gathering—of 175 people who do not oppose cockfighting and are New Mexicans—not one was polled.

I would like to know, of the 66 percent who opposed cockfighting, how many are native New Mexicans, and not transplants from other states, and in which counties the poll was gathered from.

I would guess that the poll was taken in a large city in New Mexico and in one or two counties. The people that oppose this are people who take it upon themselves to tell other people what traditions to follow and, basically, try to control another group of people. Rural New Mexicans should not be dictated to by big-city people who think that only their way is best. . . .

I hope that Gov. Richardson will see that New Mexico has bigger issues and problems than cockfighting. We have major water issues, economic and job problems, alcohol and drug abuse, education for our children, threats from terrorists and medical coverage for our people.

Cockfighting does not seem that important in comparison to these issues. Why pick on a group of people who mind their own business and who think of cockfighting as their heritage? Why is it that when we go to Santa Fe [the capital of New Mexico], the gallery is full of people who want to protect their sport and their heritage and only a handful show up to ban it.

The agenda of this group of people is to eliminate all sports involving animals and to control all aspects of our lives and our traditions. What will be next? Matanzas [a Hispanic tradition of slaughtering a pig and roasting it for a party]? Other traditions that embarrass them because it is not in their culture? This is New Mexico, the last state they can screw up. I, for one, am not going down without a fight. If you don't like New Mexico with its traditions and its culture, then either leave or learn to live with them. Do not try to ram your ideas or try to make the native rural people conform to your way of thinking just because you think it is right. I, for one, will not put up with it.

Richard Lopez, *El Defensor Chieftain*, October 16, 2004

For the following exercises, identify the analogy and explain how a generalization is needed to make it good.

33. Dick: What do you think about getting one of those Blauspot rice cookers?
Zoe: It's not a good idea. Remember, Maria got one and she had to return it twice to get it fixed.

34. Of chimpanzees fed 1 pound of chocolate per day in addition to their usual diet, 72% became obese within two months. Therefore, it is likely that most humans who eat 1% of their body weight in chocolate daily will become obese within two months.

35. 

Further Study Courses on statistics explain the nature of sampling and generalizing. A course on inductive logic in a philosophy department will study more fully the topics of this chapter and the next. Many disciplines, such as sociology, marketing, or the health sciences, give courses on the use of sampling and generalizing that are specific to their subject.

Since people started using cell phones primarily, polling has gotten much harder: many people won't answer, and older folks are difficult to reach because they're not as likely to have cell phones. You can read about that in two articles: https://www.washingtonpost.com/blogs/govbeat/wp/2014/03/12/the-problem-with-modern-polling-in-one-chart/ and http://theweek.com/articles/617109/problem-polls.

Two good books about statistics in reasoning with lots of examples are *Flaws and Fallacies in Statistical Thinking* by Stephen K. Campbell and *How to Lie with Statistics* by Darrell Huff.

15 Cause and Effect

Maria caused the accident. Smoking causes cancer. Gravity causes the moon to stay in orbit. These are ***causal claims***. We make lots of them, though they may not always contain the word "causes" or "caused," for example, "Jogging keeps you healthy" or "Taking an aspirin every other day cuts the risk of having a heart attack." And every time someone blames you, you're encountering a claim that you caused something that was bad and, apparently, avoidable.

What does a claim about causes look like? How do we judge whether it's true?

A. What Is the Cause?

1. Causes and effects

What exactly is a *cause*? Consider what Dick said last night:

Spot caused me to wake up.

Spot is the thing that somehow caused Dick to wake up. But it's not just that Spot existed. It's what he was doing that caused Dick to wake up:

Spot's barking caused Dick to wake up.

So barking is a cause and waking is an effect? What exactly is barking? What is waking? The easiest way to describe the cause is to say:

Spot barked.

The easiest way to describe the effect is to say:

Dick woke up.

Whatever causes and effects are, we can describe them with claims. And we know a lot about claims: whether they're objective or subjective, whether a sentence is too vague to be a claim, how to judge whether an unsupported claim is true.

So now we have:

Spot barked $\xrightarrow{\text{caused}}$ Dick woke up

What is this relationship of being caused?

It has to be a very strong relationship. Once Spot barked, it had to be true that Dick woke up. There's no way (or almost no way) for "Spot barked" to have been true and "Dick woke up" to be false.

We know about that relationship—it's the relationship between the premises and conclusion of a valid or strong argument. But here we're not trying to convince anyone that the conclusion is true. We know that Dick woke up. What we can carry over from our study of arguments is how to look for all the possibilities—all the ways the premises could be true and the conclusion false—to determine if there is cause and effect. But there has to be more in order to say there's cause and effect.

2. The normal conditions

A lot has to be true for it to be (nearly) impossible for "Spot barked" to be true and "Dick woke up" to be false:

> Dick was sleeping soundly up to the time that Spot barked.
> Spot barked at 3 a.m.
> Dick doesn't normally wake up at 3 a.m.
> Spot was close to where Dick was sleeping.
> There was no other loud noise at the time.

We could go on forever. But, as with arguments, we state what we think is important and leave out the obvious. If someone challenged us, we could add "There was no earthquake at the time"—but we just assume things are the way they "normally" are.

> ***Normal conditions*** For a causal claim, the normal conditions are the obvious and plausible unstated claims that are needed to establish that the relationship between the claim describing purported cause and the claim describing purported effect is valid or strong.

3. Particular causes and general causes

Spot waking Dick is a ***particular cause and effect***. This happened once, then that happened once.

To establish the causal claim, we have to consider all the possible ways Spot could have barked, under the normal conditions, and ask whether Dick would have woken up. With a physical situation like this, we could even do experiments to look at some of the possible ways the cause could be true, say, getting Spot to bark at 3:23 a.m. on a cloudless night, or getting Spot to bark at 4:18 a.m. on an overcast night. We need that every time Spot barked, Dick woke up. There has to be a ***correlation***: every time this happens, that happens. So to establish a particular cause and effect, we might try to establish a generalization.

Alternatively, we could generalize from this particular cause and effect to any situation like it:

> Very loud barking by someone's dog that's near him when he is sleeping *causes* him to wake, if he's not deaf.

This is a ***general causal claim***: for it to be true, lots of particular cause and effect claims must be true. The normal conditions for this general claim won't be specific just to the one time Spot woke Dick, but will be general. Here, too, in trying to survey the possible ways that the cause could be true, we might want to establish a generalization: "Anytime anyone's encountered these conditions—the barking, the sleeper, etc.—the sleeper woke up."

Exercises for Sections A.1–A.3

Here are two of Tom's exercises with Dr. E's comments.

> **Your teaching made me fail this class.**
>
> *Causal claim*: Your teaching caused me to fail this class.
>
> *Particular* or *general*? Particular.
>
> *Cause* (stated as a claim): You taught badly.
>
> *Effect* (stated as a claim): I failed.
>
> *You've got the idea. But why did you say the cause was "You taught badly"? Maybe it should be "You taught well but didn't slow down for unprepared students." The problem is that the original sentence is too vague.*
>
> **Drinking coffee keeps people awake.**
>
> *Causal claim*: Drinking coffee causes people to stay awake.
>
> *Particular* or *general*? General.
>
> *Cause* (stated as a claim): People drink coffee. *No.*
>
> *Effect* (stated as a claim): People stay awake. *No.*
>
> *Remember that with a general causal claim there isn't a cause and effect but lots of them. So there's no point in filling in after "cause" and "effect." When we try to figure out a particular causal claim that this general one covers, we see the real problem: Maria drank coffee yesterday, Maria stayed awake. How long did she stay awake? What would count for making this true? It's too vague.*

For each exercise here, if appropriate rewrite the sentence as a causal claim—that is, one that uses the word "causes" or "caused." If it's a particular causal claim, describe the purported cause and the purported effect with claims. Here is what you should answer:

Causal claim?
Particular or general?
Cause (stated as a claim)
Effect (stated as a claim)

1. The police car's siren got me to pull over.
2. The speeding ticket Dick got made his auto insurance rate go up.
3. Speeding tickets make people's auto insurance rates go up.
4. Because you were late, we missed the beginning of the movie.
5. The onion's smell made me cry.
6. Dogs make great pets.
7. I better not get the pizza with anchovies because every time I do, I get heartburn.
8. Someone ringing the doorbell made Spot bark.

9. Coffee keeps me from getting a headache in the afternoon.
10. Penicillin prevents serious infection.
11. If it weren't for my boyfriend, I'd have no problems.
12. My hair looked nice today until I walked outside and the wind messed it up.
13. Our airplane took off from gate number thirteen. No wonder we're experiencing so much turbulence.
14. Tom: Hey, you want to be a ballplayer, you have to do better than that.
    Lee: It was the sun that made me drop the ball.
15. The cold makes people shiver.
16. Zeke abuses animals because his parents abused him.

4. The cause precedes the effect

We wouldn't accept that Spot's barking caused Dick to wake up if Spot began barking only after Dick woke up. The cause has to precede the effect. That is, "Spot barked" became true before "Dick woke up" became true.

For there to be cause and effect, the claim describing the cause has to become true before the claim describing the effect becomes true.

5. The cause makes a difference

Dr. E has a desperate fear of elephants. So he buys a special wind chime and puts it outside his door to keep the elephants away. He lives in Cedar City, Utah, at 6,000 feet above sea level in a desert, and he confidently claims that the wind chime causes the elephants to stay away. After all, ever since he put up the wind chime, he hasn't seen any elephants. There's a perfect correlation here: "Wind chime up on Tuesday, no elephants," Dr. E notes in his diary.

Why are we sure the wind chime being up did not cause elephants to stay away? Because even if there had been no wind chime, the elephants would have stayed away. Which elephants? All elephants. The wind chime works, but so would anything else. The wind chime doesn't ***make a difference***. For there to be cause and effect, it must be that *if the cause hadn't occurred, there wouldn't be the effect*. If Spot had not barked, Dick would not have woken up. Checking that the cause makes a difference is how we make sure we haven't overlooked another possible cause.

We often need a correlation to show that there's cause and effect. But it's a mistake, a ***correlation-causation fallacy***, to claim that a correlation all by itself establishes cause and effect.

6. Overlooking a common cause

Night causes day.

This is just wrong. There is a common cause of both "It was night" and "It's now day," namely, "The earth is rotating relative to the sun."

Dick: Zoe is irritable because she can't sleep properly.
Tom: Maybe it's because she's been drinking so much espresso that she's irritable and can't sleep properly.

Tom hasn't shown that Dick's causal claim is false by raising the possibility of a common cause. But he does put Dick's claim in doubt. We have to check the other conditions for cause and effect to see which causal claim seems most likely.

7. Criteria for cause and effect

We've seen that the following conditions are necessary for there to be cause and effect—once we *describe the cause and effect with claims*.

Necessary criteria for cause and effect

- The cause happened (the claim describing it is true).
- The effect happened (the claim describing it is true).
- The cause precedes the effect.
- It is nearly impossible for the cause to happen (be true) and the effect not to happen (be false)—given the same normal conditions.
- The cause makes a difference—if the cause had not happened (been true), the effect would not have happened (been true).
- There is no common cause.

8. Three mistakes in evaluating cause and effect

a. Tracing the cause too far back

So Spot caused Dick to wake up. But Dick and Zoe's neighbor tells them that it was because of a raccoon in her yard, which shares the same fence, that Spot started barking. So really, a raccoon entering her yard caused Dick to wake up.

But it was no accident that the raccoon came into their neighbor's yard. She'd left her trash can uncovered. So *really* their neighbor not covering her trash caused Dick to wake up.

But really, it was because Spot had knocked over her trash can and the top wouldn't fit; so their neighbor didn't bother to cover her trash. So it was Spot's knocking over the trash can that caused Dick to wake up.

But really, ... This is silly. We could go backwards forever. We stop at the first step: Spot's barking caused Dick to wake up. We stop because *as we trace the cause back further, it becomes too hard to fill in the normal conditions*.

Compare what happened when Dick was taking coffee to Zoe yesterday.

Dick is just wrong. The purported cause—Spot lying next to where Dick walked—was too far away from the effect. But what does "too far away" mean? The astronomer is right when she says that a star shining caused the image on the photograph, even though that star is trillions of miles away and the light took years to arrive.

"Too far away in space and time" is just a sloppy way to say that we can't see how to fill in the normal conditions, the other claims that would make it obvious that it's (nearly) impossible for the claim describing the cause to be true and the effect false.

b. Reversing cause and effect

Consider what Tom said after the demonstration in front of the post office:

Tom: That ecology group is twisting their members' minds around.
Dick: Huh?
Tom: They're all spouting off about the project to log the forest on Cedar Mountain. All in lock step. What do they do to those guys?

Tom's got it backwards. Joining the group doesn't cause the members to become concerned about the logging on Cedar Mountain. People who are already concerned about ecological issues join the group. He's ***reversing cause and effect***.

Suzy: Sitting too close to the TV ruins your eyesight.
Zoe: How do you know?
Suzy: Well, two of my grade-school friends used to sit really close, and both of them wear really thick glasses now.
Zoe: Maybe they sat so close because they had bad eyesight.

Even if Suzy had a huge sample instead of just anecdotal evidence, it would be just as plausible to reverse the cause and effect. That doesn't mean Suzy's claim is false. It just shows that from what she said we have no good reason to believe that sitting too close to the TV ruins your eyesight.

c. Looking too hard for a cause

Every Tuesday and Thursday at 1:55 p.m., a tall redheaded lady walks by the door of Professor Zzzyzzx's classroom. Then he arrives right at 2 p.m. When Suzy says the lady walking by the door causes Professor Zzzyzzx to arrive on time at his class, she's jumping to a conclusion: it happened after, so that's the cause. We call that kind of reasoning ***post hoc ergo propter hoc*** (after this, therefore because of this).

Zoe belched loudly in the shower with the bathroom window open, and she and Dick haven't seen Spot since. Spot must have run away because she belched. That's just *post hoc ergo propter hoc*. A possible cause is being overlooked: perhaps someone left the gate open, or someone let Spot out, or . . . . *Post hoc* reasoning is just not being careful to check that it's (nearly) impossible for the cause to be true and effect false. Jumping to conclusions about causes isn't a sign of a rich imagination. ("Gee, I'd never have thought the redhaired lady caused Professor Zzzyzzx to arrive on time.") It's a sign of an impoverished imagination.

We look for causes because we want to understand, to explain, so we can control our future. But sometimes the best we can say is that it's ***coincidence***. Before your jaw drops open in amazement when a friend tells you that a piano fell on her teacher the day after she dreamt that she saw him in a recital, remember the law of large numbers: if it's possible, given long enough, it'll happen. After all, most of us dream—say one dream a night for at least 50 million adults in the U.S. That's more than 350 million dreams per week. With the elasticity in interpreting dreams and what constitutes a "dream coming true," it would be amazing if a lot of dreams didn't "accurately predict the future."

But doesn't everything have a cause? Shouldn't we look for it? For much that happens in our lives we won't be able to figure out the cause—we just don't know enough. We must, normally, ascribe lots of happenings to chance, to coincidence, or else we have paranoia and end up paying a lot of money to psychics.

Sometimes our best response to a causal claim is

- Did you ever think that might just be coincidence?
- Just because it followed, doesn't mean it was caused by . . . .
- Have you thought about another possible cause, namely . . . .
- Maybe you've got the cause and the effect reversed.
- Not always, but maybe under some conditions . . . .

Suppose two million Parisians were paired off and set to tossing coins in a game of matching. Each pair plays until the winner on the first toss is again brought to equality with the other player. Assuming one toss per second for each eight-hour day, at the end of ten years there would still be, on the average, about a hundred-odd pairs; and if the players assign the game to their heirs, a dozen or so will still be playing at the end of a thousand years! The implications are obvious. Suppose that some business had been operating for one hundred years. Should one rule out luck and chance as the essence of the factors producing the long-term survival of the enterprise? No inference whatever can be drawn until the number of original participants is known; and even then one must know the size, risk, and frequency of each commitment.

A. Alchian, "Uncertainty, Evolution, and Economic Theory"

Exercises for Section A

1. What criteria are necessary for there to be cause and effect?
2. Why isn't a correlation enough to justify cause and effect? Give an example.
3. Comparable to the unstated premises of an argument, what do we call the claims that must be true for a causal claim to be true?
4. What real problem in establishing cause and effect is usually stated badly as "That's not close enough in space and time to be the cause"?
5. Dick makes a causal claim. Zoe says it's just *post hoc ergo propter hoc* reasoning. How can he show her that he's right?
6. Explain why it's not amazing that every day a few dream predictions come true.
7. When should we trust authorities rather than figure out a cause for ourselves?

B. Examples

We have necessary conditions for there to be cause and effect. What about sufficient conditions? In practice, all we can do is check that the necessary conditions hold—being careful not to make one of the obvious mistakes—even if we're not satisfied that we can exactly state sufficient conditions for there to be cause and effect.

Example 1

The cat made Spot run away.

Cause: What is the cause? It's not just "the cat." How can we describe it with a claim? Perhaps "A cat meowed close to Spot."

Effect: Spot ran away.

Cause and effect each happened: The effect is clearly true. The cause is highly plausible: almost all things that meow are cats.

Cause precedes effect: Yes.

It is (nearly) impossible for the cause to be true and effect false: What needs to be assumed as "normal" here? Spot is on a walk with Dick. Dick is holding the leash loosely enough for Spot to get away. Spot chases cats. Spot heard the cat meow. We could go on, but this seems enough to guarantee that it's unlikely that the cat could meow near Spot and Spot not chase it.

The cause makes a difference: Would Spot have run away even if the cat had not meowed near him? Apparently not, given those normal conditions, since Dick seems surprised that he ran off. But perhaps he would have even if he hadn't heard the cat, if he'd seen it. But that apparently wasn't the case. So let's revise the cause to be "Spot wasn't aware a cat was near him, and the cat meowed close to Spot, and Spot heard it." Now we can reasonably believe that the cause made a difference.

Is there a common cause? Perhaps the cat was hit by a meat truck and lots of meat fell out, and Spot ran away for that? No, Spot wouldn't have barked. Nor would he have growled.

Perhaps the cat is a hapless bystander in a fight between dogs, one of which is Spot's friend. We do not know if this is the case. So it is possible that there is a common cause, but it seems unlikely.

Evaluation: We have good reason to believe the original claim on the revised interpretation that the cause is "Spot wasn't aware a cat was near him, and the cat meowed close to Spot, and Spot heard it."

These are the steps we should go through in establishing a causal claim. If we can show that one of them fails, though, there's no need to check all the others.

Example 2 Maria caused the traffic accident.

Analysis We're interested in who or what was involved in the cause when we go about assigning blame or fault. But it's not just that Maria exists. Rather:

Cause: Maria didn't pay attention.
Effect: The cars collided.

Is this really cause and effect? Let's assume that these claims are true. It seems the cause preceded the effect. But did the cause make a difference? If Maria had been paying attention, would the cars still have collided? Since she was broadsided by a car running through a red light where a line of cars blocked her vision, we would say that it didn't matter that she was texting at the time: the cars would have collided even if she had been paying attention, or so we all imagine. The purported cause didn't make a difference. It's not cause and effect.

Example 3 Lack of rain caused the crops to fail in Texas in 2011.

Analysis We've talked about causes as if something active has to happen. But almost any claim that describes the world could qualify as a cause.

> *Cause*: It was very hot with no rain in the summer in Texas in 2011.
> *Effect*: The crops failed.

Is this cause and effect? We better check the meteorological records and ask some farmers if there wasn't some other cause, perhaps locusts or hailstorms.

Example 4 Harry works in a laboratory where there's not supposed to be any oxygen. The materials are highly flammable. He has to wear breathing gear. Harry knows that matches won't light in the laboratory.

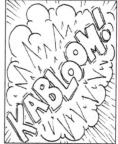

Oxygen in the laboratory caused an explosion.

Analysis It certainly isn't "normal" that Harry carried matches with him into the laboratory for a joke with a friend and then struck a match. Nor is it normal that there was a leak in his face mask.

When several claims together are taken *jointly* as the cause, we say that each is (describes) ***a cause*** or that each is a ***causal factor***.

Example 5 Running over nails causes your tires to go flat.

Analysis This is a general causal claim. But it's false. Lots of times we run over nails and our tires don't go flat.

But sometimes they do. What's correct is:

Running over nails *can cause* your tires to go flat.

That is, if the conditions are right, running over a nail will cause your tire to go flat.

The difference between *causes* and *can cause* is the difference between the normal conditions. We'll look at how to evaluate claims like this in Section D.

Example 6 When more and more people are thrown out of work, unemployment results.

Calvin Coolidge

Analysis You don't have to be smart to be president. This isn't cause and effect; it's a definition.

Example 7 Birth causes death.

Analysis In some sense this is right. But it seems wrong. Why?

What's the cause? What's the effect? The example is a general causal claim covering every particular claim like "That this creature was born caused it to die."

We have lots of inductive evidence: Socrates died. My dog Juney died. My teacher in high school died. President Kennedy died.

The problem seems to be that though this is true, it's uninteresting. It's tracing the cause too far back. Being born should be part of the normal conditions when we have the effect that someone died.

Example 8 Maria: Fear of getting fired causes me to get to work on time.

Analysis How can we describe the purported cause with a claim?

Cause: Maria is afraid of getting fired.

Effect: Maria gets to work on time.

Is it possible for Maria to be afraid of getting fired and still not get to work on time? Certainly, but not, perhaps, under normal conditions: Maria sets her alarm; the electricity doesn't go off; there isn't bad weather; Maria doesn't oversleep; . . . . Yet there's something odd in calling these the normal conditions. Isn't it supposed to be because she's afraid that Maria makes sure these claims will be true or that she'll get to work even if one or more is false?

In that case, how can we judge whether the relationship between the purported cause and effect is valid or strong? That Maria gets to work regardless of conditions that aren't normal is what makes her consider her fear to be the cause.

Subjective causes are often a matter of feeling, some sense that we control what we do. They are often too vague for us to classify as true or false.

Example 9

Dick: Hold the steering wheel.
Zoe: What are you doing? Stop! Are you crazy?
Dick: I'm just taking my sweater off.
Zoe: I can't believe you did that. It's *so* dangerous.
Dick: Don't be silly. I've done it a thousand times before.
(*crash . . . later . . .*)
Dick: You had to turn the steering wheel!? That made us crash.

Analysis The purported cause: Zoe turned the steering wheel. The effect: The car crashed. The necessary criteria are satisfied.

But as they say in court, Zoe's turning the steering wheel is a ***foreseeable consequence*** of Dick making her take the wheel, which is the real cause. The normal conditions are not just what has to be true before the cause but also what will normally *follow* the cause.

Example 10 Dick: Wasn't that awful what happened to old Mr. Grzegorczyk?
Zoe: You mean those tree trimmers who dropped a huge branch on him and killed him?

Dick: You only got half the story. He'd had a heart attack in his car and pulled over to the side. He was lying on the pavement when the branch hit him—he would have died anyway.

Zoe: But I heard his wife is going to collect from the tree company.

Analysis What's the cause of death? Mr. Grzegorczyk would have died anyway. So the tree branch falling on him wouldn't have made a difference.

But the tree branch falling on him isn't a foreseeable consequence, part of the normal conditions of his stumbling out of his car with a heart attack. As they say in court, it's an ***intervening cause***. Juries, made up of people like you, will be asked to decide what the cause of Mr. Grzegorczyk's death is. There's no clear answer, though these kinds of cases have been debated for centuries.

Example 11 Sunspots cause stock prices to rise.

Analysis Suppose your finance teacher tells you this general causal claim, and she backs it up with data showing a very good correlation between the appearance of large sunspots and rises in the Dow Jones index. But a correlation, though needed for a general causal claim, doesn't by itself establish cause and effect. It's hard to imagine a common cause, but coincidence can't be ruled out. If we look around the world long enough, we'll eventually find *some* phenomenon that can be correlated to the rise and fall in stock prices. Even if there were a very exact correlation between the size of the sunspots and the percentage of increase in the Dow Jones average two days later, we still want a theory—normal conditions that give us a way to trace how the sunspots cause the price rises—before we accept that this is cause and effect.

Example 12 The Treaty of Versailles caused World War II.

Analysis The cause: The Treaty of Versailles was agreed to and enforced. The effect: World War II occurred.

To analyze a conjecture like this, an historian will write a book. The normal conditions have to be spelled out. You have to show that it was a foreseeable consequence of the enforcement of the Treaty of Versailles at the end of World War I that Germany would re-arm.

But was it foreseeable that Prime Minister Chamberlain would back down over Hitler's invasion of Czechoslovakia? More plausible is that the signing of the Treaty of Versailles is *a* cause, not *the* cause of World War II.

Example 13 Poltergeists are making the pictures fall down from their hooks.

Analysis To accept this, we have to believe that poltergeists exist. That's dubious. Worse, it's probably not *testable*. How could you determine if there are poltergeists? Dubious claims that aren't testable are the worst candidates for causes.

Example 14 Disappointing job creation, Hungary woes send markets reeling

Headline, Associated Press, June 5, 2010

Analysis Every day news writers pick out what they consider the most prominent piece of good news if the market went up or bad news if the market went down and ascribe the change in the stock market to that. Without more evidence, that's just *post hoc* reasoning.

Example 15 Zoe: Every time I wash my car, it rains within 12 hours.

Suzy: Well, don't wash your car today. I want my picnic to be fun.

Analysis Behind Suzy's comment is a general causal claim: "Zoe's washing her car causes it to rain." We just laugh. Of course there's no connection.

But suppose it was always clear and forecast sunny for the next two days when Zoe washed her car. And it always rained within six hours. And this happened 30 times over two years. We'd have pretty good evidence for Zoe's claim.

Still, we'd be suspicious. Constant conjunction isn't enough to convince us that if the cause weren't true, the effect wouldn't be true—the conjunction might be coincidence or the result of a common cause. My pulse is evidence that I'm breathing, occurring always in conjunction with it, and if I had no pulse I would have no breath. But my having a pulse is not the cause of my breathing.

We want a general principle that connects cause and effect, some glue for the inference. The constant conjunctions give us motive to find one, but until we do we're apt to dismiss the causal claim as *post hoc* reasoning.

Example 16 Tom has a summer job doing construction work in the heat. He sweats a lot, and he drinks a lot of water. He figures he sweats so much because he drinks so much.

Analysis It seems that a common cause of both Tom sweating a lot and drinking a lot of water is that he's working outside in the heat. But if Tom stopped drinking so much, he wouldn't sweat so much. So it seems that Tom drinking a lot of water is *a* cause of his sweating so much. But then if he didn't sweat so much, he wouldn't be thirsty and drink. So sweating seems like *a* cause of his drinking so much. But he can't control his sweating. Maybe he can't control his drinking, too, if he wants to live. Here what we consider to be cause and what to be effect depend on what we consider to be the normal conditions. If we take working in the heat to be a normal condition, it seems we have cause and effect in a circle: sweating, then drinking, then sweating, then . . . . Like college students getting low grades and doing drugs, sometimes we can't break into a circle to classify cause and effect.

Example 17 Since he was adopted by staff members as a kitten, Oscar the Cat has had an uncanny ability to predict when residents are about to die. Thus far, he has presided over the deaths of more than 25 residents on the third floor of Steere House Nursing and Rehabilitation Center in Providence, Rhode Island. His mere presence at the bedside is viewed by physicians and nursing home staff as an almost absolute indicator of impending death, allowing staff members to adequately notify families. Oscar has also provided companionship to those who would otherwise have died alone. For his work, he is highly regarded by the physicians and staff at Steere House and by the families of the residents whom he serves.

David M. Dosa, M.D., *New England Journal of Medicine*, July 26, 2007

Analysis This is very sweet and mysterious. How does Oscar the Cat know the person is going to die? But reversing cause and effect is just as plausible given the evidence: Oscar the Cat visiting the person causes the person to die. Mysteries merit further investigation, not slack-jawed belief.

Exercises for Sections A and B

Here's an exercise Tom did on cause and effect.

I used Diabolic Grow on my roses and they grew great! I'll always use it.

Causal claim: (unstated) Diabolic Grow caused my roses to grow great.

Cause: The speaker put Diabolic Grow on his roses.

Effect: The roses grew great.

Cause and effect each happened? Apparently so.

Cause precedes effect? Yes.

It's (nearly) impossible for the cause to be true and effect false? Hard to say.

Cause makes a difference? It seems so, but did the cause really make a difference? Maybe they would have grown great anyway. Some years that happens when it rains at just the right time in the spring.

Common cause? For sure, no.

Evaluation: You'd need a lot more evidence to believe the claim.

Excellent! You're thinking critically!

For the exercises below, fill in answers to the following:

Causal claim:

Cause:

Effect:

Cause and effect each happened?

Cause precedes effect?

It's (nearly) impossible for the cause to be true and effect false?

Cause makes a difference?

Common cause?

Evaluation:

1. Maria: I had to slam on the brakes because some idiot pulled out in front of me.
2. Suzy: My feet hurt so bad the other day when I was cheerleading. My feet have never hurt at the other cheerleading events, but I was wearing new shoes. So it must have been my new shoes.

3. Dick: Ooh, my stomach hurts.
   Zoe: Serves you right. You really pigged out on the nachos and salsa last night. They always give you a stomachache.
4. Marriage is the chief cause of divorce.
5. I've got to go to the game. The only time I wasn't in the bleachers this season, they lost.
6. Hazards are one of the main causes of accidents. (OSHA, "Safety with Beef Cattle")
7. Zoe: The dark sky makes me really depressed today.
8. Dick: Boy, are you red.
   Zoe: Ouch! I got a terrible sunburn because the sun was so strong yesterday.
9. The emphasis on Hollywood figures in the media causes people to use drugs because people want to emulate the stars.
10. My mother missed the sign-up to get me into Kernberger Preparatory Academy, and that's why I've never been able to get a good job.
11. Maria: It's awful what's happened to Zeke.
    Lee: Why? What happened? I haven't seen him for ages.
    Maria: He started using drugs. It's because he was hanging out with that bad bunch.
12. Lou's college education helped him get a high-paying job the year after he graduated.
13. Dick: Every day I run up this hill and it's no big deal. Why am I so beat today?
    Zoe: It's 'cause you stayed out late and didn't get enough sleep.
14. Zoe: My life's a mess. I've never really been happy since all those years ago in high school you told Sally that I killed her cat Louie. She believed your stupid joke and made sure I wasn't a cheerleader. I'll never be a cheerleader. It's your fault I'm so miserable now.
    Dick: There, there.
15. Sex, drugs, and rock 'n roll are the causes of the decline in family values.
16. Suzy: Eating potato chips and sitting on the couch must be healthy. All the guys on the football team do it.
17. Lee: Yesterday my neighbor said this spring has been the worst season ever for allergies, but I told her I hadn't had any bad days. Then today I started sneezing. Darn it—if only she hadn't told me.
18. Dick: Normally my pulse rate is about 130 after exercising on this bike.
    Zoe: I can't believe you actually measure your heart rate! You're so obsessive.
    Dick: But for the past week or so it's been about 105. That's odd.
    Zoe: You stopped drinking coffee two weeks ago, remember?
19. He's stupid because his mother dropped him on his head when he was young.
20. A recent study shows that everyone who uses heroin started with marijuana. So smoking marijuana causes heroin use.
21. Dr. E: My students don't like the material at the end of this course. That's why so many have missed class the last two weeks of the course.

22. Flo: Salad makes you fat. I know 'cause Wanda's really fat and is always eating salad.
23. (An advertisement by the Iowa Egg Council in the Des Moines International Airport) Children who eat breakfast not only do better academically, but they also behave better.
    Archives of Pediatric and Adolescent Medicine

C. How to Look for the Cause

I have a waterfall in my backyard in Cedar City. The pond has a thick, rubberized plastic pond liner, and I have a pump and hose that carry water from the pond along the rock face of a small rise to where the water spills out and runs down more rocks with concrete between them. Last summer I noticed that the pond kept getting low every day and had to be refilled. You don't waste water in the desert, so I figured I'd better find out what was causing the loss of water.

I thought of all the ways the pond could be leaking: The hose that carries the water could have a leak, the valve connections could be leaking, the pond liner could be ripped (the dogs get into the pond to cool off in the summer), there could be cracks in the concrete, or it could be evaporation and spray from where the water comes out at the top of the fountain.

I had to figure out which (if any) of these was the problem. First I got someone to come in and use a high pressure spray on the waterfall to clean it. We took the rocks out and vacuumed out the pond. Then we patched every possible spot on the pond liner where there might be a leak.

Then we patched all the concrete on the waterfall part and water-sealed it. We checked the valve connections and tightened them. They didn't leak. And the hose wasn't leaking because there weren't any wet spots along its path.

Then I refilled the pond. It kept losing water at about the same rate.

It wasn't the hose, it wasn't the connections, it wasn't the pond liner, it wasn't the concrete watercourse. So it had to be the spray and evaporation.

I reduced the flow of water so there wouldn't be so much spray. There was a lot less water loss. The rest I figured was probably evaporation, though there might still be small leaks.

In trying to find the cause of the water leak at my waterfall and pond, I was using the following method.

> ***The scientific method*** Conjecture possible causes. By experiment, eliminate them by showing they don't make a difference until there is only one. Check that one:
>
> - Does it make a difference?
> - If the purported cause is eliminated, is there still the effect?
> - Is there a common cause?

I assumed there was a cause, then by a process of elimination on some conjectured causes, I fixed on one: when that occurred, the effect always did, too, and it made a difference, and I knew I could fill in the normal conditions.

But why should I assume there is a cause? Does this mean I'm assuming everything has a cause? No, I'm assuming that there is some way to stop the leak, which in this case amounts to assuming that the leak has a cause. The assumption that a particular effect has a cause is sometimes just an expression of our desire to find a way to manipulate the world.

But then doesn't this method rest on a false dilemma?

> A or B or C is the cause of E. It's not A. It's not B.
> Therefore, it's C.

No. We also have to check that C satisfies all the conditions for cause and effect, not just that it makes a difference. We must be willing to accept that our experiments will show that none of the conjectured causes satisfies all the conditions. This method cannot find the cause from nothing, but only, if we guess right, isolate it from a range of conjectured causes.

Example 18 Recently Lee found out that he has hepatitis B. None of his friends has hepatitis. He wonders how he could have gotten it.

He reasons: Since he wants to be a doctor, he volunteers to work at a hospital three times per week. Some of the patients there have hepatitis, and he often washes their bedpans and comes in contact with their body fluids, though he's always careful to wear gloves. Or at least he thought he was. A recent study he read said that 25% of health-care workers exposed to hepatitis B get it. So, he figures, he got hepatitis B from working at the hospital.

Analysis How strong is this argument? At best we can say that "Lee contracted hepatitis B from working at the hospital" is a good conjecture. We rule out all other causes we can think of. We can imagine conditions under which he could have gotten hepatitis there, but we can't specify the exact conditions that occurred that would give us the normal conditions. Eliminating all other possible causes (that we can think of) doesn't mean that we can conclude we've found the cause unless we also have:

> (*) The only ways Lee could have gotten hepatitis B
> are P, Q, R, S, T, U, or V.

There are very strong arguments that he didn't get it from Q, R, S, T, U, or V. Therefore (reasoning by excluding possibilities), he got it from P. This reasoning to a cause is just as strong as (*) is plausible.

Example 19 Tom: Ohh, I have a terrible headache. Really hungover. I drank a lot of beer last night.

Dick: Have another beer, it'll make you feel better for sure. Nothing cures a hangover like a hair of the dog that bit you.

Suzy: You're right! You can cure a hangover by drinking. So hangovers are caused by lack of alcohol.

Analysis If you think that this is stupid, consider that medical researchers have been making the same mistake:

> When it was found that psychoactive drugs affect neurotransmitter levels in the brain, as evidenced mainly by the levels of their breakdown products in the spinal fluid, the theory arose that the cause of mental illness is an abnormality in the brain's concentration of these chemicals that is specifically countered by the appropriate drug. For example, because Thorazine was found to lower dopamine levels in the brain, it was postulated that psychoses like schizophrenia are caused by too much dopamine. Or later, because certain antidepressants increase levels of the neurotransmitter serotonin in the brain, it was postulated that depression is caused by too little serotonin. . . . This was a great leap of logic . . . It was entirely possible that drugs that affected neurotransmitter levels could relieve symptoms even if neurotransmitters had nothing to do with the illness in the first place (and even possible that they relieved symptoms through some other mode of action entirely). As Carlat puts it, "By this same logic one could argue that the cause of all pain conditions is a deficiency of opiates, since narcotic pain medications activate opiate receptors in the brain." Or similarly, one could argue that fevers are caused by too little aspirin.
>
> Marcia Angell, "The epidemic of mental illness: Why?" *The New York Review of Books*, vol. LVIII, no. 11, June 23, 2011

Exercises for Section C

1. Come up with a method to determine whether there's cause and effect:
   a. Pressing the "Door Close" button in the elevator causes the doors to close.
   b. Zoe's belching caused Spot to run away.
   c. Reducing the speed limit to 55 m.p.h. saves lives.
   d. The redheaded lady walking by the classroom causes Professor Zzzyzzx to arrive at class on time.

2. Dick: (*Bending over, sweating and cursing*) There's something wrong with my bike.
   Zoe: What?
   Dick: Something's going "click, click, click" all the time.
   Zoe: Must be something that's moving.
   Dick: Duh. Here, hold it up while I turn the pedals. (*click, click, click, . . .*)
   Zoe: Yup, there it is.
   Dick: It must be in the pedals or the wheels.
   Zoe: Stop pedaling. . . . It's gone away.
   Dick: It must be in the pedals, then.

   Evaluate how Dick and Zoe have tried to isolate the cause here.

3. 
ISN'T IT AMAZING THAT OF ALL THE HOUSES IN THIS TOWN, I WAS BORN IN ONE WHERE THE PEOPLE LOOK SO MUCH LIKE ME!

What is Flo overlooking?

Tom was asked to bring in a causal claim he made recently and evaluate it. Here's his work.

> **The only time I've had a really bad backache is right after I went bicycling early in the morning when it was so cold last week. Bicycling never bothered me before. So it must be the cold weather that caused my back to hurt after cycling.**
>
> *Causal claim*: The cold weather caused my back to hurt after cycling.
>
> *Cause*: It was cold when I went cycling.
>
> *Effect*: I got a backache.
>
> *Cause and effect true*? Yes.
>
> *Cause precedes the effect*? Yes.
>
> *Valid or strong*? I think so.
>
> *Cause makes a difference*? Sure seems so.
>
> *Common cause*? None.
>
> *Evaluation*: The criteria seem to be satisfied. But now I'm wondering if I haven't overlooked some other cause. I also had an upset stomach. So maybe it was the flu. Or maybe it was tension, since I'd had a fight with Suzy the night before. I guess I'll have to try cycling in the cold again to find out.
>
> *Good. But you're still looking for* <u>*the*</u> *cause, when it may be* <u>*a*</u> *cause. Another possible cause: Did you warm up first? Another: You'll never know for sure.*

4. Write down a causal claim that you made recently and evaluate it. Have a classmate critique your evaluation.

5. Judge: I find that Maria sustained serious injuries in this accident. There is sufficient evidence that the defendant ran a red light and broadsided her car, causing the injuries. But I hold that Maria was partly responsible for the severity of her injuries in that she was not wearing a seat belt. Therefore, Maria shall collect only 50% of the costs associated with this accident.

   Explain the judge's decision in terms of normal conditions and foreseeable consequences.

6. Mickey has taken his four-wheel-drive Jeep out into the desert to explore on this hot sunny Sunday. But his two cousins want to see him dead. Bertha has put poison in Mickey's 5-gallon canteen. Richard, not knowing of Bertha's plans, has put a very small hole in the canteen.

Mickey's car breaks down. He's getting hot and thirsty. His cellular phone doesn't work because he forgot to recharge it. He goes to get some water and finds the canteen empty. . . . Overcome by guilt later in the year, both Bertha and Richard confess.

Who should be blamed for causing Mickey's death?

7. Pick out the cause and effect(s). Explain your answer.

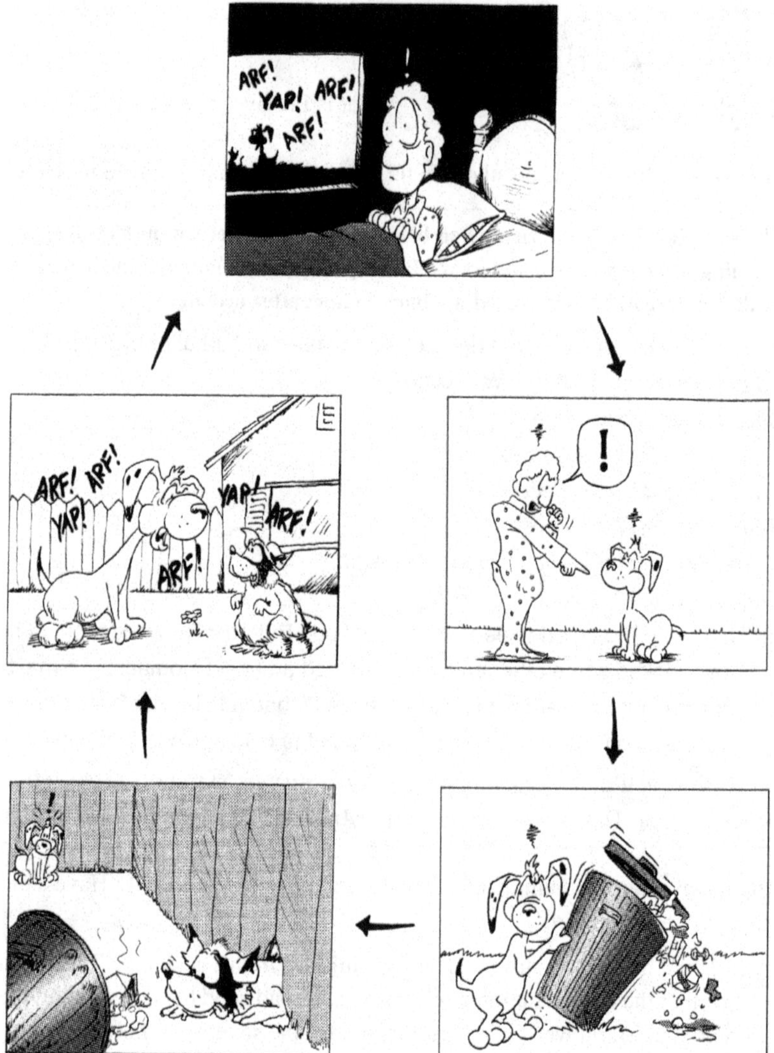

D. Cause and Effect in Populations

When we say, "Smoking causes lung cancer," what do we mean? If you smoke a cigarette, you'll get cancer? If you smoke a lot of cigarettes this week, you'll get cancer? If you smoke 20 cigarettes a day for 40 years, you'll get cancer?

It can't be any of these, since we know smokers who did all that yet didn't get lung cancer. And the cause always has to follow the effect. So what do we mean?

Cause in a population is usually explained as meaning that given the cause, there's a higher probability that the effect will follow than if there were not the cause. In this example, people who smoke have a much higher probability of getting lung cancer than nonsmokers.

That's how it's explained. But really we're talking about cause and effect just as we did before. Smoking lots of cigarettes over a long period of time will cause (inevitably) lung cancer. The problem is that we can't state, we have no idea how to state, nor is it likely that we'll ever be able to state the normal conditions for smoking to cause cancer. Other factors include one's diet, where one lives, exposure to pollution and other carcinogens, and one's genetic inheritance. But *if we knew exactly*, we'd say: "Under the conditions _________, smoking _____ (number of) cigarettes every day for _______ years will result in lung cancer."

Since we can't specify the normal conditions, the best we can do is point to the evidence that convinces us that smoking is a cause of lung cancer and get an argument with a statistical conclusion: "People who continue to smoke two packs of cigarettes per day for 10 years are ___% more likely (with a margin of error of __ %) to get lung cancer."

What kind of evidence do we use?

1. Controlled experiment: cause-to-effect

This is our best evidence. We choose 10,000 people at random and ask 5,000 of them never to smoke and 5,000 of them to smoke 25 cigarettes every day. We have two samples, one composed of those who are administered the cause, and one of those who are not, the latter called the ***control group***. We come back 20 years later to check how many in each group got lung cancer. If a lot more of the smokers got lung cancer, and the groups were representative of the population as a whole, and we can see no other *common thread* among those who got lung cancer, we'd be justified in saying that smoking causes lung cancer. The point of using a control group is to show that, at least statistically, the cause makes a difference.

But we don't do such an experiment. It would be unethical. It's not acceptable to do an experiment on humans that has a foreseeable potential for doing them harm.

So we use some animals sufficiently like humans that we feel are "expendable," like rats. We fit them with little masks and have them breathe the equivalent of 25 cigarettes per day for a few years. Then if lots of them get lung cancer, while the ones who don't smoke are still frisky, we can conclude with reasonable certainty that smoking causes cancer in laboratory rats.

So? We then argue that since rats are sufficiently similar to humans in their biological processes, we can extrapolate to say that smoking can cause cancer in humans. We argue by analogy.

2. Uncontrolled experiment: cause-to-effect

Here we take two randomly chosen, representative samples of the general population for which we have factored out other possible causes of lung cancer, such as working in coal mines. One of the groups is composed of people who say they never smoke. One group, comparable to the control group for controlled experiments, is composed of people who say they smoke. We follow the groups and 15 to 20 years later check whether those who smoked got lung cancer more often. Since we think we've accounted for other common threads, smoking is the remaining common thread that may account for why the second group got cancer more often.

This is a ***cause-to-effect*** experiment, since we start with the suspected cause and see if the effect follows. But it is uncontrolled: some people may stop smoking, some may begin, people may have quite variable diets—there may be a lot we'll have to factor out in trying to assess whether it's smoking that causes the extra cases of lung cancer.

3. Uncontrolled experiment: effect-to-cause

Here we look at as many people as possible who have lung cancer to see if there is some common thread that occurs in (almost all) their lives. We factor out those who worked in coal mines, those who lived in high pollution areas, those who drank a lot, ... If it turns out that a much higher proportion of the remaining people smoked than in the general population, we have good evidence that smoking was the cause.

This is uncontrolled because how they got to the effect was unplanned, not within our control. And it is an ***effect-to-cause*** experiment because we start with the effect in the population and try to account for how it got there.

How do we "factor out" other possible causes? How do we determine whether the sample of people we are looking at is large enough to draw conclusions about the general population? How do we determine if the sample is representative? How do we decide how many more cases of the effect—lung cancer—have to occur before it can be attributed to some cause rather than just to chance? These are the problems that arise whenever we generalize (Chapter 14), and only a course on statistics will make these issues clearer.

Until you do take such a course and have access to actual write-ups of the experiments—not just the newspaper or magazine accounts—you'll have to rely on "the experts." If the experiment was done by a reputable group, without bias, and what we read passes the obvious tests for a strong generalization, a good analogy, and a good causal argument, then we can assume that the researchers know statistics well enough to conduct proper experiments—at least until some other reputable group challenges their results.

Example 20 Reginald smoked two packs of cigarettes each day for 30 years. Reginald now has lung cancer. Reginald's smoking caused his lung cancer.

Analysis Is it possible for Reginald to have smoked two packs of cigarettes each day for 30 years and not get lung cancer? We can't state the normal conditions.

So we invoke the statistical relation between smoking and lung cancer to say it is unlikely for the cause to be true and effect false.

Does the cause make a difference? Could Reginald have gotten lung cancer even if he had not smoked? Suppose we know that Reginald wasn't a coal miner, didn't work in a textile factory, and didn't live in a city with a very polluted atmosphere—all conditions that are associated with a higher probability of getting lung cancer. Then it is possible for Reginald to have gotten lung cancer anyway, since some people who have no other risks do get lung cancer. But it is very unlikely, since very few of those people do.

We have no reason to believe that there is a common cause. It may be that people with a certain biological makeup feel compelled to smoke, and that biological make-up also contributes to their getting lung cancer independently of their smoking. But we have no evidence of such a biological factor. And we have evidence against it: people who quit smoking have lower rates of lung cancer than similar smokers who don't quit.

So assuming a few normal conditions, "Reginald's smoking caused his lung cancer" is as plausible as the strength of the statistical link between smoking and lung cancer and the strength of the link between not smoking and not getting lung cancer. We must be careful, though, that we do not attribute the cause of the lung cancer to smoking just because we haven't thought of any other cause, especially if the statistical links aren't very strong.

Example 21 Zoe: I can't understand Melinda. She's pregnant and she's drinking.
Dick: That's all baloney. I asked my mom, and she said she drank when she was pregnant with me. And I turned out fine.
Zoe: But think how much better you would have been if she hadn't.

Analysis Zoe doesn't say but alludes to the cause-in-population claim that drinking during pregnancy causes birth defects or poor development of the child. That has been demonstrated. Many cause-in-population studies have been done that show there is a higher incidence of birth defects and developmental problems in children born to mothers who drink than to mothers who do not drink, and those defects and problems do not appear to arise from any other common factor.

Dick, however, makes a mistake. He confuses a cause-in-population claim with a general causal claim. He is right that his mother's experience would disprove the general causal claim, but it has no force against the cause-in-population claim.

Zoe's confusion is that she thinks there is a perfect correlation between drinking and physical or mental problems in the child, so that if Dick's mother had not drunk alcohol he would have been better, even if Zoe can't point to the particular way in which Dick would have been better. But the correlation isn't perfect, it's only a statistical link.

Example 22 The US Bureau of Labor Statistics data from 2001 show the following:

Education and Lifetime Income

Highest Education Level Achieved	*Lifetime Income* (40 years)
Bachelor's Degree	$1,667,700
Associate Degree	$1,269,850
High School Graduate	$994,080
Not High School Graduate	$630,000

Higher levels of education payoff in lifetime income in a big way.

It is interesting to note that this relationship between education and earnings potential has been known since the 1970's, and has been consistently demonstrated by government surveys. In fact the difference in income level with education has grown significantly over the years. The Bureau of the Census has suggested that the gap in earnings between those with higher education and those with lower education will continue to grow in the future. The US Bureau of Labor Statistics has also shown that the unemployment rate steadily drops with higher levels of education. Unemployment for non-high school graduates was 6.5% in 2000, 3.5% for high school graduates, and 2.3% for those with an associate degree.

Education makes a difference!

Education Online, 2010, www.education-online_search/articles/special_topics/education_and_income/.com

Analysis There's a clear correlation between income and level of education. The website claims that this means getting more education is the cause of earning more ("payoff," "education makes a difference"). But people who finish more schooling are brighter, are either wealthier or can figure out how to get money for their education, are willing to work hard and to persevere. People like that are likely to earn more than other folks whether they get more education or not. Without more evidence, without more studies that factor out these possible common causes, this is just *post hoc* reasoning.

But even if they're right about more education leading to higher income in the past, there's no reason to think that will hold in the future. That's a bad past-to-future analogy because the job market, the kinds of skills employers want, the quality of education have all changed significantly since the 1970s—even since the 1990s. The differences matter.

Example 23 Lack of education causes poverty. Widespread poverty causes crime. So lack of education causes crime.

Analysis We often hear claims like these, and some politicians base policy on them. But they're too vague. How much education constitutes "lack of education"? How poor do you have to be? How many poor people constitute "widespread poverty"? Researchers make these sentences more precise and analyze them as cause-in-population claims, since we know they couldn't be true general causal claims: There are people with little education who have become rich; and lots of poor people are law-abiding citizens. Indeed, in the worst years of the Depression in the 1930s, when there was more widespread poverty than at any time since in the U.S., there was less crime than at any time in the last 20 years. This suggests it would be hard to find a precise version of the second sentence that is a true cause-in-population claim.

Example 24 In my backyard, indeed throughout the neighborhood where I live, the abundance of birds is limited. In other neighborhoods there are many more birds. The most important difference I can think of concerns cats. Many cats are around where I live; elsewhere there are less of them. It is probable that there will be other differences between neighborhoods which differ in bird abundance. However, in view of background information it is reasonable to infer that cats will be a causal factor. Cats eat birds and birds are afraid of cats. An experiment could provide more confirmation. If I would shoot the cats near my place and bird abundance would subsequently increase, I would feel confident that cats do influence the abundance of birds. . . .

If an experiment of this kind were indeed performed with positive results (for the birds I mean), the evidence would be telling. However, we should realize that the situations compared—before and after the shooting—may differ in other respects. Thus it is possible that, from a bird's point of view, there happens to be a long-lasting improvement of the weather after the shooting.

In view of this the following experiment would be more decisive. Suppose we identify ten neighborhoods with many cats. We could remove the cats from five randomly chosen neighborhoods, and let the cats be in the remaining ones. If bird abundance would increase in the cat-free areas, not elsewhere, that would be something. It is improbable that the two groups of neighborhoods will systematically differ in another factor that influences birds.

Wim J. van der Steen, *A Practical Philosophy for the Life Sciences*

Analysis Van der Steen proposes to use the scientific method with a cause-to-effect cause-in-population study.

Exercises for Section D

1. Describe what evidence you have for the claims below and what experiments you would devise to try to prove or disprove them. [Don't do the experiments yourself! Some of them are dangerous without adult supervision.]
   a. Universities cause students to become smarter.
   b. Hedonistic lifestyles cause premature death.
   c. Money brings happiness.
   d. Drinking alcohol causes promiscuous behavior.
   e. Unprotected sex causes disease.
2. What is the control group in the experiment proposed in Example 24?

   Explain what's wrong in Exercises 3–8.
3. Tom: Don't feed those chicken bones to Spot. Don't you know that a dog can choke and die on one of those?

   Dick: Don't be silly. I've been giving Spot chicken bones for years.
4. Suzy: Vegetarians get cancer much less than meat eaters.

Manuel: Oh, yeah, so how come Linda McCartney, a well-known vegetarian, died from cancer when she was only in her 50s?

5. Dick: Hey, Zoe. Listen to this. A Roper survey said wine drinkers are more successful than those who don't drink. Frequent wine drinkers, it says, earn about $67,000 a year, while occasional drinkers earn about $40,000. People who don't drink at all earn a little more than $30,000. You want to be successful, don't you?

   Zoe: You're not going to get me to start drinking wine that way.

6. Maria: Wives of servicemen suffer domestic abuse at the rate of 2 to 5 times that of other women.

   Suzy: Boy, I sure hope Tom doesn't join the Army.

7. [Advertisement] Studies have shown that three cups of Cheerios® a day with a low-fat diet can help lower cholesterol.

8. The number of teenagers giving birth declined 2 percent in the United States in 2008, reversing two years of increases, as older teens may have delayed starting a family because of the recession. *Albuquerque Journal*, April 7, 2010

9. One of Dr. E's dogs gets loose. He comes back the next day. He's coughing and hacking, and he vomits a couple times. Dr. E thinks maybe he ate something bad. Three days later, that dog is O.K., but his other dog, who hasn't left the yard, is coughing and hacking and vomits. Dr. E concludes that his dogs have had a flu or some illness. Explain why you think Dr. E is right or why he is wrong.

Analyze the following exercises by answering the following:

What causal claim is at issue?

Which type of cause-in-population experiment, if any, was done?

Evaluate the evidence for the causal claim.

How would you further test the claim?

10. Late nights may make teens more prone to depression and suicidal thoughts by depriving them of sleep, a Columbia University study said.

    Teens whose parents let them go to bed past midnight were 24 percent more likely to be depressed and 20 percent more likely to have contemplated suicide than peers whose parents set bedtimes at or before 10 p.m., the researchers said in the journal *Sleep*. Earlier set bedtimes may be protective because they increase the likelihood of getting enough sleep, they said. *Albuquerque Journal*, January 2, 2010

11. *A little booze does a woman's mind good*

    Women who imbibe a little wine, beer or spirits every day are less likely than teetotalers to see their memories and other thinking powers fade as they age, according to the largest study to assess alcohol's impact on the brain. The study of more than 12,000 elderly women found that those who consumed light to moderate amounts of alcohol daily had about a 20 percent lower risk of experiencing problems with their mental abilities later in life.

"Low levels of alcohol appear to have cognitive benefits," said Francine Grodstein of the Brigham and Women's Hospital in Boston, senior author of the study, which is being published in today's *New England Journal of Medicine*. "Women who consistently were drinking about one-half to one drink per day had both less cognitive impairment as well as less decline in their cognitive function compared to women who didn't drink at all."

While the study involved only women, the findings probably hold true for men, although previous research indicates that men seem to benefit from drinking slightly more—one to two drinks per day, researchers said.

The findings provide the latest evidence that indulging in alcohol, long vilified as part of an insalubrious lifestyle, can actually help people live longer, healthier lives. While heavy drinking clearly causes serious problems for many people, recent research has found that drinking in moderation protects the heart. *Washington Post*, Jan. 15, 2005

12. [Bernard] Goldberg documents the steady decline in the behavioral, emotional and physical health of America's kids that has taken place as the percentage of latchkey and day-care children has increased. Some examples:

    • From 1979 to 1988 (a period that coincides with a sizable increase in two-income families), the suicide rate for girls 10–14 rose 27 percent, while for boys it rose 71 percent.

    • In 1970, only one in 20 American girls under 15 had had sex; today, one in three is having sex, and 3 million teenagers are infected with sexually transmitted diseases every year.

    • A study of 5 million eighth-graders found that children who are left home alone more than 11 hours a week are three times more likely than kids with after-school adult supervision to abuse drugs, alcohol or tobacco.

    • A study by the National Institute of Child Health and Human Development published in 2001 found that toddlers in full-time day care tended to be more aggressive toward other children and defiant toward adults. This, the institute found, regardless of the quality.

    Goldberg acknowledges that not all the evidence is bad. Some studies on day care have found it's not bad at all. (When one considers only studies conducted by people or groups without apparent bias, however—as is the case with the above study—the results always paint a not-so-pretty picture.) And he's clear that he's talking about parents who choose to work outside the home, not those who effectively have no choice.

    John Rosemond, "Parenting," *Albuquerque Journal*, March 7, 2002

13. *Academy Award winning actors and actresses*

    (from the transcript for National Public Radio's *All Things Considered*, May 15, 2001)

    ROBERT SIEGEL, host: An article reached us today with the title "Survival in Academy Award-winning Actors and Actresses." It is not about casting or contracts. It's actually in the *Annal of Internal Medicine*, and it's about survival. Dr. Donald Redelmeier and his colleague Sheldon Singph found that actors and actresses who have won Oscars live, on average, 3.9 years longer than other performers who have never won Oscars.
    Dr. Redelmeier is in Toronto and joins us now. Dr. Redelmeier, how did you conduct this study?

DR. DONALD REDELMEIER: What we did is, we identified every actor and actress who's ever been nominated for an Academy Award in either a supporting role or a leading role over the full history of the Academy Awards since 1929.

SIEGEL: What does this tell you? What do you think is the cause of the greater longevity among those actors and actresses who won Academy Awards?

DR. REDELMEIER: One possible theory is that winning an Academy Award improves a person's self-esteem and gives them a much greater resilience to the normal stressors that confront us on a day-to-day basis. And that, in turn, causes changes in the hypothalamic, pituitary, adrenal glands of the body or the immunological systems, and so that much less damage occurs over the years.

SIEGEL: If this is true, do you think we should find then that, say, the Academy Award winners among the film editors or the special effects people would also outlive their colleagues or do you think it requires the adulation that only star actors and actresses get to add the extra 3.9 years to a life span?

DR. REDELMEIER: Well, more research is always needed. Another possibility is that it isn't due to a person's internal biology, but it reflects their external behavior—i.e., that stars live lives under continuous scrutiny, and so because of that, they need to sleep properly every night, eat a balanced diet at every meal, exercise regularly every day in order to preserve their glamorous image. And so it's those external behaviors rather than the internal peace of mind that confers a much greater survival benefit than is generally appreciated.

14. *Bad hair can give self-esteem a cowlick, study says*

People's self-esteem goes awry when their hair is out of place, according to a Yale University researcher's study of the psychology of bad-hair days.

People feel less smart, less capable, more embarrassed and less sociable, researchers said in the report released Wednesday.

And contrary to popular belief, men's self-esteem may take a greater licking than women's when their hair just won't behave. Men were more likely to feel less smart and less capable when their hair stuck out, was badly cut or otherwise mussed.

"The cultural truism is men are not affected by their appearance," said Marianne LaFrance, the Yale psychology professor who conducted the study. "(But) this is not just the domain of women."

The study was paid for by Proctor & Gamble, which makes hair-care products. The Cincinnati-based company would not discuss how much the study cost or what they planned to do with their newfound knowledge about the psychology of hair.

Janet Hyde, a psychology professor at the University of Wisconsin at Madison who studies body image and self-esteem, said personal appearance can have an enormous effect on people, especially adolescents.

But Hyde said she was surprised to hear bad hair had a stronger effect on men than on women in some cases.

For the study, researchers questioned 60 men and 60 women ages 17 to 30, most of them Yale students. About half were white, 9 percent were black, 21 percent were Asian and 3 percent were Hispanic.

The people were divided into three groups. One group was questioned about times in their lives when they had bad hair. The second group was told to think about bad product packaging, like leaky containers, to get them in a negative mind-set. The third group was not asked to think about anything negative.

All three groups then underwent basic psychological tests of self-esteem and self-judgment. The people who pondered their bad-hair days showed lower self-esteem than those who thought about something else. . . .

LaFrance, who has also studied the psychology of smiles, facial expressions and body language, said she would continue to look into the effects of bad hair. "We all do research that at first pass might seem quite small," she said. "Yes, some of my colleagues said, 'That's interesting, ha, ha.' But then, when we talk about it, people are interested."

Associated Press, January 27, 2000

15. *Two new studies back value of high-fiber diet*

New research has revived the notion that a high-fiber diet may protect against colon cancer. Long-standing recommendations for high-fiber diets have taken a hit over the last few years after a handful of carefully conducted studies failed to find a benefit.

But experts say two major studies published this week in *The Lancet* medical journal—one on Americans and the other on Europeans—indicate previous research may not have examined a broad enough range of fiber consumption or a wide enough variety of fiber sources to show an effect.

"These two new findings show that the fiber hypothesis is still alive," said the leader of the American study, Ulrike Peters of the U.S. National Cancer Institute.

Figuring out the relationship between nutrition and disease has proved difficult, but experts say fiber is particularly complicated because there are various types and they all could act differently.

Fiber is found in fruits, vegetables and whole grains. Americans eat about 16 grams a day, while Europeans eat about 22 grams. The new studies indicate fiber intake needs to be about 30 grams a day to protect against colon cancer.

There are 2 grams of fiber in a slice of whole meal bread. A banana has 3 grams and an apple has 3.5 grams, the same as a cup of brown rice. Some super-high fiber breakfast cereals have as much as 14 grams per half cup.

In the American study, investigators compared the daily fiber intake of 3,600 people who had precancerous growths in the colon with that of around 34,000 people who did not. People who ate the most fiber had 27 percent lower risk of precancerous growths than those who ate the least.

In the European study, the largest one ever conducted on nutrition and cancer, scientists examined the link in more than 500,000 people in 10 countries. Those who ate the most fiber, about 35 grams a day, had about a 40 percent lower risk of colorectal cancer compared with those who ate the least, about 15 grams a day, the study found.

"In the top quintile (group) they were eating 15 grams of cereal fiber, which is equivalent to five or six slices of whole meal bread, plus they were eating seven portions of fruit and vegetables a day, which is basically the Mediterranean levels," said the study's leader, Sheila Bingham, head of the diet and cancer group at Cambridge University's human nutrition unit.

Associated Press, May 2, 2003

16. In the mid-1970s a team of researchers in Great Britain conducted a rigorously designed large-scale experiment to test the effectiveness of a treatment program that represented "the sort of care which today might be provided by most specialized alcoholism clinics in the Western world." [reference supplied]

    The subjects were one hundred men who had been referred for alcohol problems to a leading British outpatient program, the Alcoholism Family Clinic of Maudsley Hospital in London. The receiving psychiatrist confirmed that each of the subjects met the following criteria: he was properly referred for alcohol problems, was aged 20 to 65 and married, did not have any progressive or painful physical disease or brain damage or psychotic illness, and lived within a reasonable distance of the clinic (to allow for clinic visits and follow-up home visits by social workers). A statistical randomization procedure was used to divide the subjects into two groups comparable in the severity of their drinking and their occupational status.

    For subjects in one group (the "advice group"), the only formal therapeutic activity was one session between the drinker, his wife, and the psychiatrist. The psychiatrist told the couple that the husband was suffering from alcoholism and advised him to abstain from all drink. The psychiatrist also advised the husband to stay on his job (or return to it) and encouraged the couple to attempt to keep their marriage together. There was a free-ranging discussion and advice about the personalities and particularities of the situation, but the couple was told that this one session was the only treatment the clinic would provide. They were told in sympathetic and constructive language that the "attainment of the stated goals lay in their hands and could not be taken over by others."

    Subjects in the second group (the "treatment group") were offered a year-long program that began with a counseling session, an introduction to Alcoholics Anonymous, and prescriptions for drugs that would make alcohol unpalatable and drugs that would alleviate withdrawal suffering. Each drinker then met with a psychiatrist to work out a continuing outpatient treatment program, while the social worker made a similar plan with the drinker's wife. The ongoing counseling was focused on practical problems in the areas of alcohol abuse, marital relations, and other social or personal difficulties. Drinkers who did not respond well were offered in-patient admissions, with full access to the hospital's wide range of services.

    Twelve months after the experiment began, both groups were assessed. No significant differences were found between the two groups. Furthermore, drinkers in the treatment group who stayed with it for the full period did not fare better than those who dropped out. At the twelve-month point, only eleven of the one hundred drinkers had become abstainers. Another dozen or so still drank but in sufficient moderation to be considered "acceptable" by both husband and wife. Such rates of improvement are not significantly better than those shown in studies of the spontaneous or natural improvement of chronic drinkers not in treatment.

    Herbert Fingarette, *Heavy Drinking: The Myth of Alcoholism as Disease*

Summary We encounter cause and effect claims every day. The best way to begin to evaluate them is to describe the purported cause and the purported effect with claims. Then we can use much of what we know about how to reason with claims.

For there to be cause and effect, it must be (nearly) impossible for the claim describing the cause to be true and effect false. That's the same relation as between premises and conclusion of a valid or strong argument, except that here these claims should already be plausible. As with arguments, we often need additional premises, what we call the "normal conditions," to show that the inference is valid or strong. Among those additional premises will often be a generalization establishing a correlation.

Checking that the cause makes a difference is how we rule out other possible causes. In addition, the cause has to precede the effect, and there must be no common cause. Once we've checked that all these necessary conditions for cause and effect hold, there's not much more we can do except make sure we haven't made one of the common mistakes of reversing cause and effect, or arguing *post hoc ergo propter hoc*, or mistaking correlation for causation.

When we can't specify the normal conditions for a general causal claim, we rely on statistical arguments to establish that there is some causal link. Three kinds of experiments are important for those arguments: controlled cause-to-effect, uncontrolled cause-to-effect, and uncontrolled effect-to-cause.

Key Words

causal claim
cause
effect
normal conditions
particular causal claim
correlation
general causal claim
correlation-causation fallacy
common cause
reversing cause and effect
post hoc ergo propter hoc
coincidence
causal factor
foreseeable consequence
intervening cause
scientific method
cause in a population
control group
controlled cause-to-effect experiment
uncontrolled cause-to-effect experiment
uncontrolled effect-to-cause experiment

Further Study For a fuller study of how to reason about cause and effect, see *Cause and Effect, Conditionals, Explanations*, which has more examples and a history of the subject. It's also published by ARF.

Cartoon Writing Lesson E

For each cartoon below there is a sentence that can be understood as a causal claim. Argue either for or against that causal claim, based on what you see in the cartoon and your general knowledge. Check that the necessary conditions for cause and effect are satisfied and that you have not made any of the common mistakes in reasoning about cause and effect. Compare Example 1 on p. 308.

1. 

The falling apple knocked Dick unconscious.

2. 

The wasps chased Professor Zzzyzzx because he hit their nest.

3.

Dick got burned because he put too much lighter fluid on the barbecue.

4.

Suzy failed because she stayed up late dancing.

5.

Dick crashed because of the turtle.

6.

Dick had to hitchhike because he didn't get gas.

Review Chapters 12–15

In Chapters 1–6 we considered the nature of claims and learned the fundamentals of argument analysis. In Chapters 7 and 8 we looked at how to reason with compound claims and general claims. Then we considered fallacies in Chapters 9–11. In Chapters 12–15 we looked at particular ways to reason from experience, and we looked at some common problems when using numbers in arguments.

When we reason from experience, we usually cannot get certainty. Judging arguments is more often weighing up the possibilities.

Analogies are common. We note similarities and draw conclusions. Often that's all that's done, and then the analogy is more a suggestion for discussion than an argument. To take an analogy seriously as an argument, the similarities have to be spelled out clearly, and a general principle drawing the conclusion from those similarities is needed.

Analogies lead to generalizations. We generalize when we start with a claim about some and conclude a claim about more. We saw that though we don't always know the details of how a generalization was made, we can often judge whether the generalization is good by reflecting on whether the sample is big enough, whether the sample is representative, and whether the sample is studied well.

How big the sample needs to be and whether it is representative both depend on the variation in the population. When there is a lot of variation, random sampling—not to be confused with haphazard sampling—is the best way to get a representative sample. With polls and surveys, an estimate of the likelihood of the conclusion being right and the margin of error should be given.

Analogies and generalizations play a role in perhaps the most important kind of reasoning we do every day: figuring out cause and effect. We can set out necessary conditions for there to be cause and effect. And we can survey some of the common mistakes made when reasoning about cause and effect. The most pernicious is *post hoc ergo propter hoc* reasoning (after this, therefore because of this). Often the best we can say with our limited knowledge is that it's a coincidence.

When we reason about cause and effect in populations with large variation, it's hard, if not impossible, to specify the normal conditions. Typically a statistical causal link is established. Considering the three main kinds of experiments used for those arguments, we can see that, as with generalizations, a little thought allows us to make judgments about the truth of the conclusion.

Review Exercises for Chapters 12–15

1. What is an argument?
2. What three tests must an argument pass to be good?
3. What is a weak argument?
4. Is every valid or strong argument with true premises good? Explain.
5. What does a bad argument tell us about its conclusion?
6. What is reasoning by analogy?
7. What are the steps in evaluating an analogy?
8. Define, for a collection of numbers:
   a. The average.
   b. The mean.
   c. The median.
   d. The mode.
9. What is a "two times zero is still zero" claim? Give an example.
10. a. What is a generalization?
    b. What do we call the group being generalized from?
    c. What do we call the group being generalized to?
11. What is a representative sample?
12. Is every randomly chosen sample representative? Explain.
13. Is it ever possible to make a good generalization from a sample of just one? Give an explanation or example.
14. A poll says that the incumbent is preferred by 42% of the voters with a margin of error of 3% and confidence level of 97%. What does that mean?
15. What three premises are needed for a good generalization?
16. What do we call a weak generalization from a sample that is obviously too small?
17. List the necessary conditions for there to be cause and effect.
18. Why is a perfect correlation not enough to establish cause and effect? Give an example.
19. List the common mistakes in reasoning about causes and give an example of each.
20. List the three common types of experiments used to establish cause in populations, and give an example of each.
21. Why is it better to reason well with someone even if you could convince him or her with bad arguments?

16 Explanations

A. Inferential Explanations

1. Explanations and inferential explanations

Why does the sun rise in the East? How does electricity work? How come Spot gets a bath every week? Why didn't you give me an A on the last exam?

We give explanations as answers to lots of different kinds of questions. Our answers can be as varied as the questions. We can give a story about why the world was created. We can write a scientific treatise on how the muscles of the esophagus work. We can give instructions for how to play a guitar. We can draw a map. We can talk about our feelings. A mechanic can point to a part of your car's engine.

But just as we ignored the nonverbal when we began studying convincings, here we're going to focus here on verbal explanations about why a claim is true.

> ***Inferential explanations*** An answer to the question "Why is claim E true?" that can be understood as "Because A, B, C, . . . are true" is an *inferential explanation*. Sometimes just the claims A, B, C, . . . are called the *explanation* of E. The claim E is called the ***claim being explained***, and the claims A, B, C, . . . are called the ***explanatory claims***.

2. What counts as a good inferential explanation?

An inferential explanation is meant to show *why* a claim is true.

Example 1 Zoe: Why is Spot limping?
Dick: Here, I see. It's because he's got a tiny thorn in his paw.

Analysis This is an inferential explanation: "Spot has a thorn in his paw" is meant to explain the obviously true "Spot is limping."

Example 2 Dick: Why is it that most people who call psychic hot lines are women?
Zoe: Wait a minute. What makes you think more women than men call psychic hot lines?

Analysis Zoe can't explain what she doesn't think is true. She's responded to Dick's loaded question by asking for an argument to show that "More women than men call psychic hot lines" is true.

For an inferential explanation to be good, *the claim being explained should be highly plausible*. And the explanation should provide us with other claims from which it follows. We know what it means for one claim to follow from one or more others: that's the relation of being valid or strong. In Example 1 the relation of "Spot has a thorn in his paw" to "Spot is limping" is valid or strong, relative to other claims that Dick or Zoe could easily supply. So for an inferential explanation to be good, *it should be valid or strong*.

Example 3 Dogs lick their owners because they aren't cats.

Analysis This is a bad explanation because the relation of "Dogs aren't cats" to "Dogs lick their owners" is neither valid nor strong, and there's no obvious way to repair it.

In an inferential explanation, the claims doing the explaining are supposed to make clear why the claim being explained is true. So *the explanatory claims should be plausible* because we know that anything can follow from a false claim.

Example 4 The sky is blue because there are blue globules in the high atmosphere.

Analysis This is a bad explanation because "There are blue globules in the high atmosphere" is not plausible.

Example 5

YOU DRANK THREE COCKTAILS BEFORE DINNER A BOTTLE OF WINE WITH DINNER...
THEN A COUPLE OF GLASSES OF BRANDY. ANYONE WHO DRINKS THAT MUCH IS GOING TO GET A HEADACHE.
I COULDN'T HELP IT. ANYTHING IS BETTER THAN LISTENING TO TOM TALK ABOUT POLITICS

Analysis Zoe offers a good explanation of why Dick has a headache:

Anyone who drinks that much is going to have a headache.
Therefore (explains why), Dick has a headache.

Judged as an argument, though, this is bad because it begs the question: it's a lot more obvious to Dick that he has a headache than that anyone who drinks that much is going to have a headache.

In an argument we're trying to show that the conclusion is true. So the premises should be more plausible than the conclusion. In an explanation, the conclusion is supposed to be obviously true. So in a good explanation *at least one of the explanatory claims should be no more plausible than the conclusion*. Otherwise, we'd have an argument for the conclusion, not an explanation.

As with arguments, we also want to avoid circularity.

Example 6 Zoe: Why can't you write today, Dick?
Dick: Because I've got writer's block.

Analysis This is a bad explanation. "I've got writer's block" just means that Dick can't write. We can't explain why a claim is true by invoking the claim itself.

It's hard to state precisely what it means for an explanation to be not circular more than saying that *none of the explanatory claims should be the claim being explained, a simple rewriting of it, or equivalent to it*.

Example 7

Analysis Flo thinks she's given a good explanation. Her answer makes it clear why the claim "There is only one piece of cake in the cupboard now" is true. Yet her mother won't accept it. Flo answered "Why is there only one piece of cake in the cupboard, instead of none?" but her mother meant, "Why is there one piece of cake in the cupboard, instead of two?"

Questions are often ambiguous, and a good explanation to one reading of a question can often be a bad explanation to another. If a question is ambiguous, that's a fault of the person asking the question—we can't be expected to guess correctly what's meant. We can classify an explanation as bad because it answers the wrong question only if it's very clear what question is meant.

Here are the conditions we've seen that are needed for an inferential explanation to be good.

Necessary conditions for an inferential explanation to be good
For "A, B, C, . . . explain E" to be a good inferential explanation all of the following must hold:

- "A, B, C, . . . therefore E" is valid or strong.
- E is highly plausible.
- Each of A, B, C, . . . is plausible.
- At least one of A, B, C, . . . is not more plausible than E.
- The explanation is not circular.
- A, B, C, . . . answer the right question.

Often we say that an explanation is *right* or *correct* rather than "good" and *wrong* rather than "bad."

These are necessary conditions for an inferential explanation to be good. They allow us to rule out lots of explanations as bad. But we don't have—no one has—clearly sufficient conditions for an explanation to be good.

3. Repairing explanations

Explanations, just as arguments, are often incomplete. We don't reject them out of hand without trying to see if they can be repaired. We can invoke the Principle of Rational Discussion to get a guide to repairing explanations that's similar to the Guide to Repairing Arguments.

The Guide to Repairing Inferential Explanations Given an (implicit) inferential explanation that is apparently defective, we are justified in adding a further explanatory claim if all three of the following hold:

- The explanation becomes stronger or valid.
- The claim is plausible and would seem plausible to the other person.
- The claim does not make the explanation circular.

We may delete an explanatory claim if that doesn't make the explanation weaker.

4. Causal explanations

When an inferential explanation is given in terms of cause and effect, *if it's good causal reasoning and it answers the right question, it's a good explanation; otherwise it's bad.*

Example 8 Why did Dick wake up? Because Spot barked.

Analysis This is a good explanation (see Chapter 15.A.1).

Example 9 Zoe: Did Tom get over his cold?

Suzy: Yes, he recovered from it in one week because he took vitamin C.

Analysis This is a causal explanation but not a good one: the purported cause does not clearly make a difference.

> Proper treatment will cure a cold in seven days, but left to itself a cold will hang on for a week. —Henry G. Felsen

Let's see if the following are good inferential explanations

Example 10 Zoe: You say that this argument is bad. But why?

Dr. E: It's bad because it's weak. For example, Sheila could have been a rabbit or a herring.

Analysis Dr. E knows what he's talking about, and this is a good inferential explanation. But it's not a causal one. Explanations in terms of rules or criteria aren't causal.

Example 11 Customer: Why did you call your coffee house *The Dog & Duck*?

Owner: Because *The Duck & Dog* doesn't sound good.

Analysis What's being explained is "The owner called his coffee house *The Dog & Duck*," which is obviously true. It's explained with "*The Duck & Dog* doesn't sound good," which is plausible. But the explanation is weak and the obvious repair is to assume that those were the only choices, which is a false dilemma. So the explanation is unrepairable and bad.

Example 12 Customer: Why did you call your coffee house *The Dog & Duck*?

Owner: Why not?

Analysis Shifting the burden of proof is as bad for explanations as for arguments.

Example 13 Zoe: Why was Tom so unpleasant to us today?

Dick: Oh, don't mind him. He was just out of sorts.

Analysis This looks circular, but it's worse. Being out of sorts indeed makes people rude—if we had a clear idea of what "being out of sorts" means besides acting rudely. The purported explanation is *too vague* to be a claim.

Example 14 Suzy: Why did Dick just get up and leave the room like that in the middle of what Tom was saying?

Zoe: Because he wanted to.

Analysis This is a bad explanation. Wanting to leave the room when Tom is talking is something unusual and requires further explanation. An explanation is ***inadequate*** if it leads to a further "Why?" Even if the explanatory claims are obviously true, they may not be enough.

Example 15 —Why did the turtle cross the road?
—Because its leg muscles carried it.

Analysis This is bad because it's the wrong kind of answer. Normally we'd understand the question as asking for a ***behavioral*** explanation: claims about the motives or beliefs or feelings of a person or creature. What's been given is a premise about the physical make-up of the turtle, a ***physical*** explanation. It answers the wrong question.

Example 16 Dick: Why is your car sputtering like that?
Suzy: Because the battery is low.
Dick: C'mon. That's irrelevant.

Analysis "That's irrelevant" just means that the explanation is weak and there's no obvious repair to it. As most of us know, if a battery is low, either the car should run without sputtering or not run at all. Suzy's explanation is weak, and hence is bad.

Example 17 Psychiatrist: Where is Dr. E? It's time for his appointment.
Secretary: Don't you remember? He said he wouldn't be coming anymore.
Psychiatrist: He is resisting the understanding that I am bringing him.
Secretary: But he says it's because he can't afford your fee.
Psychiatrist: Ah! There, there's the proof that his unconscious is resisting, because I know he could borrow money from his rich uncle.

Analysis Psychiatrists often make their explanations immune to testing. If anything counts as resistance, if everything can be explained in terms of unconscious motives, there's no way to test. We might as well say that a patient won't come because gremlins are inhabiting his psyche, though that might be less effective in getting a patient to continue treatment and pay the bills. This is a bad causal explanation. *If a claim explains everything, it explains nothing because it can't be tested.*

Example 18 Harry: I can't believe my uncle Ralph gave up his partnership in his law firm. He was making really big bucks. He sold his home and bought a cabin out near Big Tree Meadow, really primitive, and he says he's meditating. He was always such a responsible guy.
Zoe: How old is he?
Harry: 45.
Zoe: He's just going through midlife crisis.

Analysis This is an inferential explanation, but we need more evidence for the claim that he's going through a midlife crisis before we accept it as good—unless you define "midlife crisis" as what Harry's uncle is doing, in which case the explanation is circular.

Example 19 Zoe: My mom is always hot and irritable now.
Dick: Why's that?
Zoe: She's going through menopause.

Analysis This is a good causal explanation because there's good evidence that women who go through menopause typically have those symptoms.

Example 20 Dick: Why won't Spot eat his dog food today?
Zoe: He hasn't been hungry all day.
Dick: I don't think so—he just ate the doggie treat I gave him.

Analysis Dick has shown that Zoe's explanation is not good in one of the ways we show an argument isn't good: he challenges the premise.

Example 21 Zoe: Why did the lights just go out?
Dick: The transformer down the street must have blown again. I'll have to call the electric company.
Zoe: Don't bother—I can see the lights are still on where Flo lives, and the streetlights are working.

Analysis Zoe has used reducing to the absurd to refute Dick's explanation. If Dick's explanation were right, then from it we could conclude "The streetlights and all the lights on the block are out." But that claim is false. So his claim is false. So it's a bad explanation.

Example 22 Dr. E: I won't accept your homework late.
Maria: But I had a meeting I had to attend at work.
Dr. E: So? I don't count problems with employment as an adequate excuse for handing in late work.

Analysis Maria has explained why she did not hand in the homework on time. She thinks she's also given an excuse, but Dr. E disabuses her of that. What your employer will count as an excuse for being late may be unclear until you try a couple. What counts to a police officer as an excuse for speeding is pretty limited. *An explanation is not an excuse.*

Exercises for Section A

1. What is an inferential explanation?
2. Give an example of an explanation you reckon is good that isn't inferential.
3. What do we call a request for an explanation of a claim that is not highly plausible?
4. What do we mean when we say an explanation is circular?
5. Why is a good explanation not a good argument?

6. What are the necessary conditions we've seen for an inferential explanation to be good?
7. a. What is a causal explanation?
   b. When is a causal explanation good?
8. Why do we say that an untestable claim is a bad explanation?
9. a. Give an example of an explanation you recently offered as an excuse.
   b. What's the difference between an explanation and an excuse?
10. Bring to class examples of the following that you have encountered or heard. Exchange with a classmate to see if he or she can decide which is which.
    a. A causal explanation.
    b. A good inferential explanation that is not causal.
    c. A circular explanation.
    d. An explanation that answers the wrong question.

Here's some of Tom's work, along with Dr. E's comments.

Zoe: Why is Spot barking?
Dick: Because that stupid cat Puff is on the other side of the fence.

Inferential explanation? (yes or no) Yes.
Claim being explained: Spot is barking.
Explanatory claims: Puff is on the other side of the fence.
Is it a good explanation? Yes, since it happens all the time.

You've got the first three right, but is Puff on the other side this time? It won't be a good explanation if one of the premises is false.

Wanda: I can't figure out why I can't lose weight.
Suzy: Try eating less.

Inferential explanation? (yes or no) Yes.
Claim being explained: Wanda can't lose weight.
Explanatory claims: She should eat less.
Is it a good explanation? Looks good to me.

No! Maybe Wanda is asking for an explanation of why she can't lose weight, but Suzy hasn't given one. Advice isn't an explanation. Suzy hasn't offered any claim from which the truth of "Wanda can't lose weight" might follow.

The reason that Puff is mangy is because Suzy doesn't feed him fish.

Inferential explanation? (yes or no) Yes. *Good!*
Claim being explained: Puff is mangy.
Explanatory claims: Suzy doesn't feed him fish.
Is it a good explanation? Beats me. It looks like it's causal, but I don't know anything about cats eating fish except that a lot of them like tuna.

For the exercises below answer the following:

Inferential explanation? (yes or no)

Claim being explained:

Explanatory claims:

Causal? (yes or no)

Is it a good explanation?

11. Zoe: How did Tom get strep throat?
    Dick: Suzy had it last week.

12. Tom: Why did the match ignite?
    Harry: Because I struck it on the matchbook.

13. (Heard on National Public Radio) Birds sing in the morning because it keeps other birds away, to announce their territory.

14. Maria: Why can't my math teacher stick to the book?
    Lee: Because he's a bad teacher.

15. Dick: Why did Suzy just get up and leave the class?
    Tom: Oh, she probably had to go to the bathroom.
    Dick: But then why was she crying?

16. Lee: Why did Mr. Johns, the owner of that fast-food restaurant where your mom works, lower prices on all the meals?
    Suzy: It's because he's got a good heart and wants poor people to be able to enjoy his food.
    Zoe: I don't think so. He was the one who opposed soup kitchens in town.
    Suzy: He's just covering up. He's afraid of being thought a nice guy. He can't face his unconscious wish to be loved.

17. Zoe: I wish I could help Wanda. What's the reason for her weight problem?
    Dick: Gravity.

18. Dogs eat meat because they are carnivores.

19. Dick: Darn. My bread landed butter-side down.
    Flo: You buttered the wrong side of the bread.

B. Explanations and Associated Arguments

Dick, Zoe, and Spot are out for a walk in the forest. Spot runs off and returns after five minutes. Dick notices that Spot has blood around his muzzle. And they both really notice that Spot stinks like a skunk. Dick turns to Zoe and says, "Spot must have killed a skunk. Look at the blood on his muzzle. And he smells like a skunk." Dick has made a *good argument*:

> Spot has blood on his muzzle. Spot smells like a skunk.
> Therefore,
> Spot killed a skunk.

He's left out some premises that are as obvious to Zoe as to him:

Spot isn't bleeding.
Normally when Spot draws a lot of blood from an animal that is smaller than him, he kills it.
Only skunks give off a characteristic odor, an odor that drenches whoever or whatever is near if they are attacked.
Dogs kill animals by biting them and typically drawing blood.

Zoe replies, "Oh, that explains why he's got blood on his muzzle and smells so bad." That is, she takes Dick's conclusion and uses it as a *good explanation*, relative to the same unstated premises:

Spot killed a skunk.
Explains why,
Spot has blood on his muzzle and smells like a skunk.

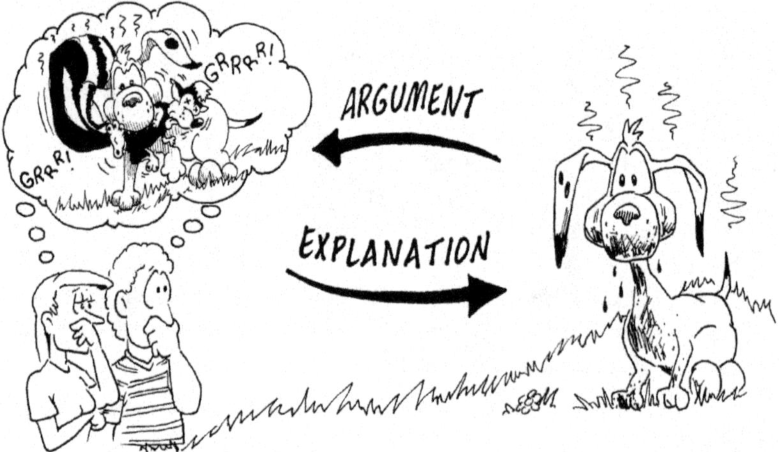

For an explanation "E because of A, B, C . . ." we can ask what evidence we have for A. Sometimes we can supply all the evidence we need just by reversing the inference. For Zoe's explanation to be good, "Spot killed a skunk" must be plausible. And it is, because of the argument that Dick gave—they needn't wait until they find the dead skunk.

> ***Explanations and associated arguments*** For an inferential explanation
>
> A, B, C, . . . explains E
>
> the ***associated argument*** to establish A is:
>
> E, B, C, . . . therefore A
>
> The explanation is ***independent*** if each explanatory claim is plausible or can be established by an associated argument. Otherwise it is ***dependent***.

If an explanation is dependent, it lacks evidence for at least one of its explanatory claims that can't be supplied by an associated argument.

Example 23 Spot chases cats because he sees them as something good to eat and because cats are smaller than him.

Analysis "Cats are smaller than Spot" is clearly true. But "Spot sees cats as something good to eat" is not. The associated argument for it is:

> Spot chases cats and cats are smaller than Spot.
> Therefore, Spot sees cats as something good to eat.

This is weak. Without more evidence for "Spot sees cats as something good to eat" we shouldn't accept the explanation. The explanation is dependent.

Example 24 Why was there a drought in the Midwest in 1995? Because of El Niño, the warming of the ocean currents off the west coast of Latin America.

Analysis This is a causal explanation. The explanation is dependent, because we need some evidence that "The ocean currents off the west coast of Latin America warmed up" is true. Is it a good explanation? That's just to ask whether it's good cause-and-effect reasoning.

Example 25

Analysis Dick offers an explanation:

> Light is bent where the water meets the air
> *explains why* the oar appears bent.

The claim doing the explaining here is a generalization: "Light is bent where the water meets the air." Zoe hasn't taken a physics course, so the only reason she has to believe that claim is the associated argument:

> The oar appears bent.
> *Therefore* Light is bent where the water meets the air.

This is a weak generalization, needing more examples to convince. So Dick's explanation is dependent.

Dick, though, has taken a physics course and has studied lots of other examples where light is refracted through various media. So he does have other evidence for his claim that he can offer to Zoe to make this explanation good.

Exercises for Section B

1. a. What is an independent explanation?
   b. What is a dependent explanation?
2. a. Give an associated argument of "Puff tries to catch mice because they are smaller than Puff and move fast, and cats are genetically predisposed to chase anything that is smaller than them and moves fast."
   b. Give another associated argument for that explanation.
   c. Is either a good argument?
   d. Is the explanation independent or dependent?
3. Give to a classmate two explanations to evaluate, one that is independent, and one that is dependent.

Here are two of Tom's exercises on evaluating explanations, with Dr. E's comments.

Lee: How come your car is vibrating and shaking so much?
Dick: Oh, Zoe hit a speed bump going 40 miles per hour.

Inferential explanation? (yes or no) Yes.
Claim being explained: Dick's car is vibrating and shaking a lot.
Explanatory claims: Zoe hit a speed bump going 40 miles per hour.
Causal? Yes.
Independent or dependent? Independent—since Dick is trustworthy.
Evaluation: I think it's pretty good. After all, when you hit a speed bump that fast you know you're going to knock the alignment off, and that makes a car shake. I bet Lee knows that, too.

Good. But since this is causal, don't forget to check the rest of the conditions for there to be cause and effect.

Manuel: I can't believe Wanda failed critical thinking. How did that happen?
Maria: She failed the final exam.

Inferential explanation? (yes or no) Yes.
Claim being explained: Wanda failed critical thinking.
Explanatory claims: Wanda failed the final exam.
Causal? No.
Independent or dependent? Dependent. You have to know that in Dr. E's class you have to pass the final to pass the course.
Evaluation: Looks good to me.

Good. But you also need to know that Wanda was in my class. Possibly this could be understood as causal, too.

For the exercises below answer the following:

Inferential explanation? (yes or no)

Claim being explained:

Explanatory claims:

Causal? (yes or no)

Independent or dependent?

(If independent and it needs an associated argument to establish one of the explanatory claims, state it. If dependent, supply additional explanatory claims if you can.)

Evaluation:

4. Flo: Why do sunflowers always point towards the sun?
   Suzy: Because if they didn't, we wouldn't call them sunflowers.

5. Dick: Why is Harry so depressed?
   Zoe: Because he didn't get that summer intern job at the Adams Foundation.

6. Zoe: Why did the lights go out?
   Dick: Because my eyes were hurting from the glare.

7. Suzy: Why do classes last only 50 minutes instead of an hour?
   Maria: Because students need time to get from one class to another.

8. Zoe: I can't understand what's happening with the garbage can.
   Suzy: What's wrong?
   Zoe: I put it out on Sunday for the garbageman to pick up early Monday, and every Monday I find it's been turned over and I have to pick up garbage that's been strewn all down the street.
   Suzy: It's 'cause where you live. My grandma told me about it. There are wee little leprechauns around here, in the woods, and they like to play tricks on people.

9. Flo: Why should there be a "g" in earth?
   Dick: But there isn't a "g" in "earth."
   Flo: Why not?
   Dick: Why should there be a "g" in "earth"?
   Flo: That's what I asked.

C. Comparing Explanations

Suppose we have two explanations of the same claim. Which is better?

Example 26 Dick: Darn it. Those two pictures we put on the wall have fallen down again.

Zoe: Those hooks we bought just aren't strong enough for those frames.

Suzy: I bet it's because of the fairies that live in the woods here. They don't like the pictures of dogs.

Analysis Zoe's explanation is better because the explanatory claim is more plausible and is testable.

Example 27 Zoe: You say that the oar in the water appears bent because the light rays are—what?—"refracted" in the water? Sounds crazy to me. I think that it's because our eyes don't see so well through water.

Analysis Dick's explanation, when it's filled out, is long and complicated, and its explanatory claims are far from plausible to most of us. Zoe's is simpler and shorter. But Dick's is better because from his claims we can explain a lot of other true ones, while Zoe's is no help in explaining why a toothpick appears different in vinegar or acetone.

We don't have good criteria for comparing explanations. What counts as simpler depends on how much background knowledge you have. What counts as plausible may depend on what you know about the subject. Still, we can often get agreement on what counts as the better explanation in a given situation. But being the better, or even the best explanation we have doesn't make the claims any more plausible. We judge whether an explanation is good by whether its explanatory claims are plausible; we don't judge the explanatory claims plausible because the explanation is good. That would be arguing backwards: from the premises we can deduce true claims, so the premises are true.

> ***Fallacy of inference to the best explanation*** The *fallacy of inference to the best explanation* is to reason that since these claims give the best explanation of this obviously true claim, they're true.

Example 28 Me: Why do I have such pain in my back? It doesn't feel like a muscle cramp or a pinched nerve.

Physician: A kidney stone would explain the pain. Kidney stones give that kind of pain, and it's in the right place for that.

Analysis When I went into the emergency room one night, the doctor gave me this explanation. It would have been a good one if he'd had good reason to believe "You have a kidney stone." But at that point the only reason he had was the associated argument, and that wasn't strong. Still, it was the best explanation he had.

So the doctor made predictions, reasoning by hypotheses: "A kidney stone would show up on an X-ray," "You'd have an elevated white blood cell count," "You would have blood in your urine." He tested each of these and found them false. He then reasoned by reducing to the absurd that if the explanation were true, these would very likely be true; they are false; therefore, the explanation is very likely false.

Nothing else was found, so by process of elimination the doctor concluded that I had a severe sprain or strain, for which massage and exercise were the only remedy.

If the doctor had believed "You have a kidney stone" just because that was the best explanation he had, there would have been no point in doing tests. And then I would have undergone needless treatment or even surgery.

Example 29 Tom: The AIDS epidemic was started by the CIA. They wanted to get rid of homosexuals and blacks, and they targeted those groups with their new disease. They started their testing in Africa in order to keep it hidden from people here. The government once again tried to destroy people they don't like.

Analysis That the AIDS epidemic was started by the CIA would explain a lot. But that's no reason to believe it's true. Every conspiracy theory depends on thinking that what explains a lot is true.

D. Teleological Explanations

One day while cleaning out the small pond in my backyard, I asked myself:

> Why is there a filter on this wet-dry vacuum?

The wet-dry vacuum has a sponge-like filter, but the vacuum sucked up water a lot faster without it. I wondered if I could remove the filter. I wanted to know the function of the filter. I suppose a causal explanation could be given starting with how someone once designed the vacuum with the filter, invoking what that person thought the function of the filter was. But most of that would be beside the point. I didn't want to know why it's *true* that there's a filter on the vacuum, even though the truth of that claim is assumed in the question. I wanted to know what the *function* of the filter is. Some explanations should answer not "Why is this true?" but "What does this do?" or "Why would he or she do that?"

> ***Teleological explanations*** As explanation is *teleological* if it invokes goals or functions or uses a claim that can come true only after the claim being explained becomes true.

Example 30 Why is the missile going off in that direction?
Because it wants to hit that plane.

Analysis It's a bad anthropomorphism to ascribe goals to a missile: people, not missiles, have goals. We should replace this teleological explanation with an inferential one: "The missile has been designed to go in the direction of the nearest source of heat comparable to the heat generated by a jet engine. The plane over there in that direction has a jet engine producing that kind of heat." Often a teleological explanation is offered when an inferential one should be used.

Example 31 Dick (picking his nose): Why do humans get snot in their nose that dries up and has to be picked away? I can't understand what good it does.

Zoe: What makes you think there's a purpose? Can't some things just be? Maybe it just developed along with everything else. And would you please stop that!

Analysis When an explanation assumes that some object has a function or that some person or thing has a goal or motive, we have to ask why we should believe there is a function or motive. Often there simply is no motive, no function, no goal, or at least none we can discern.

> ***The teleological fallacy*** A teleological fallacy is an argument that uses or requires as premise "This occurs in nature, therefore it has a purpose."

Example 32 Why do we dream? Dreams serve as wish fulfillments to prevent interruption of sleep, which is essential to good health.

Analysis According to Freudians, this is a good explanation. And it's teleological. There seems to be no way to construe it as inferential, at least not in accord with the rest of Freud's theory.

Opinion now divides. Either this is an example of a good explanation that is truly teleological, or this example shows that Freudian theories of the unconscious are no good because they yield only teleological explanations.

Example 33 Why does the blood circulate through the body?

(1) Because the heart pumps the blood through the arteries.
(2) In order to bring oxygen to every part of the body tissue.

Analysis The first explanation is a good causal one, if it answers the right question. The second is a good teleological one, if it answers the right question.

Example 34 —Why did Ponce de Leon wander all over the area we call "Florida"?
—Because he was looking for the fountain of youth.

Analysis This is a teleological explanation. But we don't have to puzzle over how something that did not exist caused Ponce de Leon to travel so far. What explains Ponce de Leon's wanderings is his *belief* that there was a fountain of youth, along with his belief that he could find it in Florida. Those assumptions can be put into an inferential explanation.

Example 35 Tom: Why is this towel under the door?
Suzy: In order to keep the draft out.

Analysis This is a teleological explanation in terms of the function of the object. But what if there is a draft under the door even with the towel there? We can talk about functions and unfulfilled functions, but it seems easier to answer the question by saying, "Because Suzy thought that putting the towel under the door would keep out the draft." That can be used as a premise of an inferential explanation.

Example 36 —Why did Harry just stick his foot out like that?
—So that he could catch his balance.

Analysis This is a teleological explanation. But where's the claim that's doing the explaining? If we used "Harry wanted to catch his balance," then it's probably false. Harry probably didn't want or believe anything about his foot and his balance—his action was merely reflex. If he did think about what he was doing, then we can analyze the example as we did the previous two.

If it was just a reflex action, then perhaps we can understand this example as an inferential explanation by adding:

When falling off balance, humans usually try to right themselves with the least effort or in the most habitual manner they can.

Harry was falling off balance.

(*) For Harry, sticking out his foot requires little effort to catch his balance or is habitual with him when he loses his balance.

But what reason do we have to believe (*) except this one instance of Harry falling off balance? The explanation would be dependent and not very good. The original teleological explanation seems better, and we can convert the phrase into the claim "The function of Harry sticking out his foot like that is to catch his balance." That seems right, but it doesn't seem much of an advance.

Even though we use teleological explanations a lot, often we can't agree whether one is good. Part of the problem is that if one of the premises can be true only after what's being explained, the explanation can't be causal (the cause has to precede the effect) and it would seem that the future is somehow affecting the past. Another problem is that we're often not clear about what counts as the function of an action or a thing. And claims asserting motives or goals are subjective and difficult to establish. At best, we have these minimal conditions for a teleological explanation to be good:

- The claim being explained is highly plausible.
- The explanation answers the right question.
- The explanation is not circular.
- The explanation does not ascribe motives, beliefs, or goals to something that doesn't or can't have those.
- The explanation does not assume that because something occurs in nature, it therefore has a purpose.

Summary An explanation is an answer to a question. When the answer is meant to show why a claim is true, it's an inferential explanation. We saw necessary conditions for an inferential explanation to be good. A causal claim is also an inferential explanation, which is good just in case it's good causal reasoning.

Sometimes the claims of an inferential explanation are all plausible. Sometimes all but one is plausible, and that one can be established by an argument associated with the explanation: reversing the role of that explanatory claim with the claim being explained. In either case we say that the explanation is independent. Otherwise, the explanation depends on giving some other evidence for at least one of the premises in order for it to be good.

Saying that the premises of an explanation are true because the explanation is good or even "the best" is just reasoning backwards.

Teleological explanations do not answer why a claim is true but rather what the function or goal of something is, often invoking claims that become true after the claim being explained is true. We try to avoid teleological explanations because they are not causal and because we don't have clear criteria for judging what the function of something is. A teleological explanation that ascribes goals or motives to something that can't have them is definitely wrong.

Key Words

inferential explanation
circular explanation
causal explanation
repairing an explanation
inadequate explanation
behavioral explanation
physical explanation
associated argument
independent explanation
fallacy of inference to the best explanation
teleological explanation
teleological fallacy

Exercises for Chapter 16

1. a. What is the fallacy of inference to the best explanation?
   b. Give an example that you've heard or found on the internet.
2. Why do we prefer to avoid teleological explanations?
3. Go to a health food store and get a clerk to explain how some herb or medication works that's sold there. Analyze and present the explanation in class.
4. Rewrite Example 34 as an inferential explanation.

For the exercises below answer the following:

Explanation? (yes or no)

Claim being explained:

Claim(s) doing the explaining:

Inferential (yes or no)?

Independent or dependent?

(If independent and it needs an associated argument to establish one of the explanatory claims, state it. If dependent, supply additional explanatory claims if you can.)

Causal? (yes or no)

Teleological? (yes or no)

If teleological, if possible rewrite it as inferential.

Evaluation

5. Ellen DeGeneres is loved by more people than Jerry Springer. That's why she gets paid more.

6. Why are there valves in our veins? So the blood can flow only one way in them.

7. Flo: What makes dogs chase cats?
   Dr. E: Cats are Satan's emissaries on Earth. Dogs, the protectors of the way of righteousness, sense this and try to rid the world of them.
   Flo: But then why does Fido get along with Puff?
   Dr. E: Some cats have tried to redeem their souls, and dogs encourage them in the way of righteousness.
   Zoe: Thank you for your deep insight, Dr. E.

8. Flo: Why do dogs like cats so much?
   Suzy: Because they're both mammals.

9. In many states the letter "O" is not used in license plates. Why? Well, it could easily be confused with the numeral "0". By not using the letter, there is a better chance that recording and reporting of license plate numbers will be accurate.

10. Lee: Why did your great uncle go to fight in Vietnam?
    Maria: He had no choice, he was drafted.

11. Lee: Why did your grandfather go to fight in Vietnam?
    Tom: He wanted to do his duty for his country.

12. Lee: Why did your grandfather go to fight in Vietnam?
    Manuel: Because some old Anglos in power decided to send our boys over there to be killed.

13. Lee: Why don't you support affirmative action for entry to universities?
    Tom: Because the minorities in this country have it too easy already.

14. Suzy: Why are students required to take a foreign language to get a degree here?
    Prof. Zzzyzzx: Because the faculty senate passed the regulation.

15. Zoe: Why don't they require university professors to take courses on how to teach?
    Dr. E: Because by the time someone gets a Ph.D. he already knows how to teach well.

16. Zoe: Why don't they require university professors to take courses on how to teach?
    Maria: Because they want to make our lives miserable.

17. Zoe: Why don't they require university professors to take courses on how to teach?
    Harry: Because the professors are too powerful and entrenched, and the administration can't overcome their resistance to it.

18. Why is there so much evil in the world? The world is too complex for us to understand. Only God can see all. He has surveyed all possible ways the world could be and has chosen this one, the actual world, because in it there is the least evil. If He had made the world differently, there would be more evil, not less.

19. —Why is Spot crouching in front of that hole?
    —So he can catch a mouse.

20. Lee: Why is the mouse trap gone?
    Maria: None of us took it. And it's in a really inaccessible place here in the attic. It must be because a mouse got trapped but not killed and dragged it away.

21. How do we catch colds? Well, cold viruses are around us all the time, in the air, in the water, we even carry them in ourselves. Only sometimes do we get colds, and that happens when we unconsciously wish to be sick.

22. Dr. Smyrn: Now for checking your heart. Do you feel that?
    Dr. E: Ow! Sure. But what has pricking my finger got to do with heart disease?
    Dr. Smyrn: The heart is on the left side of the body, and in heart attacks the victim will normally get a pain in his left arm.
    Dr. E: Gee, that hurts, too.
    Dr. Smyrn: I believe that we can predict heart disease by testing the little finger of the left hand for pain sensitivity. So I compare reactions to pricking the little finger of the left hand to pricking other fingers.
    Dr. E: Really? Ouch. That sounds wacky.
    Dr. Smyrn: I have been sending patients with unusual sensitivity in that finger to a cardiologist to follow up.
    Dr. E: And? Ow!
    Dr. Smyrn: So far he has found indications of heart disease in only 2 of the 32 people I have sent. But that is because my test is more sensitive than his. I can spot that there is incipient heart disease before any other known test.

Further Study An excellent source of interesting explanations from ordinary life is the collection *The Last Word*, published by Oxford University Press.

We'll look at explanations in science in Chapter 5S.

MAKING DECISIONS

17 Risk

A. Weighing Risk

> ***Risk*** A risk is a possibility in the future that we deem bad and that would be a consequence of some action we take or don't take.

Example 1 Dick likes to let Spot run free when they go for a walk. A risk associated with doing so is that Spot could chase a cat into traffic and get hit by a car. Perhaps Dick never thought of that risk, in which case he's not very thoughtful about what he does. But he has considered it, and he's decided that letting Spot run free is ***worth the risk***: the good that might come from it outweighs, by more than a little, the bad that might come from it. If Dick doesn't let Spot run free, Spot never gets a chance to get any real exercise, and Dick doesn't think it's very likely that Spot will run out into traffic. He's a good dog.

Tom disagrees. He's seen Spot go crazy around cats, and he knows that's not the only reason Spot might run into traffic. Tom also knows there are other ways for Spot to get exercise: Dick could lead him on a leash while Dick is bicycling or jogging, or Dick could take Spot to the countryside a few times a week to run free. Tom is weighing the likelihood of the risk differently and is seeing more choices for accomplishing the good that Dick wants.

> ***Evaluating Risk*** To evaluate a course of action we need to:
> - Weigh how likely a good outcome is.
> - Weigh how likely the risk is.
> - Weigh how much we want to avoid the risk versus how much we want the possible good outcome that might come from our action.
> - Weigh how hard it would be to accomplish the good by other means.

Only rarely can we put numbers to these evaluations. How much we want to avoid a risk or get a good outcome is a subjective or, at best, an intersubjective evaluation.

Example 2 Harry is a hardworking student, and he'd really like to make $5,000. He knows a stock that he's sure is undervalued that he could buy for $5,000 and make at least that much in a few months. But he doesn't want to make money so much that he's willing to risk losing all of his savings. In comparison, for a billionaire like Bill Gates, losing $5,000 would be a negligible risk while making $5,000 would be O.K. but hardly worth the trouble.

How hard it would be to accomplish the good by other means usually depends on subjective criteria, too.

Example 3 It would be easy for Tom to jog or bicycle with Spot on a leash by his side, since Tom plays football and enjoys exercising. But for Dick, who doesn't get much exercise, that would be hard to do. It would be easier for Dick to ask Tom to take Spot for a run, since it was Tom's idea anyway.

Example 4 Dick: Zoe! Did you hear the weather report? There's a serious chance of a tornado in the next hour.

Zoe: We better open some windows and get into the basement. Grab a flashlight and the radio.

Analysis A tornado is certainly bad, but it's not a risk because it's not a consequence of something we do or don't do. Insurance companies call a tornado a natural disaster or an ***act of God***. The risk here is what might happen to Dick and Zoe if they don't go into the basement.

Example 5 The Union of Scientists Worried about Nuclear War estimates there's a 1 in 10 chance of a nuclear war somewhere in the world this year.

Analysis Many people view the possibility of a nuclear war as if it were a natural disaster, completely out of their control. But whether it happens or not depends on what we do, all of us, from a person who doesn't vote, to a diplomat, to the president. To think of nuclear war as an act of God is to imagine ourselves powerless in the face of unseen forces, when the forces are of our own creation.

B. How Likely Is the Risk?

Sometimes we have a pretty good sense of how likely the risk is. Tom thinks it's not at all unlikely that Spot will run off into traffic if Spot's not on a leash, and his evaluation seems more accurate than Dick's wishful thinking. In comparison, Harry can't even begin to guess how likely it is he could lose most of his money if he invests in that stock.

These evaluations of likelihood of a risk or of a good outcome are evaluations of how likely possibilities are, which we've been doing all along in evaluating arguments and causal claims. It's weighing how strong the inference is that starts with the premises about what we believe is the case now and concludes with that outcome. For example, Tom thinks that the inference from "Dick lets Spot run free on a walk" to "Spot runs into traffic and gets hit by a car" is much stronger than Dick does. On the other hand, Harry doesn't have a clue how strong the inference is from "I invest $5,000 in a stock, and the stock appears to me to be undervalued" to "I lose most of my money."

Sometimes, though, we can make a very good estimate of how likely the risk is.

Example 6 Dick: I'll bet you $5 on the next flip of this coin.
Tom: You're on.

Analysis Tom knows that the likelihood he'll lose $5 is 50% and the likelihood he'll win $5 is 50%.

Example 7 Zoe: You're buying a lottery ticket?
Dick: Sure. Why not?
Zoe: Can't you do the math? There's less than one chance in 200 million that you'll win. There's a greater chance that you'll be struck by lightning twice this year than that you'll win.
Dick: That's stupid. I don't want to be hit by lightning. And you can't buy a ticket for that.

Analysis Dick's chance of losing $1 is almost certain; his chance of winning is only a tiny bit better than not buying a ticket at all. Yet he still buys a ticket. He reckons that the possible good that can come from buying a ticket, which includes a week of daydreams, outweighs what he considers the minimal loss. He also consoles himself that the money he loses will go to schools, though much less than half of it does. Others, however, would classify as a bad outcome Dick passing his time daydreaming what he'd do with millions of dollars.

Example 8 Dick: You thought I was crazy to buy a lottery ticket, yet you just bought six of them.
Zoe: Yes, but the jackpot is up to $460 million!

Analysis Buying six tickets gives Zoe six times more chances to win than buying one ticket—but that's still only a miniscule chance. Either knowing the numbers associated with the risk doesn't matter to Zoe, or else she considers the outcome of winning so much money versus the usual $25 million to be many million times more good to her. It isn't that the lottery is a tax on people who don't understand mathematics. Rather, people motivated by greed are willing to weigh a positive outcome much more than the risk, if the risk doesn't cost much.

Example 9 Lee: So you got that Chihuahua.

Wanda: Yes, isn't he cute? His name's Pepe.

Lee: Nice doggy. (*fierce barking*) Yikes.

Wanda: He's a great guard dog.

Lee: If you want to keep away very small people.

Wanda: But I'm worried about taking care of him. My aunt's dog had to have surgery and it cost $2,300. That's a lot. I'm going to buy pet insurance that will cover all his vet bills—it's only $39.95 per month.

Lee: You might want to buy insurance for covering the cost of him biting someone, too.

Analysis Wanda's Chihuahua is just a pup. So if she continues to buy insurance for his whole life, it could add up to more than $5,000. The odds of one dog needing $7,000 in medical treatments (there's always a deductible) are fairly low. The sorts of hereditary or chronic conditions likely to lead to large veterinary bills, like hip dysplasia, are rarely covered by pet insurance.

But that's how insurance companies work: they look at data on mortality and illness and use the law of large numbers to generalize that enough of their customers (in this case, dogs without pre-existing conditions) are very likely in the long run to cost them a lot less than the premiums their customers pay. Even though the insurance company will have to pay more than $5,000 for some sick dogs, those costs are more than offset by the profits they make on healthy ones.

Wanda, however, knows that if her little dog gets hurt or ill, she'll want to help him, and she knows that she'll never have enough money to pay for big vet bills. So she'll pay just a bit every month for the insurance to cover emergencies. She might come out ahead if she just put that much money in a savings account each month—unless Pepe needs a big operation next year.

C. Mistakes in Evaluating Risk

Example 10 Tom: I'm thinking of joining the Army.

Zoe: That's really dangerous.

Tom: No it isn't. The death rate for soldiers in Afghanistan is lower than the death rate in New York City.

Analysis Tom is comparing apples and oranges. The death rate for people in New York includes all the old people there, all the sick people, all the homeless. To evaluate the risk, Tom should compare the death rate for healthy New Yorkers who are of military age to that for soldiers in Afghanistan and then factor in the rate of serious injury, particularly brain injury, for those two groups.

Example 11 Zoe: Look in the newspaper! There was a plane crash in New York and all 168 people on board died. When we go to visit my mom this year, let's drive and not fly. It'll be a lot safer.
Analysis This is a case of selective attention. The likelihood of being killed in an auto accident per miles traveled is about 70 times greater than for flying—it's just that we don't read about so many people dying all at once. There's also the illusion that because we're driving we can control the risk more than in a plane. But an airplane pilot is much better trained and careful at flying than most of us are at driving, and there are also air traffic controllers and a co-pilot for backup.

Example 12 Dick: I read that most car accidents occur within three miles of the driver's home. So if we do drive to see your mom, we don't need to be so careful once we're out of town.
Analysis Of course most car accidents happen within three miles of the driver's home because that's where people drive the most. It's the rate of accidents that indicates the likelihood of the risk.

Example 13 Tom: I just read in the paper that a third of all avalanche deaths in the U.S. occur in Colorado. I'm definitely not going skiing there.
Harry: Try Florida. They didn't have any avalanche deaths there last year.
Tom: Duh. They don't have any snow.
Harry: And Colorado is where most people are skiing.

Analysis Tom thinks that the important figure for determining his risk while skiing is the number of deaths per state. Harry shows he's wrong. It's how many people are killed of those who are skiing.

Example 14 Tom: The price of gas is way too high. We need to open up the Arctic for drilling, and all along the coasts, too, and even in the national parks. We'll have more oil then, and the price will go down.
Analysis Tom's right that if we open up all these places to drilling there will be more oil. And he's probably right that if there's more of it, the price will come down. But he's fallen into the ***fallacy of scale***: saying that some consequence of a proposed action would be good (or bad) without considering the size of the consequence. Yes, it might bring the price down, but not much. There's so much demand now, and the amount of oil that would be produced is so small in comparison to that growing demand, there's no reason to think the price would go down much. Worse, Tom is looking only at the good consequences of drilling in all those places: lower prices for gas for him. He's not considered the risks: destroying parts of the country that cannot be reclaimed for generations and encouraging people not to conserve

energy. Nor has he considered an obvious alternative way to increase the supply of gas and lower the prices: reduce the speed limit to 55 mph as we did in the 1970s.

Example 15 Zoe: You drink the tap water here? Don't you know that it's high in arsenic?

Zoe's mother: It hasn't killed me yet.

Analysis Sure she hasn't died yet—too much arsenic in drinking water won't kill you instantly. Its effect is cumulative. If you drink too much over a long time you'll get cancer. Zoe's mother is confusing short-term risk with long-term risk.

Example 16 Lee's grandfather: It's been 30 years since I smoked and I still crave a cigarette. I'm 75 now, and that's the life expectancy of a man. So I might as well start smoking—the worst it can do is kill me.

Analysis Lee's grandfather's fatalism is misplaced. Saying that the life expectancy of a man is 75 means a newborn male will, on average, live that long. But if a man is 75, on average he'll live another 10.5 years. And by saying that the worst it can do is kill him, he's choosing to ignore the other risks of smoking: it'll make it harder for him to breathe and make his last years much worse even if it doesn't kill him.

Example 17 Lee: I've been checking out how I'll finance going to medical school. I'll have to take a loan. By the time I'm finished, I'll owe about $250,000.

Zoe: That's a lot!

Lee: Really, it's not so bad. I read that the average doctor makes nearly that much every year. So I'll be able to pay it off pretty quickly.

Zoe: Yeah. You're at least average. We're all above average.

Analysis Zoe has pointed out one problem with Lee's evaluation of the risk of owing more money than he'll be able to pay: he's assuming he'll earn what the average doctor does. But the average isn't necessarily the most likely. And the average of what doctors earn is for all doctors, not ones who've just graduated. Worse, Lee hasn't considered the interest he'll have to pay on the loan—even if it's just 4% that would be $10,000 per year. Let's hope that Lee gets some advice from a financial counselor at the medical school he plans to attend.

D. Evaluating Risk in Health-Care Decisions

In decisions about our health, we're often given figures that seem to make clear exactly what the likelihood of the risk is versus a good outcome. But how we understand those numbers and whether those numbers really do tell us what we need to know are crucial for us to make good decisions.

Example 18 Suppose major league baseball has a test to detect steroid use that correctly identifies users 95% of the time yet misidentifies nonusers 5% of the time. 400 players are tested, and Ralph's test comes out positive. Should he be suspended?

Analysis Sure, we think, there's a 95% chance he's using steroids. But that's not right. Previous testing showed that only about 5% of baseball players use steroids. So of the 400 players who were tested:

Likely 20 (5%) are users, 380 are not users.
Of the 20 users, 19 (95%) are likely correctly identified as users.
Of the 380 nonusers, 19 (5%) are likely incorrectly identified as users.

So there's only a 50% chance that Ralph, one of the 38, tested positive because he uses steroids. It isn't just the accuracy of the test but also what proportion of players who use steroids that determine how likely a positive test is right. That's why they repeat the test before suspending someone. After a second test given to these 38, of the 19 false positives at most we'd expect one false positive again (5%), while of the ones that were users, 17 would likely test as being users (95%). After a third test, there's almost no chance that a person who isn't a user will be classified as one, and it's almost certain that someone who tests positive is a user. *To evaluate the outcome of a test, we need to consider not just how reliable the test is but also what we know about what proportion of the population actually is or does what's tested.* This background information about the prior probability of what's being tested is called the *base rate*.

Example 19 Doctors report that, in treating men with cancer that has started to spread beyond the prostate: Survival is significantly better if radiation is added to standard hormone treatments. The new study assigned 1,200 men to get hormones plus radiation or hormones alone. After seven years, 74 percent of the men receiving both treatments were alive versus 66 percent of the others. Those on both treatments lived an average of six months longer than those given just hormones. *Albuquerque Journal*, June 7, 2010

Analysis Suzy's grandfather has prostate cancer that's begun to spread. After reading this, she urged him to get radiation therapy along with hormones. She told him, "You'll live six months longer!"

Her grandfather pointed out that the report doesn't talk about the bad effects of taking radiation therapy, which could make a man wish he hadn't lived six months more. Considering only the possible good is no basis for making a decision.

Example 20 Zoe: I can't believe you're taking St. John's wort!
Zoe's mom: They say it's good for depression. And it helped my friend Sally. Besides, it can't hurt. They sell it at the natural foods store.

Analysis Evaluating risk is evaluating reasoning. Who are "they"? Is Zoe's mom just repeating what she heard somewhere? To think that Sally got better after taking it because she took St. John's wort is just *post hoc* reasoning. And the idea that if something is sold at a natural foods store then it can't hurt you is nonsense. With a little searching on the Web, Zoe can show her mom that researchers at Duke University Clinical Research Institute found that St. John's wort can interfere with other medications. And even if it were harmless, taking it instead of seeking professional help for depression can be harmful. Saying "Oh well, it can't hurt" is just a way to avoid thinking seriously about bad consequences.

Example 21 A vaccine for shingles was licensed in 2006. In clinical trials, the vaccine prevented shingles in about half of people 60 years of age and older.

"Shingles vaccine: What you need to know"
Website of the Centers for Disease Control and Prevention, September 12, 2006

Analysis This is an authoritative source, and it seems to make clear that if someone 60 years old or older takes the vaccine, he or she will reduce the chance of getting shingles by 50%. But elsewhere on the website of the CDC, it says that 1 in 3 people that age develop shingles in their lifetime. So there's a 2/3 chance someone that age won't develop shingles anyway. The only reading of their statement that makes any sense is that one-half as many people in the trial got shingles as would have been expected without taking the vaccine. That means that if you're 60 or older, your chance of getting shingles is 1/3 without the vaccine, and 1/6 with the vaccine—if you don't know in advance whether you are one of those who is not likely to get shingles (if you haven't had chickenpox, the document says, you won't get shingles). But there are also possible side effects from taking the vaccine, the risks of which can be clearly quantified, and those are risks for everyone who takes the vaccine.

What seems to be a clear presentation of the likelihood of reducing a serious risk turns out to be so badly stated as to be worthless without more information.

Example 22 Zoe's mother: Should I get a mammogram?

Doctor: It's up to you. Statistics show that it reduces the risk of dying from cancer by 25%.

Analysis That sounds like it's well worth the risk of doing the screening. One out of 4 being saved from cancer is a terrific bet. But that's wrong. What the statistics show is that of 1,000 women who participate in screening, 3 will die from breast cancer within 10 years, whereas from 1,000 women who do not participate, 4 will die. The difference between 4 and 3 is 25%, the ***relative risk reduction***. But the figure that the doctor needs to tell Zoe's mother is the ***absolute risk reduction***, which is 1 in 1,000 who are helped—just 0.1%. And Zoe's mother needs to know the possible risk from the screening itself, such as damage from one more X-ray or an unnecessary biopsy and treatment of a slow-growing cancer.

The *number needed to treat* is another way to measure how effective a treatment is. It's the number of patients a physician would need to treat to help just one. (See the website <www.thennt.com>.) In this example, it's 1,000.

Key Words	risk	fallacy of scale
	worth the risk	relative risk reduction
	act of God	absolute risk reduction

Summary Risk is the bad that can happen because of what we do or don't do. Before we can take it into account in making decisions, we need to be able to evaluate it well. Evaluating risk uses all our reasoning skills.

Exercises for Chapter 17

1. What is a risk?
2. What does it mean to say that some course of action is worth the risk?
3. What are the four steps in weighing a risk?
4. a. Why is weighing risk subjective?
   b. Give an example of an outcome that would be a risk for you but wouldn't be a risk for some member of your family or some friend.
5. Give an example where you can calculate exactly a risk for yourself.
6. Give an example where it's impossible to calculate exactly a risk for yourself, but you can rank it against other possible outcomes.
7. a. What is an act of God? Give an example.
   b. Give an example where you or someone you know has classified something bad that happened or might happen as an act of God, yet it seems clear that it was within someone's or some group's power to make it not happen.
8. Why isn't it accurate to say that the lottery is a tax on people who can't do math?
9. Give an example of a time when you evaluated a risk badly.
10. Give an example of evaluating risk in some sport.
11. Your friend is at the doctor's office and has to make a decision about having surgery versus chemotherapy for her cancer. What should she ask her doctor to help her evaluate the risk?
12. On February 27, 2011, Melissa Jones, a senior on the Baylor women's basketball team, injured her eye in a basketball game. She hit her head on the floor, damaging her optic nerve, and she lost her sight in one eye for a while. Apparently there is a good chance she'll be able to regain her sight. But she wants to finish her basketball career. As quoted by the *Dallas Morning News* (March 24, 2011), she said:

    I don't tend to live my life in a glass box. I feel like you have the same opportunity getting hurt crossing the street that you do in a skydiving accident. I feel that you want to live your life, do what you want to do and have fun with it.

    Suppose you were a friend of Melissa Jones. What would you tell her about how she's evaluating risk?
13. Suzy: I'm going to bet $5 on "Wily Nag" to win in the seventh race.
    Dick: Why? He's at 100 to 1. There's so little chance of winning.
    Suzy: But if I win, it'll be a lot. And if I bet 100 times on horses like him, I'm sure to win at least once.

a. What risk is Suzy taking?
b. What fallacy is Suzy making that affects her evaluation of risk?

14. Zeke got tested for HIV last week and it came out positive. The test is 99% accurate: when someone has HIV, the test detects it 99% of the time. The test has a false positive rate of 1%: 1 out of 100 times when someone who doesn't have HIV is tested, the result will say that he or she does have HIV. Reliable public health statistics estimate 0.6% of the population is HIV positive.

a. What's the probability that Zeke is HIV positive?
b. If Zeke tests positive on a second test, what's the chance he has HIV?

15. In 1997, the *Cassini* spacecraft was scheduled to be launched from Florida for a mission to Saturn. The power for the spacecraft, once it left the earth, was to be provided by the heat from a core of plutonium. There was an outcry about this from the public because, though the plutonium was not the type that could cause an explosion, if the launch failed and the spacecraft reentered and broke up in the atmosphere, the plutonium would be dispersed widely, causing many cases of cancer from its inhalation. In one scenario prepared by scientists, the plutonium would be spread over about 2,000 square kilometers, causing 2,300 cancer deaths over 50 years. Other scenarios were for somewhat fewer cancers. In the end, *Cassini* was launched. The mission has been a success.

Mark E. Eberhart, a professor of chemistry and an expert in materials science discusses in his book *Why Things Break* the risk of this mission.

> When I awoke on the morning of August 15, 1997, I was confronted with many potential hazards. If I had considered these and ranked them from most probable to least probable, the list would look something like this:
>
> 1. Suffering an injury while riding my bicycle during lunch hour.
> 2. Being in an automobile accident while commuting either to or from work.
> 3. Having an accident at home—slipping in the shower or falling down stairs.
> 4. Daily exposure to toxins from the polluted air of Denver.
> 5. Exposure to second-hand smoke.
> 6. Exposure to radon.
> 7. Eating fatty foods.
> 8. Becoming a victim of crime.
> 9. Having a work-related accident.
> 10. Being struck by lightning.
> 11. Getting caught in a flash flood.
> 12. Being injured by a tornado or high winds.
> 13. Suffering an attack by a mountain lion or bear.
> 14. Inhaling plutonium from the reentry of *Cassini* during earth fly-by.
>
> I am not opposed to minimizing risk, but if I am to approach the problem of minimizing risk as a scientist, those things that pose the greatest risk to life and health should receive the greatest portion of our attention.

Explain what is wrong with Eberhart's analysis.

16. [After a chemical explosion at a plant, where one man was killed by the explosion and four were injured, a man who worked in that section of the plant was interviewed. He had been on vacation at the time.]

    Powell said the idea of working every day in a plant filled with toxic chemicals hasn't worried him, and he plans to return when his vacation is over.

    "There are toxic chemicals in your house under your sink," he said. "There is constant training on how to handle them, and if you follow those guidelines, you're O.K. Every job has a potential hazard." Tyson Hiatt, *The Spectrum,* July 31, 1997

    Suppose you were a friend of Mr. Powell. What would you tell him about how he's evaluating risk?

17. *Pascal's wager*

    (Blaise Pascal was a 17th-century mathematician and philosopher who had a religious conversion later in his life. Here, roughly, is his argument.)

    We have the choice to believe in God or not to believe in God. If God does not exist, you lose nothing by believing in Him. But if He exists, and you believe in Him, you have the possibility of eternal life, joyous in the presence of God. If you don't believe in Him, you are definitely precluded from having everlasting life. Therefore, a prudent gambler will bet on God existing. That is, it is better to believe that God exists, since you lose nothing by doing so but could gain everlasting life.

    a. What risk is Pascal evaluating?
    b. What mistakes is he making that affect his evaluation of risk?

18 Making Decisions

The skills you've learned here can help you make better decisions.

Making a decision is making a choice. You have options. When making a decision you can start as you would on a writing exercise. Make a list for and against the choice—all the pros and cons you can think of. Make the best argument for each side. Then your decision should be easy: choose the option for which there is the best argument. Making decisions is no more than being very careful in constructing arguments for your choices.

But there may be more than two choices. Your first step should be to list all the options and give an argument that these really are the only options and not a false dilemma.

Suppose you do all that, and you still feel there's something wrong. You see that the best argument is for the option you feel isn't right. You have a gut reaction that it's the wrong decision. Then you're missing something. Don't be irrational. You know that when confronted with an argument that appears good yet whose conclusion seems false, you must show that the argument is weak or a premise is implausible. Go back to your pro and con lists. Your gut reaction could be right, but it could also be prejudice or wishful thinking. Don't bend the evidence where you want it to go; go where the best evidence leads you.

Now at the end of this course your reasoning has been sharpened, you can understand more, you can avoid being duped. And, we hope, you will reason well with those you love and work with and need to convince. And you can make better decisions. But whether you will do so depends not just on method, not just on the tools of reasoning, but on your goals, your ends. And that depends on virtue.

Exercises for Chapter 18

1. Decide whether you should cook dinner at home tonight.
2. Decide whether and what kind of dog you should get.
3. Decide whether you should buy a car next year.
4. Decide whether you should recommend this course to a friend.

5. If you don't have a job, decide whether you should get one next semester.
   If you have a job, decide whether you should quit.
6. Decide what career you should have.
7. If you're not married, decide whether you should ever get married.
   If you are married, decide whether you should get divorced.
8. If you have children, decide whether you should have more.
   If you don't have children, decide whether you ever should.
9. If you're doing drugs, decide whether you should stop.
10. If you've slept with your friend's lover, decide whether you should tell your friend.
11. Decide whether you should be honest for the rest of your life.
12. Decide whether you should try to be rich and famous or be known for having a good heart.
13. Decide whether you should keep this book or sell it back at the end of the term.

Key Words virtue
the love of wisdom

Composing Good Arguments

By now you've learned a lot about how to compose an argument. Here is a summary of some of the main points.

- If you don't have an argument, literary style won't salvage your essay.
- If the issue is vague, use definitions or rewrite the issue to make a precise claim to deliberate.
- Don't make a clear issue vague by appealing to some common but meaningless phrase, such as "This is a free country."
- Beware of questions used as claims: the reader might not answer them the way you do.
- Your premises must be highly plausible, and there must be glue, something that connects the premises to the conclusion. Your argument must be impervious to the questions: So? Why?
- Don't claim more than you actually prove.
- There is often a trade-off: you can make your argument valid or strong, but perhaps only at the expense of a rather dubious premise. Or you can make all your premises clearly true but leave out the dubious premise that is needed to make the argument valid or strong. Given the choice, opt for making the argument valid or strong. If it's weak, no one should accept the conclusion. And if it's weak because of an unstated premise, it is better to have that premise stated explicitly so it can be the object of debate.
- Your reader should be able to follow how your argument is put together. Indicator words are essential.

- Your argument won't get any better by weaseling with "I believe that" or "I feel that." Your reader probably won't care about your feelings, and your feelings won't establish the truth of the conclusion.
- Your argument should be able to withstand the obvious counter-arguments. It's wise to consider them in your essay.
- For some issues, the best argument may be one which concludes that we should suspend judgment.
- Slanters turn off those you might want to convince: you're preaching to the converted. Fallacies just convince the careful reader that you're dumb or intending to mislead.
- If you can't spell, if you can't write complete sentences, if you leave words out, then you can't convince anyone. All the reader's effort will be spent trying to decipher what you intended to say.

You should be able to distinguish a good argument from a bad one. Use the critical abilities you've developed to read your own work. Learn to stand outside your work and judge it, as you would an exercise in this text.

If you reason calmly and well, you will earn the respect of others, and you may learn that others merit your respect, too.

Writing Lesson 11

Let's see how much you've learned in this course. Write an argument for or against the following.

> *Student athletes should be given special leniency when the instructor assigns course marks.*

Your Cartoon Writing Lesson

Take a photo or make a very short video. Write a claim about what you see there, something someone might infer from the picture that isn't just a description of what's obviously in it. Exchange with a classmate, writing the best argument for or against the claim, or saying why you should suspend judgment.

More Cartoon Writing Lessons

For each of the following, write the best argument you can that has as its conclusion the claim that accompanies the cartoon. List only the premises and conclusion. If you believe the best argument is only weak, explain why.

1.

Manuel is angry.

2.

Lee is allergic to bee stings.

3.

Professor Zzzyzzx is trying to lose weight.

4.

Harry's rabbit was pregnant.

5.

Dr. E grew a beard.

6.

A. The man at the car in the parking lot is the person who ran over the bicycle.

B. The man in the car knew he ran over the bicycle and purposely didn't stop.

7.

This is a school for the handicapped.

8.

Dick shouldn't get a haircut here.

9.

The guy isn't shooting blanks.

10.

Spot ran away.

REASONING in the SCIENCES

When scientists reason, they make arguments, they make definitions, they deduce from hypotheses, they generalize, they look for cause and effect, they offer explanations.

The language that scientists use is intimidating, so it's hard to see that you already have the skills to understand and evaluate much of what they're doing. That's why in the first two chapters here you'll get some practice with how scientists talk.

Then you'll see how scientists use experiments to establish claims and how those relate to the theories and models they build. When you finish these chapters, you'll be ready to begin any science course, and you'll be able to understand much of what you read about science in the popular press or on the internet.

Have fun!

A Science Journal Article

Do you know how to evaluate reasoning in science? Write a (maximum) one page report evaluating the following journal article.

Cyclic Variations in Grass Growth

by V. D. Irby, M. S. Irby
Department of Physics and Astronomy
University of Kentucky, Lexington, KY

Grass exhibits a cyclical growth pattern surprisingly different from any other known plant. In this study, average grass blade heights have been measured, on a daily basis, over a 10 week period. Measurements were taken, utilizing vernier calipers, of the height of one hundred individual grass blades randomly chosen in a 10 foot square area positioned in front of an apartment complex in the Lexington, Kentucky area. (Measurements were also repeated with a different set of calipers to ensure reproducibility on a different apparatus.) The average of these measurements was computed and experimental error was taken as the standard deviation of the mean divided by the square root of the number of grass blades in the average. The procedure was repeated on a daily basis for a period of 10 weeks.

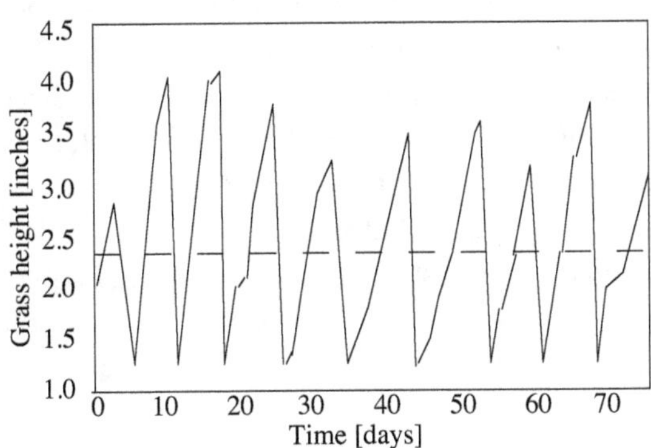

Figure 1: Experimental measurements of average grass height are plotted versus time. Solid line represents experimental data. Short dashed line indicates a "constant grass height" calculation and is normalized to the experimental data to produce the best fit.

Results and Discussion

The average grass heights, measured in this work, are plotted as a function of time in Figure 1. As one can readily see, there exists a periodic variation in average grass height with an approximate cycle of 7 to 10 days. Another intriguing observation is that there exists a minimum grass height, or "grass baseline," of about 1.3 inches.

Since the cyclic period of the grass is 7 to 10 days, one may conclude that grass height varies on a "week-about" basis. The physical mechanism responsible for this cyclic grass height phenomenon is not clearly understood at this time.

Annals of Improbable Research, vol. 1, no. 4, 1995

1S Getting Started in Science

Here are some examples to see that despite the technical language that scientists often use, we can understand and evaluate a lot of what they're doing.

Example 1 The feeding strategies of amphibians include their choice of prey and the ways in which they locate, capture, and ingest prey. Amphibians generally are considered to be feeding opportunists with their diets reflecting the availability of food of appropriate size. This may be true for some, but results of field and laboratory studies show that some species are selective in their feeding. W. E. Duellman and L. Trueb, *Biology of Amphibians*

Analysis The authors of this textbook intend for you to believe what they're saying. But they present no argument here, no reason to believe the claims they are making beyond their supposed authority.

Example 2 The causative agents of some diseases may be found in all parts of the carcasses of animals dying from those diseases. Therefore, carcasses should be disposed of as quickly and thoroughly as possible, by burning, sterilizing with heat, or burying deeply to prevent feral animals from disturbing the carcasses and further spreading the disease.
J. H. Galloway, *Farm Animal Health and Disease Control*

Analysis This is an argument. The word "therefore" cues us to that. The conclusion is "Carcasses (of animals dying from those diseases) should be disposed of as quickly and thoroughly as possible, by burning, sterilizing with heat, or burying deeply." One premise is "The causative agents of some diseases may be found in all parts of the carcasses of animals dying from those diseases." Another is "Disposing of carcasses prevents feral animals from disturbing the carcasses of animals dying from diseases and further spreading the disease," as it's meant as a reason to believe the conclusion. There's some rewriting here, but it doesn't change our understanding of what's said.

Example 3 Maria mixes some chemicals in a flask. She gets a new compound that is pink, just as she predicted. She goes to Manuel and says, "See, I was right" and points to the liquid in the flask.

Analysis Maria is attempting to convince Manuel. But pointing by itself isn't convincing at all: Manuel has to know what Maria is pointing at, what claim she is trying to show is true, and why the pointing matters for the truth of that claim. The attempts to convince in science that we're interested in are those that can be put into claims.

Example 4 I wish that everybody could feel the confidence of being alive in a fairly benign world, because I know that most of the advice and conclusions that scientists—

scientists not being very scientific about it—have made concerning our planet and the perilous journey we're on, is all bullshit. Because the place is very good at taking care of itself. We don't have to take care of it. And only by being able to read and understand the articles in places like *Science* and *Nature* and *Scientific American* can you really come to that conclusion. You're surrounded by this total barrage of faulty information that's been driven for economic reasons, information that's been basically made up for purposes of getting grants.

Kary Mullis, 1993 Nobel Laureate in chemistry,
Annals of Improbable Research, vol. 5, no. 2, 1999

Analysis This guy is a Nobel Laureate, so he's an expert. So now we can stop worrying about climate change? No. Mullis is making an argument, and we can use our critical thinking skills to see that it's weak, the premises are implausible, and there's no obvious repair. Scientists can be just as prejudiced and full of hot air as anyone else.

Example 5 From an article about attempts to program robots to learn as children learn:

> Such basic skills [forging links between different sensory perceptions] are essential for children because they pave the way for more complex tasks later. To appreciate this, take the seemingly simple job of understanding what someone is referring to when they point at an object. Only other apes and dolphins are able to grasp that there's something "over there" worth looking at, and then find the object of interest. This is one form of a skill, called joint attention, which [the robot] needs to have because so much social interaction depends on it, says Scasselati [a cognitive scientist and one of the robot's principal architects].
>
> *New Scientist*, "Booting up baby," May 22, 1999, pp. 43–46

Analysis I read this and said to myself: this is false. Dogs understand pointing very well, if we can judge by their behavior. That's how they hunt in packs, by following the gaze of other dogs. With a little effort I got my dogs to look at my gaze and pick out an animal they should chase when hunting. It took a little more effort to get them to look where I pointed with my hand. But the prestige of the journal made me doubt my own experience and reasoning! I had to remind myself that personal experience is my best guide.

Exercises for Chapter 1S

1. Bring in a copy of the first page of a chapter from some science textbook and mark any sentence in it that is *not* a claim.

For Exercises 2–8, identify whether it's a claim. If it is, give a contradictory for it.

2. If some laboratory rat lives longer than four years, then a paper will be written about it.

3. What a wonderous spectacle is the complex and highly evolved chemistry of the living world!
M. Olomucki, *The Chemistry of Life*

4. Butterflies go through the following stages in their lifetime:
egg → caterpillar → pupa → adult → butterfly.

5. (*The gas law*) $PV = kT$ where P stands for the pressure, V for the volume, and T for the absolute temperature of a fixed volume of gas, and k is a constant.

6. Given a quantity of radium, after 1,620 years, approximately half the radium atoms in the quantity will have transmuted into radon atoms.

7. When a steady current is flowing through a conductor, the strength of the current is proportional to the potential difference between its ends.

8. (Mendel) When a large number of pea plants having round, yellow seeds are crossed with a large number of pea plants having wrinkled, green seeds, the second generation of round to wrinkled and of yellow to green is approximately 3:1.

For Exercises 9–17 answering the following:

Argument? (yes or no)

Conclusion (if unstated, add it):

Premises:

Evaluation:

9. An organism is composed essentially of macromolecular compounds, among which are nucleic acids and proteins. Even the smallest organism contains a few thousand different species of macromolecules. The simplest organism is therefore a relatively complex machine.
André Lwoff, *Biological Order*

10. Vaccination has been a practical method of protection against transmissible disease since Pasteur developed vaccines against some of the common diseases of livestock and poultry, among them some of the diseases which are most important today. No vaccine is absolutely safe or completely effective all the time; however, the practical value of vaccines has been demonstrated in many millions of protected animals.
J. H. Galloway, *Farm Animal Health and Disease Control*

11. The insane notoriously give way to all their emotions with little or no restraint; and I am informed by Dr. J. Crichton Browne, that nothing is more characteristic of simple melancholia, even in the male sex, than a tendency to weep on the slightest occasion, or from no cause. They also weep disproportionately on the occurrence of any real cause of grief. The length of time during which some patients weep is astonishing, as well as the amount of tears which they shed.
Charles Darwin, *The Expression of Emotions in Man and Animals*

12. The universe began with a big bang. Therefore, there was an instant when all matter was energy.

13. Suzy: Boy, Ralph's donkey sure likes broccoli.
Tom: Why do you say that?
Suzy: Because when Ralph went over to her just now with some broccoli, she came running to him and ate it real quickly. Then she started nuzzling the bag that Ralph has the broccoli in.

14. So we understand the reasons for the ongoing evolution of matter toward more complex and more perfected forms. Progress is not accomplished "actively," guided by some predetermined "plan" or "goal," but by the elimination of the least well-adapted structures by what could be called an upward leveling. Natural selection applies not only to living organisms but also to molecules, even small ones: any chemical entity exists only if the conditions in its environment allow it. The chemical development of matter was easier in that Nature did not have to show a great deal of creativity in this area.
    Martin Olomucki, *The Chemistry of Life*

15. Our atmosphere is unique in the solar system. It is composed of 78 percent nitrogen, 21 percent oxygen, and minor amounts of other gases. The earliest atmosphere was much different and consisted largely of hydrogen, carbon dioxide, and water vapor. The present atmosphere began to form as soon as organisms evolved and through photosynthesis developed the ability to extract carbon dioxide from the air and expel oxygen. Thus, the oxygen in today's atmosphere is and was produced by life.
    W. K. Hamblin, *Introduction to Physical Geology*

16. In eclipses the outline is always curved: and, since it is the interposition of the earth that makes the eclipse, the form of this line will be caused by the form of the earth's surface, which is therefore spherical. Again, our observations of the stars make it evident, not only that the earth is circular [spherical], but also that it is of no great size. For quite a small change of position to south or north causes a manifest alteration of the horizon. There is much change, I mean, in the stars which are overhead, and the stars seen are different, as one moves northward or southward. Indeed, there are some stars seen in Egypt and the neighborhood of Cyprus which are not seen in the northerly regions; and stars, which in the north are never beyond the range of observation, in those regions rise and set. All of which goes to show not only that the earth is circular in shape, but also that it is a sphere of no great size: for otherwise the effect of so slight a change of place would not be so quickly apparent.
    Aristotle, *On the Heavens*, II.14.297, translated by Richard McKeon

17. The liver is not the seat of the soul, as was believed by many of the ancients. The proof is that the liver can be removed and another transplanted and the person's soul remains the same. Indeed, every part of the human body can be removed, or removed and transplanted, and, except for the degradations of suffering, the person's soul remains unchanged. All that is, save one: the brain. Damage that even a little, and you will see the person's soul in throes. Thus, the brain is the seat of the soul.

Evaluate the following arguments and refutations.

18. UFO enthusiasts often claim that the flying saucers they "observe" are held suspended in the air and obtain their propulsion from a self-generated magnetic field. However, it is not possible for a vehicle to hover, speed up, or change direction solely by means of its own magnetic field. The proof of this lies in the fundamental principle of physics that nothing happens except through interactions between pairs of objects. A space vehicle may generate a powerful magnetic field, but in the absence of another magnetic field to push against it, it can neither move nor support itself in midair. The earth possesses a

magnetic field, but it is weak—about 1% of that generated by a compass needle. For a UFO to be levitated by reacting against the earth's magnetic field, its own field would have to be so enormously strong that it could be detected by any magnetometer in the world. . . . And, finally, as the magnetic UFO traveled about the earth, it would induce electrical currents in every power line within sight, blowing out circuit breakers and in general wreaking havoc. It would not go unnoticed.

Milton A. Rothman, *A Physicist's Guide to Skepticism*

19. Conscious states, so defined, are real and irreducible; you cannot get rid of them. But consciousness as intrinsically subjective, qualitative, unified, and intentional is an embarrassment to a certain old-fashioned, materialist conception of the world, and there have been many attempts to get rid of it by denying its existence or pretending it was something else. Behaviorism said that consciousness was nothing but publicly observable behavior; physicalism said that it was nothing but physical states of the brain; functionalism said it was just a causal mechanism mediating between input stimuli and output behavior; and Strong Artificial Intelligence said it was no more than a number of computer programs that happen to be running in the brain but could be implemented in any sufficiently complex hardware. One has only to state these views clearly for their implausibility to seem obvious. Future generations considering late-twentieth-century intellectual life will surely wonder how serious people could have believed such stuff.

John R. Searle, "Consciousness: What we still don't know"
The New York Review of Books, January 13, 2005

2S Definitions in Science

Agreeing on a good definition in science is an important step to starting research. Consider, for example, what E. Mayr says in *Populations, Species and Evolution*:

> Species are groups of interbreeding natural populations that are reproductively isolated from each other.

Now there are two kinds of crows in Europe: the black crow and the hooded crow. The former is completely black, while the latter is part black and part gray. These used to be called different species, but some intermediate forms occur due to interbreeding in various places. Biologists now classify those kinds as subspecies. It seems that they take the word "isolated" in Mayr's definition to mean "total isolation"; by that definition species can't interbreed. Other biologists point to species that are highly isolated but do interbreed, just in very restricted areas and only rarely. They are interpreting Mayr's definition in terms of relative isolation. For them, species can interbreed. The "deep" question about whether species can interbreed turns into a question about how to *define* "species."

Exercises for Chapter 2S

State clearly any definitions in the following passages.

1. Sterility means *incapable of reproduction,* and so, in the hygienic sense, the complete absence of any form of life. The word is sometimes used more loosely to indicate absence of pathogens, ignoring the small number of harmless microorganisms which may not be destroyed. The word *sterility* should always be used in its strict sense.
   J. H. Galloway, *Farm Animal Health and Disease Control*

2. Subjective data might be described as the individual's perspective of a situation or a series of events. This information cannot be determined by the nurse independent of interaction or communication with the individual. Subjective data are frequently obtained during the nursing history and include the client's perceptions, feelings, and ideas about self and personal health status. Examples include the client's descriptions of pain, weakness, frustration, nausea, or embarrassment.

   Objective data consist of observable and measurable information. This information is usually obtained through the senses—sight, smell, hearing, and touch—during the physical examination of the client. Examples of objective data include respiratory rate, blood pressure, presence of edema, and weight. *Nursing Process and Nursing Diagnosis*, 3rd edition, P. Iyer, B. Taptich, D. Bernocchi-Losey

3. Metamorphic rocks are rocks that have been altered by heat, pressure, and the chemical action of pore fluids (water and early melted mineral matter) to such an extent that new minerals are formed that are stable in an environment of higher temperature and pressure.
   W. K. Hamblin, *Introduction to Physical Geology*

Are the following good definitions?

4. Communication is the process by which the behavior of one animal affects the behavior of others; that is, it changes the probability distribution of other animals' behavior.
   Claud A. Bramblett, *Patterns of Primate Behavior,* 2nd edition

5. Communication is when one animal intentionally affects the behavior of another.

6. A ghost is a translucent being that lives in abandoned houses.

7. Compare the following.
   a. Since the time of thalidomide, it has become widely recognized that drugs consumed by a mother during pregnancy can alter the development of the fetus. Drugs that cause such malformations are called teratogens (literally, "monster makers").
      William A. McKim, *Drugs and Behavior*, 5th edition
   b. Teratogens are environmental agents (such as drugs or viruses), diseases (such as German measles), and physical conditions (such as malnutrition) that impair physical development and lead to birth defects and even death.
      Richard A. Griggs, *Psychology*

8. Evaluate this disagreement.
   Lee: Single cell animals have a nervous system because they have a way to transmit electrical signals in the cell.
   Maria: Boy, are you wrong. Nervous systems are composed of cells, so clearly single cell animals can't have a nervous system.

9. *Definitions of "nursing"*
   Evaluate the following definitions from *Nursing Process and Nursing Diagnosis,* 3rd edition, P. Iyer, B. Taptich, D. Bernocchi-Losey, pp. 3–6 (the proposer of the definition is given in parentheses).
   a. Assisting the individual, sick or well, in the performance of those activities contributing to health or its recovery (or to peaceful death) that s/he would perform unaided if s/he had the necessary strength, will or knowledge. (Virginia Henderson)
   b. A human interaction whose goal is the promotion of wholeness for all people, well or sick. (Myra Levine)
   c. A science with an organized body of abstract knowledge arrived at by scientific research and logical analysis; it is an art in the imaginative and creative use of the body of knowledge in human service. (Martha Rogers)
   d. The practice of nursing as a registered professional is defined as diagnosing and treating human responses to actual or potential physical and emotional health problems through such services as casefinding, health teaching, health counseling, and provision of care supportive or restorative of life and well being . . . and executing medical regimens as prescribed by a licensed or otherwise legally authorized physician or dentist. (New Jersey Nurse Practice Act, 1993)

10. Bring in and evaluate a definition from a science course you have taken or are taking.

3S Experiments

A. Evidence and Experiments

What counts as evidence in science?

> ***Observational claim*** An observational claim is one that is established by personal experience or observation in an experiment.
>
> ***Evidence*** Evidence is usually the observational claims that are used as premises of an argument. Sometimes the term refers to all the premises.

What do we mean by "observation in an experiment"?

A physicist might say that she saw an electron traverse a cloud chamber, when what she actually saw was lines on a computer monitor. A biologist may say he saw the nucleus of a cell, when what he saw was an image projected through a microscope. In both cases these people are not reporting on direct personal experience but on deductions made from that personal experience. However, those claims made by deduction from the perceptions arising from certain types of experiments are, by consensus in that area of science, deemed to be observations.

Within any one area of science there is a high level of agreement on what counts as an observational claim. But from one area of science to another that standard may vary. A physicist beginning work in biology may well question why certain claims are taken as "obvious" deductions from experience, such as the reality of what you see through a microscope. But after the general form of the inference —from such direct claims about personal experience to the observational claims— is made explicit once or twice, she is likely to accept such claims as undisputed evidence. If she doesn't, she's questioning the basis of that science.

When new techniques are introduced into a science or when a new area of science is developing, there is often controversy about what counts as an observational claim. Galileo's report of moons around Jupiter was received with considerable skepticism because at that time telescopes distorted a lot. In ethology, the study of animal behavior in natural settings, there is no agreement yet on what counts as an observational claim, and you can find different journal articles using different standards. For example, consider:

Some would describe this as an incident of the first chimpanzee getting angry and chasing the second one away, and then the second returning to pacify and re-establish bonds with the first. That's what they saw. But others say that such a description is loaded with assumptions that have not been established, such as that chimpanzees have emotions sufficiently similar to humans to label as anger and that chimpanzees intend to accomplish certain ends, rather than just acting instinctually.

One constraint we impose on reports of observations is that they should be reproducible. We believe that nature is uniform. What can happen once can happen again *if* the conditions are the same. Scientists typically won't accept reports on observations they are unable to reproduce.

> ***Duplicable experiments and reproducible results*** An experiment is *duplicable* if it is described clearly enough that others can follow the method to obtain observations. The *results* of an experiment are *reproducible* if whenever the experiment is duplicated the observations of the new experiment are in close agreement with the observations of the original experiment.
>
> When an experiment has been duplicated and the results reproduced, it's said that the experiment was *replicated*.

The difficulty is to specify exactly what conditions are required and what counts as close enough agreement. It's fairly easy in chemistry and physics; less so in biology; much more difficult in psychology or ethology. It's virtually impossible in history and economics, which means history and economics are not sciences, except to the extent that we can describe very general conditions that may recur.

Examples Are the procedures described in the following passages clearly enough described that they could be duplicated?

Example 1 *A recipe from a famous coffeehouse*

Vegetarian Chili

2 cans each (include liquid): Pinto beans, Chili beans, Great Northern beans
Red beans, Kidney beans

1 # 10 can diced tomatoes
Garlic, 6-8 cloves chopped
Bell pepper, 1 chopped
Jalapeño peppers, 3 chopped
Chili powder 2 soup spoons
Onions, 2 chopped or in food processor
Paprika, 1 soup spoon

Put in soup tureen and heat to boil for 1 hour. Take care the beans don't stick to the bottom.

Analysis Any expert in the subject (any person who has worked in a commercial kitchen) will know what a #10 can of tomatoes is. Though "chopped" and "soup spoon" may be unclear, anyone who saw the chili being made would be able to duplicate the preparation.

Example 2 *Feeding behavior of primates*

General Methodology

Data were collected simultaneously on both the activity of the animals and the forest strata at which this activity took place. Counts were made at five-minute intervals of the numbers of individuals engaged in each of the six activities and the level of the forest in which the activity was performed. The following activities were recorded: feeding—the animal actually in the process of ingesting or picking a food item; grooming—mutual and self-grooming were distinguished for certain analyses; resting—no body displacement, or feeding, or grooming, sunning, etc.; moving—movement of an individual, including individual foraging; travel—movement of the group; and other—e.g., sunning, play, fighting. These data were collected only after the animals under observation were reasonably habituated to the observer. Each observation of an animal constituted an individual activity record (IAR) collected in a given five-minute time sample. Because of the focus of the study and the difficulty in keeping continuous contact with an individual animal, no attempt was made to follow individual animals nor to collect statistical data on specific age or sex classes. Statistical analyses of the data were complicated by the fact that some of the activity records were not independent of each other. The methods used for the statistical analyses are reported in Sussman *et al.*

To determine levels of the forest, I used Richards' (1957) categories of forest stratification as a model and assigned numbers of one to five to the forest layers. Level 1 is the ground layer of the forest; it includes the herb and grass vegetation. Level 2 is the shrub layer, from one to three metres above the ground. This layer is usually found in patches throughout the continuous canopy forest, but is much more dense and is the dominant layer in the brush and scrub regions. Level 3 of the forest consists of small trees, the lower branches of larger trees, and saplings of the larger species of trees. This layer is about three to seven metres high. Level 4 is the continuous or closed canopy layer. It is about five to 15 metres high. The dominant tree of the closed canopy, at all three forests, is the kily (*Tamarindus indica*). Level 5 of the forest is the emergent layer and consists of the crowns of those trees which rise above the closed canopy. It is usually over 15 metres high.

All three forests in which I made intensive studies were primary forests and the tree layers were quite distinct. In most cases, the particular level in which an animal was observed could be distinguished easily. If I could not determine the forest level unambiguously, I did not record it.

Observations recorded in this manner may be biased because animals that are active in certain levels of the forest may be more difficult to see than those active at other levels. I attempted to minimize this problem by following a relatively small number of animals (usually from five to ten) throughout a period of continuous observation, keeping track of all the animals. For *Lemur fulvus* this usually included the whole group, which was small and, for the most part, moved together. It was more difficult to do this when observing *Lemur catta,* for which it was often necessary to follow and observe subgroups of the larger group. The larger group would disperse, especially during foraging and feeding, and during afternoon rest periods.

Day ranges were mapped by following a group from one night resting site in the morning to the time it settled in another night resting site in the evening. The location of the group was plotted throughout the day on a prepared map of the forest and the amount of time the group spent in each location was recorded. Home ranges include the sum of all the day ranges. The data on home ranges are limited, however, and probably do not represent total home ranges of the groups, since the study in each area was limited to a few months.

"Feeding behaviour of *Lemur Catta* and *Lemur Fulvus*"
R. W. Sussman, in *Primate Ecology,* ed. T. H. Clutton-Brock

Analysis It is difficult to be more precise than this in ethology. The description of the methodology is clear enough to count as duplicable, perhaps even by someone who isn't an expert in the subject. Whether the observations are reproducible will depend on how closely we expect them to agree with the ones in this paper.

Note that the author has not stated what time of year the observations were made, nor the percentage of males versus females in the groups he studied. These are not part of the conditions that need to be duplicated; implicitly, the author is saying that they don't matter. If it turns out in duplicating this experiment different observations are obtained at different times of the year, then the time of year would have to be added as part of the conditions that are important and have to be duplicated.

Example 3 *The refraction of light rays*

In the wall or window of a room let *F* be some hole through which solar rays *OF* are transmitted, while other holes elsewhere have been carefully sealed so that no light enters from any other place. The darkening of the room, however, is not necessary; it only enables

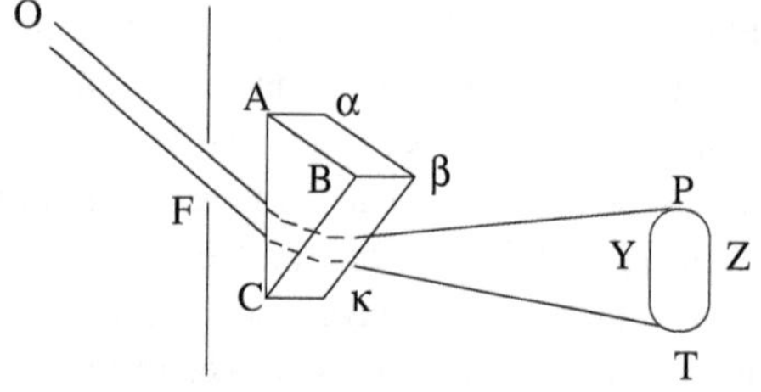

the experiment to turn out somewhat more clearly. Then place at that hole a triangular glass prism AαBβCκ that refracts the rays *OF* transmitted through it toward *PYTZ*.

From *Optica,* Part 1, Lecture 1 by Isaac Newton, 1670, translated from the Latin in *The Optical Papers of Issac Newton,* ed. Alan E. Shapiro

Analysis This is very clear because of the diagram. It can be and often has been duplicated, and the results were reproduced.

Example 4 *Measurement of photon bunching in a thermal light beam*

The experimental setup . . . is shown in Fig. 1. A light beam from a low-pressure Hg^{198} gas discharge lamp passed through a pin-hole *P* (diameter 0.54 mm), an optical filter F_1 that isolated the blue 5461-Å line, and a linear polarizer F_2. The beam fell on a 56 AVP photomultiplier through a rectangular aperture *S* (0.37 x 0.47 mm^2), whose dimensions were small enough to ensure a degree of coherence of at least 90% across the beam.

The pulses from the photomultipler were shortened by reflection in a 1-nsec clipping line, and were fed to a specially designed gated pulse counter, which registered an output whenever two pulses appeared at the anode of the photomultiplier with a time separation lying between t_1 and t_2. The time t_1 was determined by the difference of two cable lengths, and could be varied by varying one of the lengths. t_1–t_2 was determined by the width of the gating pulse, and remained constant and equal to about 7.5 nsec as t_1 was varied.

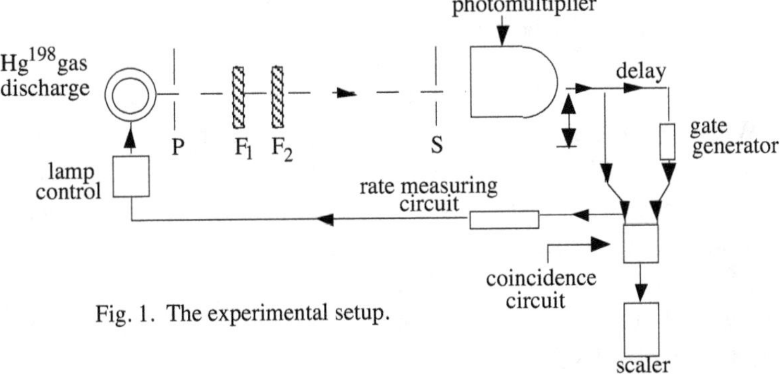

Fig. 1. The experimental setup.

From *Phys. Rev. Lett*., 1965, by B. L. Morgan and L. Mandel

Analysis If this is duplicable, you'd have to be an expert to follow the directions.

Example 5 *Testing for anomalous cognition* (*ESP*)

The vast majority of anomalous cognition experiments at SRI [Stanford Research Institute] and SAIC [Science Applications International Corporation] used a technique known as remote viewing. In these experiments, a viewer attempts to draw or describe (or both) a target location, photograph, object, or short video segment. All known channels for receiving the information are blocked. Sometimes the viewer is assisted by a monitor who asks the viewer questions; of course, in such cases the monitor is blind to the answer as well. Sometimes a sender is looking at the target during the session, but sometimes there is no sender. In most cases the viewer eventually receives a feedback in which he or she learns the correct answer, thus making it difficult to rule out precognition [knowing the future] as the explanation for positive results, whether or not there was a sender.

Most anomalous cognition experiments at SRI and SAIC were of the free-response type, in which viewers were asked simply to describe the target. . . .

The SAIC remote-viewing experiments and all but the early ones at SRI used a statistical evaluation method known as rank-order judging. After the completion of a remote viewing, a judge who is blind to the true target (called a blind judge) is shown the response and five potential targets, one of which is the correct answer and the other four of which are "decoys." Before the experiment is conducted, each of those five choices must have had an equal chance of being selected as the actual target. The judge is asked to assign a rank to each of the possible targets, where a rank of 1 means it matches the response most closely, and a rank of 5 means it matches the least.

The rank of the correct target is the numerical score for that remote viewing. By chance alone the actual target would receive each of the five ranks with equal likelihood, since, despite what the response said, the target matching it best would have the same chance of selection as the one matching it second best and so on. The average rank by chance would be 3. Evidence for anomalous cognition occurs when the average rank over a series of trials is significantly lower than 3. (Notice that a rank of 1 is the best possible score for each viewing.)

This scoring method is conservative in the sense that it gives no extra credit for an excellent match. A response that describes the target almost perfectly will achieve the same rank of 1 as a response that contains only enough information to pick the target as the best choice out of the five possible choices.

"An assessment of the evidence for psychic functioning"
by Jessica Utts, *The Journal of Parapsychology,* vol. 59, no. 4, 1995

Analysis What does the author mean by "All known channels for receiving information are blocked"? We need to know the exact layout of the room where the experiment was done. "In most cases the viewer eventually receives feedback"—how often, under what circumstances, exactly when? We need to know how close the "decoys" were to the true target. Who are the judges? This is crucial because different judges from different backgrounds may classify differently. The experiment is not duplicable. Even if you watched the experiment being done, you couldn't duplicate it because it's not clear what the author considers important and what she considers irrelevant in the setup.

Even if it were possible to duplicate the experiment and get the same results, it's not clear that by chance alone the actual target would not receive each of the five ranks with equal likelihood. Perhaps this experiment would show the opposite.

Example 6 *The growth of living nerve cells in vitro*

The immediate object of the following experiments was to obtain a method by which the end of a growing nerve could be brought under direct observation while alive, in order that a correct conception might be had regarding what takes place as the fibre extends during embryonic development from the nerve center out to the periphery.

The method employed was to isolate pieces of embryonic tissue known to give rise to nerve fibres, as for example, the whole or fragments of the medullary tube or ectoderm from the branchial region, and to observe their further development. The pieces were taken from frog embryos about three mm. long, at which stage, i.e. shortly after the closure of the medullary folds, there is no visible differentiation of the nerve elements. After carefully dissecting it out the piece of tissue is removed by a fine pipette to a cover slip upon which is a drop of lymph freshly drawn from one of the lymph sacs of an adult frog. The lymph clots very quickly, holding the tissue in a fixed position. The cover slip is then inverted over a hollow slide and the rim sealed with paraffin. When reasonable aseptic precautions are taken, tissues will live under these conditions for a week and in some cases specimens have been kept alive for nearly four weeks. Such specimens may be readily observed from day to day under highly magnifying powers.

Ross Harrison, *Proceedings of the Society for Experimental Medicine and Biology*, vol. 4, 1907 (quoted in *The Origins and Growth of Biology,* ed. Arthur Rook)

Analysis This is the first method ever recorded for maintaining living cells outside the body. It is very much like the recipe from the *Dog & Duck*. Even for an expert it would have been difficult to duplicate it from just reading this.

The morals of these examples

- It's hard to describe an experiment clearly enough to duplicate it.
- What is described in an experiment is what needs to be duplicated. What is not described is deemed irrelevant to obtaining similar observations.
- What counts as duplicable is going to be relative to the particular scientific discipline. Expert knowledge in the area may make some descriptions clear.
- What counts as close enough agreement for observations to be deemed reproducible is going to depend on the particular scientific discipline.
- New experimental designs are often sketchily described, but they are accepted because people go to the lab, see how it is done, then go back to their labs and do the experiment, and then pass that on to other people.

B. Experiments to Test a Generalization

Flo: Spot barks. And Wanda's dog Ralph barks. And Dr. E's dogs Anubis and Buddy bark. So all dogs bark.

Becky: Yeah. Let's go over to Maple Street and see if all the dogs there bark, too.

Flo is generalizing. Relative to her experience it's a pretty good generalization. Becky wants to test the generalization.

Suppose that A, B, C, D are given as inductive evidence for a generalization G. (Some other plausible unstated premises may also be needed, but we'll keep those in the background.) Then we have that G explains A, B, C, D.

But if G is true, we can see that some other claims must be true, instances of the generalization G, say L, M, N. If those are true, then G would explain them, too. For example, Rodolfo barks, Lady barks, Fido barks, . . .

That is, G *explains* A, B, C, D and *predicts* L, M, N, where the difference between the explanation and the prediction is that in the explanation we know that the claim being explained is true, whereas we don't know if the prediction is true.

Suppose we devise experiments and find that L, M, N are indeed true. Then "A, B, C, D + L, M, N therefore G" is a better argument for G than we had before. At the very least it has more instances of the generalization as premises.

But how do more instances of a generalization prove the generalization better? They can if (i) they are from different kinds of situations, that is A, B, C, D + L, M, N cover a more representative sample of possible instances of G than do just A, B, C, and D. And this is typically what happens. We deduce claims from G for situations that we had not previously considered.

And (ii) because we had not previously considered the kind of instances L, M, N of the generalization G, we have some confidence that we haven't arrived at G by manipulating the data, selecting situations that would establish just this hypothesis.

One of the best ways to test an hypothesis-generalization is to try to falsify it. Trying to falsify a generalization just means that we are consciously trying to come up with instances of the generalization to test that are as different as we can imagine from A, B, C, D. Trying to falsify is just a good way to ensure (i) and (ii).

C. Experiments Start with a Question

Example 7 Professor Shibokbok asks each of the 103 students in her psychology class to interview at least two people, asking what they've thought during the last two days. Then she and her students examine the answers, going over them again and again, classifying the responses. Eventually they find a correlation—between the weight of the person and his or her view of public transportation.

Analysis There's always some correlation you can find if you look long enough at some mass of observations. But that's going backwards. Unless you start with a question, and have some criteria for what counts as an observation, and follow the usual rules for generalizing and causal reasoning, it's nonsense.

Example 8 Suzy: I've been studying this astrology book seriously.
I think you should definitely go into science.
Lee: I've been thinking of that, too, but what's astrology got to do with it?
Suzy: Your birthday is in late January, so you're an Aquarian?
Lee: Yeah, January 28.
Suzy: Well, Aquarians are generally scientific but eccentric.
Lee: C'mon. That can't be right.
Suzy: Sure it is. Copernicus, Galileo, and Thomas Edison were all Aquarians.

Analysis Suzy's looking at some "data" and drawing a conclusion. But to justify her claim, she should start with a large sample and see whether there's a correlation between those who are Aquarians and those who are scientific but eccentric. Here it's just selective attention, a bad generalization based on anecdotal evidence.

Observations are meant to answer a question, to test an hypothesis, to give some evidence to believe or disbelieve a claim. Otherwise, there would be no justification for the conclusions you'd draw.

> ***The fallacy of mining the data*** It is a mistake in reasoning to comb through a mass of observations looking for some correlation when the data was not collected for the purpose of studying that correlation, and then claim that the correlation is significant.

Key Words	experiment	reproducible results
	observational claim	replicated experiment
	evidence	prediction
	duplicable experiment	mining the data

Exercises for Chapter 3S

1. What is an observational claim?
2. What counts as evidence in science?
3. a. What does it mean to say that an experiment is duplicable?
   b. What does it mean to say that the results of an experiment can be reproduced?
   c. What does it mean to say that an experiment is replicated?
4. You want to repeat an experiment you've read about. What do you need to duplicate?
5. What is the difference between an explanation and a prediction?
6. Give a prediction that is not about the future. How would you check whether it is true?
7. How can we show that a general claim used as an explanation is true?
8. a. What is "mining the data"?
   b. Why is that not good science?
9. What question is the experiment for growing nerve cells in Example 6 meant to answer?
10. Watch someone cooking a special dish. Write down a recipe so that someone else could make the same dish. Give it to a classmate to prepare the dish. Was it the same?
11. For five minutes watch two dogs that are active. Write down what you see. Give it to a classmate to evaluate whether what you wrote were your perceptions or what you deduced from your perceptions. (Extra credit if you introduce a cat into the experiment.)
12. Harry: You have beautiful blue eyes.
    Suzy: Huh? My eyes are brown.
    Harry: No, they're blue.

Suzy: You're crazy, they're brown.
Harry: How do you know?
Suzy: I've looked at them in the mirror every day. And eyes don't change color.
Harry: But how do you know that mirrors don't change the color of your eyes? After all, you can't ever see them without a mirror.

Devise an experiment and an argument to convince Suzy that Harry is wrong.

13. An electron is no more (and no less) hypothetical than a star. Nowadays we count electrons one by one in a Geiger counter, as we count the stars one by one on a photographic plate. In what sense can an electron be called more unobservable than a star? I am not sure whether I ought to say that I have seen an electron; but I have just the same doubt whether I have seen a star. If I have seen one, I have seen the other. I have seen a small disc of light surrounded by diffraction rings which has not the least resemblance to what a star is supposed to be; but the name "star" is given to the object in the physical world which some hundreds of years ago started a chain of causation which has resulted in this particular light-pattern. Similarly, in a Wilson cloud chamber I have seen a trail not in the least resembling what an electron is supposed to be; but the name "electron" is given to the object in the physical world which has caused this trail to appear. How can it possibly be maintained that a hypothesis is introduced in the one case and not in the other? Sir Arthur Eddington, *New Pathways in Science*

Argue for one (or more) of the following:

a. An electron is not real like a star is real.
b. An electron is just as real as a star.
c. Neither a star nor an electron is as real as a dog.

Evaluate the arguments in Exercises 14 and 15 by answering the following:

Argument? (yes or no)

Conclusion:

Premises:

Additional premises needed to make it valid or strong (if none, say so):

Method of refutation?

Classify: valid strong ——— weak

Good argument?

14. Thus it is observed by the easy experiment of opening an artery at any time in living animals that blood is contained in the arteries naturally.

In order that on the other hand we may be more certain that the force of pulsation does not belong to the artery or that the material contained in the arteries is not the producer of the pulsation, for in truth this force depends for its strength upon the heart. Besides, we see that an artery bound by a cord no longer beats under the cord, it will be permitted to undertake an extensive dissection of the artery of the groin or of the thigh, and to take a small tube made of reed of such thickness as is the capacity of the artery and to insert it by cutting in such a way that the upper part of the tube reaches higher into the cavity of the artery than the upper part of the dissection, and in the same manner also that the lower portion of the tube is introduced downward farther than the lower part of the dissection, and thus the ligature of the artery which constricts its calibre above the cannula is passed by a circuit.

To be sure when this is done the blood and likewise the vital spirit run through the artery even as far as the foot; in fact the whole portion of the artery replaced by the canula beats no longer. Moreover, when the ligature has been cut, that part of the artery which is beyond the cannula shows no less pulsation than the portion above.

Andreas Vesalius, *Fabrica,* VII. 19, written in 1543, translated by S. Lambert (also in *The Origins and Growth of Biology,* ed. Arthur Rook, p. 120)

15. *Copernicus on whether the earth rotates*
It is claimed that the earth is at rest in the center of the universe . . . Ptolemy feared that the earth and all earthly things if set in rotation would be dissolved by the action of nature, for the functioning of nature is something entirely different from artifice, or from that which could be contrived by the human mind. But why did he not fear the same and indeed in much higher degree, for the universe, whose motion would have to be as much more rapid as the heavens are larger than the earth? Or have the heavens become infinite just because they have been removed from the center by the inexpressible force of the motion; while otherwise, if they were at rest, they would collapse? Certainly if this argument were true the extent of the heavens would become infinite. For the more they were driven aloft by the outward impulse of the motion, the more rapid would the motion become because of the ever increasing circle which it would have to describe in the space of twenty-four hours; and conversely, if the motion increased, the immensity of the heavens would also increase. Thus velocity would augment size into infinity, and size, velocity. But according to the physical law that the infinite can neither be traversed, nor can it for any reason have motion, the heavens would, however, of necessity be at rest.

Copernicus, *Dialogue on the Two Chief World Systems,* translated by Stillman Drake (also in *The Origins and Growth of Physical Science,* eds. D. L. Hurd and J. J. Kipling, pp. 106-107)

Many experiments in science are designed to find out whether there is cause and effect, like cause-in-population studies (Chapter 15.D). Evaluate Exercises 16 and 17 by answering:

What causal claim is at issue?

What type of cause-in-population experiment, if any, was done?

Evaluate the evidence for the causal claim.

How would you further test the claim?

16. Several studies indicate that people who smoke cigarettes have an increased risk for low back pain and prolapsed disk [references given]. Individuals who have not smoked for more than a year, however, do not appear to have an increased risk, as least for prolapsed lumbar disk [reference given]. Table 6 shows that current smokers have almost twice the risk for prolapsed lumbar disk as those who have never smoked or who are former smokers. In the same study [reference given] it was estimated that the risk in current

smokers is increased by about 20% for every 10 cigarettes smoked per day on the average. Possible mechanisms for the association between smoking and low back pain and prolapsed disk include decreased diffusion of nutrients into the intervertebral disk among smokers [reference given], and increased pressure on the low back from the frequent coughing experienced by many smokers.

Table 6. Estimated Relative Risk for Prolapsed Lumbar Intervertebral Disk According to Cigarette Smoking Status, Connecticut

Smoking Status	Estimated Relative Risk	95% Confidence Limits
Never smoked (referent group)	1.0	—
Current smoker (smoked in past year)	1.7	1.0–2.5
Former smoker (smoked, but not in past year)	1.0	0.6–1.7

*Relative risk = risk in those exposed to factor divided by risk in those not exposed (referent group).

Jennifer L. Kelsy, Anne L. Golden, Diane J. Mundt
Rheumatic Disease Clinics of America, vol. 16, no. 3, 1990

17. *Sleepwalking and spontaneous parapsychological experiences: a note*
Two studies were conducted in which a questionnaire in Spanish with a true and false response format was used. It included, among other items, five questions about parapsychological experiences (waking ESP, dream ESP, apparitions, out-of-body experiences, and auras) and one question about somnambulism as follows: Some people have told me that I have sometimes walked in my sleep. The studies were conducted at the Centro Caribeno de Estudios Postgraduados, a private institute of graduate psychology studies in San Juan, Puerto Rico. In the first study, 120 questionnaires were collected by masters and doctoral students taking a graduate psychology course offered by the author. The students collected questionnaires from family, friends, and acquaintances outside the institution. In the second study, 52 questionnaires were collected by a colleague in two of his graduate courses. To measure frequency of psi [parapsychological] experiences, an index was formed from the above-mentioned five questions, assigning a score of 1 for true and a score of 0 for false answers.

The composite parapsychological experiences measure produced scores with the following characteristics: Study 1 (N = 120, M = 2.03, Range: 0–5, SD = 1.59); and Study 2 (N = 52, M = 1.48, Range: 0–4, SD = 1.23). The frequency of positive replies to the sleepwalking question was 17% for Study 1 (N = 119) and 24% for Study 2 (N = 51).

In the first study, those participants who replied affirmatively to the sleepwalking question (N = 20) obtained a mean of parapsychological experiences of 2.60, as compared to a mean of 1.94 for those who replied negatively, (N = 99), t(117) = 1.70, p = .045 (one-tailed), r = .16. In the second study, those with sleepwalking experiences (N = 12) obtained a mean of parapsychological experiences of 2.00, as compared to a mean of 1.28 for those without, N = 39, t(49) = 1.80, p = .039 (one-tailed), r = .25. The combined assessment of the p values in both studies produced a Stouffer z of 2.45, p = .01 (one-tailed). The combined effect size, using a Fisher z transformation [reference given] was .21. The difference between the effect sizes of Study 1 (r = .16) and Study 2 (r = .25) was not significant, z = –.52, p = .603 (two-tailed).

The results support the idea that sleepwalking is related to the frequency of parapsychological experiences. This, in turn, provides further evidence of a low-magnitude association between parapsychological experiences and dissociation. Further work should be conducted using better measures of sleepwalking, probing for both the frequency of experiences and for the stage in the experiencer's life in which sleepwalking took place or was most frequent. Habitual sleepwalkers should also be compared to nonsleepwalkers in future studies. . . .

Carlos S. Alvarado, *Journal of Parapsychology*, vol. 62, no. 4, 1998

4S What Can Go Wrong with Experiments?

There are lots of ways experiments and interpretations of experiments can go wrong besides bad sampling and bad causal reasoning.

A. Lying

Example 1 In 2004 the highly respected journal *Science* published an article by Hwang Woo-suk detailing how he and his team had for the first time ever cloned human embryonic stem cells. That had been thought impossible. Hwang, a veterinarian and researcher, was already well-known for having cloned a cow and, for the first time, a dog, Snuppy.

In 2006 Hwang admitted that the research papers had faked data. He was convicted by a court in Korea of embezzlement of millions of research dollars and of bioethical violations (taking human eggs from his research assistants).

Example 2 In 1988 *The Lancet*, one of the most respected medical journals, published an article by Dr. Andrew Wakefield and twelve other authors. It said that they had found a link between children receiving the triple vaccine for measles, mumps, rubella (MMR) and developing autism. The paper did not claim that there was cause and effect. But before it was published, Wakefield held a press conference in which he said that vaccinations using MMR should be suspended until further research was done. A lot of people stopped vaccinating their children. Outbreaks of measles became more common.

But no one else was able to reproduce his results. More and more cause-in-population studies showed the safety and efficacy of the MMR vaccinations.

In 2011 the medical journal *The BMJ* published an article showing that Wakefield's study misrepresented or altered the medical histories of the twelve children studied in it. As Brian Deer, a reporter for the *London Sunday Times* said, Wakefield was responsible for "falsifying medical histories of children and essentially concocting a picture, which was the picture he was contracted to find by lawyers hoping to sue vaccine manufacturers." According to *The BMJ*, Wakefield received $674,000 from the lawyers. Wakefield lost his license to practice medicine in the United Kingdom, and *The Lancet* retracted the article.

Money and the hope of prestige can corrupt scientists, too.

B. Self-Deception

Example 3 In the late 1800s a German mathematics teacher, Wilhelm von Osten, was convinced that animals have reasoning skills and intelligence. He tried to test his hypothesis with cats, but they were indifferent. His horse, Hans, however learned how to answer simple addition and multiplication problems by tapping his hoof the correct number of times. He could even do problems with fractions, which are beyond many high school students. After much skepticism was voiced, Germany's board of education organized a committee of a psychologist, a horse trainer, several school teachers, and a circus manager to investigate. They concluded there was no trickery. Then Oskar Pfungst, a psychologist, was called to study Hans. He found that it didn't matter whether von Osten or others questioned Hans: the answers were always correct. Unless, that is, the person didn't know the answer or was not visible to the horse. Eventually, Pfungst was able to show that each questioner, even when advised not to, showed a slight relaxation of tension when the horse tapped the correct number, which was what cued "Clever Hans" to stop. Clever Hans wasn't doing mathematics; he was clever only in reading people's expressions.

Analysis Von Osten wasn't deceptive. He continued to believe that Clever Hans could do mathematics. But he was overlooking possibilities. That an animal's behavior can be influenced by subtle and unintentional cues from a questioner is called the ***Clever Hans effect***. It also holds for humans being questioned, who might not even be aware that they are picking up on unintentional cues.

In Example 5 of the last chapter there's no reason to think that Jessica Utts meant to mislead in her experiment on psychic functioning. She, too, just didn't see that more could be important than she took into account in setting up her experiment.

But sometimes the problem is that there is less that is important.

Example 4 Lee is one of 200 students in an experiment on psychic effects done by Professor Shibokbok. She asks each student to predict whether a coin flipped by a machine will land heads or tails. Each student does this 20 times. Most are right about 50% of the time, but 20 of them are right 15 or more times, including Lee. Those, she reckons, are the ones most likely to have psychic abilities. So she tests them again, and 4 of them, including Lee, are right more than 15 times out of 20. She tests those 4 again. Lee gets 16 right, and the others get less than 10. Now Professor Shibokbok wants to know whether Lee has precognition (can predict the future) or whether he's influencing the flip of the coin by telekinesis. The next day she tests Lee again, and he predicts only 6 flips out of 20. Then again, and he predicts only 4 out of 20. Somehow, Professor Shibokbok says, his psychic abilities have deteriorated overnight.

Analysis Lee hasn't lost his psychic abilities because he never had any. With 200 people, it's likely that someone will predict correctly more often than 50% of the time, especially with so few flips. Professor Shibokbok didn't test those who weren't predicting correctly who might have suddenly "gained" psychic powers. In a long enough run of tests, Lee, as the other students, will have a run of correct predictions. But eventually the sum of all his predictions will tend toward 50%, the average or mean of what is predicted as occurring by chance. Though it's often difficult to rule out chance as an explanation in an experiment, in this case it's not.

Professor Shibokbok couldn't get her work published in a reputable journal because it was obvious to the ***referees***, other scientists who judge articles submitted to journals, that she didn't understand probability. She was denied tenure and has now moved to a position in administration.

> ***Regression to the mean*** When experimental results are found that are far from the average predicted to occur by chance, and in subsequent trials the results tend to that average, it's a case of *regression to the mean*.

Regression to the mean is just an application of the law of large numbers.

C. The Power of Suggestion

Example 5 A young psychologist from Hamburg, Germany named Krüger had been to a market and a gypsy woman gave him a description of his character. He was amazed how well it suited him. He showed it to his colleague, Zietz, without telling him where he'd gotten it and who gave it to him. Zietz thought it applied to himself. Both being of the conviction that they were very different people personality-wise, they decided to investigate the matter more closely. Krüger told the students in one of his psychology classes that he wanted to do a graphological experiment. All the students had to hand in a handwriting sample. To make the experiment look serious Krüger waited 4 weeks before he gave the students their answers. They were called into a separate room where they were handed a typed up version of the character description given to Krüger by the gypsy woman. Not one of the 39 students were dissatisfied with the evaluation of their character. Some thought that minor points were a little off, but most were astounded by the accuracy of the description. Afterwards the students were told that they had all received the same description. The experiment has been repeated many times, with the same result. Here is the description given by the gypsy woman:

> Deep down you are a sincere and honest person, and it is not in your nature to hold back your feelings and opinions. This quality has already earned you many disappointments. You can, however, be very reserved with people you

feel less sympathetic towards. In the presence of people who are close to you, you are cheerful and even high-spirited, and you can give yourself fully to the moment. There are times, though, when you need to be alone, when you need to overcome dark moods and doubts about yourself. You are social with a lot of people, but it is only superficially. You only reveal your true self to a select few. To these people you are a faithful and sincere friend they can depend on.

In general you know how to remain calm. However slight changes in mood are not rare in you. You can be very sensitive, but you do not let on. You do however feel a need to confide in certain people who are close to you. To these people you will from time to time speak of your hidden despondencies.

You are serious about the questions in life, even though many people might not expect this from you. But you have your own thoughts on life, gather knowledge about other people and try to fathom their essence. You do not simply live superficially, but you seek to clarify all.

You are no pedant or fussbudget, but you do try to carry out your duties conscientiously. In your work, you do not care to be under the supervision of others, you are too much of an independent person for that. You are ambitious and your strong desire to assert yourself occasionally borders on vanity, even though you don't like to admit it.

It is impossible to hide that there are certain less flattering features of your character. For example, you will from time to time get very upset. There is a disconnectedness in you that borders on the intemperate. You must continue your efforts to master these traits.

At the moment there is a certain pressure in your situation that inhibits the full development of your essence and creates a certain obscurity in your entire personality. However, your personal destiny is on the rise.

From *Mennesker og Høns* by Edgar Rubins at skeptica.dk/artikler/?p=8366, translated from the Danish by Rasmus Ploug

Analysis Once you know the story behind this description it's hard to take it seriously. But it does work. Try it on some of your friends, it's fun!

Taking fortune-tellers' predictions seriously or following the daily astrology predictions may seem like intellectual peccadilloes, not serious problems of the power of suggestion. Until, that is, you lose all your money in the stock market. But the power of suggestion can ruin scientific experiments involving humans, especially in testing medications. Special precautions have to be taken to avoid having the expectations of both the subjects and the experimenters skew the results. Here's what Frederick J. Evans says:

> In studying new drugs, there is a problem that some people will report improvement of symptoms if given only sugar pills. That is why the control group is administered a *placebo*. Neither the subjects in the experiments nor those administering the drug or placebo are told which is a placebo and which a drug—that's the definition of a *double blind trial*.

> The anecdotal and empirical accounts of the potency of the placebo effect are legion. For example, in one study, 30% of a large number of patients reported decreased sex drive, 17% increased headache, 14% increased menstrual pain, and 8% increased nervousness and irritability. These were all side effects of the administration of a placebo in a double-blind study of oral contraceptives [reference given]. In a double-blind study of a cold vaccine, 7% of patients in both groups reported toxic side effects requiring additional medical intervention. Double-blind studies will often list iatrogenic [i.e., induced by medical procedure] side effects found in the placebo group, but these symptoms will differ markedly from study to study. In contrast to the study of oral contraceptives, it is not surprising that in double-blind studies with antihistamines, fatigue and sleepiness are reported. Obviously the target symptoms monitored are different. In an antihistamine study, it is unlikely that the investigators would inquire about decreased sex drive and headaches among females.
>
> "Expectancy, therapeutic instructions and the placebo response," in *Placebo*, Leonard White, Bernard Trusky, and Gary Schwartz, eds.

But the studies Evans cites don't show that the people had those symptoms. They show only that they reported that they had the symptoms. There's a big difference. And given the looseness of what we count as a headache, people may report what they wouldn't normally call a headache simply in order to have something to report. Wanting to please the researcher can distort responses, too. Further, even a sugar pill can have some effect, perhaps enough to make one a little happier and so have something to report. It's extraordinarily hard to define "placebo effect" well, but roughly this is what we use.

Placebo A *placebo* is any substance or treatment given to some participants in a controlled cause-to-effect cause-in-population medical study that is assumed to have no effect.

Placebo effect A reported or experienced physical change that follows from a person being given a placebo.

Double-blind trial A controlled cause-to-effect cause-in-population study in which neither the subjects nor those administering the drug or placebo are told which is a placebo and which a drug.

With the slipperiness of what really is a placebo, all we can do is use double-blind studies with large enough populations. This allows us to compare the responses of those given the drug or treatment with those in the control group to see if there is a statistically significant difference. If there is, that's taken to be the effect of the drug or treatment.

With uncontrolled cause-to-effect experiments involving people, the expectations of the people involved can result in an unrepresentative sample. No matter how carefully studies are made on the effectiveness of different female contraceptives, they will be only marginally useful in helping women choose which method to use. That's because women who most want to avoid pregnancy choose the contraceptive they think will be most effective. So the women using the pill, which they are told is a highly effective way to avoid pregnancy, will be more motivated to follow the instructions for its use and always use it, while those who use contraceptive foam are likely to be more lax in following the method. According to the scientists who devise these studies (see the article "Data Called Misleading in Rating Contraceptives," *New York Times*, December 1, 1987), there doesn't seem to be any way to correct for this bias in the analysis of the data.

> ***Self-selection bias*** Self-selection bias occurs when those in the sample done for a survey or experiment select themselves to participate.

Self-selection bias isn't only with people. When an ethologist studies only the chimpanzees that come to a feeding station, the sample of chimpanzees she's studying is self-selected.

D. Positive Publication Bias

Suppose that Professor Fergamitz and Professor Lyle, at different universities and unknown to each other, have each done an experiment to the highest standards. They've examined their observations using the best statistical analyses.

> Professor Fergamitz: I just found out that there's no correlation between being fat and being left-handed.
>
> Professor Lyle: I just found out that there's a 12% greater chance of being fat if you're left-handed.

There's no hope that Professor Fergamitz can get his work published. Who would think that there would be a correlation? However, Professor Lyle got his work accepted by a respected medical journal because it's such a surprising result.

Journals will publish new positive results but rarely new negative ones—unless, that is, to refute someone's experiment that is famous, like Andrew Wakefield's (Example 2). If Professor Lyle's paper starts lots of research on left-handed people, Professor Fergamitz will likely be able to get his work published.

Journals—and researchers—tend to take positive results more seriously than negative ones. So when there are many people publishing, and only the positive results are published, we get a skewed picture of what's proved.

Example 6 Dr. Joseph Banks Rhine was a famous ESP researcher from Duke University. He devised an experiment using cards with five easily distinguishable symbols: a square, circle, cross, star, and wavy lines. Used in decks of 25 cards,

5 for each symbol, the person being tested was asked to predict which symbol will be drawn.

> Let us imagine that one hundred professors of psychology throughout the country read of Rhine's work and decide to test a subject. The fifty who fail to find ESP in their first preliminary test are likely to be discouraged and quit, but the other fifty will be encouraged to continue. Of this fifty, more will stop work after the second test, while some will continue, more will stop work after the second test, while some will continue because they obtained good results. Eventually, one experimenter remains whose subject has made high scores for six or seven consecutive sessions. *Neither experimenter nor subject is aware of the other ninety-nine projects, and so both have a strong delusion that ESP is operating.* The odds are, in fact, much against the run. But in the total (and unknown) context, the run is quite probable. (The odds against winning the Irish sweep-stakes are even higher. But someone does win it.) So the experimenter writes an enthusiastic paper, sends it to Rhine who publishes it in his magazine, and the readers are greatly impressed.
>
> Martin Gardner in *Fads and Fallacies in the Name of Science*

Analysis There's no deception here and no self-deception. The one experimenter did his work well. Still, a reputable scientific journal wouldn't publish his results unless they were reproduced by many experimenters, since they contradict so much else we know. Good referees are alert to the possibility of chance being at work.

Still, not every negative result is significant.

Example 7 The famous Michelson-Morley experiment in the 19th century showed that the speed of light did not vary according to whether it was measured in the same path as the earth's movement or across that path. This was the observation that led Albert Einstein to formulate his theory of relativity based on the assumption that the speed of light is the same for every observer. In the 1920s, 40 years after Michelson and Morley, a reputable physicist named Dayton C. Miller repeated the experiment and found slight variations in the speed of light, sufficient to question the theory of relativity. He repeated the experiment many times, always with the same results. He published articles about his work in scientific journals. But no one accepts that his experiment refutes the claim that the speed of light is constant.

Analysis The Michelson-Morley experiment has been duplicated many times in virtually all technologically advanced countries, at differing altitudes, with different kinds of equipment. Except for Miller's work, the results always show that the speed of light, at least to the accuracy of the instruments involved, is the same. Even now no one knows why Miller's observations were different. It isn't bias toward positive results to conjecture that there was something odd in his equipment or that he, perhaps unconsciously, made errors recording the observations. Yes, it's possible that in that one place, at those particular times, there were differences in the speed of light. But no reputable scientist would accept that, not because he or she would be intimidated by the scientific community but because all the weight of evidence is against it.

E. Should We Ever Believe Scientists?

One experiment is published; another contradicts its results. Should we just suspend judgment? Is there no standard we can use?

Some say that because scientists differ in evaluating some experiments and because there is no clear line between good work and bad work, between science and pseudoscience, we should suspend judgment on all scientific theories and consider them all to be just hypotheses: the theory of evolution is no more to be trusted—or discounted—than astrology. That's a drawing the line fallacy. In the extremes, and those extremes are not far from the middle muddle, we can clearly distinguish between a theory that is very likely to be accurate and one that is very likely to be wrong.

Work in science is distinguished by constant testing. No observation, no result, no theory will long be accepted as both correct and important until it has been tested again and again. Yes, scientists make mistakes. Like all of us, they are sometimes careless, sometimes self-deceived, sometimes misled by mistaking chance for significance, and sometimes seduced by hope of money and power. But the community as a whole acts as a skeptical audience. Some call the testing, checking, and revising in science the "scientific method." But that's just a fancy name for all that scientists do, from their first training as students in a critical thinking course to their laboratories and theoretical analyses. Testing, checking, and revising is what all of us would do for all the important decisions in our lives if we had the time and money—and energy.

> . . . when you encounter a new medical theory, universally condemned by the "orthodox," you will do well to take [the orthodox people's] word for it. It is always possible, of course, that the self-styled genius *may* be what he claims to be—another Pasteur, years ahead of stubborn colleagues. But the odds are heavily against it. For every quack who later proves to be a genius, there are ten thousand quacks who prove later only to be quacks. Many of them . . . are brainy men who write and speak with great authority and persuasion. . . . You may keep your mind open, but to rely on the consensus of informed medical men is the soundest and sanest course of action.
>
> Martin Gardner, *Fads and Fallacies in the Name of Science*, 1952

Key Words

- Clever Hans effect
- referee
- regression to the mean
- placebo
- placebo effect
- double-blind trial
- selection bias
- positive publication bias

Exercises for Chapter 4S

1. a. What is regression to the mean?
   b. Explain why doing more studies with larger sample sizes can show that a result of an experiment is due to chance.

2. a. What is a placebo?
   b. What is a double-blind study?
   c. What is the role of a double-blind study in countering the placebo effect?
   d. Look at the insert for two medications that you or a friend have taken and list the possible side-effects. Were those found with a double-blind trial?
   e. Report on a medical experiment that used a double-blind trial.

3. a. Find a blog or report on the internet posted recently that asserts that MMR vaccinations cause autism. Is the author ignorant, willfully blind, or just evaluating the evidence badly?
   b. A friend of mine refused to have her daughter vaccinated for any disease. She'd heard about the research of Andrew Wakefield and firmly believed that vaccinations are dangerous, possibly leading to autism. After all, her sister works in an alternative medicine clinic where that's what they say. I tried to convince her that those studies were bogus. In the end she said, "You have your evidence, and I have mine."
   What would you say to her?

4. What is the Clever Hans effect?

5. a. What is self-selection bias?
   b. How does self-selection bias differ from haphazard sampling?
   c. Find an example on the internet of a study that is bad because of self-selection bias.

6. a. What is positive publication bias?
   b. Go to a recent issue of a medical journal and count how many articles report on a positive correlation and how many on a lack of a correlation. How many of the latter are responding to previously published reports of a positive correlation?

7. If an experiment has been duplicated many times and the results reproduced, why don't we accept one report of a duplication of the experiment with different results as refuting the claims of the original experiment?

8. How does the scientific community try to counter the effects of bias and mistakes?

9. a. On the internet find a definition of "confirmation bias" from a reputable source.
   b. Is it precise enough that you could use it to determine when there is confirmation bias?
   c. By that definition, would any of the examples in this chapter illustrate confirmation bias?

10. Select one of the following to report to your class on how fraud in science was handled.
   a. Michael LaCour, a political scientist who couldn't produce his data on changing people's minds about gay equality: <http://science.sciencemag.org/content/early/2015/05/27/science.aac6638>.
   b. Scott Reuben, a Tufts medical researcher who faked data in at least 21 articles: <https://www.scientificamerican.com/article/a-medical-madoff-anesthestesiologist-faked-data/>.

c. Peter Chen, an engineer at Taiwan's National Pingtung University, who exploited Thomson Reuters' lax peer review procedures to review and recommend his own research: <http://www.nature.com/news/publishing-the-peer-review-scam-1.16400>.

11. Report on the difficulty of getting good studies of the effects of diet on health as described in Edward Archer et al., "The Inadmissibility of What We Eat in America and NHANES Dietary Data in Nutrition and Obesity Research and the Scientific Formulation of National Dietary Guidelines," *Mayo Clinic Proceedings*, 2015, 90 (7): 911-926, and N.V. Dhurandhar et al.," Energy Balance Measurement: When Something Is Not Better than Nothing," *International Journal of Obesity*, 2015, 39: 1109-1113.

Further Study Jonah Lehrer in "The Truth Wears Off" (*The New Yorker*, Dec. 13, 2010, <http://www.newyorker.com/magazine/2010/12/13/the-truth-wears-off)>) reports on a problem that when an experiment gets a positive result, more experiments get progressively fewer positive results until (almost) no effect at all is measured. Though this seems to be just regression to the mean, Lehrer gives examples where that doesn't seem to be the explanation of what is called *the decline effect*.

An excellent article about confirmation bias, with good examples, is "Confirmation Bias in Science: How to Avoid It" by Chris Lee at <http://arstechnica.com/science/2010/07/confirmation-bias-how-to-avoid-it/>.

Retraction Watch (<http://retractionwatch.com/>) is a blog that tracks scientific studies that get withdrawn by journals. It's run by the Center for Scientific Integrity, a non-profit organization devoted to good practices in scientific research and publication.

For an entertaining critical review of the evidence for the placebo effect and the importance of double-blind trials, see Robert Ehrlich, *Eight Preposterous Propositions*.

Science Arguments for Analysis

Exercises 1–4 depend on analogies. Evaluate them by answering the following:

Argument? (yes or no)

Conclusion (if unstated, add it):

Comparison:

Premises:

Similarities:

Additional premises (make the comparison explicit, add a general principle):

Classify (with the additional premises): valid strong ———— weak

Good argument? (look for differences or ways the general principle could be false)

- It's good (passes the three tests).
- It's valid or strong, but you don't know if the premises are true, so you can't say if it's good or bad.
- It's bad because it's unrepairable (state which of the reasons apply).

1. The mass of the water of the sea presses with its weight that part of the earth which is beneath it; if it surrounded the whole earth instead of only a part, its weight would press upon the whole surface of the earth. In the same way, since the mass of the air covers the whole face of the earth, its weight presses upon the earth at every point.

   Blaise Pascal, *The Physical Treatises* (*Treatise on the Weight of the Mass of Air*, Chapter 1) pp. 242–3 of *The Origins and Growth of Physical Science*

2. To make it clear how the weight of the mass of air causes the resistance encountered in opening a bellows from which the air is excluded, I will point to a similar resistance due to the weight of water. It needs only to be remembered, as I said in the *Equilibrium of Liquids,* that if a bellows with a tube twenty or more feet long is set in a tank full of water with the tip of the nozzle extending above the surface, it is hard to open; and the greater the depth of water above it the harder it is to open. This is obviously due to the weight of the water above: for if there is no water there, it is easy to open. The more water you pour in, the greater is the resistance, which is always equal to the weight of the water sustained. The reason is that the nozzle projects above the water, and therefore excludes it, the bellows cannot be opened without raising and holding up the whole mass of water. The water that is pushed aside in the act of opening cannot enter the bellows, is forced to find room elsewhere, and thus raises the water level—a process attended with some difficulty—whereas if the bellows were so perforated that water could get in, it could be freely opened and closed because the water could enter through the perforations as fast as room was made for it, and would not, therefore, be lifted. I do not think that anyone can be tempted to ascribe this resistance to the abhorrence of a vacuum. It is absolutely certain that it is due solely to the weight of water.

   Now what we say about water must be taken to apply to any other liquid; for if the bellows is set in a vessel full of wine, the same resistance to its opening will be experienced; likewise with milk, oil, quicksilver, and indeed any liquid whatsoever. Thus it is a general rule and a necessary effect of the weight of liquids, that if a bellows is so immersed in any one of them that the liquid is excluded from its interior, the weight of the liquid above makes it impossible to open the bellows without overcoming the resistance due to the fact that it has to be lifted. Applying this general rule to air in particular, it follows as a certain consequence that when a bellows is so sealed as to exclude all air, the weight of the air above prevents its opening without overcoming some resistance, since it cannot be opened without lifting the whole mass of air. But as soon as a perforation is made in the bellows, it can be freely opened and closed, because now the act of opening no longer lifts the mass of the air. All this is completely analogous to the action of the bellows immersed in water.

Whence it is evident that the difficulty in opening a sealed bellows is but a particular case of the general rule that it is hard to open a bellows in any liquid whatsoever that is prevented from entering it.

Blaise Pascal, *The Physical Treatises* (*Treatise on the Weight of the Mass of Air*, Chapter II, part 2) pp. 249–250 of *The Origins and Growth of Physical Science*

3. There is great interest in the possibility that animals may share with us psychological states such as consciousness and self-awareness, as well as the ability to perceive cause and effect relationships and to base behavior upon intentions. Coupled with this great interest, however, is controversy. To deal with these topics at the human level is not without problems, so it is understandable that to attempt definition and study of them at the animal level is certain to cause disagreement. In fact, there are respectable quarters of the fields of psychology and animal behavior that would hold these mental states to be at best epiphenomena [events or things that occur with, but are neither cause nor effect] and at worst nothing but irrational projections of subjective, anthropocentric flights of fantasy that explain nothing. But considering the degree to which animals are similar to us in so many other ways, it is reasonable to suspect that they might also have certain mental states quite similar to ours, and if this is so then it is very important that we explore them. As we attempt to do so, we might learn how to better understand these states that seem to control so much of our own lives.

   All forms of life are, of course, unique—it is their uniqueness that defines their taxonomy. Nonetheless, no life form is without similarities to other forms, and it is generally acknowledged that similarity increases with relatedness. This frame of reference is broadly accepted for physical attributes—apes look more like humans than do monkeys, for example. It is less generally recognized that the same principle holds for psychological attributes. Just as evolution has brought about emergent physical characteristics, so it has surely brought about emergent psychological characteristics—both evolve together as they contribute to survival and reproductive success. And just as physical similarity increases with genetic relatedness, it is reasonable to believe that psychological processes become more similar with genetic relatedness. Therefore, whatever we believe about the important attributes of human cognitive processes, many of the same conclusions are probably true for other animals, and, in particular, they are likely to be true for animals closely related to humankind. This means that they are more likely to be true for the ape than for any other animal. Whatever we ascribe to the dimensions of our experience—awareness, purposeful communication, perception of cause and effect relationships, the ability to formulate rules and principles from our experience, the ability to base our actions on intentions, and so on—we are most likely to find traces of these abilities in the psychological characteristics and behaviors of the animal that is most closely related to us, the chimpanzee (*Pan troglodytes* and *Pan paniscus*).

Duane M. Rumbaugh and Sue Savage-Rumbaugh, in *Animal Intelligence,* eds. Hoage and Goldman, pp. 57–58

4. Every species of plant or animal is determined by a pool of germ plasma that has been most carefully selected over a period of hundreds of millions of years.

   We can understand now why it is that mutations in these carefully selected organisms almost invariably are detrimental. The situation can be suggested by a statement made by Dr. J. B. S. Haldane: my clock is not keeping perfect time. It is conceivable that it will run better if I shoot a bullet through it; but it is much more probable that it will stop altogether. Professor George Beadle, in this connection, has asked: "What is the chance that a typographical error would improve *Hamlet*?"

   Linus Pauling, *No More War*

To evaluate the following longer arguments, use the methods described in the section "Analyzing Complex Arguments" on pp. 237–245.

5. ***The promise of cloning for human medicine***

   The production of a sheep clone, Dolly, from an adult somatic cell [reference given] is a stunning achievement of British science. It also holds great promise for human medicine. Sadly the media have sensationalised the implications, ignoring the huge potential of this experiment. Accusations that scientists have been working secretively and without the chance for public debate are invalid. Successful cloning was publicised in 1975 [reference given], and it is over eight years since Prather et al. published details of the first piglet clone after nuclear transfer [reference given].

   Missing from much of the debate about Dolly is recognition that she is not an identical clone. Part of our genetic material comes from the mitochondria in the cytoplasm of the egg. In Dolly's case only the nuclear DNA was transferred. Moreover, we are a product of our nurture as much as our genetic nature. Monovular twins are genetically closer than artificially produced clones, and no one would deny that such twins have quite separate identities.

   Dolly's birth provokes fascinating questions. How old is she? Her nuclear DNA gives her potentially adult status, but her mitochondria are those of a newborn. Mitochondria are important in the aging process because aging is related to acquired mutations in mitochondrial DNA, possibly caused by oxygen damage during an adult's life [reference given]. Experimental nuclear transfer in animals and in human cell lines could help elucidate mechanisms for many of these questions.

   Equally extraordinary is the question concerning the role of the egg's cytoplasm in mammalian development. Once the quiescent nucleus had been transferred to the recipient egg cell, developmental genes expressed only in very early life were switched on. There are likely to be powerful factors in the cytoplasm of the egg that make this happen. Egg cytoplasm is perhaps the new royal jelly. Studying why and how these genes switch on would give important information about both human development and genetic disease.

Research on nuclear transfer into human eggs has immense clinical value. Here is a model for learning more about somatic cell differentiation. If, in due course, we could influence differentiation to give rise to targeted cell types we might generate many tissues of great value in transplantation. These could include skin and blood cells, and possibly neuronal tissue, for the treatment of injury, for bone marrow transplants for leukaemia, and for degenerative diseases such as Parkinson's disease. One problem to be overcome is the existence of histocompatibility antigens encoded by mitochondrial DNA [reference given], but there may be various ways of altering their expression. Cloning techniques might also be useful in developing transgenic animals—for example, for human xenotransplantation [organs from non-human animals].

There are also environmental advantages in pursuing this technology. Mention has been made of the use of these methods to produce dairy herds and other livestock. This would be of limited value because animals with genetic diversity derived from sexual reproduction will always be preferable to those produced asexually. The risk of a line of farm animals prone to a particular disease would be ever present. However, cloning offers real prospects for preservation of endangered or rare species.

In human reproduction, cloning techniques could offer prospects to sufferers from intractable infertility. At present there is not treatment, for example, for those men who exhibit total germ cell failure. Clearly it is far fetched to believe that we are now able to reproduce the process of meiosis, but it may be possible in future to produce a haploid cell from the male which could be used for fertilisation of female gametes. Even if straight cloning techniques were used, the mother would contribute important constituents—her mitochondrial genes, intrauterine influences, and subsequent nurture.

Regulation of cloning is needed, but British law already covers this. Talk of "legal loopholes" [reference given] is wrong. The Human Fertilisation and Embryology Act may need modification, but there is no particular urgency. A precipitate ban on human nuclear transfer would, for example, prevent the use of in vitro fertilisation and preimplantation diagnosis for those couples at risk of having children who have appalling mitochondrial diseases [reference given]. Self regulation and legislation already work well. Apart from any other consideration, it seems highly unlikely that doctors would transfer human clones to the uterus out of simple self interest. Many of the animal clones that have been produced show serious developmental abnormalities [reference given], and apart from ethical considerations, doctors would not run the medicolegal risks involved. Transgenic technology has been with us for 20 years, but no clinician has been foolish enough to experiment with human germ cell therapy. The production of Dolly should not be seen as a moral threat, but rather as an exciting challenge. To answer this good science with a knee jerk political reaction, as did President Clinton recently [reference given], shows poor judgment. In a society which is still scientifically illiterate, the onus is on researchers to explain the potential good that can be gained in the laboratory.

Robert Winston, *British Medical Journal,* vol. 314, 1997, pp. 913–914

6. *Ethics of using animals for experimental studies*

Every year we slaughter over 4 billion animals for meat and euthanize more than 10 million as unwanted pets. We have distanced ourselves far enough from the farm to forget that chicken, beef, fish, leather, and other animal products were once living, feeling beings. This distance allows us to behave irresponsibly, and to be influenced by extreme and inappropriate opinions. On one hand, we tend to dehumanize all animals and at the opposite extreme we treat other species as human surrogates.

The mythical garden of Eden in which there are no predators and consequently no prey does not exist on this planet. While the relationship between a snake and a mouse may seem ruthless and cruel, it is a part of the biology that supports the complex ecosystems of this planet. It is not a matter of choice. Every living animal costs other living things something, somewhere in their ecosystem.

Ethical convictions need not be logical, but when we put them into practice they at least need to be adaptive. Both dogs and monkeys were used in the development of the rabies vaccine, and that vaccine protects both owners and pets worldwide. The cost-benefit ratio of such research is favorable from most points of view. To not conduct the research is to put all who live in the future at avoidable risk.

Research should not be wasteful and it should be conducted with care, empathy, and respect. Primates should be used only for subjects that cannot be studied in more inexpensive species. However, if one wishes to learn about the specific biology of a particular primate, that species must, of course, be investigated.

Investigators do make mistakes, they have the same human foibles as the rest of the populace. Consequently, institutional monitoring, critical proposal reviews, and national standards of care are important to prevent abuse, waste, or neglect. Primatologists, especially interested in behavior, have a reputation among researchers as animal advocates in their institutions.

Captive breeding is the only alternative for species that no longer have a natural habitat, and with sponsorship from Conservation International, there is a global captive action plan formulated by the International Union for Conservation of Nature and Natural Resources. Funding for captive breeding is minimal, and the reality is that financial resources tend to be invested in those species that are in demand as research subjects. Habitat loss due to the expansion of the human population is the most serious threat to many, if not all nonhuman primate species. We must understand our world and ultimately make compromises between short-term and long-term sustainability if we are to be intelligent, responsible custodians.

Claud A. Bramblett, *Patterns of Primate Behavior,* 2nd edition, pp. 4–5

7. *Consciousness*

Neurophysiologists [did not] find it necessary to recognize the scientific legitimacy of consciousness: they did just fine by regarding the brain as a wholly physical system, a complex of neurons and their biochemistry. Even the nascent computer-based theories of the mind had no place for consciousness, since computers can perform their information-processing operations without benefit of conscious awareness. Consciousness seemed like a phenomenon it was not necessary to consider, and hence possible to deny—common sense notwithstanding. Other subjects took up the intellectual space that one might have thought would be occupied by consciousness: overt physical behavior, environmental "stimuli," internal states of the nervous system, abstract computations. In principle, as they have defined "principle," the sciences of human nature need make no reference to consciousness and suffer no explanatory or predictive inadequacy.

Yet to any sensible person consciousness is the essence of the mind: to have a mind precisely is to endure or enjoy conscious states—inner, subjective awareness.

Colin McGinn, "Can we ever understand consciousness?"
New York Review of Books, Vol. XLVI, no. 10, 1999, p. 44

8. *Galileo on the acceleration of falling bodies–1*

Simplicius: I believe that a falling body acquires force in its descent, its velocity increasing in proportion to the space, and that the momentum of the falling body is doubled when it falls from a doubled height . . .

Salviati: And yet [it is] false and impossible as that motion should be completed instantaneously; and here is a very clear demonstration of it. If the velocities are in proportion to the spaces traversed, or to be traversed, then these spaces are traversed in equal intervals of time; if, therefore, the velocity with which the falling body traverses a space of eight feet were double that with which it covered the first four feet (just as the one distance is double the other) then the time-intervals required for these passages would be equal. But for one and the same body to fall eight feet and four feet in the same time is possible only in the case of instantaneous [discontinuous] motion; but observation shows us that the motion of a falling body occupies time, and less of it in covering a distance of four feet than of eight feet; and therefore it is not true that its velocity increases in proportion to the space.

Galileo, *Dialogues Concerning Two New Sciences,*
translated by Henry Crew and A. DeSalvio
(also in *The Origins and Growth of Physical Science,*
eds. D. L. Hurd and J. J. Kipling, pp. 170–171

Further Study A good book to see how science reasoning matters in the law is *Galileo's Revenge: Junk Science in the Courtroom* by Peter W. Huber.

5S Models and Theories

A. Examples

Example 1 *A map of Minersville, Utah—reasoning by analogy*

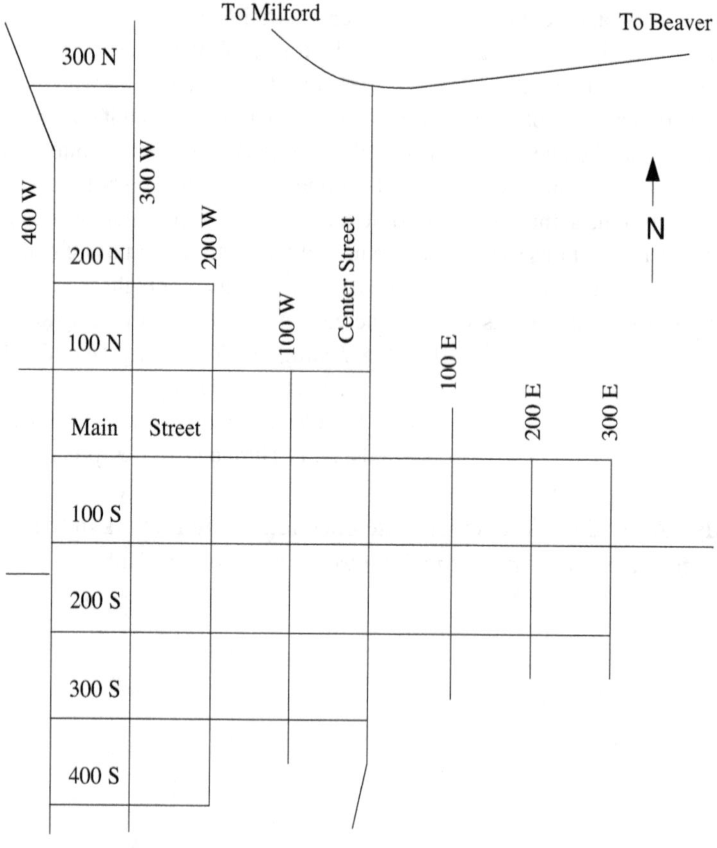

This is an accurate map of Minersville, Utah. Looking at it we can see that the streets are evenly spaced. For example, there is the same distance between 100 N and 200 N as between 100 E and 200 E. The last street to the east is 300 E. There is no paved road going north beyond Main Street on 200 E.

That is, from the map we can deduce claims about Minersville, even if we've never been there. But there is much we can't deduce: Are there hills in Minersville? Are there lots of trees? How wide are the streets? How far apart are the streets? Where are there houses? The map is accurate for what it pays attention to: the relative location and orientation of streets. But it tells us nothing about what it ignores.

Reasoning about Minersville from this map is reasoning by analogy. The map is similar to Minersville in the relative position of streets and their orientation to north. The differences between the map and Minersville aren't important when we infer that the north end of 200 W is at 200 N.

Perhaps you've seen a scale model of a city or a mountain. Such a model abstracts less from the actual terrain: height and perhaps placements of rivers and trees are there. We say a model ***models more*** than another if there are more similarities between the model and what it's modeling. The map of Minersville ***abstracts more*** from the actual terrain than a scale model of the city would—that is, it ignores more.

To use this model is to reason by analogy. *We can draw conclusions when appropriate similarities are invoked and the differences don't matter.* The general principle, in this example, is not stated explicitly. The discussion above suggests how we might formulate one, but it hardly seems worth the effort. We can "see" when someone has used a map well or badly.

Example 2 *Models of the universe—getting a better model*
Here is a sketch of the model of the universe that the Egyptian astronomer Ptolemy proposed in the second century A.D.

Ptolemy's model

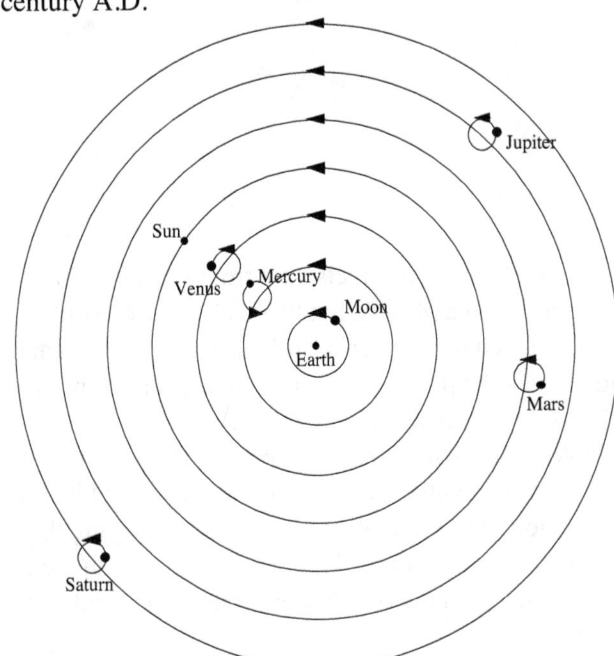

This "map" of the universe is meant to show the relative positions of the planets, sun, and moon, and the ways that they move. We can't deduce anything about, say, the size of the planets or the distances between them or the speeds at which they move because this model ignores those. According to this model, the moon, sun, and each of the planets revolve around the Earth in a circular orbit, all moving in the same direction. Along that orbit, each planet also revolves in a smaller circle, called an "epicycle." The sun, Earth, and Venus are always supposed to be in a line as shown in the picture.

Ptolemy made a lot more claims about the planets, Earth, and sun that were to be used in making predictions, but for our purposes this sketch of his model will do.

Ptolemy's model accorded pretty well with observations of the movements of the planets and was the generally accepted way to understand the universe for many centuries. But in 1543 the Polish astronomer Copernicus published a book with a different model of the universe.

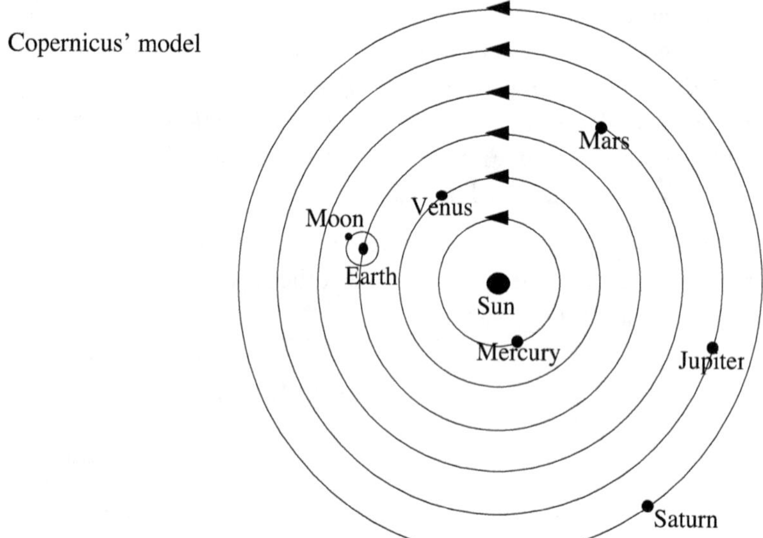

Copernicus' model

This sketch, too, abstracts a lot from what is being modeled. The sun is shown to be larger than the planets, but that's all we see about their relative sizes. We can't tell from the picture whether the orbits are all on the same plane or on different planes. We do see that the planets all revolve in the same direction, and that the Earth, sun, and Venus do not always stay lined up.

Ptolemy accounted for the motion of the planets and the stars in the sky by saying that they revolved around the Earth every 24 hours. Copernicus accounted for the motion of the sun, planets, and stars by saying that the Earth revolved around its own axis every 24 hours. How could someone in the late 16th century decide between these two models? Both were in accord with the observations that had been made.

In the early 1600s the telescope was invented, and in 1610 Galileo built his own telescope with a magnification of about 33 times, using it to study the skies. One of his students suggested an experiment that might distinguish between the Ptolemaic and Copernican models. Venus was too far from the Earth to be seen as anything other than a spot of light. But according to Ptolemy's model, viewed from the Earth, at most only a small crescent-shaped part of Venus will be illuminated by the sun. From Copernicus' model, however, we can deduce that from the Earth, Venus should go through all the phases of illumination, just like the moon: full, half, crescent, dark, and back again. Galileo looked at Venus through his telescope for a period of time and saw that it exhibited all phases of illumination, and this he took to be proof that Copernicus' model was correct.

Not a lot of people were convinced, however. Telescopes were rare and not very reliable: they introduced optical illusions, such as halos, from the imperfections in the glass and the mounting. Why should astronomers have trusted Galileo's observations?

It was more due to Newton that something like Copernicus' model of the universe was finally accepted. Newton deduced from his laws of motion that the orbits of the Earth, sun, and planets would have to be ellipses, not circles. And the distances between them would have to be much greater than supposed. Using Newton's laws, Edmond Halley predicted correctly the return of a comet that had been observed in 1682. Telescopes were better, with fewer optical illusions, and they were common enough that most astronomers could use one, so better and better observations of the planets and stars could be made. Those observations could be deduced from the Copernican-Newtonian model, while new epicycles had to be invented to account for them in the Ptolemaic model.

Note that each model is supposed to be similar to the universe in only a few respects, ones that would have an effect on how we could see from the Earth the objects in the universe. Differences, such as whether Venus is rocky or gaseous, are not supposed to matter for those observations. If the model is correct, then reasoning by analogy—very precise analogy—certain claims can be deduced.

Example 3 *The kinetic theory of gases*
—getting true predictions doesn't mean the model is true

This theory is based on the following postulates, or assumptions.

1. Gases are composed of a large number of particles that behave like hard, spherical objects in a state of constant, random motion.

2. The particles move in a straight line until they collide with another particle or the walls of the container.

3. The particles are much smaller than the distance between the particles. Most of the volume of a gas is therefore empty space.

4. There is no force of attraction between gas particles or between the particles and the walls of the container.

5. Collisions between gas particles or collisions with the walls of the container are perfectly elastic. Energy can be transferred from one particle to another during a collision, but the total kinetic energy of the particles after the collision is the same as it was before the collision.

6. The average kinetic energy of a collection of gas particles depends on the temperature of the gas and nothing else.

J. Spencer, G. Bodner, and L. Rickard, *Chemistry*

Here is a picture of what is supposed to be going on in a gas in a closed container.

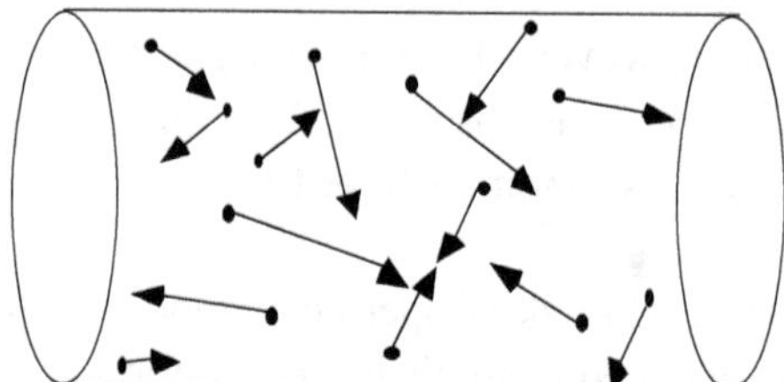

The molecules of gas are represented as dots, as if they were hard spherical balls. The length of the line emanating from a particle models the particle's speed; the arrow models the direction in which the particle is moving. The kinetic energy of a particle is defined in terms of its mass and velocity: kinetic energy = .5 mass x velocity^2. The model defines what is meant for a collision to be elastic. In contrast, here is a picture of what happens in an inelastic collision between a rubber ball and the floor.

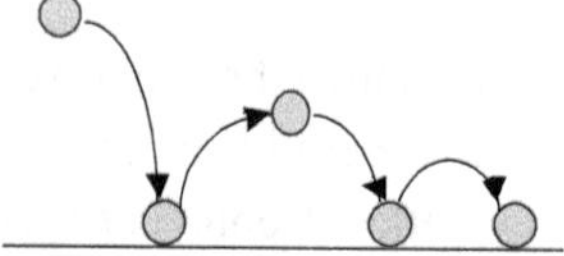

Each time the ball hits the ground, some of its kinetic energy is lost either through being transferred to the floor or in compressing the ball.

What are we to make of these assumptions? Some are false: molecules of gas are not generally spherical and are certainly not solid; the collisions between molecules and the walls of a container or each other are not perfectly elastic; there is some gravitational attraction between the particles and each other and also with the container. How can we use false claims in a model?

The model proceeds by abstraction, much like in analogy: to the extent that we can ignore how molecules of gases are not spherical, and ignore physical attraction between molecules, and ignore . . . we can draw conclusions that may be applicable to actual gases. To the extent that the differences between actual gases and the abstractions don't matter, we can draw conclusions. But how can we tell if the differences matter?

The model suggests that the pressure of a gas results from the collisions between the gas particles and the walls of the container. So if the container is made smaller for the same amount of gas, the pressure should increase; and if the container is made larger, the pressure should be less. So the pressure should be proportional to the inverse of the volume of the gas. That is, the model suggests a claim about the relationship of pressure to volume in a gas. Experiments can be performed, varying the pressure or volume, and they are close to being in accord with that claim.

Other laws are suggested by the model: Pressure is proportional to the temperature of the gas, where the temperature is taken to be the average kinetic energy of the gas. The volume of the gas should be proportional to the temperature. The amount of gas should be proportional to the pressure. All of these are confirmed by experiment.

Those experiments confirming predictions from the model do not mean the model is more accurate than we thought. Collisions still aren't really elastic; molecules aren't really hard spherical balls. The kinetic theory of gases is a model that is useful, as with any analogy, when the differences don't matter.

Example 4 *The acceleration of falling objects —an equation can be a model*

Galileo argued that falling objects accelerate as they fall: they begin falling slowly and fall faster and faster the farther they fall.

> You say the experiment appears to show that immediately after a heavy body starts from rest it acquires a very considerable speed: and I say that the same experiment makes clear the fact that the initial motions of a falling body, no matter how heavy, are very slow and gentle. Place a heavy body upon a yielding material, and leave it there without any pressure except that owing to its weight; it is clear that if one lifts this body a cubit or two and allows it to fall upon the same material, it will, with this impulse, exert a new and greater pressure than that caused by its mere weight; and this effect is brought about by the [weight of the] falling body together with the velocity acquired during the fall, an effect which will be greater and greater according to the height of the fall, that is according as the velocity of the falling body becomes greater. From the quality and intensity of the blow we are thus enabled to accurately estimate the speed of a falling body. But tell me, gentlemen, is it not true that if a block be allowed to fall upon a stake from a height of four cubits and drives it into the earth, say four finger-breadths, that coming from a height of two cubits it will drive the stake a much less distance, and from the height of one cubit a still less distance; and finally if the block be lifted only one finger-breadth how much more will it accomplish than if merely laid on top of the stake without percussion? Certainly very little. If it be lifted only the thickness of a leaf, the effect will be altogether imperceptible. And since the effect of the blow depends upon the velocity of this striking body, can anyone doubt the motion is very slow and the speed more than small whenever the effect [of the blow] is imperceptible?

Galileo, *Dialogues Concerning Two New Sciences,* translated by Henry Crew and A. DeSalvio (also in *The Origins and Growth of Physical Science,* eds. D. L. Hurd and J. J. Kipling)

Galileo also said that the reason a feather falls more slowly than an iron ball when dropped is because of the resistance of air. He argued that at a given location on the earth and in the absence of air resistance, all objects should fall with the same acceleration. He claimed that the distance traveled by a falling object is proportional to the square of the time it travels. Today, from many measurements, the equation is given by:

(*) $d = 9.80 \text{ meters} / \text{sec}^2 \cdot t^2$

Equation (*) is very precise; with it we can make calculations. For example, if you drop a ball bearing from the Empire State Building, after 4 seconds it should travel:

$$d = 9.80 \text{ m} / \text{sec}^2 \cdot (4 \text{ sec})^2$$
$$= 9.80 \text{ m} \cdot 16 = 156.8 \text{ m} \quad \text{(about 517.5 feet)}$$

In what sense is equation (*) an analogy? It says that if we compare a falling object to a mass as if it were a single point that is falling to the earth with no air resistance, any calculation (which is really a deduction) that holds from the equation also will hold for the object. The differences don't matter. Or rather, they don't matter very much, since air resistance does slow down an object: if you drop a cat from a hot air balloon, it will spread out its legs and reach a maximum velocity when the force of the air resistance equals the force of acceleration. And it matters, too, where on earth you are: an object dropped from a 100 foot building in San Francisco will accelerate more than an object dropped from a 100 foot building in Denver, which is 5,000 feet above sea level.

With this model there is no visual representation of the part of experience that is being described. There is no point-to-point conceptual comparison, nor are we modeling a static situation. The model is couched in the language of mathematics; equations can be models, too.

Mathematical equations are essentially analogies because we can draw conclusions from them (use them to calculate) when the differences don't matter. The mass of the object being dropped doesn't matter because the results of the calculations using (*) will be close enough for most of our purposes. But we can't use (*) for calculating how the moon moves relative to the earth because the differences do matter: the moon has a mass that is large enough compared to the earth to be significant.

Example 5 *Newton's laws of motion and Einstein's theory of relativity —how a false theory can be used*

Newton's laws of motion are taught in every elementary physics course and are used daily by physicists. Yet modern physics has replaced Newton's theories with Einstein's and quantum mechanics. Newton's laws, physicists tell us, are false.

But can't we say that Newton's laws are correct relative to the quality of measurements involved, even though Newton's laws can't be derived from quantum mechanics? Or perhaps they can if a premise is added that we ignore certain small effects. Yet how is that part of a theory?

A theory is a schematic representation of some part of the world. We draw conclusions from the representation (we calculate or deduce). The conclusion is said to apply to the world. The reasoning is legitimate so long as the differences between the representation and what is being represented don't matter. Newton's laws of motion are "just like" how moderately large objects interact at moderately low speeds; we can use those laws to make calculations so long as the differences don't matter. Some of the assumptions of that theory are used as conditions to tell us when the theory is meant to be applied.

Example 6 *Ether as the medium of light waves*
—an experiment can show that an assumption of a theory is false

In the 19th century, light was understood as waves. In analogy with waves in water or sound waves in the air, a medium was postulated for the propagation of light waves: the ether. Using that assumption, many predictions were made about the path and speed of light in terms of its wave behavior. Attempts then were made to isolate or verify the existence of an ether. The experiments of Michelson and Morley showed those predictions to be false. When a better theory was postulated by Einstein, one which assumed no ether and gave as good or better predictions in all cases where the ether assumption did, the theory of ether was abandoned.

Example 7 *Euclidean plane geometry—a model that can't be true*

Euclidean plane geometry speaks of points and lines: a point is location without dimension, a line is extension without breadth. No such objects exist in our experience. But Euclidean geometry is remarkably useful in measuring and calculating distances and positions in our daily lives.

Points are abstractions of very small dots made by a pencil or other implement. Lines are abstractions of physical lines, either drawn or sighted. So long as the differences don't matter, that is, so long as the size of the points and the lines are very small relative to what is being measured or plotted, we can deduce conclusions that are true.

No one asks (anymore) whether the axioms of Euclidean geometry are true. Rather, when the differences don't matter, we can calculate and predict using Euclidean geometry. When the differences do matter, as in calculating paths of airplanes circling the globe, Euclidean plane geometry does not apply, and another model, geometry for spherical surfaces, is invoked.

Euclidean geometry is a deductive theory: a conclusion drawn from the axioms is accepted only if the inference is valid. It is a purely mathematical theory, which taken as mathematics would appear to have no application since the objects of which it speaks do not exist. But taken as a model it has applications in the usual way, arguing by analogy where the differences don't matter.

B. Models, Analogies, and Abstraction

We've seen models of static situations (the map) and of processes (acceleration of falling objects). We've seen examples of models that are entirely visual and of models formulated entirely in terms of mathematical equations. We've seen models in which the assumptions of the model are entirely implicit (the map), and we have seen models in which the assumptions are quite explicit (Newton's laws of motion).

In all the examples either the reasoning is clearly reasoning by analogy or can be seen to proceed by abstraction much as in reasoning by analogy. We do not ask whether the assumptions of a theory or model are true, even if that was the intention of the person who created the theory. Rather, we ask whether we can use it in the given situation: do the similarities that are being invoked hold and do the differences not matter? Even in the case of Newton's laws of motion, where it would seem that what is at stake is whether the assumptions are true, we continue to use the model when we know that the assumptions are false in those cases where, as in any analogy, the differences don't matter. In only one example (the ether) did it seem that what was at issue was whether a particular assumption of the theory was actually true of the world. And that wouldn't have mattered if the theory had yielded accurate predictions.

The assumptions of theories in science are false when we consider them as representing all aspects of some particular part of our experience. The key claim in every analogy is false in the same way. When we say that one side of an analogy is "just like" the other, that's false. What is true is that they are "like" one another in some key respects that allow us to deduce claims for the one from deducing claims for the other.

The term ***model*** is typically applied to what can be visualized or made concrete, while ***theory*** seems to be used for examples that are fairly formal with explicitly stated assumptions. But in many cases it is as appropriate to call an example a theory as to call it a model, and there seems to be no definite distinction between those terms.

Example 8 The atomic model of matter has gone through many refinements. At one time or another, atoms were imagined to be tiny spheres with hooks on them (to explain chemical bonding), or as tiny billiard balls continually bouncing against each other. More recently, the "planetary model" of the atom visualized the atom as a nucleus with electrons revolving around it, just as the planets revolve around the sun. D. C. Giancoli, *Physics,* 2nd edition

Analysis Giancoli describes various models of the atom as they were used to help visualize the working of something we can't see. What isn't mentioned, however, are all the other claims about the workings of the atom that were made in conjunction with those pictures, claims from which predictions about the behavior of chemical compounds could be made. Those claims, along with the similarities between atoms and the models that were proposed, constituted the atomic theory of that time.

C. Confirming a Theory

From theories we can make predictions. When a prediction turns out to be true, we say it ***confirms*** (to some degree) the theory. This is not the same as confirming a generalization in an explanation, for it rarely makes sense to say that the claims that make up a theory—the assumptions of the theory—are true or false.

We cannot say that verifications of the relation of pressure, temperature, and volume in a gas confirm that molecules are hard little balls and that all collisions are completely elastic. Nor does fitting a carpenter's square exactly into a wooden triangle that is 50cm x 40cm x 30cm confirm the theorem of Pythagoras. Nor can we say that finding a tree at the corner of 100 W and 100 S in Minersville disconfirms the model given by the map. The map wasn't meant to give any information about trees, so it doesn't matter that it shows no tree there.

Except in rare instances where we think (usually temporarily) that we have hit upon a truth of the universe to use as an assumption in a theory, we do not think that the assumptions of a theory are true or false. We can only say of a theory such as Euclidean plane geometry or the kinetic theory of gases whether it is ***applicable*** in a particular situation we are investigating.

To say that a theory is applicable is to say that, though there are differences between the world and what the assumptions of the theory state, those differences don't matter for the conclusions we wish to draw. Often we can decide if a theory is applicable only by attempting to apply it. We use the theory to draw conclusions in particular cases, claiming that the differences don't matter. If the conclusions—the predictions—turn out to be true (enough), then we have some confidence that we are right. If a prediction turns out false, then the model is not applicable there. We do not say that Euclidean plane geometry is false because it cannot be used to calculate the path of an airplane on the globe; we say that Euclidean plane geometry is inapplicable for calculating on globes.

When we make predictions and they are true, we confirm a ***range of application*** of a model. When we make predictions and they are false, we disconfirm a range of application—that is, we find limits for the range of application of a model. More information about where the model can be applied and where it cannot be applied may lead, often with great effort, to our describing more precisely the range of application of a model. In that case, the claims describing the range of application can be added to the theory. We often use mathematics as a language to make this art of analogy precise. But in many cases it is difficult to state precisely the range of application. Reasoning using models is reasoning by analogy, which is likely to require judgment.

Sometimes it's said that a theory is valid, or is true, or that a theory holds. These are just different ways to assert that a particular situation or class of situations to which we wish to apply a theory is within the range of that theory.

Theories are tools, not statements of facts.

D. Good Theories and Modifying Theories in the Light of New Evidence

The criteria for whether one theory is good or better than another cannot in general include whether the assumptions of the theory are true or "realistic." That would rule out the kinetic theory of gases. So besides getting true predictions, what criteria can we use to evaluate theories? Consider what we do when we discover that a prediction made from a theory is false.

When Newton's laws of motion resulted in inaccurate predictions for very small objects, we noted that the theory had been assumed true for all sizes and speeds of objects and then restricted the range of application. But when the theory of the ether resulted in false predictions, no modification was made to the theory, for none could be made. That theory did not abstract from experience, ignoring some aspects of situations under consideration, but postulated something in addition to our experience, which we were able to show did not exist. The theory was completely abandoned.

If a theory has been made by abstraction—that is, many aspects of our experience are ignored and only a few are considered significant—then tracing back along that ***path of abstraction*** we can try to distinguish what difference there is between our model and our experience that matters. What have we ignored that cannot in this situation be ignored? If we cannot state generally what the difference is that matters, then at best the false prediction sets some limit on the range of application of the model or theory. We cannot use the theory here—where "here" means this situation or ones that we can see are very similar.

But our goal will be to state precisely the difference that matters and try to factor it into our theory. We try to devise a complication of our theory in which that aspect of our experience is taken into account. As with Einstein's improvement of Newton's laws, we get a better theory that is more widely applicable and that explains why the old theory worked as well as it did and why it failed in the ways it failed. We improve the map: by adding more assumptions, we can pay attention to more in our experience, and that accounts for the differences between the theories.

True predictions are never enough to justify a theory. Indeed, we do not "justify" a theory, nor show that it is "valid." What we do in the process of testing predictions is show how and where the theory can be applied. And for us to have confidence in that, either (i) we must show that the claims in the theory are true, or (ii) show in what situations the differences between what is being modeled and the abstraction of it in the theory do not matter. True (enough) predictions help in that. But equally crucial is our ability to trace the path of abstraction so that we can see what has been ignored in our reasoning and why true predictions serve to justify our ignoring those aspects of experience. Without that clear path of abstraction, all we can do is try to prove that the claims in the theory are actually true.

Sometimes we are confronted with two theories that both yield good predictions for a class of situations and for both there is a clear path of abstraction. In that case, we say that one theory is better than another if:

- Its assumptions are simpler.
- It yields clearer derivations of the claims the theories are meant to derive.
- It has a wider range of application.

For example, Ptolemy's model can be improved by adding more epicycles to predict the movements of the planets and sun. Using the computing power we now have, we'd see that the predictions come out true—in geometry we can always shift the origin of an axis system. But we prefer Newton's model because of these criteria.

Example 9 Consider the density of leaves around a tree. I suggest the hypothesis that the leaves are positioned as if each leaf deliberately sought to maximize the amount of sunlight it receives, given the position of its neighbors, as if it knew the physical laws determining the amount of sunlight that would be received in various positions and could move rapidly or instantaneously from any one position to any other desired and unoccupied position. Now some of the more obvious implications of this hypothesis are clearly consistent with experience: for example, leaves are in general denser on the south than on the north side of trees but, as the hypothesis implies, less so or not at all on the northern slope of a hill or when the south side of the trees is shaded in some other way. Is the hypothesis rendered unacceptable or invalid because, so far as we know, leaves do not 'deliberate' or consciously 'seek,' have not been to school and learned the relevant laws of science or the mathematics to calculate the 'optimum' position, and cannot move from position to position? Clearly, none of these contradictions of the hypothesis is vitally relevant; the phenomena involved are not within the 'class of phenomena the hypothesis is designed to explain'; the hypothesis does not assert that leaves do these things but only that their density is the same *as if* they did. Despite the apparent falsity of the 'assumptions' of the hypothesis, it has great plausibility because of the conformity of its implications with observation. We are inclined to 'explain' its validity on the ground that sunlight contributes to the growth of leaves and that hence leaves will grow denser or more putative leaves survive where there is more sun, so the result achieved by purely passive adaptation to external circumstances is the same as the result that would be achieved by deliberate accommodation to them. This alternative hypothesis is more attractive than the constructed hypothesis not because its 'assumptions' are more 'realistic' but rather because it is part of a more general theory that applies to a wider variety of phenomena, of which the position of leaves around a tree is a special case, has more implications capable of being contradicted, and has failed to be contradicted under a wider variety of circumstances.

Milton Friedman, "The Methodology of Positive Economics"

Analysis Friedman's hypothesis about leaves seeking to maximize the amount of sunlight they receive cannot be used for reasoning by analogy or abstraction. It does not begin by either (a) looking at a real situation and comparing it to the growth of leaves, allowing us to distinguish what are the similarities and what are the differences, or (b) abstracting from experience to state what are the points of similarity that are supposed to hold, ignoring all else.

Rather, what he has posited is not an abstraction but the addition of properties to a given situation. We are asked to suppose that leaves behave anthropomorphically with the skills of a terrific calculator. And then we are asked to ignore that as well. This doesn't make sense as a method of reasoning: why should we have confidence that predictions made from such an hypothesis will be accurate? That some of the predictions turn out to be accurate cannot be enough, any more than they are in astrology. We need to know why they turn out accurate in order to have confidence in the theory or model.

The alternative hypothesis of passive adaptation that Friedman presents is better, but not for the reasons he gives. It is better for the reason he says is not meaningful: we have better reason to accept the alternative hypothesis precisely because we can see that in this case it is reasonable to believe it is true. No clearly false assumption incapable of fitting into reasoning by analogy or abstraction has been made.

Key Words

model	a prediction confirms a theory
theory	range of application of a theory
models more	path of abstraction
abstracts more	

Exercises for Chapter 5S

1. Explain how the map of Minersville, Utah, is used to reason by analogy.
2. Does the use of the kinetic theory of gases to make true predictions show that its assumptions are true? Explain.
3. Why can we use Newton's laws of motion even though we know they are false?
4. What does it mean to say that a true prediction confirms a theory?
5. Several similar predictions are made from a theory, and by experiment they are all shown to be false. Explain under what circumstances we should then abandon the theory. If we do not abandon the theory, explain how the false predictions can be used to make a better theory.

6. How could one confirm astrology?
7. Explain why theories are tools, not statements of facts.
8. Evaluate the following and explain what is meant by "animal models."

   Rats with damaged brains could help forgetful humans

   Rats with amnesia have provided a new insight into the biochemical basis of forgetfulness. The finding may lead to drugs for treating memory loss associated with aging, say researchers in the US.

   Researchers have known for decades that they can make rats forgetful by creating lesions in their fornix, a bundle of nerves in the brain connected to the hippocampus. When normal rats learn to avoid a dark chamber that gives them an electric shock through their feet, they remember for several days to choose the safe, bright chamber. But rats with lesions on their fornix only remember to avoid the dark chamber for a few hours, suggesting that they can form short-term memories but not long-term ones.

   No one knew how the fornix consolidated long-term memories, but a new experiment suggests a biochemical explanation. Cristina Alberini and her colleagues at Brown University in Providence, Rhode Island, decided to look at how fornix lesions affect the activation of a protein called CREB in the hippocampus during learning. CREB can exist in "active" or "inactive" forms, and previous studies in sea snails and fruit flies suggested that active CREB is essential for the creation of long-term memories.

   In rats with no fornix lesions trained in the light and dark chambers, hippocampal levels of CREB activation soared to around 150% of levels in control animals that had received no training. These levels remained high for as long as nine hours after training. Rats with fornix lesions, however, showed no increase in CREB activation compared with controls (*Nature Neuroscience,* vol. 2, p. 309). "The importance of this finding is that for the first time, we now know that CREB-dependent response in the hippocampus is modulated via the fornix," says Alberini. "This provides a possible molecular basis for amnesia associated with fornix and related structures."

   In November last year, Daniel Storm and his colleagues at the University of Washington in Seattle also showed that training rats activates CREB in their hippocampus as they lay down long-term memories. But while that study showed CREB activation in rats who could remember, this one shows that activation fails to occur in forgetful rats. "It's the other side of the coin and it's a good piece of work," Storm says of Alberini's latest research.

   "What is new is the disappearance of CREB with the amnesiac mode," agrees Jerry Yin of Cold Springs Harbor Laboratory in New York. Four years ago, Yin and a colleague Tim Tully gave fruit flies the equivalent of photographic memory by genetically engineering them to produce extra CREB.

   "There's a lot of us that believe it's a very good drug target site," says Storm, who advises a company called Helicon Therapeutics, founded by Yin and Tully. The company hopes to develop drugs that treat memory disorders by boosting CREB activity. After screening around 200,000 drug candidates, it recently found one promising enough to test in simple animal models. "It looks very hopeful," says Yin.

   Nell Boyce, *New Scientist,* no. 2179, March 27, 1999

9. Give a detailed description of a model used in some area of science.
   a. State the similarities that can be used in making deductions.
   b. State what deductions have been made and confirmed from the model.
   c. Give at least one example of a difference between the model and what's being modeled.
   d. State a claim that cannot be deduced because of that difference.

   Here are some models you could choose to describe.

   - William Harvey's model of the circulation of blood compared to a pump.
   - The tinker-toy model of the structure of crystals.
   - Blueprints used in architecture.
   - The mathematical model used in economics of supply and demand.
   - The wave model of light.
   - The Watson-Crick double-helix model of DNA
     (include why Watson and Crick abandoned the triple-helix model).

6S Explanations in Science

A. Is a Theory an Explanation?

Sometimes it's said that a theory gives a good explanation of some claim. For example, it's said that Einstein's general relativity explains why there is no difference in speed between light moving with the direction of the earth and light moving transversally to the path of the earth. But that's a loose way of talking. A theory does not explain; a deduction from a theory can be an explanation.

Here's an example of how Karl Popper in *Objective Knowledge* conflates theories with explanations.

> The new theory, although it has to explain what the old theory explained, *corrects* the old theory, so that it actually *contradicts* the old theory: it contains the old theory, *but only as an approximation*. Thus I pointed out that Newton's theory contradicts both Kepler's and Galileo's theory—*although it explains them,* owing to the fact that it contains them as approximations; and similarly Einstein's theory contradicts Newton's, which it likewise explains, and contains as an approximation.
>
> Karl Popper, *Objective Knowledge*

Wrong. You can't explain anything using false claims, and you certainly can't explain a claim that contradicts the claim doing the explaining. Here, as with many theories, it makes no sense to say that the premises are true but rather that the theory as a whole is applicable.

It's only when we think that the premises of a theory are or can be true that we can say that (a deduction from) the theory is a good explanation. In that way we can make sense of how Carl G. Hempel in *Aspects of Scientific Explanation* compares a theory as an explanation and predictions made from the theory.

> Consider the explanation offered by Torricelli for a fact that had intrigued his teacher Galileo; namely, that a lift pump drawing water from a well will not raise the water more than about 34 feet above the surface of a well. To account for this, Torricelli advanced the idea that the air above the water has weight and thus exerts pressure on the water in the well, forcing it up the pump barrel when the piston is raised, for there is no air inside to balance the outside pressure. On this assumption the water can rise only to the point where its pressure on

> the surface of the well equals the pressure of the outside air on that surface, and the latter will therefore equal that of a water column about 34 feet high.

Torricelli offered an explanation, but the only evidence he had for the explanation, which was a generalization, was the claims being explained.

> The explanatory force of this account hinges on the conception that the earth is surrounded by a "sea of air" that conforms to the basic laws governing the equilibrium of liquids in communicating vessels. And because Torricelli's explanation presupposed such general laws it yielded predictions concerning as yet unexamined phenomena. One of these was that if the water were replaced by mercury, whose specific gravity is about 14 times that of water, the air should counterbalance a column about 34/14 feet, or somewhat less than $2^1/_2$ feet, in length. This prediction was confirmed by Torricelli in the classic experiment that bears his name. In addition, the proposed explanation implies that at increasing altitudes above sea level, the length of the mercury column supported by air pressure should decrease because the weight of the counterbalancing air decreases. A careful test of this prediction was performed at the suggestion of Pascal only a few years after Torricelli had offered his explanation: Pascal's brother-in-law carried a mercury barometer (i.e., essentially a mercury column counterbalanced by the air pressure) to the top of the Puy-de-Dôme, measuring the length of the column at various elevations during the ascent and again during the descent; the readings were in splendid accord with the prediction.

Predictions are made of further instances of the generalization or of consequences of the claim doing the explaining; those are shown to be true; the claim doing the explaining thus become more plausible because the associated argument for it is strengthened.

B. Insight and General Laws

An explanation is not meant to convince that the claim doing the explaining is true. It's meant to give us some insight into why what's being explained is true. But what do we mean by "insight"?

> From accounts given by gunners, I was already aware of the fact that in the use of cannon and mortars, the maximum range . . . is obtained when the elevation is 45° . . . ; but to understand why this happens far outweighs the mere information obtained by the testimony of others or even by repeated experiment.
>
> Galileo, *Dialogues Concerning Two New Sciences*

The insight, it's often said, is a law that connects the claim being explained to other experiences.

It seems that for inferential explanations some law, some general principle is needed among the premises, whether stated or added via the Guide to Repairing Inferential Explanations (p. 340). Yet no one has a clear idea what we should mean by "a general principle." And in many cases, as with some of the cause-and-effect examples in Cartoon Writing Lesson E for Chapter 15, we have no idea what general principle would be needed even though we're sure there is cause and effect.

We cannot say more now than that the claim doing the explaining must somehow link what's being explained to other claims we know to be true, somehow place what's being explained within our general knowledge. A good inferential explanation must show what the claim being explained follows from and must lead us to a place where we can stop asking "Why?" That, often is the role of a theory, connecting many explanations into one general view of a part of the world.

C. Inference to the Best Explanation in Science

Some scientists think that if you have the best explanation, one that explains a lot, it must be true.

> It can hardly be supposed that a false theory would explain, in so satisfactory a manner as does the theory of natural selection, the several large classes of facts above specified [the geographical distribution of species, the existence of vestigial organs in animals, etc.]. It has recently been objected that this is an unsafe method of arguing; but it is a method used in judging of the common events of life, and has often been used by the greatest natural philosophers.
>
> Charles Darwin, *On the Origin of Species,* p. 476

But if Darwin was right, why did scientists spend the next hundred years trying to confirm or disprove the hypothesis of natural selection? Only now do we believe that a revised version of Darwin's hypotheses are true. Darwin fell into the fallacy of inference to the best explanation. He's not alone.

Example 1 Dick: There. See! The sign for the western menswear store: "Real Men Don't Browse".

Zoe: Yeah. So?

Dick: It's true. We're genetically programmed that way. Long ago when humans were evolving, men were stronger and went out to hunt. The women gathered fruit and berries. When we're hunting we take the first thing we can get, maybe just a rabbit, even if we're looking for a mastodon, 'cause we don't know if there'll be another chance that day. When women went out to get berries there were lots of choices, so they'd pick the best and discard ones that weren't quite so good. That's why women like to shop and men just go in and buy the first thing that looks good and then leave.

Analysis This explains why men don't browse and women do. But it doesn't explain it well. It's an example of the fallacy of inference to the best explanation, an evolutionary *just-so story*, like Kipling's "How the Leopard Got Its Spots."

Silly, you say? Then consider the next example.

Example 2 Male U.S. high school students score higher than female students on the geometry questions on the SAT. Some psychologists gave an evolutionary explanation for this. Back in the cave man days, the men went out hunting while the women stayed in the cave to cook and tend the children. Thus, it was evolutionarily adaptive for men to develop spatial reasoning skills, but no such pressure was put on women, and this led to men being better at spatial reasoning and geometry.

Analysis This story didn't sit well with evolutionary neuroscientists. They reviewed studies from biology, neuroscience, and psychology on spatial and geometric knowledge, and they found an interesting pattern. Bears (which are well known for having excellent spatial memory) explore and remember large tracts of land. However, female bears explore less than male bears and have a smaller home-range size. The same pattern was found in several species. So, by analogy, we should expect the same in humans: men should be better at geometry and spatial memory than women. But some species defy this trend. In particular, female hyenas have a larger home-range size than male hyenas. Hyenas, it turns out, differ from bears, dogs, and humans in that females have much higher testosterone levels than males. So the neuroscientists hypothesized that geometry skills are connected to testosterone levels. Testosterone is produced in the hippocampus. The hippocampus is responsible for long-term memory formation and especially spatial memory. So it seems that testosterone levels are connected to the size and activity of the hippocampus, which in turn is tied to geometry skills.

The cave men story is bogus. The same pattern we see in humans is also found in mice, so it didn't evolve uniquely in humans. Perhaps the higher spatial reasoning skills may not have been selected at all, just coming along with the use of higher testosterone levels in reproduction.

Scientists have high hopes for their hypotheses and are motivated to investigate them if they appear to provide a better explanation than current theories. But the scientific community will soon correct a scientist if he or she thinks that just making an hypothesis establishes it as true. Torricelli had more sense than that.

This the best explanation we have.
= *This is a good hypothesis to investigate*.

Exercises for Chapter 6S

1. Evaluate the following argument for why we should believe the law of gravitation and the laws of Galileo and Kepler.

   If you accept the law of gravitation, the laws of Galileo and Kepler, the lunary motions and the tides will, as a matter of course, be systematically explained and cast into a universal mechanics.

   But why should I? The empirical truth of the law is not directly obvious, nor can what it asserts be easily grasped.

Because if you accept it all these things will, as a matter of course, be systematically explained and cast into a universal mechanics. What could be a better reason?
Russell Norwood Hansen, *Patterns of Discovery*

For Exercises 2 and 3 answer the following:

Explanation? (yes or no)
Claim being explained
Claims doing the explaining
Inferential or teleological? *If teleological, can it be rewritten as an inferential*?
Causal? (yes or no)
Evaluation

2. The call of a male Majorcan midwife toad keeps females ripening their eggs in anticipation of sex, a new study shows.

   Jerry Lea, a postgraduate student at the Open University in Milton Keynes, has studied three groups of female Majorcan midwife toads, *Alytes muletensis*. All the toads had ripening eggs in their ovaries. To one group, Lea played a synthesized version of the male calls. A second group heard the call of a different species, while the third heard no calls.

   After a month, females from the first group had many eggs that were ripe and ready for ovulation, while the females in the other two groups had hardly any ripe eggs. Lea speculates that stimulation of the female's auditory nerve fibres causes hormone release in the part of the brain that controls reproductive behavior.

   The finding makes sense given the sex roles of Majorcan midwife toads, says Lea. The males are in short supply because after fertilising the eggs they are celibate for a month while they raise the brood on their own. "The males carry the eggs down the cliff faces to the pools where they develop into tadpoles," says Lea.

   Meanwhile, females squabble over remaining males, who advertise their readiness to mate by calling. Some females don't find a partner for the entire breeding season. There's no point in wasting energy ripening eggs that have no hope of being fertilised, Lea says. Alison Motluk, *New Scientist*, May 15, 1999

3. Like multiple sclerosis, poliomyelitis in its paralytic form was a disease of the more advanced nations rather than of the less advanced ones, and of economically better off people rather than of the poor. It occurred in northern Europe and North America much more frequently than in southern Europe or the countries of Africa, Asia or South America. Immigrants to South Africa from northern Europe ran twice the risk of contracting paralytic poliomyelitis than South-African-born whites ran, and the South-African-born whites ran a much greater risk than nonwhites did. Among the Bantu of South Africa paralytic poliomyelitis was rarely an adult disease. During World War II in North Africa cases of paralytic poliomyelitis were commoner among officers in the British and American forces than among men in the other ranks. At the time various wild hypotheses for the difference were proposed; it was even suggested that it arose from the fact that the officers drank whiskey whereas men in the other ranks drank beer!

   We now understand very well the reason for the strange distribution of paralytic poliomyelitis. Until this century poliomyelitis was a universal infection of infancy and infants hardly ever suffered paralysis from it. The fact that they were occasionally affected is what gave the disease the name "infantile paralysis." With the improvement of hygiene in the advancing countries of the world more and more people missed infection in early childhood and contracted the disease for the first time at a later age, when the risk that the infection will cause paralysis is much greater.

This explains why the first epidemics of poliomyelitis did not occur until this century and then only in the economically advanced countries.

G. Dean, "The multiple sclerosis problem," *Scientific American*, 1970

4. "Why do birds fly? Because it was a useful trait that helped them survive."
   a. This is an example of a teleological explanation. What unstated assumptions are needed?
   b. How does the theory of evolution avoid invoking a guiding intelligence in its (apparently) teleological explanations?

5. In the 17th century it was believed that worms and flies were spontaneously generated from mud and rotting or putrefying material. Here is how Francisco Redi argued against that.

   > I began to believe that all worms found in meat were derived directly from the droppings of flies, and not from the putrefaction of meat, and I was still more confirmed in this belief by having observed that, before the meat grew wormy, flies had hovered over it, of the same kind as those that later bred in it. Belief would be in vain without the confirmation of experiment, hence in the middle of July I put a snake, some fish, some eels from the Arno and a slice of milk-fed veal in four large wide-mouthed flasks; having well closed and sealed them, I then filled the same number of flasks in the same way, only leaving these open. It was not long before the meat and fish, in these second vessels, became wormy and flies were seen entering and leaving at will; but in the closed flasks I did not see a worm though many days had passed since the dead flesh had been put in them. Outside on the paper cover there was now and then a deposit, or a maggot that eagerly sought some crevice by which to enter and obtain nourishment. Meanwhile the different things placed in the flasks had become putrid and stinking.
   >
   > Francisco Redi, *Experiments in the Generation of Insects* (1688), translated by Mab Bigelow, 1909, in *The Origins and Growth of Biology*, ed. Arthur Rook

   a. What other explanation could there be for why there were no worms in the sealed containers?
   b. What other experiment(s) could you perform to show whether Redi is right? Remember that in Redi's time reliable microscopes were not available.
   (See Redi's paper for the other possibilities that Redi thought of.)

7S Ways of Knowing

There are many ways of knowing. Science claims to be the best. But religions claim insights known only through revelation that science cannot lead us to. The Zen master claims to teach without words, by actions, an insight deeper than words can give. The shepherd training his dog learns from his dog and knows the nature of his dog and sheep in a way that science cannot describe. There are many ways of knowing.

But there are also ways of pretense and confusion. The charlatan preys on the gullibility of the many to convince them she knows the spirits of the dead. The ESP researcher has so much faith in what he wishes to show that he convinces himself that what is accidental is sure.

Why do scientists claim pride of place in the ways of knowledge? Because they are willing to test every belief they have. No claim is above suspicion. Even the rules of logic can and have been challenged. To be a scientist is, above all, to make claims that you are willing to test, to leave open to disproof, to make public. Science is a public kind of knowledge, and a verbal kind of knowledge.

Religion differs. Some claims are beyond challenge. You cannot hope to gain insight through the religion if you do not accept those claims. And those claims cannot be tested. Or, in the case of Zen and the roads of mysticism, knowledge comes only when all claims have been thrown away.

Magic seeks a middle way, invoking powers that cannot be shown through the methods of science. Magic, not the magic of the circus or Las Vegas but magic that believes, attempts to control the universe. That is what science does, too. But science attempts control through understanding the mechanisms via experiments, arguments, and explanations. Magic attempts to control through rituals and incantations. Any failure of an attempt to control is explained away.

Science is supposed to lead to understanding, prediction, and control of the world in which we live. Religion is supposed to lead to understanding, but control is only in the hands of higher powers. Magic is supposed to lead to control, but understanding is only understanding of the rituals that work to control. The lines between science, magic, and religion are not so clearly drawn that we cannot doubt that science ending at points beyond its understanding does not merge with religion, or that religion that leads to nonverbal understanding does not share many methods with science. And magic shares so many traits with both that we have a spectrum, not a division of ways of knowing. But it is the fallacy of drawing the line to say that because we cannot make a sharp division between science, magic, and religion, there is no difference.

I have stressed in the presentation of the methods of science that to reason well we must use our imagination: imagine the possibilities. Yet there are possibilities that science will not countenance because they are not verbal or cannot be tested, either directly or through their consequences, and it is a narrow mind that ignores too many possibilities.

The insight—more than feeling—that strikes us on a quiet riverside at dusk when birds are settling in the trees, the sun setting above the leaves of the oaks, is not to be discounted because it cannot be replicated or even expressed. The insight that strikes suddenly on a crowded street in traffic, in the midst of pushing and bright lights, that changes a life in an instant is not to be derided for being ineffable. There are good reasons to believe that are not public, that are not verbal, that are not in the path of science—this is beyond doubt. Even science itself in psychology can establish that there are tasks we cannot perform, such as driving, if we reflect and try to say what we are doing.

But to wish to know is not to know, and to wish to believe is not good reason to believe. The false ways of knowing, the charlatans, the self-duped, the too eager to be convinced, their ways we can avoid, and the methods of this book are useful tools in the fight to avoid self-deception.

There are many ways of knowing. Here we've learned one of them.

Exercises for Chapter 7S

1. Give an example of when you used magic in your daily life recently (for example, you wore a special shirt to your football team's game so they'd win, or you tossed spilled salt over your shoulder). Analyze it using the methods of science. Then decide whether the methods of science do or should apply.

2. Give marks that distinguish science, magic, and religion. That is, note characteristics that would definitely mark a belief or practice as being in one of those categories only, even though not all instances of science, magic, or religion have that mark—sufficient but not necessary conditions for a belief or practice to be labeled science, magic, or religion. Exchange with a classmate and see if you can find exceptions to the characterizations he or she provided.

3. Zoe's friend Marvin belongs to the First Church of Cat. Zoe attends a ceremony of Marvin's Church where he sacrifices a songbird to ensure health in his home for the coming winter. Two months later in January, Zoe visits Marvin in the hospital where he and his daughter are recovering from pneumonia. Marvin has almost recovered, so Zoe challenges him, saying that his belief in an all-powerful Cat whose favor can be ensured by ritual sacrifice of songbirds is unfounded, as shown by his illness. Marvin responds that his faith is not shaken and that he is certain the ritual was somehow imperfect. He notes that Zoe did not believe in the ritual, so her attendance may have contaminated the appeal to Cat.

   Evaluate Marvin's response. What standards have you used? Justify the use of those standards in this context.

4. Evaluate the following argument:

   If the Big Bang theory of the universe is correct, then there was a beginning to the universe. Everything that begins to exist must have a cause. So the universe must have a cause. Therefore, God exists.

5. Dick tried the following test with Spot every day for the last six weeks.

   > At mealtime you might put out two feedpans instead of one for your dog or cat. The feedpans should be located so that they are equally convenient to the animal. They should be placed six to eight inches apart. Both should contain the same amount of food and avoid using a feedpan the animal is familiar with. Pick the dish you wish the animal to eat from and concentrate on it. In this test, the animal has a 50% chance of choosing correctly half the time. You may want to keep a record of his responses over several weeks to determine how well your pet has done.
   >
   > Martin Ebon, ed., *Test Your ESP*

   Dick found that Spot chose the right dish 30 of the 42 times. Now he's sure that Spot and he can communicate telepathically. Did his experiment really confirm his explanation for why Spot chose the right dish so often?

6. Evaluate the following experiment and the criticism of it.

   Strangers' prayers don't benefit health, study finds

   Does praying for a sick person's recovery do any good?

   In the largest scientific test of its kind, heart surgery patients showed no benefit when strangers prayed for their recovery.

   And patients who were being prayed for had a slightly higher rate of complications. The researchers could only guess why.

   Several scientists questioned the concept of the study. Science "is not designed to study the supernatural," said Dr. Harold G. Koenig, director of the Center for Spirituality, Theology, and Health at the Duke University Medical Center. The researchers emphasized that their $2.4 million study could not address whether God exists or answers prayers made on another's behalf. The study could only look for an effect from the specific prayers offered as part of the research, they said.

   The study "did not move us forward or backward" in understanding the effects of prayer, said Dr. Charles Bethea, a co-author and cardiologist at the Integris Baptist Medical Center in Oklahoma City. "Intercessory prayer under our restricted format had a neutral effect."

   Researchers also said they didn't know why patients who knew they were being prayed for had a higher rate of complications than patients who only knew that such prayers were a possibility. Maybe they became anxious by the knowledge that they had been selected for prayers, Bethea said: "Did the patients think 'I am so sick that they had to call in the prayer team?' "

   The researchers said family and friends shouldn't be discouraged from telling a patient about their plans to pray for a good recovery. The study only focused on prayers by strangers, they said.

It's the largest and best designed study ever to test the medical effects of intercessory prayers—praying on behalf of someone else. But critics said the question of God's reaction to prayer simply can't be explored by a scientific study.

The study followed about 1,800 patients at six medical centers. It was financed by the Templeton Foundation, which supports research into science and religion, and one of the participating hospitals. It will appear in Tuesday's issue of the American Heart Journal.

The research team tested the effect of having three Christian groups pray for particular patients, starting the night before surgery and continuing for two weeks. The volunteers prayed for "a successful surgery with quick, healthy recovery and no complications" for specific patients.

Malcolm Ritter, The Associated Press, March 31, 2006

8. Compare:
   - Latin prayers said by a priest that the people in the church don't understand.
   - Hebrew prayers said by a rabbi that the people in the synagogue don't understand.
   - Ritual incantations said by a magician that those attending the ceremony do not understand.

Further Study A good survey of the issues here is *Magic, Science, Religion, and the Scope of Rationality* by Stanley Jeyaraja Tambiah. See also "Rationality" by Charles Taylor and "Tradition and modernity revisited" by Robin Horton in *Rationality and Relativism*, edited by M. Hollis and S. Lukes. In my paper "Language-Thought-Meaning" (on the ARF website) you can read more about ways of knowing that are not verbal.

Evaluating Reasoning

Here's a summary of the methods of evaluating reasoning we've studied.

Arguments

1. Decide if there is an argument. If so, identify the conclusion, and identify each sentence or clause that might be a claim.
2. For each of those, decide:
   - Is it ambiguous or too vague to be a claim?
   - If it's vague, could we clear that up by looking at the rest of the argument? Are the words implicitly defined?
   - If it's too vague, scratch it out as noise.
   - If it uses slanters, reword it neutrally.
3. Identify the claims that lead directly to the conclusion.
4. Identify any subarguments that are meant to support the claims that lead directly to the conclusion.
5. See if the obvious objections have been considered.
   - List ones that occur to you as you read the passage.
   - See if they have been answered.
6. Note which claims in the argument are unsupported, and then evaluate whether each is plausible. If one is not plausible, can it be deleted without making the argument weaker?
7. Decide whether each subargument is valid or strong.
   - Note if it is a valid type or one of the fallacies we've seen.
   - If it is not valid or strong, can it be repaired?
   - If it can be repaired, do so and evaluate any added premises.
8. Evaluate whether the entire argument is valid or strong.
   - Note if the argument is a valid type or one of the fallacies we've seen.
   - If it is not valid or strong, can it be repaired?
   - If it can be repaired, do so and evaluate any added premises.
9. Decide whether the argument is good.

Analogies

1. Is this an argument? What is the conclusion?
2. What is the comparison?
3. What are the premises (one or both sides of the comparison)?
4. What are the similarities?
5. Can we state the similarities as premises and find a general principle that covers the two sides?
6. Does the general principle really apply to both sides?
   Do the differences matter?
7. Evaluate the entire argument using the procedure for arguments.

Generalizing

1. Is this an argument? What is the conclusion?
2. Identify the sample and the population.
3. Are the three premises for a generalization plausible?
   - The sample is representative.
   - The sample is big enough.
   - The sample is studied well.
4. Evaluate the generalization using the procedure for arguments.

Cause and Effect

1. Identify what appears to be the causal claim.
   If it is not too vague, rephrase the cause and effect as two separate claims.
2. Decide whether the purported cause and effect happened (the claims are true).
3. Decide whether the purported cause precedes the effect.
4. Evaluate whether it is (nearly) impossible for the claim describing the cause to be true and the claim describing the effect to be false, relative to normal conditions that you could provide.
5. Decide whether the cause makes a difference: if there were no cause, would the effect still have happened?
6. Decide whether there is a common cause.
7. Make sure that none of the obvious mistakes are made:
   - Cause and effect are not reversed.
   - It's not *post hoc ergo propter hoc*.
   - It's not tracing the cause too far back.
8. Decide whether you can conclude that there is cause and effect.

Cause in Populations

1. Identify the kind of experiment that is used to support the conclusion: controlled or uncontrolled; cause to effect, or effect to cause.
2. Decide whether you should accept the results of the experiment.
   - Was it conducted well?
     (Use the methods for evaluating generalizations.)
   - Does it really support the conclusion?
     (Use the steps for evaluating arguments and cause and effect.)
3. Decide whether the argument is good.

Evaluating Risk and Making Decisions

1. List all the choices.
   Not just the choices that are "within reason," but all the choices you can think of. Remember: Doing nothing is a choice, too.
2. For each choice, list:
   - What are the consequences of choosing it?
   - What are the consequences of not choosing it?
3. Rank the choices in order from the one you want the most to the one you want the least. Or if it is not a personal decision, rank the choices in order from which is most desirable to which is the least desirable.
   These rankings should be arguments. That is, you should argue why a particular choice is desirable and another is not desirable. In doing so, consider the risks associated with the consequences of making one choice versus another.
4. For each choice, list:
   - The obstacles to accomplishing it.
   - What might make it easy to accomplish.
5. Review (3) in light of (4).
   Are some of the obstacles there because it is (or should be) less desirable? Do some of the reasons it is easy to accomplish reflect why it is (or should be) desirable?
6. Rank the choices in order from which is easiest to accomplish and which is hardest. These rankings should be arguments.
7. Make a decision by weighing (6) against (3).
   One choice may be easy to accomplish, yet not very desirable. While another may be highly desirable, yet harder to accomplish. If your choice is hard to accomplish, you will have to argue that it is so desirable that it is worth overcoming the obstacles in its way. If your choice is not very desirable, you will have to argue that the other choices are too difficult to accomplish.

Evaluating Explanations

Inferential explanations

1. Decide whether this is an attempt to explain why some claim is true.
   If so, identify the claim that's being explained and number every sentence or clause that might be a claim.
2. For each numbered part, decide:
   - Is it too vague or ambiguous to be a claim?
   - If it's vague, could we clear that up by looking at the rest of what's said? Are the words implicitly defined?
   - If it's too vague, scratch it out as noise.
   - If it uses slanters, reword it neutrally.
3. Check that the claim being explained is clearly true.
4. Evaluate whether each explanatory claim is plausible.
   - If not, can it be established by the associated argument?
   - If the associated argument won't do, can it be established by another argument?
5. Check that at least one of the explanatory claims is not more plausible than the conclusion.
6. Evaluate whether the explanation is valid or strong.
7. Check whether the explanation is circular.
8. Decide whether the explanation answers the right question and whether it is adequate.
9. Decide whether the explanation is good.

Teleological explanations

1. Decide whether this is an attempt to explain how some claim is true in terms of goals or functions, or whether it uses explanatory claims that can be true only after the claim being explained becomes true.
2. Decide whether the explanation can be recast as an inferential one that is better.
3. Check that the necessary conditions for a teleological explanation to be good are satisfied:
   - The claim being explained is highly plausible.
   - The explanation answers the right question.
   - The explanation is not circular.
   - The explanation does not ascribe motives, beliefs, or goals to something that doesn't or can't have those.
   - The explanation does not assume that because something occurs in nature, it therefore has a purpose.
4. Decide whether you have good reason to accept the explanation.

Glossary

Absolute risk reduction The percentage of all people who take the treatment, whether ill or not, who would be helped by the treatment.

Abstracts more One model abstracts more than another if it ignores more about the part of the world it is meant to model. *See also* Path of abstraction.

Abstraction A theory is made by abstraction when we ignore many aspects of our experience for reasoning by analogy. *See also* Path of abstraction.

Applicable A theory is applicable in a situation if the differences between the world and the assumptions of the theory don't matter for the conclusions we wish to draw from the theory. *See also* Range of application.

Act of God A natural disaster not due to human actions.

Ad baculum An appeal to fear. *See* Appeal to emotion.

Ad hominem ("Against the person") A general name used to refer to any one of *Mistaking the person for the argument, Mistaking the person for the claim, Phony refutation.*

Ad misercordiam An appeal to pity. *See* Appeal to emotion.

Ad verecundiam A bad appeal to authority.

Affirming the consequent Reasoning in the form: If A, then B; B; so A. Usually weak.

All Usually means "every single one, no exceptions." Sometimes "all" is best understood as "every single one, and there is at least one."

Alternatives The claims that are the parts of an "or" claim.

Ambiguous sentence A sentence that can be understood in two or a very few obviously different ways.

Analogy, reasoning by A comparison becomes reasoning by analogy when it is part of an argument: on one side of the comparison we draw a conclusion, so on the other side we should conclude the same.

Anecdotal evidence Claims about a sample of one or very few that clearly do not constitute a big enough sample that are used as evidence for a generalization. The claims about the sample in a hasty generalization.

Antecedent The claim A in a conditional claim "If A, then B."

Appeal to authority An argument that uses or requires as premise: (Almost) anything that _______ says about ______ is true.

Appeal to common belief An argument that uses or requires as premise: If (almost) everyone else (in this group) believes it, then it's true.

Appeal to emotion An argument that uses or requires as premise: You should believe or do _______ if you feel _______ (e.g., fear, pity, spite, . . .).

Appeal to fear. *See* Appeal to emotion.

Appeal to ignorance Arguing that because we don't know more, we can conclude that the claim is true (or that it is false). Confusing that there is no reason to believe a claim is true with having a reason to believe it's not true.

Appeal to pity. *See* Appeal to emotion.

Appeal to spite. *See* Appeal to emotion.

Appeal to tradition An argument that uses or requires as premise: You should believe or do because it's a tradition.

Appeal to vanity. *See* Appeal to emotion. *See also* Apple polishing.

Apple polishing A feel-good argument that appeals to vanity.

Apples and oranges A comparison of different kinds of things where there's no common basis for comparison.

Arguing backwards Reasoning that a premise of an argument is true because the conclusion is true and the argument is valid or strong. *See also* Affirming the consequent.

***Arguing backwards with* all** Reasoning in the form: All S are P; *a* is P; so *a* is S. Usually weak. *See also* Affirming the consequent.

***Arguing backwards with* almost all** Reasoning in the form: Almost all S are P; *a* is P; so *a* is S. Usually weak.

***Arguing backwards with* no** Reasoning in the form: All S are P; no Q is S; so no Q is P. Usually weak. *See also* Denying the antecedent.

Argument An attempt to convince someone (possibly yourself) that a particular claim, called the *conclusion*, is true by giving one or more other claims as reasons.

Assertion A claim that is put forward as true.

Associated argument For an inferential explanation "A, B, C, . . . explains E", the associated argument to establish A is "E, B, C, . . . therefore A." *See also* Dependent explanation; Independent explanation.

***Average* (*or mean*)** *of a collection of numbers* The number obtained by adding all the values and then dividing by the number of items.

Bandwagon fallacy An appeal to common belief.

Begging the question An argument that uses a premise that is not more plausible than the conclusion. Sometimes called *petitio principii*.

Behavioral explanation An explanation in terms of the motives or beliefs or feelings of a person or creature.

Biased sample A sample that is not representative.

Burden of proof. *See* Shifting the burden of proof.

Calling in your debts An argument that uses or requires as premise: You should believe or do _______ if you owe _______ a favor.

Causal claim A claim that is or can be rewritten as "— causes (or caused) —." *See also* Cause and effect, necessary criteria for; General causal claim; Particular causal claim.

Causal factor One of several claims that jointly qualify as describing the cause.

Cause. *See* Cause and effect, necessary criteria for.

Cause and effect, *necessary criteria for*

- The cause happened (the claim describing it is true).
- The effect happened (the claim describing it is true).
- The cause precedes the effect.
- It is (nearly) impossible for the cause to happen (be true) and the effect not to happen (be false), given the normal conditions.
- The cause makes a difference—if the cause had not happened (been true), the effect would not have happened (been true).
- There is no common cause.

Cause makes a difference If the cause had not occurred, there wouldn't be the effect.

Cause in a population A claim which says that if the cause is present, then there is a higher probability the effect will follow than if the cause were not present.

Circular argument An argument in which a premise is equivalent to or supposes the conclusion; a variety of *begging the question*.

Claim A declarative sentence used in such a way that it is either true or false (but not both).

Clever Hans effect The effect that an animal's or person's behavior can be influenced by subtle and unintentional cues from an experimenter.

Composition, fallacy of Reasoning that what is true of (or good for) the individual must also be true of (or good for) the group, or vice-versa. The latter is sometimes called the *fallacy of division*.

Compound claim A claim composed of other claims but which has to be viewed as just one claim.

Conclusion The claim whose truth an argument is meant to establish.

Conditional claim A compound claim that is either in the form *If A, then B* or is equivalent to one in that form.

Conditional proof. *See* Reasoning from hypotheses.

Confidence level The percentage of the time that the same sampling method would give a result that is a true generalization. The strength of the generalization.

Confirming a theory When a prediction made from a theory turns out to be true, we say it confirms (to some degree) the theory. *See also* Range of application.

Confusing objective and subjective Calling a claim objective when it is really subjective, or vice-versa.

Consequent The claim B in a conditional claim "If A, then B."

Content fallacy An argument that uses or requires for repair a particular kind of (generic) premise that if false or dubious classifies the argument as a fallacy.

Contradictory of a claim A contradictory of a claim is one that has the opposite truth-value in all possible circumstances. Sometimes called a *negation* of a claim.

- Contradictory of "A or B" is "Not A and not B."
- Contradictory of "A and B" is "Not A or not B."
- Contradictory of "If A, then B" is "A but not B."

Contrapositive The contrapositive of "If A, then B" is "If not B, then not A." It is equivalent to the original conditional.

Control group. *See* Controlled experiment: cause-to-effect.

Controlled experiment: cause-to-effect An experiment to establish cause in a population. Two randomly chosen samples are used. One is administered the cause, and the other, called the *control group,* is not administered the cause. *See also* Uncontrolled experiment.

Correlation Every time this happened, that happens.

Correlation-causation fallacy To claim that a correlation all by itself establishes cause and effect.

Criteria for accepting or rejecting an unsupported claim In the order in which they should be applied:

Accept: We know the claim is true from our own experience.
Reject: We know the claim is false from our own experience.
(Exceptions: We have good reason to doubt our memory or our perception; the claim contradicts other experiences of ours; and there is a good argument against the claim.)
Reject: The claim contradicts another claim we know is true.
Accept: The claim is made by someone we know and trust, and the person is an authority on this kind of claim.
Accept: The claim is made by a reputable expert on this kind of claim who has no motive to mislead.
Accept: The claim is put forward in a reputable journal or reference source.
Accept: The claim is in a media source that's usually reliable and has no obvious motive to mislead, if the source is named.

Critical thinking Evaluating whether we should be convinced that some claim is true or some argument is good, as well as formulating good arguments.

Deduction An inference meant to be judged as valid or invalid.

Definition An explanation or stipulation of how to use a word or phrase. A definition is not a claim. *See also* Good definition; Persuasive definition.

Denying the antecedent Reasoning in the form: If A, then B; not A; so not B. Usually weak.

Dependent explanation *See* Independent explanation.

Descriptive claim A claim meant to describe what is, was, or will be. *Compare* Prescriptive claim.

***Direct way of reasoning with* all** Reasoning in the form: All S are P; *a* is S; so *a* is P. Valid.

***Direct way of reasoning with* almost all** Reasoning in the form: Almost all S are P; *a* is S; so *a* is P. Usually strong.

Direct way of reasoning with conditionals Reasoning in the form: If A, then B; A; so B. Valid. Also called *modus ponens*.

***Direct way of reasoning with* no** Reasoning in the form: All S are P; no Q is P; so no Q is S. Valid.

Direct ways of refuting an argument. *See* Refuting an argument directly.

Disjunction. *See* Or-claim.

Disjunctive syllogism. *See* Excluding possibilities.

Double blind trial A controlled cause-to-effect cause-in-population study in which neither the subjects nor those administering the drug or placebo are told which is a placebo and which a drug.

Downplayer A word or phrase that minimizes the significance of a claim.

Drawing the line fallacy A type of bad argument which assumes that if you can't make the difference precise, then there is no difference.

Dubious claim. *See* Implausible claim.

Duplicable experiment An experiment that is described clearly enough that others can follow the method to obtain observations. *See also* Replicated experiment; Reproducible results.

Dysphemism A word or phrase that makes something sound worse than a neutral description. *See also* Euphemism.

Effect. *See* Cause and effect, necessary criteria for.

Equivalent claims Claims that in all circumstances have the same truth-value.

Equivocation A bad argument that depends on an ambiguity.

Euphemism A word or phrase that makes something sound better than a neutral description. *See also* Dysphemism.

Evidence A claim or claims that give some reason to believe another claim. *See also* inductive evidence.

Evidence (in science) The observational claims that are used as premises of an argument.

Excluding possibilities Reasoning in the form: A or B; not A; so B (can use more alternatives). Valid. Also called *disjunctive syllogism*.

Explanandum In a verbal explanation, the claim meant to be explained.

Explanation. *See* Inferential explanation; Teleological explanation.

Explanatory claims In an inferential explanation, the claims from which the claim being explained is supposed to follow.

Explanans In a verbal explanation, the claims meant to do the explaining.

Fallacy An argument of one of the types that have been agreed to be so bad as to be unrepairable. *See also* Content fallacy; Structural fallacy.

Fallacy of scale Saying that some consequence of a proposed action would be good (or would be bad) without considering the size of the consequence.

False dilemma A use of excluding possibilities where the "or" claim isn't plausible. Sometimes the false or dubious "or" claim itself is called the "false dilemma."

Feel-good argument An argument that uses or requires as premise: You should believe or do _______ if it makes you feel good.

Follows from The conclusion follows from the premises if the argument is strong or valid.

Foreseeable consequence of a cause A claim that becomes true after the cause, yet because it is a consequence of that cause, it is not counted as part of the cause.

Gambler's fallacy An argument that uses or requires as premise: A run of events of a certain kind makes a run of contrary events more likely in order to even up the probabilities.

General causal claim A causal claim that is true if and only if many particular cause-and-effect claims are true. *See also* Particular causal claim.

General claim A claim that asserts something about all or a part of a collection.

Generalizing Concluding a claim about a group, the *population*, from a claim or claims about some part of it, the *sample*. To generalize is to make an argument. Sometimes the general claim is called the *generalization*; sometimes that word is used for the whole argument. The claims describing the sample are called the *inductive evidence* for the generalization. *See also* Premises needed for a good generalization.

Good argument A good argument is one in which the premises give good reason to believe that the conclusion is true. *See also* Tests for an argument to be good.

Genetic fallacy. *See* Mistaking the person for the claim; Mistaking the person for the argument.

Good definition A definition in which (1) the words doing the defining are clear and better understood than the word or phrase being defined, and (2) the word or phrase being defined and the words doing the defining can be used interchangeably.

Guide to Repairing Arguments Given an (implicit) argument that is apparently defective, we are justified in adding a premise or conclusion if it satisfies all three of the following:

- The argument becomes stronger or valid.
- The premise is plausible and would seem plausible to the other person.
- The premise is more plausible than the conclusion.

If an argument is valid or strong, we may delete a premise if doing so does not make the argument weaker. *See also* Unrepairable arguments.

Guide to Repairing Inferential Explanations Given an (implicit) inferential explanation that is apparently defective, we are justified in adding a further explanatory claim if all three of the following hold:

- The explanation becomes stronger or valid.
- The claim is plausible and would seem plausible to the other person.
- The claim does not make the explanation circular.

We may delete an explanatory claim if that doesn't make the explanation weaker.

Haphazard sampling Choosing a sample with no intentional bias. Not usually reliable for generalizing. *Compare* Random sampling.

Hasty generalization Generalizing from a sample that is much too small.

Hyperbole An extreme version of an up-player; a gross exaggeration.

Hypothetical syllogism. *See* Reasoning in a chain with conditionals.

Ignoratio elenchi ("Ignorance of the conclusion") A hopelessly weak argument. *See* Irrelevant premise.

If and only if "A if and only if B" means "If A, then B; and if B then A."

Implausible claim A claim that we do not have good reason to believe is true.

Implying. *See* Inferring and implying.

Inadequate explanation An explanation that leads to a further "Why?"

Independent explanation A explanation is independent if each explanatory claim is plausible or can be established by an associated argument. An explanation that is not independent is *dependent*

Indicator word A word or phrase added to a claim to tell us the role of the claim in an argument or what the speaker thinks of the claim or argument. Not part of a claim.

Indirect way of reasoning with conditionals Reasoning in the form: If A, then B; not B; so not A. Valid. Also called *modus tollens*.

Induction A term that is used to mean sometimes (i) a generalization, or (ii) any argument from experience, or (iii) a causal inference, or (iv) an inference that is not meant to be judged as valid/invalid. Not used in this text..

Inductive evidence. *See* Generalizing.

Inference to the best explanation To reason that since these claims give the best explanation of this obviously true claim, they are true. A fallacy.

Inferential explanation An answer to the question "Why is claim E true?" that can be understood as "Because A, B, C, . . . are true". The claim E is called the *claim being explained* and the claims A, B, C . . . are called the *explanatory claims*.

Inferential explanation, necessary conditions to be good For "A, B, C, . . . explain E" to be a good inferential explanation all of the following must hold:

- "A, B, C, . . . therefore E" is valid or strong.
- E is highly plausible.
- Each of A, B, C, . . . is plausible.
- At least one of A, B, C, . . . is not more plausible than E.
- The explanation is not circular.
- A, B, C, . . . answer the right question.

Inferring and implying When someone leaves a conclusion unstated, he or she is implying the conclusion. When you decide that an unstated claim is the conclusion, you are inferring that claim. We also say someone is implying a claim if in context it's clear he or she believes the claim. In that case we infer that the person believes the claim.

Innuendo A concealed claim that is particularly unpleasant.

Intersubjective claim A subjective claim that (nearly) everyone agrees is true or that (nearly) everyone agrees is false.

Intervening cause A claim that becomes true after the cause and before the effect that is not a foreseeable consequence of the original cause and that qualifies as a cause, too.

Invalid argument An argument that is not valid. Classified from strong to weak.

Irrelevant premise(s) A premise or premises that can be deleted from an argument without making the argument any weaker. *See also* Relevance.

Issue A claim that is being debated.

Judging claims (***three choices for whether to believe a claim is true***)

- Accept the claim as true.
- Reject the claim as false.
- Suspend judgment.

Law of large numbers If the probability of something occurring is X percent, then over the long run the number of times that happens will be about X percent.

Loaded question A question that conceals a dubious claim that should be argued for rather than assumed.

Margin of error In a generalization, the range within which the actual number for the population is claimed to fall.

Mark of irrationality If you recognize that an argument is good, then it is irrational not to accept the conclusion.

Mean. *See* Average.

***Median** of a collection of numbers* The midway mark: the number in the collection such that there are as many items above it as below it in the collection.

Mining the data Combing through a mass of observations for some correlation when the data was not collected for the purpose of studying that correlation, and then claiming that the correlation is significant. A fallacy.

Misdirection Directing a person's attention away from what you want to conceal.

Mistaking the person for the argument An argument that uses or requires as premise: (Almost) any argument that _____ gives about _____ is bad.

Mistaking the person for the claim An argument that uses or requires as premise: (Almost) anything that _____ says about _____ is false.

***Mode** of a collection of numbers* The number that appears most often in the collection.

***Model**. See* Theory.

Models more One model models more than another if there are more similarities between the model and what it is modeling. *See also* Abstracts more.

Modus ponens ("way of putting"). *See* Direct way of reasoning with conditionals.

Modus tollens ("way of taking"). *See* Indirect way of reasoning with conditionals.

***Naturalistic fallacy**. See* You can't get "ought" from "is."

Necessary and sufficient conditions A is *necessary* for B means that "If not A, then not B" is true. A is *sufficient* for B means that "If A, then B" is true.

***Negation of a claim**. See* Contradictory of a claim.

No "No *S* is *P*" means "Not even one *S* is *P*," "every single *S* is not *P*."

No-matter-what argument Reasoning in the form: If A, then B; if not A, then B; so B. Valid.

Normal conditions For a causal claim, the obvious and plausible unstated claims that are needed to establish that the relationship between the claim describing purported cause and the claim describing purported effect is valid or strong.

Objective claim A claim that is not subjective. That is, its truth-value does not depend on what someone (or something) thinks, believes, or feels.

Observational claim A claim that is established by personal experience or observation in an experiment.

Only "Only S are P" is equivalent to "All P are S."

Only if "A only if B" is equivalent to "If not B, then not A." It is also equivalent to "If A, then B."

Or-claim A claim that is either of the form "A or B" or is equivalent to one in that form. Sometimes called a *disjunction*.

***"Ought" from "Is"**. See* You can't get "ought" from "is."

Particular causal claim A claim that this particular cause caused this particular effect. *See also* General cause and effect.

Path of abstraction The specific choices for what to ignore about our experience (the world) in devising a theory.

Perfectionist dilemma An argument with the (possibly unstated) premise: Either the situation will be completely perfect if we do this, or we shouldn't do it.

Persuasive definition A claim that should be argued for but which is made to sound like a definition.

Petitio principii. *See* Begging the question.

Phony refutation Concluding that an argument is bad because the person who made the argument has done or said something that shows he or she (apparently) does not believe one of the premises or the conclusion of the argument. A fallacy.

Physical explanation An explanation in terms of the physical make-up of a person, creature, or part of the world.

Plausible claim A claim that we have good reason to believe is true.

Placebo Any substance or treatment given to some participants in a controlled cause-to-effect cause-in-population medical study that is assumed to have no effect.

Placebo effect A reported or experienced physical change that follows from a person being given a placebo.

Poisoning the well A strawman in which someone tries to forestall an impartial hearing of another's argument by asserting something negative about him or her.

Population. *See* Generalizing.

Positive publication bias The tendency of scientific journals to publish articles that show a correlation rather than papers that show there is no correlation.

Post hoc ergo propter hoc ("After this, therefore because of this.") Claiming that there is cause and effect solely because this happened after that.

Premises The claims in an argument that are meant to establish that the conclusion is true.

Premises needed for a good generalization
- The sample is representative.
- The sample is big enough.
- The sample is studied well.

Prescriptive claim A claim meant to describe what should be. *Compare* Descriptive claim.

Principle of Rational Discussion We assume that the other person who is discussing an issue with us or whose arguments we are reading:
- Knows about the subject under discussion.
- Is able and willing to reason well.
- Is not lying.

Proof substitute A word or phrase that suggests the speaker has a proof but no proof is actually offered.

Qualifier A word or phrase that restricts or limits the meaning of other words.

Random sampling Choosing a sample so that at every choice there is an equal chance for any of the remaining members of the population to be picked. *Compare* Haphazard sampling.

Range of application of a theory Those possible situations or parts of the world for which the theory can be applied—that is, for which deductions from the theory will be true (enough).

***Reasoning in a chain with* all** Reasoning in the form: All S are P; all P are Q; so all S are Q. Valid.

***Reasoning in a chain with* almost all** Reasoning in the form: Almost all S are P; almost all P are Q; so almost all S are Q. Usually weak.

Reasoning in a chain with conditionals Reasoning in the form: If A, then B; if B, then C; so if A, then C. Valid. Sometimes called a *hypothetical syllogism*. *See also* Slippery slope argument.

Reasoning in a chain with "some" Reasoning in the form: Some S are P; some P are Q; so some S are Q. Usually weak.

Reasoning from hypotheses If you start with an assumption or hypothesis A that you don't know to be true and make a good argument for B, then what you have established is "If A, then B." Sometimes called *conditional proof*.

Red herring Any weak argument in which the premises are used to distract attention from whether the conclusion is true, as a red herring dragged across a path that a dog is following can lead the dog off the true scent.

Reducing to the absurd Showing that at least one of several claims is false or dubious, or collectively they are unacceptable, by drawing a false or unwanted conclusion from them.

Reductio ad absurdum. *See* Reducing to the absurd.

Referee An expert chosen by a journal to decide whether an article is correct and worth publishing.

Refuting an argument Showing an argument is bad.

Refuting an argument directly

- Show that at least one of the premises is dubious.
- Show that the argument isn't valid or strong.
- Show that the conclusion is false.

Refuting by analogy Using the crucial premise of an argument in a different argument to get an absurd conclusion.

Regression to the mean When experimental results are found that are far from the average predicted to occur by chance, and in subsequent trials the results tend to that average, it's a case of *regression to the mean*.

Relative risk reduction A comparison of how many people who are actually ill who would be helped with a treatment to those who get no treatment.

Relativist Someone who believes that all prescriptive claims are subjective and/or that all value standards are subjective.

Relevance To say that the premises of an argument are irrelevant just means that the argument is so bad you can't see how to repair it. *See also* Irrelevant premise.

Repairing arguments. *See* Guide to Repairing Arguments; Unrepairable arguments.

Replicated experiment An experiment that has been duplicated and the results are in close agreement with the observations of the original experiment.

Representative sample A sample in which no one subgroup of the whole population is represented more than its proportion in the population.

Reproducible results The results of an experiment that whenever the experiment is duplicated are in close agreement with the observations of the original experiment. *See also* Duplicable experiment; Replicated experiment.

Risk A possibility in the future that we deem bad and that would be a consequence of some action we take or don't take. ***See also*** Worth the risk.

Sample. *See* Generalizing.

Scare tactics An appeal to fear. *See* Appeal to emotion.

Scientific method A way to find a cause. Conjecture possible causes. By experiment eliminate them by showing they don't make a difference until there is only one. Check that (1) it makes a difference, (2) if the purported cause is eliminated the effect is, too, (3) there is no common cause.

Self-selection bias If those in a sample done for a survey or experiment are chosen by themselves to participate, there is no good reason to believe the sample is representative.

Selective attention Generalizing from some experiences because you remember them best, though they might not be representative.

Shifting the burden of proof Saying that the other person should disprove your claim, rather than proving it yourself.

Slanter Any attempt to convince by using words that conceal a dubious claim.

Slippery slope argument An argument that uses a chain of conditionals at least one of which is false or dubious. A bad form of reducing to the absurd.

Smokescreen. *See* Red herring.

Some Often taken to mean "at least one." Sometimes "some" is best understood as "at least one, but not all."

Sound argument A valid argument with true premises.

Statistical generalization A generalization that says that the same proportion of the whole as in the sample will have the property being investigated.

Strawman An attempt to refute a claim or argument by arguing against another claim that is easier to show false or against another argument that's easier to show is bad. Putting words in someone's mouth.

Strong and weak arguments Invalid arguments are classified on a scale from strong to weak. An argument is *strong* if it is possible but unlikely for the premises to be true and the conclusion false (at the same time). An argument is *weak* if it is possible and not unlikely for the premises to be true and the conclusion false (at the same time).

Structural fallacy An argument whose form alone guarantees that it is a fallacy.

Subjective claim A claim whose truth-value depends on what someone (or something) thinks, believes, or feels.

Subjectivist fallacy Arguing that because there is a lot of disagreement about whether a claim is true, it is therefore subjective.

Sufficient condition. *See* Necessary and sufficient conditions.

Support A claim or claims that give some reason to believe another claim.

Teleological explanation An explanation that invokes goals or functions or uses a claim that can come true only after the claim being explained becomes true.

Teleological fallacy An argument that uses or requires as premise "This occurs in nature, therefore it has a purpose."

Tests for an argument to be good

- The premises are plausible.
- The premises are more plausible than the conclusion.
- The argument is valid or strong.

Theory A collection of claims used as premises in reasoning by abstraction about the world. Often called a *model* if it uses a physical or visual description, though those terms are usually interchangeable.

Truth value The quality of being true or of being false.

Tu quoque ("You, too"). *See* Two wrongs make a right. *See also* Phony refutation.

Two times zero is still zero A comparison in which the base is not given.

Two wrongs make a right A bad argument which appeals to the bad that someone else has done in order to justify the bad that you are doing.

Unbiased sample. *See* Representative sample.

Uncontrolled experiment: cause-to-effect An experiment to establish cause in a population. Two randomly chosen samples are used. In one the cause is (apparently) present, in the other (apparently) not, and they are followed over time.

Uncontrolled experiment: effect-to-cause An experiment to establish cause in a population. A sample of the population in which the effect is present is examined to see if the cause is also present and other possible causes are not present.

Unrepairable arguments We don't repair an argument if any of the following hold:

- There's no argument there.
- The argument is so lacking in coherence there's nothing obvious to add.
- The obvious premise to add would make the argument weak.
- The obvious premise to add to make the argument valid or strong is false.
- A premise is false or dubious and cannot be deleted.
- Two of its premises are contradictory, and neither can be deleted.
- The conclusion is clearly false.

Up-player A word or phrase that exaggerates the significance of a claim.

Vague sentence A sentence is too vague to be a claim if there are different ways to understand it and we can't settle on one of those without the speaker making it clearer.

Valid argument An argument in which it is impossible for the premises to be true and the conclusion false (at the same time).

Weak argument. *See* Strong and weak arguments.

Weaseler A claim that is qualified so much that the apparent meaning is no longer there.

Wishful thinking A feel-good argument used on oneself.

Worth the risk The good that might come from doing some action outweighs, by more than a little, the bad that might come from it. *See also* Risk.

You can't get "ought" from "is" There is no good argument all of whose premises are descriptive and whose conclusion is prescriptive.

Answers to Selected Exercises

Chapter 1

1. Convincings/arguments.
3. We can convince others; others can convince us; we can convince ourselves.
4. a. Yes.
   b. Depends on what you mean by "expensive." We'll look at this more in Chapter 2.
   e. Yes, but it might not have the same truth-value as (d).
   k. Yes.
7. To convince (establish) that a particular claim is true.
8. *Given an argument,* the *conclusion* is the claim that someone is attempting to establish is true, while the *premises* are the claims that are used in trying to establish that.
9. Commands, threats, entreaties ("Dr. E, Dr. E, please, please let me pass this course"), etc. are not arguments.
12. Depends on whether she's talking to herself. We can't tell. Arguments use language.
14. *Argument*? Yes.
    Conclusion: You shouldn't eat at Zee-Zee Frap's restaurant.
    Premise: I heard they did really badly on their health inspection last week.
    NOTE: The premise isn't "They did really badly on their health inspection last week."
    Someone hearing that it's so and it being so aren't the same claim.
16. *Argument*? No.
19. *Argument*? No. No conclusion is stated (though it's implicit—we'll talk about when we're justified in supplying a missing conclusion in Chapter 5).
27. *Argument*? Yes.
    Conclusion: The gas tank is full.
    Premises: The gas stopped pumping by itself. Zoe can't get it to pump any more gas.
29. **Virtue**.

Chapter 2

Section A

2. b. O.K.
   d. O.K. Just because *you* don't know what the entire cost is doesn't mean it's vague.
   h. O.K. It's just a funny way of saying "Jane is really attractive."
   j. Too vague. (Which brands? Which sizes?)
   l. Too vague (but see the next section).
   q. Too vague. (You thought it was easy to be an instructor at a college?)
4. It's an example of the drawing the line fallacy.
7. b. Americans—individually or collectively? Compare Example 10, p. 16.
   f. Ambiguous: Each player on the team had a B average. The average of all the grades of the members of the team was B.
   h. Vague, not ambiguous.
   l. Too vague.
10. a. Suzy can't understand what "argument" means.
    b. No quotes needed.
    c. Ambiguous until we know whether the word "murder" is meant literally or metaphorically (without quotes or with quotes).

d. O'Brien says that there are seven "legal" ways to never pay taxes. (Unfortunately, this may not need scare quotes now.)

Section B

1. a. Subjective = Its truth-value depends on what someone or something thinks/believes/feels.
   b. Objective = not subjective.
   c. No.
3. When describing our own feelings, we don't have awfully precise language to use. So "It's hot" may be the best we can do in describing how we feel. But it's too vague to be an objective claim.
5. a. Objective.
   d. Subjective (even though Dr. E thinks it's objective and true).
   k. Objective in the Middle Ages, when people believed demons existed. Now probably understood as demons in the mind, so subjective.
   l. Objective since "insane" is now a technical term of the law.
   m. Whether it's subjective or objective depends on what standard you're using for "intelligent." Since that's not clear, it's too vague to be a claim.
   n. Objective.
   r. Objective.
   s. Subjective.
8. a. Tom made an objective claim about the statistical likelihood of a teenage girl getting into an automobile accident. He may be wrong, or he may have sexist motives for saying it, but that's not what the claim says. Zoe takes it to be subjective.
9. Zoe is not right. Dick has objective standards, even if he can't explicitly state them just then. Dick should point out at least one way in which his claim could be taken as objective (the tires skidded and you had to over-correct, . . .) .

Section C

2. *Prescriptive or descriptive*? Prescriptive, since we shouldn't do what is cruel and immoral.
   Standard needed? Yes, namely, "What is cruel and immoral is wrong/shouldn't be done."
3. *Prescriptive or descriptive*? Descriptive.
   Standard needed? No.
4. *Prescriptive or descriptive*? Prescriptive.
   Standard needed? Yes. Perhaps "Incest is wrong."
5. *Prescriptive or descriptive*? Prescriptive.
6. *Prescriptive or descriptive*? Prescriptive.
   Standard needed? Yes. Perhaps "You should not steal."
11. *Prescriptive or descriptive*? Prescriptive.
    Standard needed? Assumed in the reason given for the claim is the standard, "We should require courses for students to improve their comprehension in all courses."
12. *Prescriptive or descriptive*? This is an objective value judgment! And true.

Section D

1. The definition and the original phrase can be used interchangeably, and the words in the definition are clear and better understood than the words doing the defining.
2. Because they settle a debate before it's started. They are concealed claims.
3. c. Persuasive definition.
   d. Definition. No longer classifies correctly, but it once did.
   f. Not a definition.
   i. Yes, a definition of "fusiform."

Exercises for Chapter 2

1. Here are all the possibilities (+ example):
   claim + objective
   claim + subjective
   definition + not a claim
   ambiguous or too vague + not a claim
   persuasive definition + claim + objective
   persuasive definition + claim + subjective
3. Definition, not a claim.
7. Objective claim.
11. Too vague, not a claim.
16. Subjective claim.

Chapter 3

Sections A–D

4. No. *Invalid* arguments are classified from strong to weak.
5. No. The premises could be false. Even if the premises are true, they might be less plausible than the conclusion.
9. We've got good reason to believe it.
10. Nothing.

14. d. 15. d. 16. c. 17. d. 18. d. 19. c.

Exercises for Chapter 3

1. a. Come up with a (possibly imagined) situation in which the premises are true and the conclusion false.
   b. Come up with a (possibly imagined) *likely* situation in which the premises are true and the conclusion false.
3. a. i. premise, ii. premise, iii. premise, iv. conclusion
   b. i. conclusion, ii. premise, iii. premise, iv. premise
   f. i. premise, ii. premise, iii. conclusion
4. Nothing.
6. No. See the parakeets example in Section B.
8. *Conclusion*: Flo got a haircut.
   Premises: Flo's hair was long. Now Flo's hair is short.
   Note: "So" is not part of the conclusion.
   Invalid: Flo might have got her hair caught in a lawn mower. But it's strong. Good if premises are plausible.
13. Valid and good.
16. Weak, bad. We could change the price tomorrow to $120 like other critical thinking textbooks.
18. Weak, bad. Spot could be a penguin or a cockroach.
19. Not an argument.
20. Weak, bad. They might want to hire conservatives for balance. Or conservatives are hired, but they become liberal over time. Or Maria just hasn't met enough professors. (Or, you could say that the premise is too vague for it to be an argument.)
21. Weak. Professor Zzzyzzx may have changed his grading, or the school may have required him to become harder, or he may just never have had a student as bad as Suzy.
25. Valid and good if premises are plausible. (Maybe Louie bought it on credit? Then the first premise is false.)

Chapter 4

Sections A and B.1

2. Accept as true, reject as false, suspend judgment.
3. Because it's impossible for the premises to be true and the conclusion false.
6. No. It's just the experience of other people.
10. We have good reason to doubt our memory, or the claim contradicts experiences of ours and there is a good argument (theory) against the claim. Also, beware of confusing memory with deductions from experience.
16. Our memory.
17. Nothing.

Section B

3. a. The criteria go from ones closest to our own experience to those furthest.
21. You're being foolish if you buy the root extract. There's no reason to believe the clerk knows anything about the subject; most likely he or she is just parroting what he or she has heard. And the "Well, it can't hurt" line is just plain false: Lots of quack cures sold at health-food stores can hurt you. You could end up spending thousands of dollars following quack cures before you do something useful for yourself. On the other hand, you might want to get a second opinion.
23. a. Reject (common knowledge that it's false).
    b. Reject—if you know anything about toads and warts. Change doctors.
    c. Reject (personal experience. You *did* notice it rises in the east?).
    f. Accept if you haven't been looking at your speedometer, or if you have and you know you were speeding. Reject if you've been monitoring your speed, saw the speed limit sign, and you weren't speeding. (But don't sass back.)
    g. Suspend judgment (biased source, and "all forests" seems an exaggeration).
    j. Accept!! You can't reject this on personal experience, since no personal experience you have will tell you who got sick worst from which pets in the U.S. during the last year. Cats can transmit a disease to pregnant women that causes birth defects, and they also cause untold cases of severe asthma each year. And that's not even counting the infections from clawing.
    m. Accept (reliable source).
    o. This sounded really interesting. So I wrote to the public relations office of DePauw University for further information and received the following reply:

    As far as I am aware, I think the study to which you refer can best be classified as an "urban legend." No such study has been done during my 12 years at DePauw, and I can find no one here who has ever heard of such a study.

    Larry Anderson, Director of Public Relations, DePauw University

    It was later reprinted in the *Ukiah Daily Journal*, Ukiah, CA, Jan. 4, 1982, in the *Kerrville Times*, Kerrville, TX, Dec. 11, 1998 and Dog knows by how many other gullible editors.

Section D

2. Never.
5. He's confused the person with the argument, thinking that if a person *apparently* doesn't believe the conclusion of his own argument, the argument is bad.
7. Suzy really blew it! She's taking the word of an expert over her own experience. Above all, you should trust your own experience.
12. Suzy is right! She says that she has no good reason to believe me, since I'm not an expert on virtue (I'm a logician, after all). She's not suggesting that I'm wrong but only that she has no reason to accept the claim. (Of course, if Suzy knew me better, she'd revise her opinion.)

16. Just a comment on the speaker's *apparent* inconsistency.
18. Prof. Zzzyzzx is challenging his doctor's unstated assumption that he needs to do those things to stay healthy. Nothing wrong with that.
20. Appeal to common belief (*not* authority—they aren't referring to a review). Good, if Lee has found in the past that books on the *New York Times* Best Seller list are what he likes. Bad otherwise.

Chapter 5

Section C

3. Nothing.
4. If the argument is still strong without the false premise, the conclusion is likely true. Otherwise, you have no more reason to believe the conclusion than you did before you heard the argument.
5. Deleting it doesn't make the argument weaker, and there's no obvious way to link it to the conclusion.
6. *Conclusion*: Dr. E is a man.
   Premises: Dr. E is a teacher. All teachers are men.
   Valid, bad, unrepairable: second premise is false.
7. "Anything that walks like a duck, looks like a duck, and quacks like a duck, is a duck" or "If it walks like a duck, looks like a duck, and quacks like a duck, it's a duck."
10. *Conclusion*: You didn't get the flu from me.
    "The person who shows symptoms of the flu first got the flu first. If you get the flu first, you can't have gotten it from someone who didn't have it." Valid.
    The first added premise is probably false, but it's the only way the argument could be repaired. So the argument is unrepairable.
    You *can't* add "The person who shows symptoms of the flu first *probably* got the flu first." The word "impossible" indicates the speaker thinks he or she is making a valid argument, so you can't repair it as a strong argument.
13. This is an argument: You can't ignore what the speaker intends, and "so" shows that the speaker meant it as an argument. Can't be repaired (see Example 8).
14. "Ralph barks" will make this valid. But we don't know if it's plausible. All we can do here is point out what's needed.
15. "(Almost) the only way you can inherit blue eyes is if both your parents are blue-eyed" is the obvious premise to add to make the argument valid. But that's false. So it's unrepairable.
22. Not an argument. If you try to interpret it as an argument, it's hopelessly bad, and that should convince you not to think of it as an argument.
27. *Conclusion*: "Cigarettes are not a defective product that causes emphysema, lung cancer, and other illnesses." The premises in the quote contradict each other, so the argument is bad.

Section D

4. *Conclusion*: Zoe should go to law school.
   Premise: Zoe wants to make a lot of money.
   "(Almost always) people who go to law school make a lot of money."
   That's implausible. But worse, what's the standard? "You should do what's most likely to make you lots of money"? That's even more implausible—Zoe should rob a bank? The argument is unrepairable.

Section E

1. a. The guy she's talking to is fat.
   b. She thinks I'm fat.
6. Only an Hispanic can represent Hispanics (properly). False and very ugly.

Chapter 6

Exercises for Chapter 6

1. No. All I've shown is that the student is (apparently) being irrational.
2. Raising objections to parts of an argument to show the argument is bad or to a claim to show it's false.
3. Nothing!
4. Answer the objections by showing that they are false or do not destroy the support for your conclusion. OR you could say, "I hadn't thought of that. I guess you're right." OR you could say, "I'll have to think about that."
8. Sex is the answer to almost everyone's problems.
   Unsubstantiated claim. Dick's "Why?" asks for support. It's an invitation to Zoe to give an argument.

   It takes away your tension.
   Zoe offers support for her conclusion.

   It doesn't if you're involved with someone you don't like.
   Dick shows her support is false or dubious.

   Sex makes you feel better.
   Zoe gives up on that support and offers another.

   It doesn't if it's against your morals. Heroin makes you feel good.
   Dick's first comment shows Zoe's claim is dubious. His second comment shows that the relation of Zoe's claim to the conclusion is weak (he's challenging the unstated premise "If it feels good, it's good to do").

   It's healthy and natural, just like eating and drinking.
   Zoe gives one last try to support her conclusion.

   You can catch terrible diseases. Sex should be confined to marriage.
   Dick shows that support is dubious, too. Then he asserts his own view, which is somewhat supported by his previous claims.
11. Showing that at least one of several claims is false or dubious, or collectively they are unacceptable, by drawing a false or unwanted conclusion from them.
13. Ridicule is not an argument.
15. a. Putting words in someone's mouth. Refuting an argument or claim that the other person didn't really say.
16. Tom's presented a strawman. Lee is for equal rights, not preferences. Tom has mistakenly identified equal rights laws with affirmative action programs. Doesn't refute.
19. Reducing to the absurd.
22. This shows how important it is to master the material in this chapter if you want to be a good CEO. We can classify this hopelessly bad attempt at a refutation as *blustering*. A few years later his company went bankrupt.
28. Suzy is attempting to refute by analogy. If the only reasons Tom had for wanting a big dog are those he gave, then indeed Suzy would have refuted him. It's a challenge to Tom to give more reasons for why he wants a big dog. Maybe he wants a big one to scare away Puff.
30. Wanda is committing the subjectivist fallacy.
31. Reduce to the absurd. Maria probably won't accept it, but it should give her pause to clarify what she means by "decide life and death."

Review Chapters 1–6

Review Exercises for Chapters 1–6

1. A collection of claims intended to show that one of them, the conclusion, is true.

2. A declarative sentence used in such a way that it is true or false.
3. a. A claim whose truth-value does not depend on what anyone or anything thinks/believes/feels.
4. Yes, depending on the context.
5. a. A claim that says what should be (versus a descriptive claim that says what is).
6. No. A definition is an instruction for how to use a word or words.
7. a. A claim phrased to sound like a definition.
8. An argument that uses as a (stated or unstated) premise: If you can't make the difference precise, then there is no difference.
9. The premises are plausible.
   The premises are more plausible than the conclusion.
   The argument is valid or strong.
10. a. A valid argument is one in which it is impossible for the premises to be true and the conclusion false (at the same time).
11. a. A strong argument is one in which it is very unlikely for the premises to be true and the conclusion false (at the same time).
12. Yes. See the answer to Exercise 9.
13. Give a likely example where the premises are true and the conclusion false.
14. No, unless the argument is still strong without the false premise.
15. Nothing.
16. No. It could beg the question. Or a premise could be false or dubious.
17. No. See the parakeets example in Chapter 3.
18. Our personal experience.
19. Accept as true; reject as false; suspend judgment.
20. We know the claim is true from personal experience.
    The claim is made by someone we know and trust and who is an expert on this kind of claim.
    The claim is made by a reputable authority whom we can trust as being an expert about this kind of claim and who has no motive to mislead.
    The claim is put forward in a reputable journal or reference source.
    The claim is in a media source that's usually reliable, has no obvious motive to mislead, and names the original source.
21. We know the claim is false from personal experience.
    The claim contradicts other claims we know to be true.
22. When we do not have good reason to believe a claim, and we do not have good reason to think that the claim is false.
23. He or she believes the premises are true because the argument is valid or strong and the conclusion is true.
24. He or she says an argument is bad just because of who said it.
25. Never.
26. Never.
27. Rejecting an argument because the speaker's actions or words suggest that he/she does not believe the conclusion of his/her own argument.
28. We assume that the other person who is discussing with us or whose arguments we are reading: 1. Knows about the subject under discussion, 2. Is able and willing to reason well, and 3. Is not lying.
29. Someone recognizes that an argument is good but does not believe the conclusion.
30. Given an (implicit) argument that is apparently defective, we are justified in adding a premise or conclusion if: 1. The argument becomes stronger or valid, and 2. The premise is plausible

and would seem plausible to the other person, and 3. The premise is more plausible than the conclusion. If the argument is valid or strong, yet one of the premises is false or dubious, we may delete the premise if the argument remains valid or strong.

31. The obvious premise to add to make the argument strong or valid is false.
    The obvious premise to add would make the argument weak.
    A premise it uses is false or dubious and cannot be deleted.
    Two of its premises are contradictory and neither can be deleted.
    The argument is so lacking in coherence that there's nothing obvious to add.
    There's no argument there.
    The conclusion is clearly false.
32. There's no good argument with a prescriptive conclusion and only descriptive premises.
33. a. A word or phrase added to a claim telling us the role of the claim in an argument or what the speaker thinks of the claim or argument.
    b. No.
34. It helps you avoid making your argument weak, and it shows others that you have considered the other side.
35. Show that one of the premises is dubious; show that the argument isn't valid or strong; show that the conclusion is false.
36. Only if the additional premises you have used are all true and the argument is valid. If the additional premises are only plausible, or the argument is only strong, you've only shown that it's very likely that one of the original premises is false or collectively they lead to an absurdity.
37. Ridicule is not an argument.

Chapter 7

Sections A.1 and A.2

1. A claim composed of other claims but which has to be viewed as just one claim.
6. Because each has to be true anyway for the argument to be good.
7. *Alternatives*: Inflation will go up. Interest rates will go up.
   Neither will inflation go up nor will interest rates go up.
10. *Alternatives*: You're for me. You're against me.
    You're neither for me nor against me.
14. Not a claim.

Section A

6.

9. *Argument*? Yes.
   Conclusion: Lee will vote for the Republican.
   Premises: Either you'll vote for the Republican or the Democratic candidate for president. Lee won't vote for the Democrat.
   Additional premises needed: None.
   Classify: Valid.
   Good argument? No. It's a false dilemma. There are other choices for Lee (the candidate for the Libertarian Party or the Green Party).

10. *Argument*? Yes.
    Conclusion: Manuel and Tom went to the basketball game.
    Premises: Manuel and Tom went to the basketball game if they didn't go to the library.
        (= Manuel and Tom went to the basketball game or they went to the library.)
        They didn't go to the library.
    Additional premises needed: None.
    Classify: Valid.
    Good argument? Good if the premises are true.

Section B.1

1. a. A claim that can be rewritten as an "if . . . then . . ." claim that always has the same truth-value.
   b. Yes.
4. Here are two samples. Come up with your own.
   Don't come home and there'll be hell to pay.
   When you get married it means that you can no longer date anyone else.
6. A, but not B.
7. a. Suzy studies hard, but she doesn't pass Dr. E's class.
   b. Both (b) and (*) could be true (if Dr. E has a kind heart).
   c. Both (c) and (*) could be true.
   d. Both (d) and (*) could be true in the case that Suzy doesn't study hard, since neither tells us what happens then.
9. *Conditional*? (yes or no) Yes.
   Antecedent: Spot barks.
   Consequent: Puff will run away.
   Contradictory: Spot barked, but Puff didn't run away.
10. *Conditional*? (yes or no) Yes.
    Antecedent: Dick will help Lee with his English exam.
    Consequent: Lee will take care of Spot next weekend.
    Contradictory: Dick will help Lee with his English exam, but Lee will not take care of Spot next weekend.
14. *Conditional*? (yes or no) No. An argument. No contradictory.
15. *Conditional*? (yes or no) Yes.
    Antecedent: You'll get me some cake mix.
    Consequent: I'll bake a cake.
    Contradictory: You get me some cake mix, but I won't bake a cake.
18. *Conditional*? (yes or no) Yes.
    Antecedent: If Dick takes Spot for a walk, Dick will do the dishes.
    Consequent: Dick won't take Spot for a walk.
    Contradictory: If Dick takes Spot for a walk, Dick will do the dishes, and Dick did take Spot for a walk.

Section B.2

1. a. If Flo doesn't have to take a bath, then she didn't play with Spot.
2. a. Neither necessary nor sufficient.
   c. (i) sufficient for (ii).
6. a. If Suzy didn't go with Tom to the library, then he didn't get out of practice by 6. A sufficient condition for Tom to go to the library with Suzy is that he gets out of practice by 6. (Or: For Tom to get out of practice by 6 it's necessary that Suzy went with him to the library.)

7. a. If Zoe gets a transcript, then she paid her library fines.
   Or: If Zoe doesn't pay her library fines, then she won't get her transcript.
8. a. If Maria buys a new dress, then she got a bonus this month.
   A necessary condition for Maria to buy a new dress is that she gets a bonus this month.

Section C

6. Flo came over early to play. (Direct way)
7. Spot didn't bark. (Indirect way)
11. None. Appears to be Affirming the Consequent.

Exercises for Chapter 7

3. Excluding possibilities, the direct way of reasoning with conditionals, the indirect way of reasoning with conditionals, reasoning in a chain with conditionals, (and in an exercise: no matter what).
4. Affirming the consequent, denying the antecedent.
5. Affirming the consequent, denying the antecedent, false dilemmas, slippery slope arguments, (in an exercise: perfectionist dilemma).
9. a. If Dr. E isn't rich, then he didn't win the lottery.
   If Dr. E isn't rich, then his book didn't sell a million copies.
   If Dr. E isn't rich, then he didn't marry a rich woman.
   b. Dr. E won the lottery, but he isn't rich.
   Dr. E's book sold a million copies, but he isn't rich.
   Dr. E married a rich woman, but he isn't rich.
   d. Dr. E winning the lottery is sufficient for Dr. E to be rich.
   Dr. E's book selling a million copies is sufficient for Dr. E to be rich.
   Dr. E marrying a rich woman is sufficient for Dr. E to be rich.
   e. Dr. E being rich is necessary for Dr. E winning the lottery.
   Dr. E being rich is necessary for Dr. E's book selling a million copies.
   Dr. E being rich is necessary for Dr. E marrying a rich woman.
10. *Argument*? Yes.
    Conclusion: Suzy won't break up with Tom.
    Premises: If Suzy breaks up with Tom, then she'll have to return his letter jacket. Suzy won't give up that jacket.
    Additional premises needed: None.
    Classify: Valid.
    Form: Indirect Way.
    Good argument? Yes.
12. *Argument*? Yes.
    Conclusion: If you take issue with current Israeli policy, you're an anti-Semite.
    Premises: If you take issue with current Israeli policy, then you're criticizing Israel. If you criticize Israel, then you're anti-Israel. If you're anti-Israel, you're an anti-Semite.
    Additional premises needed: None.
    Classify: Valid.
    Form: Reasoning in a chain with conditionals.
    Good argument? No. Unrepairable. Last premise is false.
15. *Argument*? Yes.
    Conclusion: It's the ebola virus (in Uganda).
    Premises: People in Uganda are dying of some fever where they hemorrhage a lot.
    If people in Uganda are dying of hemorrhagic fever, then it's the ebola virus.

Additional premises needed: None.
Classify: Valid. Direct way.
Good argument? Yes, if premises are true.

16. *Argument*? Yes.
Conclusion: I should not allow questions in my class.
Bad argument. Slippery slope.

19. *Argument*? Yes.
Conclusion: Columbus didn't discover America.
Premises: Only if Columbus landed in a place with no people in it could you say he discovered it. The Americas, especially where he landed, were populated. Columbus met natives.
Additional premises needed: If Columbus met natives, then where he landed was populated.
Classify: Valid.
Form: Indirect way of reasoning with conditionals (rewrite the "only if" claim as an "if . . . then . . ." claim).
Good argument? Yes.

22. *Argument*? Yes.
Conclusion: If you lock up someone, he should be locked up forever.
Premises: Every criminal either is already a hardened repeat offender or will become one. Criminals learn to be hardened criminals in jail. We don't want any hardened criminals running free on our streets.
Additional premises needed: *First argument*: If a criminal is not a hardened repeat offender and goes to jail, then he will learn to be a hardened repeat offender.* If a criminal goes to jail, then he will be a hardened repeat offender. Every criminal who is locked up will become a hardened repeat offender.
Second argument: If we don't want any hardened criminals running free on our streets, then if we lock up a criminal, we should lock him up forever.
Classify: *First argument*: Valid—no matter what.
Second argument: Valid—direct way.
Good argument? No. Premises are dubious, especially *. It's a false dilemma.

25. *Argument*? Yes.
Conclusion: Lee didn't get a ticket.
Premises: If the car's bumper isn't crumpled, Lee wasn't speeding.
Additional premises needed: The car's bumper isn't crumpled. If Lee got a ticket, he was speeding.
Classify: Weak. The last added premise is implausible.
Form: Direct and indirect ways.
Good argument? Bad.

26. *Argument*? Yes.
Conclusion: (unstated) Tom will get a dog.
Premises: Dick heard that Tom is going to get a pet. The only pets allowed in this town are dogs or cats or fish. Tom can't stand cats. Tom doesn't like a pet that you just contemplate. Tom won't get a fish.
Additional premises needed: If Dick heard that Tom is going to get a pet, then Tom is going to get a pet. (1st conclusion) Tom is going to get a pet. If Tom gets a pet, then it will have to be a dog or cat or fish. (2nd conclusion) Tom will get a dog or cat or fish. If Tom can't stand cats, then he won't get a cat. (3rd conclusion) Tom won't get a cat. If Tom doesn't like a pet that you just contemplate, then Tom won't get a fish. (4th conclusion) Tom won't get a fish. (5th conclusion) Tom will get a dog.

Classify: Valid.

Form: Direct way (four times) and excluding possibilities.

Good argument? Possibly. Arguments are valid or strong and premises are plausible except for one unstated premise: "If Dick heard that Tom's going to get a pet, then Tom is going to get a pet."

27. *Argument*? No. Zoe is just trying to show her Mom is wrong by stating the contradictory. But she gets the contradictory wrong.
29. *Argument*? Yes.
    Conclusion: They shouldn't raise tuition again.
    Bad argument. Slippery slope.

Chapter 8

Section A

1. Dogs eat meat. Every dog eats meat. Everything that's a dog eats meat.
2. At least one cat swims. There is a cat that swims. There exists a cat that swims.
5. Everything that flies is a bird.
6. No one who is a police officer is under 18 years old. All police officers are not under 18 years old. Not even one police officer is under 18 years old. Nothing that's a police officer is under 18 years old.
7. Dogs and only dogs are domestic canines.
8. Nothing that's a pig can fly. Pigs can't fly.
9. c. Don't confuse this with "Some textbooks fall apart after one semester." You cannot know whether this example is true from your personal experience unless you've worked for a publisher.
   d. False. I've seen Crest in some stores.
10. (There are other correct answers.)
    a. Some student doesn't like to study.
    b. Some woman is a construction worker.
    c. Some CEO of a Fortune 500 company is not a man.
    d. This textbook is not used in some section of critical thinking.
    e. Some exam is suitable for all students.
    f. All exams really test a student's knowledge.
    g. All drunk drivers get in accidents.
    h. Some donkeys don't eat carrots.
    i Some people who die young aren't good.
    j. Someone who is a teacher is not allowed to grade exams, or someone who grades exams is not a teacher.
    k. Something both barks and meows.
    l. Tom is not injured and he will not start some football game.
    m. There is a football player who is a vegetarian, and his coach doesn't hate him. (See Chapter 7.)
    n. Some decisions about abortions should not be left to the woman and her doctor.
    o. Some cowboy had a friend named "Tonto," and the cowboy wasn't the Lone Ranger.
11. a. Sometimes when Dr. Wallace is irritated with his students, he doesn't give an exam.
    b. Sometimes it rains in Seattle in July.
    c. Spot will always chase Puff.
    d. There are flocks of birds along the river at times other than in the winter.

Section B

1. Invalid.

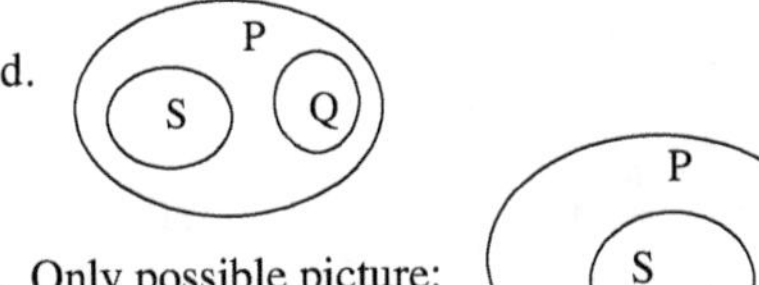

2. Valid. Only possible picture:

3. Valid. Must have:

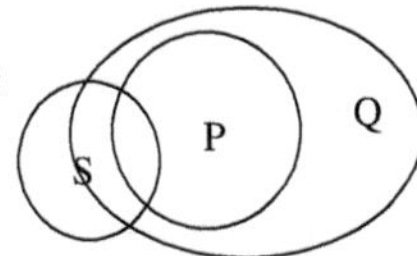

(S could be entirely within P or Q, but still the conclusion would be represented as true.)

4. Invalid.

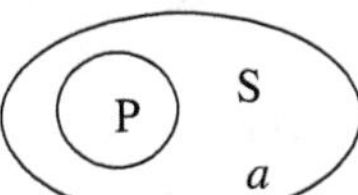

5. Invalid.

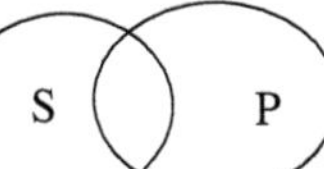

6. Valid.

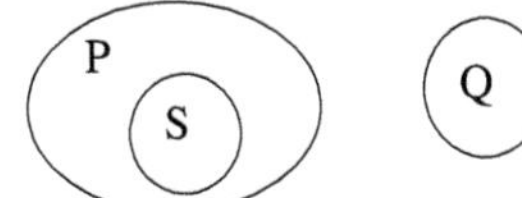

7. c.
8. d
9. c
10. c
11. d
12. d.
13. e.
14. d.
15. Invalid. Lee could be one of the ones who does attend lectures. Not every ≠ every not.
16. Invalid

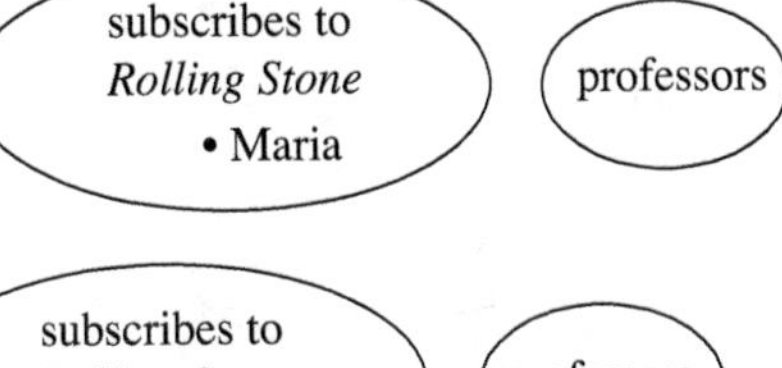

17. Valid

18. Invalid. No picture, but it could be that dogs bite only postal workers who are cowardly and would never bite back, and the postal workers who bite dogs are so tough they never get bitten. So there's no postal worker and dog that bite each other.
19. Invalid.

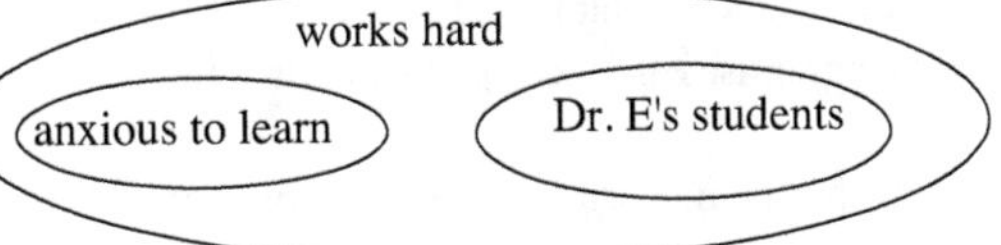

21. Invalid.

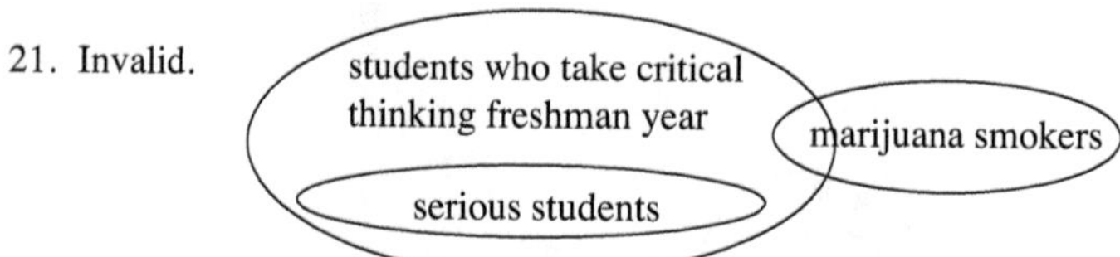

23. Invalid. George could be mute.

25. Invalid.

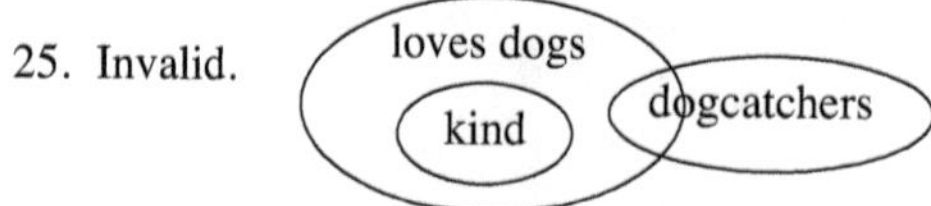

26. Invalid. The premise is *not* "all hogs grunt." Don't mistake your knowledge of the world for what's actually been said. It's reasoning in a chain with "some."
30. Valid. No picture. Dr. E has a dog. That dog must love its master. So that dog loves Dr. E. So Dr. E is loved.
31. Invalid. Only janitors have access does not mean that all janitors have access. Paul could be one of the day janitors who doesn't have access.
33. Valid. The Direct Way of Reasoning with No. If you think the conclusion is false, which premise isn't true?
34. For example,
    a. If it's a cat, then it coughs hairballs.
    b. If something is a donkey, then it eats hay.
    c. If something is made of chocolate, it's good to eat.
    d. If it's a duck, then it likes water.

Section C

1. All but a very few teenagers listen to pop music.
   Nearly every teenager listens to pop music.
   Only a very few teenagers don't listen to pop music.
2. Almost all adults don't listen to classical music.
   Very few adults listen to classical music.
   Almost no adult listens to classical music.
3. Strong.
4. Not strong. Arguing backwards with "very few."
5. Not strong. Here's a picture drawn to scale:

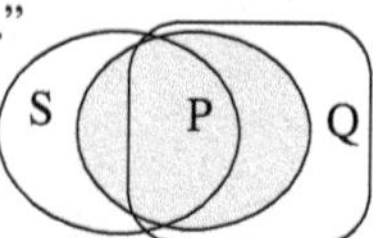

6. Strong.
7. Strong.
8. Weak.
9. Strong.
12. Weak. Reasoning in a chain with "almost all."
13. Strong.

Review Chapters 7 and 8

1. An argument is a collection of claims, one of which is called the "conclusion," and the others of which, called the "premises," are meant to establish or prove that the conclusion is true.
2. The premises are plausible. The premises are more plausible than the conclusion. The argument is valid or strong.
3. A valid argument is one for which it is impossible for the premises to be true and conclusion false (at the same time).

4. A strong argument is one for which it is almost impossible for the premises to be true and the conclusion false (at the same time).
5. No. The premises could be false or it could beg the question. You should provide an example of a bad valid argument.
6. Provide a likely example where the premises are true and the conclusion false.
7. No. It could beg the question. You should provide an example.
8. A compound claim is one made up of other claims but that has to be viewed as just one claim.
10. a. The contradictory of a claim is another claim that must have the opposite truth-value.
11. Yes.
12. A false dilemma is an "or" claim that seems to be true but isn't, because there is another possibility that it does not state.
13. Yes. 14. Yes. 15. No. 16. No.
17. No. It could be a slippery slope argument.
18. a. "A is a necessary condition for B" means that "If B, then A" is true.
19. A slippery slope argument is bad and doesn't refute.
27. Excluding possibilities.
    The direct way of reasoning with conditionals.
    The indirect way of reasoning with conditionals.
    Reasoning in a chain with conditionals.
    The direct way of reasoning with "all."
    Reasoning in a chain with "all."
    The direct way of reasoning with "no."
28. Affirming the consequent.
    Denying the antecedent.
    Arguing backwards with "all."
    Arguing backwards with "no."
    Reasoning in a chain with "some."
    Arguing backwards with "almost all."
    Reasoning in a chain with "almost all."

Chapter 9

16. "Only" is a downplayer, suggesting that this is very few. Seems like a lot to me.
17. Baldness is not a disease.
19. Nothing wrong here.
20. Weaseler: Zoe didn't apologize!
21. Innuendo, suggesting that economists are horrible at predicting.
24. This implies but does not state that in our part of the world people don't react with emotions and wouldn't be as easily manipulated as Arabs. That's implausible.
30. There is no slanter in this highly disparaging remark about foreign-exchange dealers. It's all upfront ridicule.
34. "Despite" is an up-player. Why "despite"?
36. "Gaming" is a euphemism for "gambling." Sure you'd say, "Honey, let's go out gaming tonight."
41. Euphemism: unspoiled wilderness area = uninhabited area.
43. Implies without proof that junkies, rape, and bad families are "real life." But no slanters.
45. Euphemisms: resettled = forcibly moved to *and* internment camps = prison camps (it's a dysphemism to call them "concentration camps"). Innuendo: at last.
47. Anytime you see a comparison to Hitler or the Nazis you should suspect that it's hyperbole, which is what we have here.

50. The word "profess" here conceals the claim that northern workers—on the whole—are duplicitous. They say they're trying to help their southern counterparts when they're really motivated by self-interest. But the authors have given no reason to believe that those workers are not sincere. By noticing how the authors have used a slanter here, we can be on the alert for this bias against workers in their book.

Chapter 10

8. Zoe's argument: appeal to pity. Premise: You shouldn't experiment on animals if you feel sorry for the dogs. GREAT!

   Dick's argument: appeal to spite. Premise: You should experiment on cats if they make you sneeze. EVEN BETTER!
9. Feel-good argument. Weak because a politician might care for the same things you do but be totally incompetent.
14. Appeal to patriotism (subspecies of feel-good argument). Generic premise: You should believe that democracy is the best form of government if you love the U.S. (and think it's the greatest country). Bad argument.
16. Appeal to fear. You might think it's O.K. because a senator is supposed to worry about how his votes will be perceived by his constituents. But it's bad: we have a *representative* democracy, so a senator is supposed to vote as he or she thinks best. And the children whose votes the writer is threatening the senator with aren't voters yet.
18. Appeal to fear. Without more premises, it's bad.
19. Wishful thinking. Bad. That way of thinking may be useful, though, to motivate her to lose weight.

Chapter 11

1. The argument must be valid or strong; we must have good reason to believe its premises; the premises must be more plausible than the conclusion.
4. No. It could beg the question, or a premise could be implausible even though true.
5. Only if the false premise can be eliminated and the argument remains strong.
6. Nothing.
7. Our own experience.
8. The argument has a valid form. But some of the premises are false or collectively too dubious.
9. It's a valid argument form. But the "or" claim is false or dubious.
10. An attempt to reduce to the absurd is pretty clearly an argument. With ridicule there's no argument at all.
29. A strawman is putting words in someone's mouth, attempting to refute an argument by refuting a different one.
30. Because they are also clearly bad ways to convince, though they aren't arguments.

Short Arguments for Analysis

2. Shifting the burden of proof. Bad. But you probably knew that even before reading it.
4. Dick's response to Zoe's comments looks like an attempt to reduce to the absurd. But not enough argument is given, so it's just ridicule.
5. Not an argument; there's no attempt to convince.
7. Tom's argument has a prescriptive conclusion: You should get a small pig. Everything he says may be true, but it won't get him the conclusion unless he has some prescriptive premise. You figure out what that should be and if it's plausible.

   Dick makes an argument that Lee shouldn't accept Tom's argument. Dick is mistaking the person for the argument.

9. Conclusion: Maria's alarm didn't go off. Premise: She's still asleep. Unstated premise: If Maria's still asleep, her alarm clock didn't go off. Direct way of reasoning with conditionals. Good if the premises are plausible.
12. Shifting the burden of proof. The candidate who's speaking has to show inflation is a serious risk.
13. Conclusion (as question): We should become nudists. All the premises are false. Bad.
14. No argument here. You're supposed to believe this because of Mao's authority.
17. It looks like Zoe is concluding that these cookies will be awful. If so, it's reasoning in a chain with "some," and it's bad.
18. Conclusion: You should employ Mr. Abkhazian as your lawyer.
    Premise: He's been doing accident cases for 20 years.
    Unstated premises: If he's been doing accident cases for 20 years, he's good at doing that. You should go to someone who's good at accident cases.
    Bad argument. First unstated premise is dubious.
20. Suzy draws a conclusion from Zoe's comment: You don't care about people. Weak and no way to make it better. Bad.
21. Strawman (Ms. F is putting words in the student's mouth). Bad.
26. Premises: Israel had 23 casualties. The combat took a long time.
    Conclusion: Great efforts were made by the IDF to conduct the operation carefully in an effort to bring to an absolute minimum the number of Palestinian civilian casualties.
    Unstated premises: Israel has a huge military advantage. Israel could heavily bomb the refugee camp at Jenin. If a military operation in an urban setting takes a long time and the strong attacking force has a number of casualties, then a great effort was made to keep civilian casualties to a minimum.
    The last premise is highly implausible (a conditional form of a false dilemma), unless "great effort" means doing anything other than bombing a refugee camp flat. Since we can assume that the people in the IDF can reason, this appears to be evidence that they don't adhere to the Principle of Rational Discussion.
29. Appeal to pity. With an unstated prescriptive premise that family responsibility is more important than fleeting pleasure, it's good.
30. Bad appeal to authority. The attorney general has motive to mislead. It's just too much to think that a political appointee never lies and always investigates thoroughly. But that's not to say the conclusion is false.
31. This conspiracy theory illustrates that possibility ≠ plausibility. The interior minister has given no reason to believe anything he's said. This is so bad that it's either an attempt to confuse people, or it shows that the Saudi minister can't reason. Either way, don't bother to engage him in rational discussion.
38. With appropriate unstated premises, it's excluding possibilities, and it's good.
40. Ridicule. Bad. Or maybe it's reducing to the absurd, and good, depending on what Lee believes.
41. Begging the question. Bad.
42. Bad. Reasoning backwards with "all": Only tenants have a key = All people who have a key are tenants. Harry might be a tenant who doesn't have a key.
43. DOGS ARE GOOD. CATS ARE BAD.
44. Conclusion: Suzy or one of her friends on the squad will get a contract. Reasoning in a chain with "some." Bad.
46. Implied but unstated: Women heads of credit unions are not qualified—otherwise, Headlee would see that there are plenty of women in Utah who are qualified. Convincing without an argument with innuendo. Bad.

47. We can make this argument fairly strong by adding premises: Society should do what it can to prevent young people from engaging in sexual activities before they are emotionally prepared and before they understand the health risks. Young people who know about the mechanics of sex will not be as likely to engage in risky sexual activities. Teaching young people to refrain from sexual intercourse will lessen the likelihood that they will engage in sexual intercourse before they are emotionally prepared.

    All these are plausible. But what about the third premise of the original argument? The unstated premise needed to link it to the conclusion is something like "Society should do what it can to prevent young women from becoming pregnant before they are 20" and/or "Becoming pregnant before age 20 is bad." Those are at best dubious (in parts of the U.S. it is considered a religious duty to start a family right after high school).

    Though the original premise is not itself dubious, trying to incorporate it into the argument will make the argument worse. Since we already have a moderately strong argument, we delete this premise, just as we would a false premise that isn't essential to the strength of the argument. If the speaker feels it is crucial, then he or she will have to link it to the conclusion.
48. Bad appeal to authority. It's the reverse of "If you're so smart, why aren't you rich?"
49. Bad argument. Proved the wrong conclusion! (Compare the last sentence to the first one.) Also bad generalizations, which we'll study in Chapter 14.
51. Lee is reasoning backwards with "no." Also, first premise is dubious. Bad.
54. Perfectionist dilemma or bad appeal to common practice. Bad.
58. Bad. Affirming the consequent.
59. Good argument with unstated premises which you can add. (Prescriptive conclusion, so it'll need a prescriptive premise.)
60. Bad. Maybe Dr. E went out with Ms. Fletcher, who has a cat. You can't add "Dr. E would never go out with someone who hates cats" because that's not a repair; it's making a new argument.
61. Good. Direct way of reasoning with "no."
62. Bad. Reasoning backwards with "all": "Only A are B" is equivalent to "All B are A." Sam might be one of the managers not allowed behind the bar because he doesn't have a bartender's license since he normally only works with food.
63. They're debating a vague sentence that has no truth-value. (Maybe Suzy thinks that arriving on time means within an hour.) Or they're trying to make a subjective claim objective.
64. Maria's argument is pretty good with the added claim: If the factory farms are awful, you shouldn't eat meat. But that's too vague: what does she mean by "awful"? Maybe what's awful for her isn't awful to Suzy. Suzy responds with the "ostrich technique": If I don't see it, it's not there. She doesn't fulfill the Principle of Rational Discussion.
68. *Conclusion*: We have saved hundreds of thousands of lives.

    Premises: It took only 20 terrorists to kill 3,000 people.
    We've killed hundreds of people in an offensive against Al-Qaida fighters.

    Unstated premises: All, or at least the great part, of the people we killed were Al-Qaida fighters (and not innocent villagers boosting the death toll). Everyone who is an Al-Qaida fighter could be a terrorist who could kill 150 or more people, like the terrorists who flew the planes into the World Trade Center. Hundreds of people killed times 150 per person is hundreds of thousands of people.

    Each of the unstated premises is false or highly dubious. In particular, the last unstated premise shows that Maj. Bryan Hilferty not only can't reason, he can't do simple arithmetic, either. Bad argument.

    Note: Brian Hilferty has since been promoted to Colonel and U.S. Army Central Chief of Public Relations. Your tax dollars at work.

Analyzing Complex Arguments

1. My neighbor should be forced to get rid of all the cars in his yard. *1* People do not like living next door to such a mess. *2* He never drives any of them. *3* They all look old and beat up, *4* and (they) leak oil all over the place. *5* It is bad for the neighborhood, *6* and it will decrease property values. *7*

   Argument? Yes.

   Conclusion: *1*

   Additional premises needed? Yes. If someone drives a car occasionally, he'd have the right to keep it on his property. *a* So he doesn't have a right to keep the cars on his property. *b* Cars that leak oil on the land are an environmental hazard. *c* Environmental hazards should not be allowed to continue. *d* If a person has something on his property that his neighbors do not like, that is an environmental hazard, that he does not have a right to keep in his yard, and that decreases property values, then he should get it off his property. *e*

   Identify any subargument: *3* and *a* support *b*. *5* and *c* support *d*. Then *2, 7, c,* and *e* yield *1*. Note that *4* can be deleted without making the argument weaker. And *6* is too vague.

   Good argument? Claim *7* is not clearly true—it depends on the neighborhood (it could be an industrial area). Everything rides on claim *e,* which on the face of it looks pretty plausible. In that case the argument is valid and good.

2. I'm on my way to school. *1* I left five minutes late. *2* Traffic is heavy. *3* I'll be late for class. *4* I might as well stop and get breakfast. *5*

   Argument? Yes.

   Conclusion: *5*

   Additional premises needed? Whenever I'm on my way to school and I'm 5 minutes late and traffic is heavy, I will be late for my class. *a* If I'm late for class, I might as well be very late or miss the class. *b*

   Identify any subargument: *1, 2, 3,* and *a* support *4*. Then *4* and *b* support *5*.

   Good argument? Depends on whether *b* is true.

3. Las Vegas has too many people. *1* There's not enough water in the desert to support more than a million people. *2* And the infrastructure of the city can't handle more than a million. *3* the streets are overcrowded *4* and traffic is always congested; *5* the schools are overcrowded *6* and new ones can't be built fast enough. *7* We should stop migration to the city by tough zoning laws in the city and county. *8*

   Argument? Yes.

   Conclusion: *8*

   Additional premises needed? (You must know what "infrastructure" means to make sense of this argument.)

   Las Vegas has close to a million people. *a* If streets are crowded and schools are crowded, then the infrastructure is inadequate. *b* If infrastructure is inadequate and there is not enough water for more people, there are too many people. *c* If there are too many people, new migration to the city should be stopped. *d* The best way to stop migration is by tough zoning laws. *e* (Can't add: The *only* way to stop migration to the city is by tough zoning laws—you could arm gangs or raise building fees.)

   Identify any subargument: *4, 5, 6, 7,* and *b* are dependent as support for *3*. *2, a, 3,* and *c* support *1*. *1, d,* and *e* support *8*.

   Good argument? Everything is plausible with the exception of *e*. If that can be shown to be true, it's good.

Chapter 12

2. We need to draw a conclusion based on the comparison.
3. No. They typically lack a statement of a general principle that would cover both (or all) cases.
4. State the conclusion. Then look for similarities that suggest a general principle.
6. This is a comparison, not an argument. What conclusion could we draw?
7. Zoe is refuting Dick's argument that it's O.K. to throw a banana peel out the window by showing the same argument would work for justifying throwing a newspaper out the window.
10. This is not really an analogy. It's questioning whether the person believes the general principle he or she espouses.
12. We can fill this out to be an argument: We don't sell sunshine. Trading water is like selling sunshine. So we *shouldn't* sell water.

    It's a very bad analogy. First, we do sell sunshine: In some big cities, there are laws and various covenants about blocking windows/views when building. Second, we *can't* sell sunshine in the same way we sell water, allocating a supply. And the prescriptive premise that's needed here is unclear.
14. This is reasoning by disanalogy, using the differences to argue for the conclusion. Tom is confusing the ideal perpetrated by business people with reality. Big businesses have lots of incompetent employees, take risks with money that a person who is being trusted shouldn't, and are plenty inefficient. Moreover, Tom isn't taking into account the big difference between businesses and colleges: businesses are out to make money, while a college's goal is (purportedly) to educate students. Consider the differences between consumers and students.
16. Selling stocks is compared to offering you a sure-fire way to pick up $100 bills on the street. But no competent stockbroker is going to tell you that he or she can make you money for sure, without fail. So investing well with a stockbroker isn't like picking up money on the street.

    Further, the general principle is: You shouldn't believe someone who says that he or she can make you a lot of money if he or she could do the same to make money. But a stockbroker might not be able to make a lot of money if he or she didn't already have a lot of money to invest—and then patiently wait for that 5–8% return.
17. This is reasoning by analogy, with unstated conclusion "It's not so hard to raise kids." The comparison seems great to me: Both kids and dogs need discipline and love. They need to be trained. They have to be housebroken. If you train them well, they will be obedient and affectionate and come when called, though they may not get into Stanford.
19. Tom is committing the fallacy of composition: what is good for the individual is good for the group. But there are major differences: spontaneous vs. organized violence is the most obvious. There are too many differences between being against all wars and unwilling to participate in wars vs. being unwilling to respond to personal violence.
22. Dick seems to be inferring that Tom is concluding we shouldn't use seat belts. But Tom doesn't say that, and it's not clear he believes that. In that case, Dick gives us food for thought, but not much more than unjustified ridicule.

    The research was done by Sam Peltzman of the University of Chicago.
23. This analogy breaks down. The person with the sense of smell will be right most of the time, in many different situations, and clearly so. No magician is going to find him out. Eventually, using brain scans and physical examinations, we could determine to some extent the mechanism behind his predictions, even if we ourselves couldn't experience them. But to date, claims about ESP can't be duplicated, even by the person claiming to have the powers; they are often debunked; they aren't right almost always but at best just a bit more than average. It's not just that we have lost motivation to investigate ESP because of so many false claims about it. We haven't even found a good candidate to study.

24. Zeke is trying to justify that it's O.K. to make snide remarks. The unstated premise he seems to assume is: If it feels good, do it. That's implausible, not least because of this comparison. Eating ice cream gives you pleasure but doesn't harm anyone else.
26. Challenge: If this isn't a good argument, how would you convince someone that others feel pain? And if you can't, what justification would you have for not torturing people?
27. A bad analogy because of the differences. We determine that a watch was made by someone because it *differs* from what we find in nature that is not crafted, such as rocks or trees. And we can deduce from its construction that it has a purpose. We can't do that for all of nature.
28. If you said "yes" for some and "no" for others, what differences are there? If you said the same for all, did you reason by analogy? What general principle did you use?
29. Did you answer this the same as Exercise 28? If so, what was your reason? Are you arguing by analogy? What is your general principle?

Chapter 13

5. average: 74.27 mean: 74.27 median: 76 mode: 88 *and* 62
7. The experts are right. All you have to do is wait until the stock market goes back up again —unless you die first. It's like doubling your bet on black with roulette every time you lose. You're sure to win in the long run. Unless you go broke or die first. The long run can be a very long time.
9. It's 45% lower than the *average* of the other brands, but 24 of those other brands could actually have less fat than this candy bar if there's just one of them that has a huge amount of fat. And what are those "leading" brands? Leading where? In Brazil?
11. This is apples and oranges because it doesn't correct for inflation: $2,000 in 1968 is equivalent to what in current dollars?
14. Wrong. It's just backwards. It should be: if you have breast cancer, there's less than a 10% chance you have the gene.
16. Don't do it, Dick. One per day ≠ average of one per day.
17. 58.1 million of them were pets? (97.8 million less 30.5 million and 9.2 million) If you look up the figures online, you'll see they've just copied it wrong.
22. Meaningless: Too much variation from one area to another. Median or mode won't be much more use.
23. A fair indication, since there's not much variation.
24. Terrible comparison: There's little variation in university professors' salaries (almost all earn between $30,000 and $100,000), but there's a huge variation in concert pianists' income ($15,000 vs. $2,000,000). The mode would be more informative.
30. By making the left-hand axis upside down, an increase looks like a decrease. This graph goes beyond misleading to outright lying.

    The source is: https://www.buzzfeed.com/katienotopoulos/graphs-that-lied-to-us?utm_term=.jtGeOLZyg#.nuW6wDyKY

Chapter 14

Section A

1. Generalizing.
   Sample: The German shepherds the speaker has met.
   Population: All German shepherds.
3. Generalizing.
   Sample: The cell phone Maria has.
   Population: All Hirangi cell phones.
4. Generalizing? Is the sample Maria's brother, or other football players she knows? Since we can't identify the sample, it's not O.K. to call it a generalization.
8. Generalizing.
   Sample: The times that Zoe has taken her clothes to be cleaned at Ricardo's.
   Population: All times anyone will take their clothes to that dry cleaner.
9. Possibly generalizing, but could be just repeating a general claim he's heard. We can't identify the sample, so don't treat it as a generalization until the speaker elaborates.
10. A general claim, but no generalizing is going on, since there's no argument.
11. Hard to say if it's generalizing. Has the speaker met Japanese guys? Or is she just repeating a stereotype she's heard?

Section B

1. One in which no subgroup of the population is represented more than its proportion in the population.
2. There is always a possibility that the members of the population which you haven't studied are different from the ones you have studied.
3. a. If the probability of something occurring is X percent, then over the *long run* the number of occurrences will tend toward X percent.
   b. The probability of getting a large sample that isn't representative is very small.
6. You can't know in advance what the "relevant" characteristics are. If you could, you wouldn't need to do a survey/experiment. You're biasing the sample towards the characteristics you think in advance are important.
8. No. Indeed, the law of large numbers predicts that eventually a randomly chosen sample of 20 students at your school will consist of just gay men. But the likelihood of a randomly chosen sample not being representative is small.

Exercises for Chapter 14

1. There is a 94% chance that between 51% and 61% of the entire population of voters actually favors your candidate.
3. a. A hasty generalization using anecdotal evidence.
   b. Yes, see the example in Section C.5, pp. 289–290. There would have to be very little variation in the population.
4. Variation.
5. 1. The sample is big enough.
   2. The sample is representative.
   3. The sample is studied well.
   Note well: The second premise is *not* "The sample is chosen randomly." That claim can support the second premise but isn't always needed. See the answer to Exercise 3.b.
9. Such a survey would be nonsense because most students don't know what the president of a college does—or can do. Do you approve of the way they're sweeping the streets in Timbuktu?
14. This is a confused attempt to generalize. Perhaps Lee thinks that the evidence he cites gives the

conclusion that if you invest in the stock market, you'll get rich(er). But that's arguing backwards, confusing (1) "If you invest in the stock market, you'll get rich" with (2) "If you're rich, then you will have invested in the stock market." The population for (1) is all investors in the stock market, not just the rich ones. It's a case of selective attention.

15. *Generalization*: (unstated) Lots of people fail Dr. E's course.
    Sample: The three people the speaker knows.
    Sample is representative? No reason to believe so.
    Sample is big enough? More like anecdotal evidence.
    Sample is studied well? Yes, they failed.
    Good generalization? No.
    Unstated premise and conclusion: You shouldn't take a course you might fail.
    You shouldn't take Dr. E's course.
19. This appears to be a report on a generalization from sampling hogs from various producers. But who knows for sure? Yet the organization would have no reason to lie. Suspend judgment.
20. Agrabah is a fictional city from Disney's *Aladdin*.
22. *Generalization*: (unstated) A high percentage of women think men with beards are sexy.
    Sample: The women who responded to the survey.
    Sample is representative? No reason to believe so. Lee doesn't even have reason to think the sample is representative of the women who read that magazine. After all, they may have got only 10,000 out of 200,000 sent out, and mostly women who like men with beards responded.
    Sample is big enough? Yes, if only we had reason to believe it is representative.
    Sample is studied well? Probably.
    Good generalization? No.
24. Tom is not making a generalization; he's using one. Almost all pro basketball players are over 6 feet tall, and people that tall won't fit into Suzy's car. Therefore, (unstated) You shouldn't use Suzy's car to pick up the basketball player. Needs an unstated premise: You shouldn't pick up someone in a car he can't fit into. Pretty good argument.
26. This is just haphazard sampling. There's no reason to believe that the people interviewed are representative of all Swiss, much less "the general public." Yet this was published in a peer-reviewed journal, albeit one that's only online and has an ad for "Science Singles" at the top of its home page (when we saw it).
27. *Generalization*: The pacifier will stop the baby from crying.
    Sample: All the times the speaker has given the pacifier to the baby.
    Sample is representative? Who knows?
    Sample is big enough? We don't know how often they've done it.
    Sample is studied well? Possibly, or possibly bad memory.
    Additional premises needed? None.
    Good generalization? Weak, but there's little risk in that course of action.
32. First, a poll is a generalization from a sample, so not everyone will be polled. I'd ask him how much soup he needs to eat before he can tell what it tastes like. Presumably, he doesn't have to eat the whole pot; he only needs a few spoonfuls. In the same way, unbiased polling of several hundred New Mexicans (randomly chosen) is very likely to give an accurate picture of what New Mexicans in general think. Asking 175 cockfighting supporters he knows if they've been polled and then concluding from that that the poll was skewed in favor of city-folk or recent arrivals is like someone in California asking 200 friends in California if they are Californian and then concluding that any poll showing Californians are only 10% of Americans must be biased.

    The rest of his letter relies on a variation of the perfectionist dilemma ("If there are bigger problems than cockfighting, then cockfighting should be left alone") and a strawman or slippery slope of non-New Mexicans bent on controlling "all aspects of our lives and traditions." Notice that he nowhere mentions or responds to arguments against cockfighting.

33. The analogy is comparing Maria's rice cooker to the one that Zoe wants to buy. The generalization needed is: (Almost) all Blauspot rice cookers will have a serious defect. Though the generalization is only anecdotal evidence, Zoe might decide that the risk is enough to go with that weak argument.
34. The analogy is between chimpanzees and humans. It requires a generalization that (almost) all chimpanzees will become obese if fed 1 pound of chocolate per day in addition to their regular diet. The analogy depends on the similarity of chimpanzee physiology to human physiology, and assumes that the equivalent of 1 pound of chocolate for a chimpanzee to 1% of body weight for a human. And how much exercise did they get? A pretty poor argument: the conclusion is more plausible than the premises.

Chapter 15

Sections A.1–A.3

1. *Causal claim*: The police car's siren caused me to pull over.
   Particular or *general*? Particular.
   Cause (stated as a claim): The police car had its siren going near me.
   Effect (stated as a claim): I pulled over.
2. *Causal claim*: Dick getting a speeding ticket caused his insurance rates to go up.
   Particular or *general*? Particular.
   Cause (stated as a claim): Dick got a speeding ticket.
   Effect (stated as a claim): Dick's insurance rates went up.
3. *Causal claim*: People getting speeding tickets causes their insurance rates to go up.
   Particular or *general*? General—generalizing over all examples like Exercise 2.
4. *Causal claim*: Your being late caused us to miss the beginning of the movie.
   Particular or *general*? Particular.
   Cause (stated as a claim): You were late.
   Effect (stated as a claim): We missed the beginning of the movie.
6. Not a causal claim. (Sometimes "make" means "causes," and sometimes not.)
7. Not a causal claim. Inductive evidence is offered for a generalization that might be used in establishing a general causal claim.
8. *Causal claim*: Someone ringing the doorbell caused Spot to bark.
   Particular or *general*? Particular.
   Cause (stated as a claim): Someone rang the doorbell.
   Effect (stated as a claim): Spot barked.
9. *Causal claim*: Drinking coffee causes me not to get a headache in the afternoon.
   Particular or *general*? General. Perhaps too vague: How much coffee?

Section A

2. The cause must make a difference. Example: The wind chimes and elephant.
3. The normal conditions.
4. We can't see how to fill in the normal conditions. It's just like when we say a premise isn't relevant to the conclusion of an argument.
7. Reread Chapter 4.

Sections A and B

1. *Causal claim*: Someone pulling in front of Maria caused her to slam on her brakes.
   Cause: Someone pulled in front of Maria.
   Effect: Maria slammed on her brakes.

Cause and effect true? Apparently so.
Cause precedes effect? Yes.
It's nearly impossible for the cause to be true and effect false? Yes, given some plausible normal conditions.
Cause makes a difference? It seems so, but we need to know more about what was happening at the time. Was Maria paying attention?
Common cause? Possibly, if the other driver was trying to avoid hitting someone.
Evaluation: Plausible if nothing else unusual was happening at the time.

2. *Causal claim*: Wearing new shoes caused Suzy's feet to hurt when she was cheerleading.
Cause: Suzy wore new shoes cheerleading.
Effect: Her feet hurt.
Cause and effect true? Apparently so. Suzy ought to know.
Cause precedes effect? Yes.
It's nearly impossible for the cause to be true and effect false? We need to know the normal conditions. Was everything like it usually is when Suzy is cheerleading? Apparently so, from what she says.
Cause makes a difference? Suzy says it did, by comparing it to all the other times when she didn't have sore feet.
Common cause? None apparent.
Evaluation: Pretty plausible.

3. *Causal claim*: Dick pigging out on nachos and salsa caused his stomachache.
Cause: Dick pigged out on nachos and salsa last night.
Effect: Dick has a stomachache.
Cause and effect true? Apparently so, but Zoe could be exaggerating.
Cause precedes effect? Yes.
It's nearly impossible for the cause to be true and effect false? We need to know more.
Cause makes a difference? Can't say without knowing more.
Common cause? No.
Evaluation: Suspend judgment.

4. *Causal claim*: Marriage causes divorce. General causal claim.
Evaluation: This is tracing too far back: getting married is part of the normal conditions for getting a divorce.

5. *Causal claim*: (unstated) My not going to the game causes the team to lose. It's a general causal claim.
Evaluation: Anecdotal evidence. *Post hoc* reasoning. No reason to believe it.

6. This isn't cause and effect; it's a definition.

7. *Causal claim*: The dark sky caused Zoe to be depressed.
Cause: The sky was dark.
Effect: Zoe got depressed.
Cause and effect true? Apparently so.
Cause precedes effect? Yes.
It's nearly impossible for the cause to be true and effect false? Can't say. We'd need to know a lot more about Zoe's psyche or else rely on a generalization that Zoe gets depressed every time it's dark in similar circumstances.
Cause makes a difference? Perhaps, but we need to know what happened to Zoe before that might have made her depressed.
Common cause? None.
Evaluation: Suspend judgment until we know more.

8. *Causal claim*: The sun being strong yesterday caused me to get a sunburn.
   Cause: The sun was strong yesterday.
   Effect: I got a sunburn.
   Cause and effect true? Apparently so.
   Cause precedes effect? Yes.
   It's nearly impossible for the cause to be true and effect false? Depends on what we call the normal conditions.
   Cause makes a difference? Yes.
   Common cause? None.
   Evaluation: This is a good candidate for *a* cause, not *the* cause. Zoe being outside with her skin exposed for a long time is not a normal condition.
12. *Causal claim*: Lou's getting a college education is *a* cause of his getting a high-paying job the year after he graduated.
   Cause: Lou graduated from college.
   Effect: Lou got a job the next year.
   Cause and effect true? Apparently so.
   Cause precedes effect? Yes.
   It's nearly impossible for the cause to be true and effect false? Unlikely.
   Cause makes a difference? Don't know. What are the normal conditions? Does Lou's dad own the factory where he got the job?
   Common cause? Perhaps Lou's parents are wealthy. Or Lou works hard.
   Evaluation: Plausible as *a* cause, if the normal conditions are right, but you'd need to know a lot about Lou and his hiring. It's not plausible as it stands. See Example 22 in this chapter.
14. *Causal claim*: Dick telling Sally that Zoe killed Louie caused Zoe to be miserable now.
   Cause: Dick told Sally that Zoe killed Louie.
   Effect: Zoe is unhappy now.
   Cause and effect true? Apparently so. Dick doesn't deny it!
   Cause precedes effect? Yes.
   It's nearly impossible for the cause to be true and effect false? Can't tell.
   Cause makes a difference? Can't tell.
   Common cause? None apparent.
   Evaluation: Tracing the cause too far back. A psychiatrist might say Zoe's right. But spelling out what she believes are the normal conditions might show she's wrong. It's like the Treaty of Versailles example on p. 312 of the text, and on top of that it's subjective. Just have broad shoulders, Dick.
20. *Causal claim*: (General) Smoking marijuana causes heroin use.
   Evaluation: First, at best it's *can cause* not *causes,* since we all know people who smoke marijuana and don't use heroin. But it's also *post hoc* reasoning. They probably all drank milk, too.
23. Clear possibility of common cause: Their parents are richer and/or spend time with them, which is why they get breakfast and do better.

Section C

2. *Causal claim*: The pedals are making a clicking sound on Dick's bike.
   Cause: The pedals are defective. ??
   Effect: There is a clicking sound.
   Evaluation: Good method, but a false dilemma starts it. The clicking could also come from the gears. Have Zoe put her ear close to the pedals when Dick is turning them.

3. There isn't a causal claim here. Rather, Flo is overlooking one. Perhaps coincidence is just our ignorance of real cause and effect. To be sure, our knowledge is limited. But not commonly as limited as with children.

Section D

6. Suzy thinks that being in the Army causes men to abuse their wives. But there's a possible common cause that hasn't been ruled out: men who are prone to abuse their wives like violence and hence are more likely to join the Army.
8. Or aliens may have been planting thoughts in their heads. Or it could have been because of global warming. This is just a *post hoc* conjecture.
10. *Causal claim*: Late nights for teens *can cause* them to have depression.
    Type of cause-in-population experiment: We're not told.
    Evaluate the evidence: We have no idea how the sample was chosen, nor how large it was, nor if it was studied well. There may be a common cause: parents who don't care enough for their children to supervise them and set bedtimes cause their children to be depressed.
    At best, if this sounds interesting it should lead you to look up the article in *Sleep*. But there's no reason here to believe the causal claim.
11. Francine Grodstein is hedging her words, suggesting that there's cause and effect when she knows she's only shown correlation between alcohol use and cognitive benefits. It's the writer of the article who goes further in the last paragraph.
    The problem is that it could be the reverse here: elderly women who are mentally alert prefer to have something to drink to slow them down to sleep better. Or there could be a common cause. It's not even clear from this article whether this was a cause-to-effect or effect-to-cause study. More studies are needed, at least from the little we learn in this write-up. So don't start drinking.
12. *Causal claim*: Suggests without saying it ("Some studies on day care have found it's not bad at all"): Day care causes behavioral, emotional, and physical health problems for children.
    Type of cause-in-population experiment: The first two bulleted items are not studies at all, just *post hoc* observations. The third bulleted item appears to be an uncontrolled cause-to-effect study, but it's hard to say, since not enough information is given. The fourth bulleted item appears to be an uncontrolled cause-to-effect study.
    Evaluate the evidence: All this is just *post hoc ergo propter hoc*. There's no reason to think there isn't a common cause of parents putting their children in day care and children's problems—namely, parents are too busy to give time to their kids. Or parents who leave their children in day care—on the whole—have pressures that make them not parent well. Or bad parents prefer to put their children in day care. Or . . . There's no reason to believe the causal claim based on what's said here.
    Further tests? Uncontrolled studies that factor out common threads. Controlled studies.
15. *Causal claim*: A high-fiber diet *can cause* less colon cancer.
    Type of cause-in-population experiment: Uncontrolled: cause-to-effect.
    Evaluate the evidence: Clear correlation. Not clear if sample is representative, though large. No mechanism given for explaining why there is the correlation. Equally likely is the reverse cause and effect: people eat more fruit and fiber because their digestion is good. Until that is ruled out, there's no reason to believe the claim.
    Further tests? Controlled studies seem in order to rule out the reverse cause and effect. Try to find an explanation for the correlation.

Review Chapters 12–15

1. A collection of claims that are intended to show that one of them, the conclusion, is true.

2. The argument must be valid or strong, the premises must be plausible, and the premises must be more plausible than the conclusion.
3. An argument is weak if there is a likely way that the premises could be true and conclusion false at the same time.
4. No. It could have a dubious premise or beg the question.
5. Nothing.
6. A comparison becomes reasoning by analogy when a claim is being argued for. On one side of the comparison we draw a conclusion, so on the other side we should conclude the same.
7.
    1. Is this an argument? What is the conclusion?
    2. What is the comparison?
    3. What are the premises? (one or both sides of the comparison)
    4. What are the similarities?
    5. Can we state the similarities as premises and find a general principle that covers the two sides?
    6. Does the general principle really apply to both sides?
       What about the differences?
    7. Is the argument strong or valid? Is it good?
8.
    a. Add all the numbers in the collection. Divide by the number of items in the collection.
    b. Same as the average.
    c. The midway number: as many numbers in the collection are greater than it as are less than it.
    d. The number that appears most often in the collection (there may be more than one mode in a collection).
9. A comparison where the base is unknown.
10.
    a. A generalization is an argument concluding a claim about a group from a claim about some part of the group.
    b. The sample.
    c. The population.
11. One in which no one subgroup of the population is represented more than its proportion of the population as a whole.
12. No. You could get a very biased sample by chance, but the likelihood of that happening is very, very small.
13. Yes. See the computer example in Section C.5 of the text.
14. There is a 97% chance that between 39% and 45% of the voters favor that candidate.
15. The sample is big enough. The sample is representative. The sample is studied well.
16. A hasty generalization. The claims about the too-small sample are called "anecdotal evidence."
17. *Describing the purported cause and effect with claims*:
    The cause happened (the claim describing it is true).
    The effect happened (the claim describing it is true).
    The cause precedes the effect.
    It is (nearly) impossible for the cause to happen (be true) and the effect not to happen (be false), given the normal conditions.
    The cause makes a difference—if the cause had not happened (been true), the effect would not have happened (been true).
    There is no common cause.
18. You still have to establish that the cause makes a difference.
19. Reversing cause and effect. *Post hoc ergo propter hoc.* Looking too hard for a cause. Tracing the cause too far back.
20. Controlled cause-to-effect. Uncontrolled cause-to-effect. Uncontrolled effect-to-cause.

21. Because arguing or persuading badly:
    Undermines your own ability to reason well.
    Helps destroy democracy.
    In the long run doesn't work as well as reasoning well.

Chapter 16

Section A

3. Bad. A loaded question.
4. The explanatory claims include one that is the same or a rewriting of what's being explained or is equivalent to what's being explained.
5. Because in a good explanation at least one of the claims doing the explaining (a premise) is not more plausible than the claim being explained (the conclusion).

7.b. When it is good causal reasoning that answers the right question.

12. *Inferential explanation*? Yes.
    Conclusion (claim being explained) The match ignited.
    Premises (claims doing the explaining) Harry struck it on the matchbook.
    Causal? Yes.
    Evaluation Inadequate, unless it wasn't obvious that the match was struck.

Exercises for Chapter 16

2. They are not causal.
   They often invoke claims that become true only after what is being explained is true.
   They often ascribe motives or goals to things that can't have them.
   We have no good criteria for deciding if what we say is the function really is the function.
6. *Explanation* Yes
   Claim being explained There are valves in our veins.
   Claim(s) doing the explaining Blood can flow only one way in our veins.
   Inferential? No
   Teleological? Yes
   If teleological, rewrite it as inferential if possible No obvious way. The inferential recasting would be weak: blood can flow only one way in our veins, so we have valves in our veins.
   Evaluation Even if you accept teleological explanations, you'd have to come up with more premises to show why valves are there rather than some other mechanism.
7. *Explanation* Yes. There are two explanations.
   Claim being explained 1. Dogs chase cats.
   2. Fido gets along with Puff.
   Claim(s) doing the explaining 1. Cats are Satan's emissaries on Earth. Dogs, the protectors of the way of righteousness, sense this and try to rid the world of them.
   2. Some cats have tried to redeem their souls, and dogs encourage them in the way of righteousness.
   Inferential? Yes.
   Independent or dependent? Both are dependent. The second, in particular, requires that Puff has tried to redeem his soul.
   Causal? Apparently so.
   Teleological? No.
   Evaluation Both are great! If you don't agree, then you are not a believer and may be forced to spend eternity in the company of cats.
10. *Explanation* Yes.
    Claim being explained Maria's great uncle went to fight in Vietnam.

Claim(s) doing the explaining Maria's great uncle was drafted.
Inferential? Yes.
Independent or dependent? Independent, if we trust Maria's word.
Causal? Yes.
Teleological? No.
Evaluation Good, if it answers the right question, since we can fill in the unstated premises to make it strong or valid.

19. *Explanation* Yes.
Claim being explained Spot is crouching in front of the hole.
Claim(s) doing the explaining Spot crouching in front of the hole has the purpose of Spot catching a mouse.
Inferential? No.
Teleological? Yes.
If teleological, rewrite it as inferential if possible Spot is crouching in front of the hole because he wants to catch a mouse.
Evaluation This is as good as the evidence for "Spot wants to catch a mouse." Right now we have only the associated argument to establish that.

Chapter 17

1. A possibility in the future that we deem bad and that would be a consequence of some action we take or don't take.
2. The good that might come from it outweighs, by more than a little, the bad that might come from it.
3. • Weigh how likely a good outcome is.
   • Weigh how likely the risk is.
   • Weigh how much we want to avoid the risk versus how much we want the possible good outcome that might come from our action.
   • Weigh how hard it would be to accomplish the good by other means.
4. a. It depends in part on what you consider to be a good outcome and how hard or easy it is for you to do the action.
11. How many people would you need to treat to cure one of them by surgery?
How many people would you need to treat to cure one of them by chemotherapy?
How many people would get better without any treatment?
Anyway, what do you mean by "cure"?
What are the bad outcomes with surgery? How often do those occur?
What are the bad outcomes with chemotherapy? How often do those occur?
How much is either of these going to cost me out of my pocket?
13. a. She'll lose $5.
    b. The gambler's fallacy (p. 285).
14. a. ON AVERAGE:
Of every 1,000 people tested, 6 will have HIV and 994 won't.
Of the 994, 1% will test positive even though they don't have HIV = 10 will test positive who don't have HIV.
Of the 6 who test positive, 99% will have HIV = 6 will test positive and have HIV.
So 16 people will test positive.
Of those, 6 actually have HIV. So there's a 6/16 chance that Zeke really is HIV positive = 37.5% chance that Zeke really has HIV.
    b. They test the 16 people.

Of the 10 false positives, there's a 1% chance that they'll test positive again, which is less than 1 of them.

Of the 6 who tested positive and do have HIV, 99% will test positive again = 6 of them.

So ON AVERAGE of the 16 people who tested positive, on average only 6 will test positive a second time, and they will all have HIV. So if Zeke tests positive a second time, it's almost certain he is HIV positive. Let's hope Zeke doesn't test positive a second time.

15. Eberhart wants to convince us that the risk of getting cancer from the reentry of the spacecraft is not worth our attention. What's wrong with that?

First, it's an example of a perfectionist dilemma. If you can't stop bigger risks, don't bother to stop a small one, even though it would be easy to do.

Second, Eberhart does not distinguish between risks we voluntarily assume, such as riding a bicycle in downtown traffic; risks we cannot avoid, such as being injured by a tornado; and risks that are imposed on us, such as some politicians and scientists deciding for us that it's O.K. if some of us die to further the space exploration program.

This is a clear example of why we don't want scientists making policy decisions, for such decisions depend on critical thinking skills and ethical sense, which are not what scientists are normally trained in.

Chapter 1S

2. *Claim*? Yes.

   Contradictory Some laboratory rat lives longer than four years, but no paper is written about it.

4. *Claim*? Yes.

   Contradictory Some butterfly does not go through those stages.

5. *Claim*? Yes.

   Contradictory Some gas at some time and place does not satisfy $PV = kT$.

7. *Claim*? Yes.

   Contradictory Sometimes when a steady current is flowing through a conductor, the strength of the current is not proportional to the potential difference between its ends.

8. *Claim*? Yes.

   Contradictory Sometimes, when a large number of pea plants having round, yellow seeds are crossed with a large number of pea plants having wrinkled, green seeds, the second generation of round to wrinkled and of yellow to green is not approximately 3:1.

14. Maybe it is an argument or an explanation. But it's really bad. Science does not tell us that some forms are "more perfected" than others; that is a value judgment. Capitalizing the word "nature" and ascribing creativity to it is a bad metaphor and an odd substitute for theology.

15. An argument.

    Conclusion The oxygen in today's atmosphere is and was produced by life.

    Premises The earliest atmosphere was much different and consisted largely of hydrogen, carbon dioxide, and water vapor. The present atmosphere began to form as soon as organisms evolved and through photosynthesis developed the ability to extract carbon dioxide from the air and expel oxygen.

    Evaluation Valid. Good if the premises are plausible.

18. *Argument*? Yes.

    Conclusion 1 It is not possible for a vehicle to hover, speed up, or change direction solely by means of its own magnetic field.

    Premises for conclusion 1 Nothing happens except through interactions between pairs of objects. A space vehicle may generate a powerful magnetic field, but in the absence of another magnetic field to push against it, it can neither move nor support itself in midair.

Conclusion 2 A flying saucer suspended in air and propelled by its self-generated magnetic field would be noticed throughout the world.

Premises for conclusion 2 The earth possesses a magnetic field, but it is weak—about 1% of that generated by a compass needle. For a UFO to be levitated by reacting against the earth's magnetic field, its own field would have to be so enormously strong that it could be detected by any magnetometer in the world. . . . As the magnetic UFO traveled about the earth, it would induce electrical currents in every power line within sight, blowing our circuit breakers and in general wreaking havoc. It would not go unnoticed.

Additional premises There is no magnetic field for a spaceship to push against that is everywhere above the surface of the earth except the earth's own magnetic field.
No such electrical effects have ever been recorded.

Method of refutation? Shows the other person's claim is false directly by an argument.

Good argument? Yes. Valid, and the premises all seem plausible.

19. The passage is one long proof substitute. Of course you wouldn't want to be old fashioned and accept such theories, would you? You want to be a serious person who won't be laughed at by future generations, so you should agree with Searle.

    Worse, the characterizations of the various views are caricatures, strawmen that are easy to disprove but aren't what researchers really say.

Chapter 2S

2. *Subjective data* is the individual's perspective of a situation or a series of events.
   Objective data consist of observable and measurable information.
3. The whole sentence is a definition of "metamorphic rock."
4. Terrible definition, since it misclassifies. It is *too broad*. For example, a dog walks by a tree, and a squirrel that the dog isn't aware of on another tree hides in its hole. Now you can call that something, but you can't call it "communication" because that word has a clear use that requires an intention to communicate.
6. To investigate whether ghosts exist, we need to be clear what would count as a ghost. This is one possible definition.

Chapter 3S

1. A claim that is established by personal experience or observation in an experiment.
2. Evidence is usually the observational claims that are used as premises of an argument. Sometimes the term refers to all the premises.
3. a. It is described clearly enough that others can follow the method to obtain observations.
   b. When the experiment is duplicated, the observations of the new experiment are in close agreement with the observations of the original experiment.
   c. It can be duplicated and the results reproduced.
5. The difference between an explanation and a prediction is that in an explanation we know that the claim being explained is true, whereas we don't know if the prediction is true.
7. We try to falsify the claim by making predictions using it and see if those are true. If true, they make the claim more plausible; if false, the claim is likely false.

8.b. It's working backwards. Without a question to guide the collection of data, you have no criteria for what counts as an observation, no way to check if you have a random sample for that issue.

17. Did you go glassy-eyed and get wowed by the statistics? The stats are meaningless. You should be able to note that the sample was not chosen randomly and has lots of room for bias. And even if the statistics did show a correlation between the responses, all that shows is that there is a correlation between the *responses people give on a questionnaire* to whether they sleepwalk and whether they have parapsychological experiences. Or rather to whether someone has *told*

them they sleepwalk. His conclusion assumes that there is a correlation between people saying they have parapsychological experiences and actually having those experiences. Even in this journal that takes for granted that there are parapsychological experiences, the correlation between reporting that you've had such an experience and actually having one has to be established. The whole study is nonsense.

Chapter 4S

1.b. The law of large numbers: in the long run the data will go to what's the statistically predicted average, and the more studies, the longer the run.

5.b. Self-selection bias is haphazard sampling, but not all haphazard sampling is due to self-selection (see the example of Tom's study in Chapter 14.B.1).

7. "Reproducible results" does not mean that anyone at any time will reproduce the results: there can be error or subtle differences in the situation that are not taken into account. If a reputable scientist cannot reproduce the results, however, that is motive for others to try to see what the problem is.

Science Arguments for Analysis

1. *Argument*? Yes.
   Conclusion: The mass of air covers the whole face of the earth and its weight presses upon the earth at every point.
   Comparison: Water pressing on the earth is like air pressing on the earth.
   Premises: The water of the sea presses with its weight that part of the earth which is beneath it. If it surrounded the whole earth instead of only a part, its weight would press upon the whole surface of the earth. Water is like air.
   Similarities: ????
   Additional premises:
   Classify: valid strong ————X— weak
   Good argument? Not yet. We need to know how water is like air. Air seems to be weightless. Of course Pascal provided that kind of evidence elsewhere in his writing.

3. *Argument*? Yes.
   Conclusion: Animals have mental states quite similar to ours.
   Comparison: First analogy: Animals are like humans. Second analogy: Physical characteristics are like psychological characteristics. (*1*) Just as evolution has brought about emergent physical characteristics, so it has surely brought about emergent psychological characteristics —both evolve together as they contribute to survival and reproductive success.
   Premises: Similarity of life forms increases with relatedness. (*2*) It is reasonable to believe that psychological processes become more similar with genetic relatedness. (*3*)
   Classify: valid strong X weak
   Good argument? Premise *2* is stupid, because the similarities between life forms are what lead us to classify them as related, not vice-versa. What is required is what the authors mean by "similar." Much later the authors say that they are talking about genetic relatedness, but again, since there are so many genetic similarities between even the fruit fly and humans, it is the physical relatedness that leads us to look for genetic markers that we can say make us "genetically related." Or at least the authors haven't countered that obvious objection.
   Premise *1* begs the question. Premise *3* is a proof substitute.
   Overall, a hopelessly bad argument.

4. *Argument*? Yes.
   Conclusion: Mutations in plants or animals are almost invariably detrimental.
   Comparison: Shooting a bullet through a clock that doesn't keep perfect time is like a mutation

in the germ plasma of a plant or an animal. Making a typographical error in *Hamlet* is like a mutation in the germ plasma of a plant or animal.

Good argument? The dissimilarities are much too great for this to be a good analogy. Clocks and *Hamlet* are man-made and are designed in advance to perform some function/achieve some goal. To change them is to tinker with their design, whether that design is good or bad. But the whole point of evolutionary theory is to replace design and goals and purposes as the causes of why plants and animals are like they are now.

Chapter 5S

2. No. The assumptions of the theory are still false. The true predictions show that the assumptions are good *abstractions*, useful for drawing conclusions when the differences don't matter. They confirm a range of applicability of the model.
4. It shows that the theory can be used in such situations to make true predictions, where "such situations" has to be made more precise by finding cases where the theory does or does not apply.
5. We should abandon the theory if it does not proceed entirely by abstracting but posits something in addition to experience, as in the case of the ether. Otherwise, we try to use the false predictions to put a limit on the range of applicability of the theory.
7. Theories are tools for making predictions and controlling the world. They do not describe the world except to the extent that we can ignore what the abstractions ignore.

Chapter 6S

4. The theory of evolution is not teleological. Instead, the basic premise is that mutations occur. Most mutations are either not expressed or lead to a form that does not survive. Sometimes, however, a random mutation occurs which leads to an organism that is better able to survive and lives long enough to reproduce. Organisms that have a better chance of reproducing are likely to spread their genes. There is no invocation of a guiding intelligence but only a process that relies on random occurrences.

Chapter 7S

7. Koenig's criticism is poorly articulated. Thinking that prayer causes healing is making a causal claim, whether it's supernatural or not. The real problem is that calling something "supernatural" is an admission of ignorance about how it works. Unless there is a clear model of how prayer works (knowing the mind of God?), it is impossible to know whether the observed differences between the groups were due to the cause or due to differences in the normal conditions. Perhaps lots of the patients were sinful people who were being righteously punished. Or maybe they were good people who needed to learn some unfathomable "lesson." Or perhaps God ignores experiment-prompted prayers for strangers. Or maybe they were praying to the wrong god and should have been offering sacrifices to CAT.

   What is miraculous here is that someone paid $2.4 million dollars for the study.

Index

Printed in the USA
CPSIA information can be obtained
at www.ICGtesting.com
JSHW050624300823
47505JS00005B/29